the cinema of LOUIS MALLE

DIRECTORS' CUTS

Other selected titles in the Directors' Cuts series:

the cinema of ROBERT ALTMAN: *hollywood maverick*
ROBERT NIEMI

the cinema of WES ANDERSON: *bringing nostalgia to life*
DEANE WILLIAMS

the cinema of CHRISTOPHER NOLAN: *imagining the impossible*
JACQUELINE FURBY & STUART JOY (eds)

the cinema of THE COEN BROTHERS: *hardboiled entertainments*
JEFFREY ADAMS

the cinema of CLINT EASTWOOD: *chronicles of america*
DAVID STERRITT

the cinema of ISTVÁN SZABÓ: *visions of europe*
JOHN CUNNINGHAM

the cinema of AGNÈS VARDA: *resistance and eclecticism*
DELPHINE BÉNÉZET

the cinema of ALEXANDER SOKUROV: *figures of paradox*
JEREMI SZANIAWSKI

the cinema of MICHAEL WINTERBOTTOM: *borders, intimacy, terror*
BRUCE BENNETT

the cinema of RAÚL RUIZ: *impossible cartographies*
MICHAEL GODDARD

the cinema of MICHAEL MANN: *vice and vindication*
JONATHAN RAYNER

the cinema of AKI KAURISMÄKI: *authorship, bohemia, nostalgia, nation*
ANDREW NESTINGEN

the cinema of RICHARD LINKLATER: *walk, don't run*
ROB STONE

the cinema of BÉLA TARR: *the circle closes*
ANDRÁS BÁLINT KOVÁCS

the cinema of STEVEN SODERBERGH: *indie sex, corporate lies, and digital videotape*
ANDREW DE WAARD & R. COLIN TATE

the cinema of TERRY GILLIAM: *it's a mad world*
JEFF BIRKENSTEIN, ANNA FROULA & KAREN RANDELL (eds)

the cinema of THE DARDENNE BROTHERS: *responsible realism*
PHILIP MOSLEY

the cinema of MICHAEL HANEKE: *europe utopia*
BEN McCANN & DAVID SORFA (eds)

the cinema of SALLY POTTER: *a politics of love*
SOPHIE MAYER

the cinema of DAVID CRONENBERG: *from baron of blood to cultural hero*
ERNEST MATHIJS

the cinema of JAN SVANKMAJER: *dark alchemy*
PETER HAMES (ed.)

the cinema of LARS VON TRIER: *authenticity and artifice*
CAROLINE BAINBRIDGE

the cinema of WERNER HERZOG: *aesthetic ecstasy and truth*
BRAD PRAGER

the cinema of TERRENCE MALICK: *poetic visions of america (second edition)*
HANNAH PATTERSON (ed.)

the cinema of ANG LEE: *the other side of the screen (second edition)*
WHITNEY CROTHERS DILLEY

the cinema of STEVEN SPIELBERG: *empire of light*
NIGEL MORRIS

the cinema of TODD HAYNES: *all that heaven allows*
JAMES MORRISON (ed.)

the cinema of DAVID LYNCH: *american dreams, nightmare visions*
ERICA SHEEN & ANNETTE DAVISON (eds)

the cinema of KRZYSZTOF KIESLOWSKI: *variations on destiny and chance*
MAREK HALTOF

the cinema of GEORGE A. ROMERO: *knight of the living dead (second edition)*
TONY WILLIAMS

the cinema of KATHRYN BIGELOW: *hollywood transgressor*
DEBORAH JERMYN & SEAN REDMOND (eds)

the cinema of
LOUIS MALLE

transatlantic auteur

edited by Philippe Met

WALLFLOWER PRESS LONDON & NEW YORK

A Wallflower Press Book
Published by
Columbia University Press
Publishers Since 1893
New York • Chichester, West Sussex
cup.columbia.edu

Copyright © 2018 Columbia University Press
All rights reserved

Wallflower Press® is a registered trademark of Columbia University Press

A complete CIP record is available from the Library of Congress

ISBN 978-0-231-18870-8 (cloth)
ISBN 978-0-231-18871-5 (pbk.)
ISBN 978-0-231-85126-8 (e-book)

Series design by Rob Bowden Design
Cover image: courtesy of AF archive/Alamy Stock Photo

CONTENTS

Acknowledgements vii
Notes on Contributors ix

Foreword   *Volker Schlöndorff*   1
Introduction   *Philippe Met*   5

TRANSVERSAL STUDIES

1   Malle Before Malle   *Guillaume Soulez*   19
2   The Art of Silence: From Documentary to Fiction   *Caroline Eades*   34
3   No Comment: Direct Cinema in *Humain, trop humain* and
    Place de la République   *Derek Schilling*   49
4   Louis Malle's Nonfiction: Tradition, Rebellion and Authorial Voice
    Alan Williams   63
5   Louis Malle's 1960s 'Star' Films   *Sue Harris*   72
6   Experimentation and Automatism in *Zazie dans le métro* and *Black Moon*
    Ian Fleishman   86
7   Louis Malle and 'His' Writers (Drieu La Rochelle, Nimier, Modiano)
    Michel Ciment   99
8   A Gendered Geography of Death: Louis Malle's Orphic Voyage
    T. Jefferson Kline   107
9   The Figure of the Mother in *May Fools*, *Au revoir les enfants* and *Murmur of the Heart*   *Justine Malle*   116
10 Jazz as Counterpoint in *Elevator to the Gallows*, *Murmur of the Heart* and
    Pretty Baby   *Jean-Louis Pautrot*   127

MONOGRAPHIC ESSAYS

11 *The Fire Within*: Touching   *Elisabeth Cardonne-Arlyck*   145
12 *Le Voleur*: (Self-)Portrait of the Filmmaker as a Thief   *Philippe Met*   159
13 Absorption and Reflexivity in *Phantom India*   *Ludovic Cortade*   174
14 Fog of War: *Lacombe Lucien* and Its Afterlives   *Steven Ungar*   185
15 Memory, Friendship and History in *Au revoir les enfants*
      Sandy Flitterman-Lewis   200
16 *Atlantic City*: When Sound Meets Utopia   *Francesca Cinelli*   210
17 Between Conversation and Conversion: *My Dinner with André*
      Tom Conley   222
18 *Vanya on 42nd Street*: Inventing a Space of Creation   *Sébastien Rongier*   232

INTERVIEW

   Truth and Poetry: An Interview with John Guare   *Philippe Met*   246

VARIA (PREVIOUSLY UNPUBLISHED MATERIAL)

   Notes for a Lecture on the Queen Elizabeth 2   *Louis Malle*   257
   'The Loner': Treatment suggested by H. James' *What Maisie Knew*
      Louis Malle (with introduction by Philippe Met)   265

   Afterword   *Wes Anderson*   303

   Filmography   305
   Index   311

ACKNOWLEDGEMENTS

This book had its inception at an international conference organized at the University of Pennsylvania by Philippe Met on 16–17 October 2015 ('The Transatlantic Cinema of Louis Malle: A Critical Reassessment, 20 Years After His Death'). It was made possible by the generous support of the University of Pennsylvania ('Conference Grant from the Provost's Interdisciplinary Arts Fund'; 'School of Arts and Sciences Conference Support Grant') as well as the assistance of Timothy Corrigan, Nicola Gentili and Saïd Gahia, not to mention the participation of many other Penn colleagues. The original number of contributions was doubled for the purpose of the volume.

My most heartfelt gratitude must go to Justine Malle. Her unfailing involvement and kind encouragement every step of the way were thoroughly instrumental to the development and completion of the project. This book is dedicated to her.

Thanks must also be extended to Jacqueline Dougherty for her diligent technical assistance with the manuscript.

Translations: chapter 1 was translated from the French by Melissa Dunlany, and chapter 18 by Samuel Martin.

Unless otherwise stated, all other translations are by the respective authors of each contribution to this volume.

For Yue.

NOTES ON CONTRIBUTORS

Elisabeth Cardonne-Arlyck is Professor Emerita of French at Vassar College. She is the author of *Véracités: Ponge, Jaccottet, Roubaud, Deguy* (2009) and two books on novelist Julien Gracq. In addition to numerous articles on French filmmakers, she co-edited, with D. Viart, *Effractions de la poésie* (2003) and was guest editor of two issues of *Contemporary French and Francophone Studies* entitled 'Writing/Filming' (2005). She is currently writing a book on tears in film.

Michel Ciment is Honorary Associate Professor of American Studies at the University of Paris VII and has been a member of the editorial board of *Positif* since 1966. He is the author of some twenty books, including *Kazan on Kazan* (1973), *Kubrick* (1980; trans. 1983), *Conversations with Losey* (1985) and *Film World: Interviews with Cinema's Leading Directors* (2003; trans. 2009). He is also a radio producer and contributor, and has been a member of numerous prestigious international film festival juries.

Francesca Cinelli is completing a PhD in French Literature and Cinema at the University of Rutgers. Her primary area of interest is the function and meaning of music in novelistic and filmic fiction. She focuses on the links literature and cinema weave with jazz and its history in France and the US, especially with regard to the notion of bodily and spiritual freedom.

Tom Conley is Lowell Professor in Visual Studies and Romance Languages at Harvard University. His many books include *Film Hieroglyphs* (1991; new ed. 2006), *Cartographic Cinema* (2007), *An Errant Eye: Topography and Poetry in Early Modern France* (2011) and *À fleur de page: Voir et lire le texte de la Renaissance* (2016). He recently published articles on James Benning, Jacques Rancière and others. He is also co-editor, with T. Jefferson Kline, of *A Companion to Jean-Luc Godard* (2014).

Ludovic Cortade is Associate Professor in the Department of French Literature, Thought and Culture at New York University. His research focuses on the intersection of literature, social sciences and film, with particular emphasis on cinematic representations of space and collective beliefs in French film theory. In addition to numerous articles, he is the author of *Antonin Artaud, la virtualité incarnée* (2000) and *Le Cinéma de l'immobilité* (2008).

Caroline Eades is Associate Professor of Film and French Culture at the University of Maryland. Her research interests include European cinema, Post-colonial studies, and film and mythology. She is the author of *Le Cinéma post-colonial français* (2006), the co-editor, with Judith Aston and Sandra Guadenzi, of *The Essay Film: Dialogue, Politics, Utopia* (2016), and has written over thrity book chapters and scholarly articles on French cinema, culture and literature.

Ian Fleishman is Assistant Professor of German at the University of Pennsylvania. He is the author of *An Aesthetics of Injury: The Narrative Wound from Baudelaire to Tarantino* (2018) and has published in *French Studies*, *Comparative Literature Studies*, *German Quarterly*, *The Germanic Review*, *Mosaic* and elsewhere on subjects ranging from the Baroque to contemporary cinema.

Sandy Flitterman-Lewis is the author of *To Desire Differently: Feminism and the French Cinema* (1990) and co-author, with Robert Stam and Robert Burgoyne, of *New Vocabularies in Film Semiotics* (1992). She has co-founded two journals, *Camera Obscura: Feminism and Film Theory* and *Discourse: Studies in Media and Culture*. She is currently assembling a collection of her essays entitled *Hidden Voices: Childhood, the Family, and Antisemitism in Occupation France*, a study of material culture and memory in World War II France.

Sue Harris is Professor of Film Studies at Queen Mary University, London. She is the author of *Bertrand Blier* (2001) and *An American in Paris* (2015), and co-author, with Tim Bergfelder and Sarah Street, of *Film Architecture and the Transnational Imagination: Set Design in 1930s European Cinema* (2007). She has written widely on French cinema, popular culture and stars, including Gérard Depardieu, Catherine Deneuve and Alain Delon.

T. Jefferson Kline is Professor of French at Boston University. He is the author of *Bertolucci's Dream Loom* (1987), *Screening the Text* (1992), *Unraveling French Cinema* (2009) and numerous essays on French and European literature and film. He is the co-editor, with Tom Conley, of *A Companion to Jean-Luc Godard* (2014) and has co-edited several volumes in the *Interviews* series for University of Mississippi Press. He has recently translated the first four volumes of Robert Merle's *Fortunes de France*.

Justine Malle, daughter of Louis Malle and Alexandra Stewart, was born and grew up in Paris. She first went to Brown University, then studied philosophy at the Sorbonne. After translating several books into French, she directed two short fictions (*Cet été là*, 2007; *Surpris par le froid*, 2008) and two short documentaries (*Shanghai Notebooks*, 2003-4; *Light in April*, 2004-5) before making her first, largely autobiographical, feature film, *Youth* (2013).

Philippe Met is Professor of French and Cinema Studies at the University of Pennsylvania where he teaches poetry, fantastic fiction and film. He is Editor-in-Chief of *French Forum* and has written widely on literature and film, including several books (as author or editor) and some ninety articles. He is most recently the co-editor, with Derek Schilling, of *Screening the Paris Suburbs: From the Silent Era to the 1990s* (2018).

Jean-Louis Pautrot is Professor of French and International Studies at Saint Louis University. He researches interrelations of music with contemporary French literature and film. His publications include *La Musique oubliée* (1994), *The André Hodeir Jazz Reader* (2006), *Pascal Quignard ou le fonds du monde* (2007) and *Pascal Quignard* (2013), as well as guest-edited journal issues (*Études Françaises, L'Esprit Créateur, Sites*). He is Editor-in-Chief of an upcoming journal in Quignard Studies.

Sébastien Rongier is a French writer and essayist with a PhD in Philosophy of Art (Panthéon-Sorbonne University, Paris I). His latest nonfiction and fiction publications are *78* (2015) and *Les désordres du monde. Walter Benjamin à Port-Bou* (2017). His most recent book-length essays include *Cinématière* (2015) and *Théorie des fantômes* (2016). He is currently completing a book entitled *Marcel Duchamp et le cinéma*.

Derek Schilling is Professor of French at Johns Hopkins University. He is the author of *Eric Rohmer* (2007), *Mémoires du quotidien. Les lieux de Perec* (2006) and of a forthcoming study on literary representations of the French suburbs between the wars, entitled *Banlieues de mémoire. Géopoétique du roman français de l'entre-deux-guerres*. He is the co-editor, with Philippe Met, of *Screening the Paris Suburbs: From the Silent Era to the 1990s* (2008).

Guillaume Soulez is Professor of Film Studies and Head of Institut de recherche sur le cinéma et l'audiovisuel (IRCAV) at University Sorbonne Nouvelle, Paris III, where he teaches film, media theory and the history of television. He is the author of *Quand le film nous parle. Rhétorique, cinéma, télévision* (2011) and co-author, with Laurent Jullier, of *Stendhal, le désir de cinéma* (2006). He is also the co-editor, with Kira Kitsopanidou, of *Le levain des médias. Forme, format, media* (2015).

Steven Ungar is Professor of Cinematic Arts at the University of Iowa, where he has also taught French and Comparative Literature since 1976. His books include *Roland Barthes: The Professor of Desire* (1983), *Scandal and Aftereffect: Blanchot and France Since 1930* (1995), *Popular Front Paris and the Poetics of Culture* (with Dudley Andrew, 2005) and *Cléo de 5 à 7* (2008). *Critical Mass: Social Documentary in France*, is scheduled for publication in 2018.

Alan Williams is Professor of French and Cinema Studies at Rutgers University. He has written numerous studies of French and American cinema, the theory and history of film sound, and the narrative analysis of film. He is the author of *Max Ophuls and the Cinema of Desire* (1980), *Republic of Images: A History of French Filmmaking* (1992), and the editor of *Film and Nationalism* (2002).

FOREWORD

Volker Schlöndorff

By 1963, at age 31, Louis Malle had already known major artistic and financial ups and downs, but suffered from a perceived lack of recognition as an 'auteur' within the *nouvelle vague*. So he set out to write an almost autobiographical screenplay when a friend, novelist Roger Nimier, accidentally killed himself on the *autoroute*, right about at the spot where the young runaways of *Elevator to the Gallows* raced to Miles Davis's horn. Malle dropped his own story and started a screenplay that would lead to *The Fire Within*, about a 30-year-old committing suicide, based on Drieu La Rochelle's novel, whom he modeled largely on himself, shooting in a friend's apartment, furnished with his own stuff – his books, his paintings and newspaper cuttings that we, his friends and assistants knew from his own bathroom. Jeanne Moreau, Alexandra Stewart and other lesser-knowns belonged to his life as much as to his films and were cast immediately. Only for his alter ego did he seem unable to find the proper 'personifier', making tests with as unlikely candidates as Christopher Plummer and Thomas Holtzmann, until he finally settled on Maurice Ronet, who was the obvious choice from the beginning. But Malle had been afraid at first that Ronet might be too self-indulgent, and he directed him with the extreme rigor of someone painting an unforgiving self-portrait; and the portrait, at that, of a person impossible to seize, for Louis was forever elusive.

On Labor Day 2016, I introduced the film at the Telluride Film Festival and thereby saw it again for the first time in maybe 25 years. Personal as it may have been by its inspiration, the film showed no self-indulgence whatsoever. I remembered how Louis, who could be so charming and easy-going – 'grace and elegance incarnate' on the sets of *Zazie dans le métro, A Very Private Affair* or *Black Moon* as well as in his social life – had been tense, demanding, never satisfied during *The Fire Within*. And by the way, again during the shooting of *Lacombe Lucien* and *Au revoir les enfants*, as if on these more personal films he were subjecting himself to a more Bressonian approach. In a sense, he was at his best when he was in a bad mood – that is, short of temper with his collaborators, DP and ADs, but of infinite patience with his actors. The reading of a line, the nuance in a relationship between characters, the way they looked at each other, always hiding part of their feelings, never 'indecent', belonged so much to his own lived life that he felt a deep obligation to get it right. Each one of these details was testimony to his own experience of life, and not to be betrayed under any pretext. This extreme severity towards himself and towards the class he came from, this unforgiving portrayal of behaviour, distinguish his films from all others of his generation. Although carefree and prone to 'teasing', Louis was deeply impregnated with the solid bourgeois education he had received at home as well as during his studies. Literature, especially French, he held in high esteem, not only for its artistic, but its moral value. Writers, from Montaigne to Bataille, from Stendhal to Proust and Drieu La Rochelle, were his guidance in choices to be made, whether in his private, public or professional life. His strong social conscience – the work he was most proud of was *Phantom India*! – was never 'ideological'. Simple decency, a sort of Kantian obligation as to what one had to do or abstain from, surfaced as soon as he felt that 'things were getting serious'. As much as he enjoyed *épater le bourgeois* ('shocking the bourgeoisie'), he refrained from practical jokes about social reality.

It was Roger Nimier who arranged for my first visit to Louis Malle. The production office was located at 'le Poste Parisien', which had been the Germans' radio station during the Occupation. The place looked like a busy police station, desks piled with documents in a spacious room overlooking the Champs-Elysées, phones ringing, impenetrable cigarette smoke and, most notably, youngsters busying themselves, prepping the shooting schedule. They were extremely well dressed – button-down collar shirts, striped ties, gray flannel suits. Snobbish French people trying to look 'British', quite unlike my Quartier Latin style – jeans, black turtle neck and parka. Louis Malle took Nimier's calling card and read the few words scribbled on the back: 'My dear Louis, being in contact with a German philosopher can't do you any harm.' Indeed, in my studies at Paris Lycée Henri IV I had won the prestigious *Concours Général* in Philosophy…

This distinction, however, did little to impress Malle, any more than my three years working at the Cinémathèque Francaise as simultaneous translator. He had two assistants already and three interns working as PAs. As I knew this was my first and possibly last chance to enter French cinema, I insisted, and Malle, just to get rid of me, sent me off to his first AD, Philippe Collin, who was even more elegant than his 'master' and allowed me to come and visit the set for a day, at Studio Joinville, where they were due to start shooting *Zazie dans le métro* the following Monday, 3 March 1960. That day was to be the beginning not only of my work in movies, but of several friendships which have lasted to this day. A minor incident, it has to be mentioned, helped me along. The parrot that was supposed to be babbling all the time in the film refused to open its mouth when set up for a close-up, until I suggested spreading mustard around its beak. The bird tried to lick it off, such permitting to lip sync any dialogue. The trick worked and I was allowed to come back the next day. In fact, by the end of the 16-week shoot, I was practically the only remaining AD.

Malle's arrival on the set was like a diva entering center stage. One unforgettable moment says a lot about his way of working, and made me understand that a director before seducing the audience has to seduce his crew. One morning, under the Eiffel Tower he came speeding on the gravel in his Renault Dauphine, stopped with a power slide and jumped out, his cap turned backwards like Buster Keaton's cameraman. 'Let's see how we will start', he said, looking up the tower where Zazie was to climb all the way to the top. The crew started making proposals and moving around equipment, when suddenly Louis stopped us, calling for a rope. Quickly, he showed the grips how to fence off the space where we were standing. 'I declare this space to be the memorial for the unknown suicide', he said, showing us on the palm of his hand drops of blood falling from the tower above us. Somebody must have jumped to their death…

While his charm allowed him to get away with any impertinence, his perfect upbringing as well as his natural modesty and self-restraint, his tact and sensitivity saw to it that he never abused his powers of seduction. With 12-year-old Catherine Demongeot *aka* Zazie he was like a brother, hardly a few years older; with Maurice Ronet he was quite 'bossy'; Brigitte Bardot he cajoled; Jeanne Moreau he adored. His directions were never given as such, nor did he provide motivations; performances he obtained by seduction and complicity – one could say, by his mere presence. For he was never seducing in an active, conventional way. There was no courtship, it was not an act: it was a bond he established with one look, being then recognised as the 'master', and it was up to the other person(s) to please him. His satisfaction he would express almost ecstatically, at the end of a take, with a long triumphant 'cou–peeez!' or, if he did not get what he was looking for, with a dry 'cut!'

Cinematographers, sound mixers and production designers were equally his comrades. He was a skilled technician himself. As a soldier his gun, he knew cameras and sound equipment inside out; he also knew how to handle them and always did the framing himself. When a scene did not work out, when the performances were not to his liking, he would not stubbornly insist, but look for another way around, interrupting the work for a while, trying a different blocking or lighting, regardless of schedule and budget, until he got what he wanted. He would frequently reshoot entire scenes after having seen the dailies, which at the time was after the next day's work, or else after a day in the cutting-room. Oftentimes on weekends. On the eve of a Bastille Day, as we, his assistants, were inviting Louis to come with us celebrate by the Marne river, next to the St. Maurice studios, he declined with regret: 'I do not have your beautiful independence' – meaning he would spend the holiday editing.

Often, I wondered how he knew all he knew about filmmaking, and about life. He had never been an assistant, never seen another director at work; all his experience, at age 25, came from 'doing' or else by birth. We were friends, and worked together until his death. I first became his assistant for half a dozen projects – for years I lived in the 'maid's room' of his Parisian apartment by the river Seine. He then co-produced my first film, *Young Törless* (*Der junge Törless*, 1966), before I became his German co-producer for *Murmur of the Heart*, *Lacombe Lucien* and *Black Moon*. He took me on recon tours to Algeria during the war, to Vietnam for a reportage just before the start of the conflict in 1961. Finally, I followed him to the United States. I lived in his footsteps – his editor Suzanne Baron worked with me, I introduced him to Sven Nykvist … to mention only the professional exchanges.

It was not always an easy relationship, for Louis was often unpredictable, in his demands as in his moods, and I must have been pretty stubborn myself. On one of the last days of shooting *Viva Maria!* in Guanajuato, Mexico – Louis being exhausted by four months of constantly juggling his two stars, Jeanne Moreau and Brigitte Bardot – he was blocking a scene and I stood on the sidelines, inaudibly murmuring something, when he turned to me and said for the whole crew to hear: 'I've had the feeling for a while now there is no longer an assistant by my side, but a judge.'

I felt humiliated and was utterly destroyed, but he was right indeed. I had started to think I knew better than him. It was about time to become a director myself. Graciously he helped me, using his older brother Jean-Francois, who was a banker in New York, to obtain the rights to *Young Törless* from the Robert Musil estate in the USA. He was interested in how I was going to cast the boarding school boys, and reminded me how hard it was to get out of bed in the early morning dormitory. He came with me to the Cannes festival for the film's opening there, but we missed the true incident during the screening. Louis had taken me off to the Blue Bar as soon as the theatre lights went out. He was of the opinion that the public should see a film without its director. It was a question of propriety; anyway, it seemed more elegant. He had won the Palme d'Or himself at 21 for *The Silent World*, together with Captain Jacques Cousteau. I was 26 and in a hurry to prove myself his equal. We drank to that. Louis and I were a bit tipsy as we snuck back to our seats in the dark, shortly before the end of the film. There was excited whispering: where had I been? There'd been a scandal! The German cultural attaché had left the theatre, protesting loudly. This was not a German film! The students' torments seemed to confirm foreign prejudices regarding Teutonic sadism; and the scene where a white mouse was slapped against a wall was simply too much. He later wrote to the foreign office: 'This sequence could have led the foreign audience to lower its opinion of Germans.'

Years later, both of us living in the States, we often met and exchanged our impressions. I was very enthusiastic, working with Miller, Hoffman and Malkovich on *Death of a Salesman* (1985), while Louis' mood pendulum was swinging from positive to increasingly cautious, and over the years to disenchanted. 'Just wait until you watch TV in bed with an American woman', he warned me. Indeed, he tried to penetrate the country working and living with a number of fine ladies, among them Barbara Steele, Susan Sarandon and finally Candice Bergen. However, back in Paris, where again we met, he was not happy either. Stubbornly, he said he was going to prove to the French how obsolete they were, and to the Americans 'how Frenchie I am!' Margarethe von Trotta once mused that he was a man without a centre, all sensibility and skin, no gut – which might be the definition of 'modern man'. In fact, he was quite lost. But not in his filmmaking. We, his friends, knew that there was much more to come, that he could and would have reinvented himself a few more times, had he not died so soon.

INTRODUCTION

Philippe Met

'There is something suspicious about a film that is unanimously acclaimed.'
– Louis Malle[1]

The fundamental aim of this volume is, simply put, to reassess the at once acclaimed, provocative and versatile transatlantic career of French director Louis Malle (1932–1995). It seeks in particular to critically rethink the place of this influential *auteur* within the history of French, American (mostly independent, but not exclusive of Hollywood) and international cinema. Just over two decades after his premature demise, and notwithstanding the continued public notoriety and appreciation it has enjoyed, the time seems opportune to redress the surprising critical neglect his oeuvre has long been subjected to. This is especially true and glaring in comparison with the output of most of the Young Turks of the French New Wave who have seemingly overshadowed Malle in the eyes of critics and scholars alike, both in France and in the US. Admittedly, an artist's enduring impact and legacy are hardly measured numerically – by, or against, raw figures and rudimentary statistics – or in terms of creation, production or reception, all the more so for one whose first foray into filmmaking earned him, at the 'ripe' age of 24, no less than an Academy Award and a Palme d'Or as co-director (and cameraman) to Jacques Cousteau on *The Silent World* (1956). The fact still remains that – outside of invaluable interviews (chief of which is Philip French's enlightening *Malle on Malle*, 1993),[2] and discounting, due to a publishing date of 1964, an otherwise cogent essay, the first of its kind, by Henri Chapier (liberally complemented by a selection of excerpted statements and scripts by Malle, film reviews, as well as testimonies from collaborators) – monographs devoted to Malle are essentially limited, on the French front, to a long-out-of-print study by René Prédal (1989) that perforce does not cover the director's last three films, and an indisputably monumental and compelling biography by Pierre Billard (2003). To a degree, English-language scholars have been more generously attentive to the entire Mallean corpus in recent years, with book-length essays by Hugo Frey (2004) and Nathan C. Southern (2006), in particular. PhD dissertations focused on Malle have been and are few and far between on either side of the Atlantic or the Channel, Stéphanie Grégoire's 'Louis Malle, un observateur minutieux de la société contemporaine. Le "détour documentaire" et le "détour américain"' being the most notable, to this day unpublished, example.[3] Academic journal articles are unsurprisingly much more numerous, but again lag far behind those dedicated to the works of Malle's former *nouvelle vague* contemporaries.

And yet, his debut feature, *Elevator to the Gallows* (1957) was arguably a precursor or a pioneering work of that very movement in terms of its shooting and production methods, starting with the long takes of Jeanne Moreau illuminated only by the light from cafés, restaurants and shops as she wanders the streets of Paris at night. It cannot be overstated here the central role of groundbreaking cinematographer Henri Decaë, who uncoincidentally went on to lens not only Malle's next endeavor, *The Lovers* (1958), and several of his 1960s features, but also founding or iconic films of the New Wave like Chabrol's *Le Beau Serge* (1958) and Truffaut's *The 400 Blows* (1959). The case of *Elevator to the Gallows* is particularly striking and revealing. On one hand, Malle was to remain an 'outlier' vis-à-vis the rest of the group (a conscious self-positioning as much as incurred 'marginalisation') after the New Wave exploded onto the international film scene and started making headlines in 1959. On the other, this debut is already, characteristically, an unclassifiable work, with its unique blend of Hitchcock and Bresson, of radical modernity (including the largely improvised jazz score courtesy of Miles Davis) and overly literate (if not literary) dialogue and narration. Recognised and lionised for his first films by the *Cahiers du cinéma* gang (for example, Truffaut comparing *The Lovers*, 'a fascinating film', to Renoir's work, but we might also look at it as a 'feminist' film *avant la lettre*), Malle soon clashed with them over Brigitte Bardot and Roger Vadim when the latter took over as director after Jean Aurel's eviction on the set of *Please, Not Now!* (*La Bride sur le cou*, 1961). His *grand bourgeois* background and his outwardly dandy, dilettante ways no doubt contributed to the subsequent estrangement – an irreparable one, it must be said, save for the rebellious coalition formed with Truffaut and Godard at the May 1968 Cannes Film Festival and the *États Généraux*, or general assembly, of Cinema, and an admiring consensus on *The Fire Within* (1963).

But Malle was too fiercely independent, versatile and peripatetic, in the first place, to let himself be enlisted, let alone encaged, in any coterie or trend. This was too often erroneously confused with, if not deliberately stigmatised as, a telltale sign of ambivalence, instability and fickleness, or even inconsistency, by his detractors throughout his life and career – or by some critics still today. Nothing could be further from the truth, ontologically speaking. Call it instead a deep-seated core of perpetual dissatisfaction (with his own achievements), an insatiable curiosity, an unquenchable thirst for new experiences and experiments, an unflinching refusal to repeat himself (or plow the same furrow) and to be pigeonholed, an inclination for *tabula rasa* with every new project.[4] And, first and foremost, a sustained, uninterrupted substratum – a veritable *basso continuo*, to use a musical metaphor – subtending his filmography from start to finish: himself. In several notes to himself kept in the archives Malle is indeed quick to acknowledge that, aside from unquestionable thematic recurrences (childhood and loss of innocence, rebellion, solitude, identity, travel, etc.) and a no less irrefutable iconoclastic penchant for controversial or transgressive material (female desire and *jouissance*, suicide, incest, collaboration in occupied France, prostitution, pedophilia – the list goes on), the one common thread or linkage – 'the only *continuity*', in his own words[5] – running through a seemingly heterogeneous, unpredictable, discrete body of work is none other than 'me'. If Malle's films are indeed the fabric of his life, and vice versa, it may however be posited that through diversity and multiplicity at least three guiding principles, rather than a mere autobiographical or confessional mode, let alone a self-centered compulsion, govern his output. The first one should be readily apparent, if only based on his 'dromomania' and his keenness on (self-)reinvention: intellectual curiosity and humanistic openness. Or, to put it in psycho-optic terms, a scopic drive receptive to becoming symmetrically the object of the Other's gaze, as is exemplified most poignantly, albeit not exclusively (Violet gazing intently at the camera in *Pretty Baby* [1978] comes to mind), in his documentaries. The second principle is the 'passion' and '*acharnement*'[6] with which Malle said he practiced his art (see Mallecot 1978: 69). Though far from excluding such other motivations, intentions or directions as, say, devotion, rigour, sincerity or professionalism, the choice of words is here nonetheless eloquent in its privileging of an intense physicality and emotionality: semantically, the French *acharnement* points to 'relentlessness' or 'unremittingness', but also 'fierceness'. In a sense Malle himself encapsulated those first two components best when he stated:

> I never have a project in the wings, or, if I do, I end up not shooting it. Every film is a slice of life, a different adventure. It crystallizes my curiosity at that moment. Somewhat like in matters of the heart, after all. In either case, I only believe in love at first sight [*coup de foudre*] (Mallecot 1978: 37).

As for the third, and possibly most determining and defining, feature acting as a strong, magnetic vector, it might be termed a constant *shuttling* between poles that are habitually regarded as distinct and distant, if not divergent or incompatible. In geo-cultural terms, Malle's 'existential restlessness' first manifested itself as wanderlust. Serendipity – or was it 'objective chance'? – came along early on when Cousteau offered the young IDHEC student an initially short-term mission onboard the *Calypso*, his oceanographic expedition vessel, that turned into an 18-month 'discovery of the Tropics, Conrad style (*Youth*)' with its peculiar, persistent mix of contentment and unease.[7] This experience was later to find extensions and ramifications, substituting the deep with terra firma, the marine animal realm with human, all too human societies. Hence a more expressly ethnographic or anthropological bent, with the TV short *Bons baisers de Bangkok* (1964) and, most of all, *Calcutta* and *Phantom India* (1969; also shot for television), the latter two clearly constituting its fullest expression. As the present volume's title underlines, a privileged axis eventually came to the fore in the late 1970s, linking France to the US. France: Le Coual, Malle's retreat-estate-cum-anchor-point in southwestern France since the late 1960s where he successively shot

Lacombe Lucien (1974) and *Black Moon* (1975), and Paris, partly out of necessity in a highly centralised nation. The US: primarily New York, and, to a much lesser extent, Los Angeles. The keywords here have to be connection, circulation and potentiality, as opposed to tension, conflict or pulling apart, where some might have expected – and, indeed, others may have read at the time – a bitter expatriation, a resigned or even 'forced' exile after the virulent polemic and the broadsides generated in France by the release of *Lacombe Lucien*.

In point of reality Malle's interest in, and attraction to, the 'land of plenty' by far predates this midlife phase, and his 'American turn' was no doubt spurred on by numerous, if not all easily identifiable or quantifiable, factors.[8] Needless to say, since the days of Maurice Tourneur, Jean Renoir and Julien Duvivier (to name but a few) and all the way to the present time (see Jean-Pierre Jeunet, Mathieu Kassovitz, Luc Besson, Michel Gondry & co.), the annals of French cinema have not been short on filmmakers emigrating temporarily or, less often, permanently across the Atlantic, some forced by circumstances, others drawn to the lure of 'making it' in Tinseltown. It bears reiterating, however, that, operating under the aegis of the New York independent scene rather than within the Hollywood blockbuster machinery, marrying an American actress (Candice Bergen, before she became a household name with the lead, eponymous role in the sitcom *Murphy Brown* [1988–1998]), and continuing his exploratory documentary work in diverse physical areas and socio-cultural strata, or local mores, of the US (not only with *And the Pursuit of Happiness* [1986] and *God's Country* [1986], but also a drama film like *Alamo Bay* [1985]), Malle's trajectory and 'thought process' were definitely of a different order. Such that the very notion of 'an American period' is arguably rendered largely inapposite or irrelevant, in the case of a career like his, by the overall impression of a *perpetuum mobile*, of an incessant and insistent swing of the pendulum – with a fair degree of overlap or 'straddling' at times as well – that, beyond strict topographical considerations, extends to many other facets of the director's professional (and personal) life.[9] This would notably hold true in terms of genres: witness the fertile, more or less perceptible 'exchanges' between invention and autobiography, as noted earlier, especially in films like *The Fire Within, Le Voleur* (1967), *Murmur of the Heart* (1971) or *Au revoir les enfants* (1987); or an opus like *Zazie dans le métro* (1960), both screwball comedy and experimental film. In terms of styles and approaches: from the radical innovation of *Zazie dans le métro* and *Black Moon* (the latter defined by its author as 'a mythological fairy tale set in the near future'), or even *My Dinner with Andre* (1981) as limit-experience, to the narrative classicism of *Murmur of the Heart* and, exemplarily, *Au revoir les enfants*, or for that matter (but isn't it rather a *drame gai* à la Renoir?) *May Fools* (1990). And, even more importantly, in terms of filmmaking practices: one cannot but be struck by the alternation of, or oscillation between, direct cinema and fiction, with documentary concerns or overtones frequently bleeding or blending into the fictional world as, emblematically, in *Atlantic City* (1980). In that regard, if *Vanya on 42nd Street* (1994) is anything but a 'testament film',[10] it nonetheless epitomises many of these central features and manages to rejuvenate the documentary-reinvested-in-fiction principle by shifting, blurring or bending the lines.

Just as Malle's many *succès de scandale* – chief among them *The Lovers*, *Murmur of the Heart*, *Lacombe Lucien* and *Pretty Baby* – too often tended to obfuscate the subtle restraint and profound melancholy of his oeuvre (in that respect, arch-*provocateur* Bertrand Blier and him are not that far part, all things considered), just as his innate proteanism and constant self-renewal were occasionally equated, when ideology got the better of even the sharpest critics of the time, with a conspicuous lack of personality (read: of an *auteurist* personality), the back-and-forth activity previously described was regularly mistaken by some for detachment or dilettantism. This volume's contributions conversely delineate a filmmaker and a corpus remarkably both varied and coherent, but ultimately unclassifiable or, more aptly, in a class all their own. It therefore hardly comes as a surprise that, while remaining an inexhaustible source of admiration and inspiration for contemporary artists like Richard Linklater and Wes Anderson, such a richly eclectic and boldly subversive body of work has not accrued a cohort of true disciples or epigones. But isn't this, after all, the hallmark of all genuine masters? If Malle may have appeared at times to contradict himself it is because he was in passionate yet honest pursuit of an inner truth (even more than of a self-identity), and because, not unlike the Walt Whitman of *Leaves of Grass*, he 'contain[ed] multitudes' ('Song of Myself').

The first section of this volume is devoted to transversal studies of Malle's career focusing on a period, a motif, a genre or a style – or a combination thereof – in two or more films.

The opening chapter examines rarely seen, let alone glossed, films and sequences shot and/or directed by Malle during his Cousteau period, including the short document-aries *Station 307* (1954) and *La Fontaine de Vaucluse* (1955), as well as underwater images for E. T. Gréville's fiction feature *House on the Water Front* (1955). It also speculates about Malle's choices and input in *The Silent World*. Adopting a 'morphological' approach Guillaume Soulez shows that while Cousteau and Malle together contributed to a watershed in deep-sea iconography and adventure filmmaking style, the latter soon resolutely moved away from a Disney-like, spectacular aesthetic and a grandiloquent, overhanging, didactic voice-over narration in favour of a social documentary, first-person observational perspective. Malle thereby opted for a more authentic, immersive or even disorientating experience. Overall, the scientific exploration film led him to refine a number of filmic forms or techniques, and to experiment with a fluid harmony of bodies, equipment and natural elements.

Addressing the switch between filmmaking practices, Caroline Eades in chapter two picks up this general line of thought (Malle's collaboration with Cousteau as training ground and foundational work for the budding director) to contend that the specific treatment of three elements – the presence of recording technology, the representation of marine life, the use of sound – pervading *The Silent World* as a documentary feature had a significant influence on Malle's narrative and aesthetic choices as soon as he turned to fiction two years later, with *Elevator to the Gallows* and *The Lovers* (and on to his early 1960s films – *Zazie dans le métro*, *A Very Private Affair*, *The Fire Within*). Malle's interest in the mediatisation of vision, his 'mechanistic' conception of cinema, his acute perception of the both representational and narrational inadequacy of verbal language, his ethnographic concern (shared with Jean Rouch) for 'an ethic of looking and listening', his disenchanted gaze on the man-machine, his shift between nature (animals) and mankind (in particular, children) – all speak to a constant engagement with issues of realism, truth and objectivity and, ultimately, to a more assertive political thrust than is ordinarily perceived in his early work.

Chapter three looks at key twin documentaries made by Malle in France in 1974. As post-May 1968 investigations of factory work and the theatricality of street life respectively, Derek Schilling argues, they set forth a model for an ethically committed, exploratory cinema, one that privileges monstration or open-ended engagement over editorialising and outlines a film praxis at odds with the militant rhetoric of the day (which claimed exclusive transformative struggle capabilities). A careful review of period assessments highlights the argument *ad hominem* and the ideological bias behind accusations of a reactionary alignment, if not collusion, with the late capitalist apparatus and discourse. A close reading of *Humain, trop humain* (1974) follows, which reveals the film to be, in the bold decision to forego (social) commentary altogether, 'a prescient essay in reverse ethnography focused on human bodies at work' in lieu of the expected indictment of the Taylorist exploitation of workers. In letting women and men express themselves with minimal interference *Place de la République* (1974) is a variation on an observational mode that other practitioners of direct cinema (Raymond Depardon chief among them) would adapt to new contexts.

Alan Williams' chapter proposes a transversal study of the Mallean documentary corpus, with eventual emphasis on his American output – *God's Country* and *And the Pursuit of Happiness* – but within the larger transatlantic context and against a criss-cross historical background of similarities and differences, idiosyncrasies and commonalities, symmetry and dissymmetry. Malle's work is thus precisely compared, across a broad time/space spectrum, now to that of his former New Wave or Left Bank peers, now to that of English-language pioneers of direct cinema like Leacock and Wiseman, now to a recent and more specific 'school of Philibert' example, Julie Bertucelli's *School of Babel* (2014). What emerges is a blend of consistency – thematically (happiness, work, immigration, war protesting) as well as formally (for example, the 'contrarian set piece' introducing 'a twist, or a new perspective on a film's previous subject matter') – and variety – in terms of approaches (involvement vs. detachment) and techniques (pre-Nagra vs. synch sound; long takes) – that ultimately reflects Malle's 'anarchic conservatism'.

In chapter five Sue Harris considers Malle's statements about a stifling 'crisis' in French cinema's star-system in the early 1970s, and his concomitant appeal for new faces on French screens (precisely at a time when he selected a non-professional unknown for the titular role in *Lacombe Lucien*). She suggests that such a stance may have originated in the practical and personal experiences attached to Malle's films of the previous decade, when his artistic reputation allowed him to have his pick of France's top talent (after being something of a starmaker in the career of Jeanne Moreau in the late 1950s). Three star vehicles from the 1960s are thus closely scrutinized: *A Very Private Affair* (1961), with Bardot and Mastroianni; *Viva Maria* (1965), with Bardot and Moreau; and *William Wilson* (1967, from the Edgar Allan Poe-inspired *Spirits of the Dead* [*Histoires Extraordinaires*] portmanteau film), with Delon and Bardot. The focus ranges from the nature of the difficulties encountered (and documented by all parties), as well as their impact on the films produced, particularly at the level of performance and narrative coherence, to production histories, biographical sources and popular film criticism of the era.

The first of two successive essays specifically addressing the complex ties between Malle's filmography and literature, Ian Fleishman's chapter is a detailed analysis of the most singular and innovative of the director's formal forays. Literary adaptations in more than the traditional sense, *Zazie dans le métro* and *Black Moon* each attempt an apparently impossible literary ruse: the first in finding cinematic equivalents for Raymond Queneau's proto-Oulipian language games and the second in giving filmic form to Surrealist automatic writing. Although thematically both films trace the fantastic, oneiric education of a young female protagonist vaguely reminiscent of Lewis Carroll's *Alice in Wonderland*, stylistically they could hardly be more different. *Zazie dans le métro* is a schizophrenic, fast-paced, slapstick number whereas *Black Moon* is slow and brooding, patient and profound. Put differently, if *Zazie dans le métro* is an exercise in control, a lesson in filmic syntax, *Black Moon* is an attempt at learning to let go. Yet both reveal how Malle negotiated between textual strategies (Oulipo and Surrealism) in order to come to a mature filmic poetics entirely his own: 'a dream of a pure cinema of the unconscious'.

In a brief but pointed and historically informative chapter, Michel Ciment chooses to study Malle's proximity and/or collaboration with a select trio of writers. The intricate relationships between Malle and a brand of literature generally associated with the political right (Roger Nimier) or even far-right (Pierre Drieu La Rochelle) – an ideological affiliation actually shared by several of the young Turks of the French New Wave, as Ciment reminds us – are considered through a close examination of *Elevator to the Gallows*, scripted by Nimier, and *The Fire Within*, adapted from Drieu La Rochelle's same-titled novel. Both films capture the *zeitgeist* (on the cusp of a new parliamentary republic) even as they reflect Malle's personal mindset (fear of failure; rejection of 'adulthood'; romantic temptation of self-destruction). Last but not least, Ciment discusses the controversy surrounding the release of *Lacombe Lucien*, an original screenplay that Malle co-wrote with young novelist and future Nobel Prize-winner Patrick Modiano, whose unsuspected commonalities with Nimier are revealed.

In adapting Josephine Hart's *Damage*, under the same title, in his next-to-last film (1992) and explicitly labeling the latter *Les Amants #2*, Malle returned in many ways to a position he had taken in his second film, *The Lovers*, over thirty years earlier. However, he mapped this time a much more violent and darkly erotic *Carte de Tendre*, an imaginary cartography serving as a utopia of gender relations in the seventeenth century and as a guiding thread of T. Jefferson Kline's argument. Connecting the death-wish to the Orpheus myth (in particular, as cinematically mediated by Cocteau) and, to a lesser extent, to Hamlet, this chapter combines psychoanalysis with mythology and symbology to re-read, via *Damage*, the core of *The Lovers* as a female-gendered 'geography of hell'. This corresponds to an Orphic journey merging *Eros* and *Thanatos* in a very pessimistic canvas of despair that feels remarkably similar to *The Fire Within* and *Elevator to the Gallows*. Malle's work more largely comes across, Kline concludes, as 'one of the most appropriate exemplars of Bazin's theory of the ontology of the filmic image: the absent presence'.

Malle is known as a filmmaker who, early on, made the rejection of his own upper bourgeois upbringing a central theme of his oeuvre. Yet, in two more or less explicitly autobiographical opuses (*Murmur of the Heart* and *Au revoir les enfants*), as well as in a third one with strong confessional components (*May Fools*), the mother is always somehow on the side of the child (albeit an 'overgrown' one in the last of the three films), against the very values and conventions of the *grande bourgeoisie*, as Justine Malle demonstrates in chapter nine. Such a paradox is only apparent since Malle's personal history mode, though classical in appearance, cannot be reduced to a documentary-like reproduction of biographical elements, but should instead be seen as an incessant attempt to explore not only his inner soul, but, beyond and through it, the collective psyche. The figure of the mother, with the fantasies and taboos attached to it, is not, in these films, a mere representation of the real Françoise Malle, but a key to the unconscious, a way of digging into this shadowy underworld which the director's entire filmography is an effort to map out.

As one of the lifelong interests that fashioned his artistic ethos, jazz features prominently in the soundtracks of numerous films by Malle, courtesy of Jelly Roll Morton, Charlie Parker, Miles Davis, Ry Cooder, Joshua Redman, Sidney Bechet, Django Reinhardt and Stéphane Grapelli, among others. Drawing inspiration from previous theoretical research, Jean-Louis Pautrot's chapter sets out to apply specific 'reading codes' to a triad of Malle's films where jazz music is a particularly pregnant marker, be it of a cultural-historical (*Pretty Baby*), affective (*Murmur of the Heart*) or ontological (*Elevator to the Gallows*) order. Such clearly defined categories, however, soon start to bleed into each other. For instance, *Murmur of the Heart* also uses jazz as a cultural marker: set in 1954 during the siege of Dien Bien Phu, it evokes the famous 'war' that pitted the 'Ancients' against the 'Moderns' by featuring Bechet and Parker. Symmetrically, with *Pretty Baby* one can find in jazz both affective and ontological markers. More largely, the three musical soundtracks are shown to contribute to structuring the films in different yet related ways, thereby imparting not only rhythm and expressivity, but also a spontaneous, instinctive quality to Malle's filmmaking style.

Following a chronological order (with the exception of *Au revoir les enfants* placed right after *Lacombe Lucien* owing to the evident historical links between the two opuses), the second section includes monographic studies of key films by Malle.

As he progresses towards his planned suicide Alain Leroy, the protagonist of *The Fire Within* (1963), claims, with increasing urgency, that he can touch neither things nor people. Yet, from the start, the film emphasises the haptic interplay between the sense of touch and the act of looking: Alain's 'unrelenting' gaze upon Lydia elicits, as it were, the tactility of the actors' skin. While growing more acute over the course of the film, especially as he moves within cluttered spaces, Alain's inability to touch is ironically touching; it invites his friends' solicitude, albeit in vain. Elisabeth Cardonne-Arlyck's meticulous analysis in chapter eleven exemplifies how the detailed attention to Alain's personal objects (the gun, the pen, the clothes, the figurines, the photographs, etc.) and the decor surrounding him (in particular, mirrors and other reflective surfaces) accentuates 'the pathos of time' as well as the inextricably physical and emotional facets of touch. It is this interaction of touching and looking that, together with 'the mise-en-scène of small gestures, the performance of muted emotions, the unspoken language of bodies, and Erik Satie's bittersweet music', creates the richly complex texture of the film and prompts our empathy.

Although generally neglected by scholars and critics alike, *Le Voleur* is arguably one of Malle's most accomplished opuses – or, as he himself defined it, his 'last classical film'. Perhaps even more importantly, as Philippe Met argues in chapter twelve, it is Malle's most profoundly and darkly autobiographical film. Archival resources and genetic material (including the multiple script versions deposited at the Bibliothèque du Film/Cinémathèque Française) are extensively exploited with a view less to illuminating an adaptational process (the film is based on a largely forgotten novel by Belle Époque anarchist Georges Darien) than to considering alternate narrative possibilities and significant choices in the self-portraiture enterprise. As both voice-over narrator and nocturnal burglar carrying a (magic) lantern that 'lights the scene and dictates frame composition', the titular thief clearly emerges to be an authorial doppelgänger. A sense of scopophilia and various metafilmic associations are symbolically attached to his persona as iconoclastic aesthete. In terms of narrative and character development the overall arc is one of increasingly crepuscular melancholy and disenchantment, implicitly framed by a Baudelairean green paradise of youthful loves and a Proustian embodiment of Time.

Inspired by the reading of Michel Leiris and Joseph Conrad, *Phantom India* is a seven-episode documentary in which Malle 'expresses an interest in the experience of foreignness and the concept of cultural relativity'. Ludovic Cortade's chapter shows how the ensemble hinges on an ambivalent relationship to reality and to the film medium, as reflected in the voice-over narration. The filmmaker is driven by the contemplative desire to be a part of the universe and to immerse himself in the moving image, but faces difficulty in coalescing with the object of his gaze: the aspiration for absorption turns out to be a vain attempt – a 'ghost'. Indeed, *Phantom India* is haunted by 'the shape-shifting specter of subjectivity that includes the awareness that the camera modifies the reality that it is supposed to capture, perpetuating a risk of ethnocentrism'. Malle is thus reminded of his own subjectivity which he ends up cultivating in the name of self-reflexivity and social criticism.

Steven Ungar's chapter provides a minute account of the evolving reception of the 1974 film since its release, at a time when the eponymous protagonist's affiliation with the self-styled French Gestapo and his affair with a Jewish girl, provocatively named France Horn, were clearly at odds with Gaullist perspectives on Vichy France. It carefully considers how *Lacombe Lucien*, far from being a mere *mode rétro* product, continues to recast the questions 'What is a collaborator?' and 'What is a Jew?' raised by Sartre some three decades earlier into a concomitant one. Historical documentation on the German Occupation of France, recent studies on collaboration and its representations in literary or cinematic fiction, and Patrick Modiano's key role in the film's genesis and production are also brought to bear on this reevaluation of the film's unique reach and the controversy it fostered.

If the child figure and the attendant theme of innocence lost tend to hold a choice place in Malle's oeuvre, they both acquire biographical resonances and partake of historical awareness in *Au revoir les enfants*. The film, indeed, revolves around a childhood wartime memory that had haunted the director for four decades and thereby evokes the fate of hidden Jewish children under the Occupation – a fate that was still barely acknowledged in the late 1980s. Sandy Flitterman-Lewis argues that, while offering 'a recognisable New Wave-like representation of childhood friendship, maternal attachment, curiosity and youthful bonding', the film is just as disturbing and powerful for today's audiences. Tracing the imprint of anti-Semitism and the Holocaust, the chapter is structured around key term concepts – Memento, Milice, Movies, Music, Murder and Memory – which are either foregrounded in specific situations or alluded to across the narrative. This brings to the fore a network of symbols and references that is integral to the film's humanistic purport.

Through detailed microanalyses of specific sequences centred on three couples (Sally and Lou, in the voyeuristic 'lemon' opening sequence; Dave and Chrissie, in a loudly animated street scene, then hitching a ride on a truck; Grace and Lou, who eventually emerge from their domestic trials and make peace with each other), Francesca Cinelli's chapter analyses how sound (mostly diegetic, but often deceptively so) and music (be it psychedelic, operatic or jazzy) are 'theatricalised' in *Atlantic City*. What is thus conveyed or amplified across two different generations, one nostalgically yearning for the glory days it enjoyed during the 1940s while the other lives in a present (the early 1980s) largely filtered through hippie sensibilities, is a disconnect between stereotypes and facts, dreams of grandeur and grim reality in the ever-changing utopia/dystopia (between demolition and (re)construction) of the titular seaside casino resort, arguably the film's true protagonist.

Tom Conley's chapter is an illuminating study of a *sui generis* film whose inherently uncinematic 'table talk' premise, far from generating boredom, led instead, overtime, to a cult following. Postulating that the film 'has the trappings of a mystical narrative, and that its form bears the attributes of a *mystic fable*' (in the vein of Marie de France's *lai*, 'Bisclavret'), Conley traces the intricate threads woven by Malle's mise-en-scène between conversation (Andre Gregory and Wally Shawn around a dinner table) and conversion (Shawn's worldview at the end being partly altered and renewed after listening to his friend's outlandish spiritual experiences around the world); between interlocution and narration; between prologue and epilogue; between visuality, aurality and scripturality; between the construction of duration and the shot/countershot montage of close-ups; between the play of reflections and the camera (or the viewer, or the waiter) as a vital intercessory third party.

Finally, Sébastien Rongier explores Malle's last feature, *Vanya on 42nd Street*, showing it to be neither a 'testament film' (notwithstanding the crepuscular thematic, it is based on energy, experimentation and renewal – not finality, closure or completion) nor a 'Chekhov adaptation'. Instead, it presents an improbable theatrical adventure and creative process, led by Andre Gregory and a small troupe of actors (including Wally Shawn). With no actual performance in sight they are working on a Chekhov play in the New Amsterdam Theater, then abandoned and dilapidated, with scant remaining traces of the old magnificent Art Nouveau décor. Filming these sessions Malle blurs or interweaves all artistic lines through not only a complex dialogue between theatre and cinema, but also the subtle foregrounding of jazz music (played by the Joshua Redman Quartet) and the repeated slippage between actor and character, run-through and reality. All in all, *Vanya on 42nd Street* proves to be an undecidable cinematic object: 'an erosion of forms'.

These eighteen chapters which make up the analytical core of the volume are followed by 'Truth and Poetry,' an extensive interview of John Guare conducted by Philippe Met in New York on 7 October 2015. An acclaimed playwright, Guare was one of Malle's closest friends and collaborators in the US. He recounts at length, and with remarkable precision, his involvement with the researching and writing of *Atlantic City* as well as with important ulterior projects of Malle's (in particular, 'Moon over Miami' and 'Dietrich and Marlene') that unfortunately never saw the light of day. Their common love of books, Malle's life and work in New York, and the relationships on the set are also all highlighted as part of the discussion.

Wrapping up this volume, two exceptional archival documents are published for the first time. One is the transcription of a feature-length script of some sixty-four typewritten pages authored by Malle, titled 'The Loner', and dated November 1990. Based on – or 'suggested by', in the director's own words – Henry James' 1897 novel *What Maisie Knew*, it not only provides a glimpse or an inkling, however approximate and incomplete, of what this adaptation might have turned out to be on the screen, but also reveals fascinating thematic resonances or ramifications with the rest of the Mallean oeuvre. The other is a collection of rough notes (transcribed as is) for a lecture that Malle delivered onboard the *Queen Elizabeth 2* in the mid-1980s. It offers invaluable insight into his career trajectory while unveiling his personal views on the art of filmmaking and the film industry's inner workings on both sides of the Atlantic.

Last but not least, the volume is bookended by two eminent filmmakers, Volker Schlöndorff and Wes Anderson, who articulate the reasons why Louis Malle was such a seminal presence and/or influence for them. I am immensely grateful to both of them for such a generous gesture and testimony.

Notes

1 Mallecot 1978: 70.
2 See also Jacques Mallecot's *Louis Malle par Louis Malle* (1978) presented in an absorbing self-portraiture mode.
3 On a more glamorously anecdotal level, one may mention Brooke Shields' senior thesis at Princeton in 1987: 'The Initiation: From Innocence to Experience – The Pre-Adolescent/Adolescent Journey in the Films of Louis Malle, *Pretty Baby* and *Lacombe Lucien*'. It might not be incongruous to read this choice of topic as a testament to the lasting impression of her encounter with the director of *Pretty Baby* when he cast her at the tender age of twelve for the leading role. A short interview between Shields and Malle is appended to the thesis.

4   Notice, for example, the recurrence of the *repartir à zéro* syntagm ('starting from scratch') in Mallecot.
5   See also this undated self-note on a loose page where, presumably musing over a quasi-Proustian project that would subsume and recapitulate his creative journey, Malle writes: 'The continuity must come from me, not from the casting or from the plot.' (Malle Archives-Bibliothèque du Film/Cinémathèque Française: MALLE 1230-B228).
6   On that specific notion see chapter eleven on *The Fire Within* in this volume.
7   See MALLE 1230-B228.
8   See, for instance, Billard 2003: 367–72 (and *passim*).
9   Interestingly, at a time when his first American feature film (*Pretty Baby*) had just been released, Malle preferred to assess his output theretofore in *cyclical* terms; see Mallecot 1978: 57.
10 See chapter eighteen in this volume.

Bibliography

Billard, P. (2003) *Louis Malle. Le rebelle solitaire*. Paris: Plon.
French, P. (1993) *Malle on Malle*. London: Faber and Faber.
Frey H. (2004) *Louis Malle*. Manchester: Manchester University Press.
Chapier, H. (1964) *Louis Malle*. Paris: Seghers.
Mallecot, J. (1978) *Louis Malle par Louis Malle*. Paris: Editions de l'Athanor.
Prédal, R. (1989) *Louis Malle*. Paris: Edilig.
Southern, N. C., with J. Weissgerber (2006) *The Films of Louis Malle*. Jefferson, NC: McFarland.

TRANSVERSAL STUDIES

CHAPTER ONE

Malle Before Malle

Guillaume Soulez

The scene of vibrantly coloured torches descending into the sea that opens *Le Monde du silence* (*The Silent World*, 1956) has been compared, most notably by Cousteau himself, to a Promethean gesture.¹ Man brings light and colour to the dark, opaque underwater space, displaying his ability to expand the limits of his knowledge and his mastery of the planet. The sea is a new area of 'conquest' for Man, and Jacques-Yves Cousteau and Louis Malle emphasise the human adventure embodied by the *Calypso*'s expeditions early in the film with the introduction of the ship and its crew – from the divers and the first mate to the galley (*Reflets de Cannes*, 1956). *Station 307* (1955), Malle's 'first short film',² opens in a similar way, with a diver wielding a jackhammer on the floor of the Red Sea. Cousteau, narrating, states that there is no reason why Man, who has explored and discovered oil on the ground onshore, should not use the same techniques under the sea; this is the scientific and technical challenge at the heart of *Station 307*.³ These two striking opening sequences lend a synoptic and generative form to their films, with *Station 307* constituting a sort of rough draft of *The Silent World*. However, notable differences can be detected early on between Malle's more understated style and Cousteau's grandiloquence. This is evidenced, for example, by Cousteau's narration in the opening credits of *Station 307*: 'The *Calypso*, our underwater expedition ship, is tasked with an extraordinary mission…', a point to which I will later return.

Indeed, Malle's formal solutions progressively emerge in alignment with Cousteau and the established genre forms of the scientific, adventure, live-televised or underwater iconography film, while keeping a distance from Cousteau's formal choices (see Machu 2011: 21).⁴ My 'morphological' hypothesis is based on the idea that unique forms can be born from a project's friction with pre-existing genres and formats by playing with the different 'formal regimes' available as well as intermedial relations – namely, photography, cinema and television (see Soulez 2005). I will thus compare *The Silent World* with Cousteau and Frédéric Dumas' photograph-rich book of the same title, along with various films and sequences filmed by Malle during his Cousteau period. These include the short documentary films *Station 307* (19'; filmed in the spring of 1954) and *La Fontaine de Vaucluse*, (14'; filmed in the summer of 1955), underwater images shot by Malle for the fiction film *Port du désir* (*House on the Water Front*, E.T. Gréville, 1955), as well as a live television programme in 1955 in which Malle may have participated.[5] Malle was not only at sea during his Cousteau period, however. His two tours aboard the *Calypso* (January–July 1954; March–June 1955) allowed him the time to take part in film projects apart from *The Silent World*, both with Cousteau (*La Fontaine de Vaucluse*) and without (*Port du désir*).[6]

The Silent World is doubly scripted, around its subject and the subject of the filming itself. Cousteau recruited Malle in the summer of 1953, and after his summer apprenticeship proved successful, Cousteau hired him for his colour film project on the *Calypso*, slated for 1954 thanks to unexpected funding from British Petroleum. The first version, *Calypso cap au Sud. Requins bleus et corail noir* (*Calypso Southerly Course: Blue Sharks and Black Coral*) was shot in 1954 in 16mm Kodachrome colour and edited as a film conference in two parts. It was broadcast in 1955 as a part of the 'Connaissance du monde' ('Knowledge of the World') series with live commentary by Cousteau (see Machu 2011: 82–3). Malle was the assistant director, but Cousteau had already entrusted him, as noted above, with the responsibility of the short film *Station 307*. In light of the film conference's great success, Cousteau decided to do a remake in 35mm Eastmancolor, following the same route as before. For the first time, the aim of one of the *Calypso*'s excursions was to make a film. Malle and Cousteau wrote the first script in 1955, building from *Calypso cap au Sud*. This script served as the basic outline for the daily directing work carried out by Malle, who was responsible for production, but also contributed numerous shots and took part in editing.[7] In 1955, the various animal species expected all showed up, some of the refilmed sequences were not kept in the final edit, a black-and-white sequence from 1954 was blown up in 35mm, and another was added, but generally speaking, the characters in the film replayed their roles, while the *Calypso* navigated the same route, encountered the same marine life and found the same ocean spaces (see Machu 2011: 88–9).

In 1955, we are still far from the vogue – and the practice – of direct cinema, despite the already present interest in 'live' televised broadcasts of the ocean depths. Indeed, even beyond the readers of adventure or popular science magazines (such as *Neige et Glace*, which sponsored *Calypso cap au Sud*; or *Science et Vie*, which covered the filming in 1955),[8] viewers of the period were accustomed to the type of documentary reconstructions or reenactments found in the *Actualités filmées* (newsreels)[9] and on television. They were also capable of sizing up the novel nature of the colour images, and it was this never-before-seen aspect, in combination with the beauty that surged from the colour images, which was the main focus of the film's glowing reviews.[10] Viewers appreciated the humanistic, and often informal, style that was commonly seen in television reports or documentaries of the time.[11] Although the film equipment was 'heavy' and the teams burdened with cables and floodlights, it was nevertheless possible to operate cameras in the water, or put them on – or in – underwater scooters. We are also far from the loaded-down scuba divers of times past (known in the jargon as '*les pieds lourds*', 'heavy feet') as demonstrated early in the film by the confrontation with sponge fishermen who use the old technique. The television-inspired 'direct style' (as opposed to the often thick use of voice-overs in the *actualités filmées*), mixing complicity and technical exploit without necessarily being *en direct* or live (see Bringuier 1961; Soulez 2005), found a fresh ground of expression, enriched by the pleasure of discovery and the prospect of adventure.[12] It was as though the film's subject, and the filming environment, had 'lightened' the film even before the development of light techniques: 'Until now we have stumbled under the weight of this material, yet it is this material that will free us of our weight. Our mountain packs contained provisions of food; now we shoulder provisions of air.'[13]

Cousteau and Malle thus invented a new art of filming the sea that remains a reference today[14] by clearing a path between the different documentary and reporting genres and sub-genres of their era.[15] Tracing the various sources of *The Silent World*, we can attempt to see how Malle's specific documentary style was forged. This three-year span was seminal for Malle, as he has indicated on a number of occasions (see Billard 2003: 140–1). It was this experience that would repeatedly push him to return to documentary on a more authentic footing than with *The Silent World*, as if he had put his finger on the possibilities offered by the *films du réel*. *Station 307* contains about a dozen sequences,[16] and we can see how each of them is inspired by and departs from an existing format. In sum, we can distinguish three movements: (i) how the adventure film is based on a desire for risk and performance, but raises the question of the limits of the spectacular for Malle; (ii) how the scientific exploration film exposes Malle to different techniques and leads him to refine several filmic forms; (iii) how Malle, in the end, faced with the imagery of didactic photography and film, moved away from it and nurtured an interest in human and social relations.

1. Filming Danger: The Adventure Film and the Limits of the Spectacular

Cousteau had no qualms about making a spectacle of his explorations, in the tradition of Jules Verne and in an effort to reach the general public. The 1955 box office results proved him right, as it were, with the success of Disney's *20,000 Leagues Under the Sea*. Fourth in the box office in France, it featured a giant squid fight scene that made quite the splash. While Malle was enthusiastic about the images shot during his first encounter with sperm whales in 1954 (see Machu 2011: 80), he wished to avoid a Disney-like aesthetic and instead curated his interest in documentary as a discovery of the unknown, an experience of immersion, even a loss of bearings.[17] A steel cage designed to protect the divers from sharks appears in *Station 307* (min. 10) and is indeed used to shield divers from two lurking sharks between minutes 14 and 15. Shots of a shark filmed from the interior of the cage are used to anchor a series of alternating shots of sharks and a distressed diver signaling to his partner to go to safety before he joins him in the cage. This dramatic sequence, without commentary, is itself preceded by a sequence at minute 12, where we watch the divers as they face a sea serpent 'whose bite would be lethal' (commentary) while a cross-cutting shot on the ship is accompanied by the commentary, 'without suspecting what was happening underneath the hull, the hydrographer uses his sextant to find the station's position (min. 13). There is, as we can see, a mounting tension built into the construction of the documentary story, as though the scene aboard the ship were a harbinger. Contact between the ship and the action underwater, moreover, is reestablished when one of the divers tugs on a rope to ask that the cage be hoisted up. Although the sequence involves staging – there is no indication that all scenes were filmed at the same location, or on the same day; the second diver who swims to the cage is filmed from the exterior, as if Malle, who is holding the camera, did not think of his own safety – the risk is real and tragedy a possibility. There is certainly a thrill of pleasure resulting from the brush with danger and the disorientation possible under the water (and related to the off-screen), but the scene is not 'manufactured' as a fictional film sequence would be. In *Station 307*, it is a question of starting from a lived experience to dramatise it, or rather to restore its dramatic force by filmic means. Malle would also be the one to film shots of the shark cage in *The Silent World* alongside Falco, who, having left the cage at one point, narrowly escapes a shark at his heels (see Billard 2003: 140).

In *The Silent World*, it is a baby whale injured by the ship's propeller that bears the brunt of the sharks' voracity, introducing a sacrificial third party between the men excited by danger and the sharks by blood. The sharks in this film have a more threatening profile, filmed in close-up along the side of the cage. The dramatisation is thus intensified from one film to the next, particularly as we now know that the second accident with the whale pup was deliberate, in contrast to the random nature of the first (see Machu 2011: 79–81; 95–6).[18] Cousteau had the final say on *The Silent World*, contractually,[19] and agreed with the editor Georges Alépée's suggestion to edit the sequences in the style of 'a line-up of circus acts' (see Grégoire 2006: 44; Machu 2011: 98).[20] 'This is a scripted film', asserted Cousteau.[21] The commentary styles of the two directors were also very different, Cousteau having created his own style, that of a smooth-talking conference speaker, post-war (see Machu 2011: 50), whereas Malle's voice was much more interior and understated, as we will see in *La Fontaine de Vaucluse*. Starting from the same basic mold, that of the underwater adventure film, Cousteau and Malle make their distinctive, and diverging, marks.[22]

2. Filming/Swimming

In *The Silent World* there is a general move to reconcile the gesture of the filmmaker with that of the athlete/explorer. Cousteau, 'the underwater mountaineer',[23] regularly worked with Marcel Ichac, founder of mountain film as a school of energy and endurance. Ichac directed the first film-explorations of the Himalayas in the 1930s, and Cousteau and Ichac shared the same cameraman, Jacques Ertaud, whom Malle replaced for *The Silent World* after his apprenticeship in the summer of 1953. It was a combined effort and a test of techniques and bodies that preceded direct cinema as *light cinema*, with its focus on portability and miniaturisation of equipment, exposure of material and bodies to extreme conditions, and coordination of technical and athletic

Fig. 1: *The Silent World* (1956): Underwater silhouettes. (Photographer: Luis Marden)

movements while filming an exploit. One of the main difficulties of underwater filming was stability and coordination between the filmed diver, the lighting, and the camera. Jérôme Salle's biopic *L'Odyssée* (*The Odyssey*, 2016) reproduces well the initial 16mm underwater camera shootings and the first public screenings of films by the three 'Mousquemers', Philippe Tailliez, Frédéric Dumas and Cousteau. In *The Silent World* it is Cousteau who films Dumas during the shipwreck sequence, but Malle soon takes the reins and films Cousteau, Dumas, Falco, and the others in turn. When Cousteau recruited him, Malle knew and admired his film *Autour d'un récif* (*Around the Reef*, 13', 1949), which was similar to another film by Jean Painlevé in terms of the way the fish were filmed, but went further to introduce the relationship between man and marine fauna (see Machu 2011: 53) and was scored with jazz (one of Malle's great passions), a choice also noted by Jean Mitry.[24] Alongside Cousteau, Malle quickly became one of the best filmmaker-divers of the time, and received multiple offers to film similar projects during and after *The Silent World*, so much so that he was initially regarded by part of the film community as a '*scaphandrier*', a deep-sea diver (see Moreau 2017: 14).

From such a perspective, a film is first and foremost a chronicle of a 'mission' or a 'campaign', a series of physical feats and technical exploits recorded in a *carnet de plongée* (a diving notebook; this was the title of a film directed by Cousteau and Ichac in 1949). We can see this at work in *Station 307*. Following the pre-credits drilling sequence, the opening credits roll as we approach the surface of the *Calypso*, which is arriving at its new territory of investigation. Next, the new mission ('Now we are approaching Station 307', min. 2), the team and the technical equipment are presented, just as in *The Silent World* where the boat,[25] its crew and tools are introduced after the pre-credits sequence. The endings of the films are also similar. We see the crew of the *Calypso* lift the anchor, and the ship sails off to new adventures – 'On the way to the 308th!' in *Station 307*, and 'One day we will go much deeper. New discoveries await us in the silent world', in *The Silent World*.

Malle faced a number of technical and equipment-related difficulties that the film obscures by highlighting the wonders of these new machines – the lighting, their mobility and the techniques themselves, in a display of modernity emblematic of the spirit of the times. A blend of control, shooting tricks (culled from the extensive experience of Cousteau and his associates) and physical fitness resulted in a fluid, albeit orchestrated production. The young Louis Malle, an accomplished athlete, was also one of the IDHEC (The Institute for Advanced Cinematographic Studies) students the most interested in technical questions (see Machu 2011: 73). The athletic aspect also came into play as a condition of filming and a performance to be filmed. Cousteau and Malle each directed a team of divers, and the shooting was done by Malle, Cousteau, Falco, Dumas and Edmond Séchan, who did the 'exterior' shots on the ship. Malle also oversaw the shooting. A paragraph from the film's press release at Cannes expresses well how the film met these physical expectations: 'the travellers who participate in the fabulous expedition of the *Calypso* glide underwater with the same ease as they would tread paths on dry land, even with more ease. They bring their air reserve, use real underwater scooters and are weightless. They go on these treks "in real life" that we have all done in our dreams, at least once.'[26] Putting techniques on display and discussing them does not detract from the documentary's aim but rather strengthens it as the harmony of bodies and equipment fills the screen. These images are all the more impressive as we can easily imagine the amount of 'trash footage' generated to get them.

One type of sequence emblematic of athletic and technical prowess on display involves marine animals that appear to play with and challenge the team's technical skills by taking their turn at performing like star athletes. The long sequence of dolphins leaping out of the sea as if in a race with the ship, dubbed the 'Olympic Games for Dolphins', is one such example.[27] There is also a parallelism established between the underwater scooters and the turtles used to tow around the divers, including a scene where Falco abandons a scooter to latch onto a turtle as it glides past. Such scenes attest to the pursuit for a fluid form combining scientific description (discovery of unexpected marine fauna and flora), athletic feats (competition between man and animal, or between men), and the technical skills needed to follow all movements without losing a scrap, as the third partner in the game (see Machu 2011: 53).

As stated in an IDHEC class note that Malle saved, 'gratuitous panoramas must be avoided *at all costs*. The camera should not pan across a line of immobile objects, but follow something in movement, even if that means inventing a movement from nothing.'[28] From this standpoint, the ideal camera movement is the forward tracking shot,[29] which mimics the diver's movement and encourages the viewer to identify with

Fig. 2: 'Down to the Andrea Doria' (The News Magazine of the Screen, Pathé Pictures Inc., 1956): Louis Malle checks out an underwater camera.

the filmer progressively discovering marine life wonders, moving his body forward in a liquid element. As Malle remarked, where a crane would have been required in the studio, 'we would do it just like breathing because it was part of the movement of the diver' (French 1993: 8). As such, the tracking shot can be considered the best formal expression of the capabilities of this 'new animal, the man-fish', as Painlevé described in referring to *Paysages du silence* (*Silent Landscapes,* 1947), one of Cousteau's first films that makes prominent use of this movement.[30] Malle uses the shot in *Port du désir* to film scuba divers exploring a shipwreck (and discovers a crime through a porthole). The scene repeats the same movements twice, in the same order, first demonstrating the horizontality of exploration, and then the verticality of discovery (with the diver perpendicular to the shipwreck), before the climb up and the revelation at the surface. In this regard, the resemblance between this forward movement and Malle's filming of the Tour de France is striking. In *Vive le Tour!* (1962), Malle seems to be searching for an equivalent effect from atop a speeding bicycle. This can be seen, for example, in the opening sequence crossing through a little town, and in the shots grazing past spectators, accompanied by commentary from former cyclist Jean Bobet, who states that the bicycles' speed can reach up to 37 mph.

Man-bicycle, man-fish. These films seek to film the way we ride, to film the way we swim – achieving a fusion between body, machine and natural elements, while at the same time defying resistance to those elements, water and air. When Cousteau elevated young Malle's position by naming him co-director, it was because he very quickly saw in him an *alter ego*.[31] The shipwreck sequence shot by Cousteau is quite beautiful and involved multiple cameras to seamlessly connect the tracking movements and objects appearing inside the wreck. But Malle developed and amplified Cousteau's model in a number of other places, to the point where Bazin considered that 'the quality of the film owed much to Malle's intelligence and directing', a mise-en-scène that arranged and rearranged but conserved the beauty of the movement as well as the co-presence of nature (shipwrecks teeming with fish) and the divers (see Bazin 1956: 38). We could perhaps venture that the success of the film is owing to the tension created between the

Fig. 3: *Silent Landscapes* (1947): 'The man fish'.

sequences carried by the elements (Malle's horizon) and the rhythm of the screenplay (Cousteau's horizon), even though the two directors both filmed and contributed to the editing.

3. Of Fish and Men

When the man-camera becomes a fish, it is also to produce an album of the ocean floor that is both scientific and otherworldly. 'The enthusiasm for this film (*The Silent World*)', said Michel Cieutat, 'was made possible by the numerous screenings of the first part of the documentaries, which raised the masses' awareness of the genre (of the scientific film)' (2005: 23). Outside of Painlevé's work and Cousteau's own films, an iconography already existed in colour. It became known through Cousteau's eponymous book (1953) before the film's release, with five million copies distributed worldwide, as well as by news stories in illustrated scientific and general public magazines. In the book, the photographs focus on the pioneers and daredevils, as well as the equipment, including underwater cameras. As in *Paysages du Silence*, Cousteau spotlights the men-fish (group profiles, slender bodies, unique postures). Most importantly, he builds a repertoire of images that subsequent films would draw from: close-ups of colourful fish and curiosities of the marine flora (enormous algae-flowers, massive corals), and a number of images of the 'encounter' between Man and animal (turtle, dolphin, big fish, octopus...) that we don't see in Painlevé's work. In Cousteau's book, man has become a marine animal in his own right, able to enter in contact with the animals. Different relational modes are present that we also find in the films: fusion of bodies, reciprocal observation, combat, even food in the way of a feast of lobster, just as in the film. It is more difficult to detect Malle's own touch in these photos as a number of them are 'snapshots' in line with Cousteau's iconography. In any case, Malle appreciated the intact beauty of the islands and the seafloor, but rejected their treatment as postcards.[32]

The most obvious example of these images involves the ship's mascot, a dog (though a pet seal was originally planned, according to a note in the initial script) face to face with a marine creature – an octopus, a lobster – on deck. This human-provoked encounter between two animal worlds is found in nearly all of Cousteau's films (whereas in *Station 307*, a sailor settles for playing with the dog during a break), as well as in TV programmes on or involving the Cousteau team. These images serve as a comic relief in contrast to more harrowing sequences involving diving accidents or the menace of sharks. They often poke fun at an oddity of nature (a fish that deflates as it empties itself of air, a plant that transforms itself before your eyes), or they anthropomorphise marine life (showing a curious fish, a gluttonous fish, a fearful fish). It is here that the musical and spectacular Disney style threatens to disrupt the poetry of deep-sea discovery.

Such requisite sequences were not particularly to Malle's taste. He seemed to prefer instead sequences that revealed man's attitude toward animals, such as the crew's eruption of violence against the sharks, which he wrote about in his correspondence, and which Edmond Séchan, in charge of the 'exterior' shots on the *Calypso*, captured through reverse angle and cutaway shots. When Malle had more control over his films, as in *Station 307*[33] and *Fontaine de Vaucluse*, he did not hesitate, as we have seen, to create dramatic ties between humans at work, in particular by intently filming the gestures between divers. He also reproduced the strong impressions of certain scenes: 'Twenty-five meters, we pass in front of the zinc boat, next to the entryway to the second room. It sunk 77 years ago during its first attempt to descend, the sight of it comforts me, I don't know why' (*La Fontaine de Vaucluse*, min. 2). He also shares his empathy for his comrades: 'Sucked in by the current, he [Goiran] got sucked in by the current, Canoë helps free him (soundtrack: 'Careful'…) I'm impressed by the composure of my three mates. […] Canoë looks disappointed, a bit annoyed. He opens his air supply, it's time to resurface (Barely audible words). Above me, the three divers consult' (min. 6). Malle's novice-like inner voice, and the attention he pays his and his companions' emotions, clearly contrast with the detached tone and dominant (but certainly benevolent) stance of '*pasha*' Cousteau.

Malle's interest in individual or collective work can also be seen in *La Galère engloutie* (*The Sunken Galley*), filmed in 1955 to be included in *The Silent World*, but eventually edited out.[34] Malle's filming of the work of Falco and the other divers at the Grand Congloué shipwreck is illustrative of this, as is his coordinated filming with Séchan, both under and above the water for Laban's accident sequence in *The Silent World*. The sequence begins with Laban making strange gestures under water, before becoming a scene of community life, ending with the lobster meal that Laban isn't allowed to partake in as he must remain in the decompression chamber. The original script had also envisioned a scene on Laban's discovery of diving (chapter 4), and a hazing scene to mark Laban's first time crossing the equator (chapter 9). As Franck Machu has remarked, *Station 307* is the first of the Cousteau team's films to turn the camera on the Captain himself, at work in front of maps with the geologist, thereby sketching the portrait of a singular man that would be taken up again in *The Silent World* (2011: 76). The focus on work in drawing the portrait of a man or a group also harks back to the effort and solidarity of the cyclists mentioned earlier, and the central role of work in questioning 'the human', which would be evident in *Humain, trop humain,* twenty years later. The scenes of group work, the analysis of fish by the onboard biologist, the moments of playing or relaxing – all these elements retained in the film contribute a new dimension to the painting of collective life, which is then played out again under water through shared experiences, looks and exchanges. Malle the filmmaker thus seems to be as much, if not more, interested in human personalities (Canoë, Cousteau, Falco, Dumas…), and the human 'group' as he is by the unseen beauty of the ocean depths (which he appreciates as a diver, or as any viewer would). For reasons that are certainly different, linked to their adoption of near-opposing genres (the model of the adventure film for Cousteau, who carries the 'we' of the script,[35] versus the social documentary perspective of Malle, who observes and creates in the first person), *The Silent World* manages to garner just as much interest for men as for fish.

In a letter to his mother, Malle writes of an 'interior'[36] adventure related to the progress of the soul in the face of discovery and danger, seen as tests that serve to strengthen and increase self-knowledge. It is this that Malle refers to later in a note conserved at the Cinémathèque française:

> For my little madeline [sic], remember the Calypso … All the time, we feel well and bad; nature takes over reason, chaos, rot, violence, and the soul's calm as well. We feel well and bad all the time. An indelible mark. It could be Calypso, it could be India. It's difficult to integrate it, but it deserves a film fitted into the whole (In the margins: I made it with *Phantom India*).[37]

But when he evokes this interior adventure, he further notes:

> I swear to no longer dream about the marvelous light of the South Seas, a sterile contemplation, when the social adventure is completely open to me. Things don't seem to be going well in France…[38]

Malle's 'petits films', which flank *The Silent World*, in addition to some of his choices in the feature film (as determined from various sources and in comparison with his short films) not only inform us about the situation of documentary and more generally film in the mid-1950s, but also give us a glimpse into some of Malle's early interrogations. For Malle, the three-year period was not only a technical and practical apprenticeship, full of marvel and adventure, but also the grounds of his first formal experiments with several documentary genres, incorporating social and political issues that would be expanded upon in his later projects.

Notes

1 'L'Invité du dimanche', ORTF, 2e chaîne, 5 October 1969. The name of this sequence in the first script was 'Descent into the unknown, fire under the sea'.

2   'My first short film. The film team was – me!' (L. Malle, *Catalogue Pyramide et NEF: Le cinéma de Louis Malle*. No page numbers or date.) The film's opening credits, at 45 seconds, state: 'A film by Jacques-Yves Cousteau – Music: Jean Wiener – Assistant director: Maryse Barbut – Direction, filming, editing by Louis Malle.' The commentary and voice are Cousteau's.

3   *Station 307*, first and second minutes.

4   A filmmaker before becoming a diver, he seeks a cinema that is neither 'romanesque à la Williamson' (a pioneer of underwater photography and film, who filmed a version of *Vingt mille lieux sous les mers* [*Twenty Thousand Leagues Under the Sea*] in 1915), nor a 'science documentary in the style of Painlevé' (Machu 2011: 31).

5   The programme was *Provence Magazine*'s 'Techniques nouvelles, essai de tournage sous-marin à partir de la *Calypso*' [New techniques, testing underwater filming with the *Calypso*], RTF, 5 November 1955. Malle also references films shot by the Ford Foundation (which sponsored American television programmes) or the BBC (see Billard 2003: 136).

6   See Billard 2003: 145. He was even briefly Bresson's assistant on *Un condamné à mort s'est échappé* (*A Man Escaped*) in the spring of 1956, before and after Cannes (see Billard 2003: 152). His 'Cousteau period' lasted from July 1953 to September 1956 (after a botched dive off the coast of the United States during which a diver died, Malle ruptured his eardrums and decided to end his collaboration with Cousteau [see Billard 2003: 123; Grégoire 2006: 52]).

7   The Malle Archives at the Cinémathèque française contains two versions of the script that are very close, one of which is divided into chapters (that I have numbered) and has served as a foundation for my work (MALLE 1230-B228).

8   These were an illustrated cover, 'Comment Cousteau a tourné *Le Monde du Silence*' ('How Cousteau filmed *The Silent World*'), and an article by Daniel Vincendon (1956).

9   One of the first programmes on Cousteau in 1944, *Par 62 mètres de fond. Un reportage de Cousteau et Cabrières* (*62 Meters Deep: A Report by Cousteau and Cabrières*), featured the scuba gear and the waterproof camera he had perfected. Cousteau did the underwater shots (*France Actualités*, 18 February 1944).

10 Press kit at the Cinémathèque française, and press kit from Cannes conserved in the Festival's archives (FIFR 155-B19).

11 It is this 'fake spontaneity' that Malle referred to in a letter to his mother. Malle, as we will see, was very critical of Cousteau's conception of cinema, and consequently of the result produced by the film. He refused to critique Cousteau publically, doubtlessly out of loyalty to the Captain and his men, with whom he learned and shared so much (see Billard 2003: 141).

12 'Without rigging, didacticism or platitudes'; 'An unforgettable spectacle' (FIFR 155-B19).

13 *Paysage du silence* (1947; around the two-minute mark), when the team and their equipment are lowered into the water. This film, whose title is not insignificant, is the first of Cousteau's films to so prominently feature the team of divers.

14 Guide from the blog *Vidéo Bleue: Make Quality Underwater Videos*, pdf document (2016: 5).
15 It should be noted that Malle contributed to financing the film as one of the associates of the company *Requins associés*, which gave him a certain amount of leeway; see Violet 1993: 137 and Billard 2003: 148.
16 The 85-minute film is rhythmed by alternating sequences of around twelve minutes each. The first script had planned for eighteen-minute sequences, revealing a choice made in favour of efficiency and coherency. One of the cut sequences on a shipwreck in the Mediterranean would later become *La Galère engloutie* (*The Sunken Galley*, 1957), in which Malle also participated in filming. Outside of the episode with the Greek sponge fishermen, the images came, for the most part, from the Red Sea and the Indian Ocean (Seychelles). Excluded were attempts at live television and images of the Arctic (Diving Under Ice – chapter 7).
17 Malle related that he opposed Cousteau's penchant 'for conventional spectacle', and that due in particular to the music used for *The Silent World*, he thought it was not documentary: 'this [was] show business … it [was] becoming like Walt Disney' (French 1993: 8).
18 See also André Laban's remarks in J. Wybon's film, *Du silence et des hommes* (*Of Silence and Men*, 2010).
19 'For an indefinite period, to expire on the day of the corporate presentation of the first copy of the film in question [*The Silent World*], you shall devote yourself, body and soul, and under my high and benevolent leadership, to the co-direction of the film.' Letter-contract signed between Cousteau and Malle, 27 February 1955 (MALLE, 1230-B228).
20 In the same vein, the film's opening torch scene, which had been planned as the closing scene in the first script, became a spectacular beginning, doubtlessly due to the influence of Alépée, and placed even more emphasis on Cousteau, who then emerged from the water removing his diving mask, and appeared again after as the Captain during the boat presentation scene. In the initial script, however, there were only a few red-light shots before the divers emerged following Cousteau's orders ('Introduction').
21 An interview in *Combat*, 8 February 1956, cited by Grégoire 2006: 34.
22 '[…] we've got what we need to show up Annapurna and Everest [an allusion to Marcel Ichac's film, *Victoire sur l'Annapurna*, 1950]. Black, color, affect, heroics … du cocorico. All that's needed for *Paris Match*! (*No kiddin*'). So long. L.' (Addressee not clearly identified; perhaps one of his brothers), 2 March 1954, Malle Archives, 1272-B234). Cousteau's position (at that time) sparked a number of controversies over time, including the recent critique of *The Silent World* by Gérard Mordillat in June 2015, in his column on the site *Là-bas si j'y suis*, which was picked up by a number of blogs and articles. Malle himself wrote in a letter to his mother in April 1955, doubtless in a moment of exhaustion or passing revolt, that he had ended up with 'a great hatred of the sea, of Cousteau, of his pomp, of his works, of the sun…'.
23 Press kit, Cannes Film Festival Archives: FIFR 155-B19.

24 'Edited to match a piece of jazz music, this explosion of pure movements [schools of fish agitated by the divers] seems to have been orchestrated by the most extraordinary of choreographers [...]. Here, the oneiric unreal is expressed as reality itself' (quoted by Violet 1993: 136).

25 'Presentation of the Calypso', in the script's first version; 'La Calypso' (including the pre-credits sequence) in the DVD chapters.

26 Press kit for *The Silent World*. Cannes Film Festival Archives, FIFR 155-B19.

27 This is the title for the chapter on dolphins in the first script, a sequence which appears near the end (chapter 17).

28 Class on technical editing (M. Laviron). Sheet no. 10 (*verso*), paragraph: 'Lois d'utilisation de la technique.' ('Laws on the use of the technique.'). Malle Archives, 1210-B218 (IDHEC).

29 As Laurent Jullier notes in his entry on *The Silent World*: 'Both the Calypso and the scooter were designed with the forward tracking shot in mind, a device fetishized by a post-modern cinema that thrives on music video effects (Luc Besson opens his *Grand Bleu* [*The Big Blue*, 1988] with a sequence in black and white featuring a cousin of Jojo the grouper [...].) Was that influenced by Louis Malle? In any event, the film also contains what will be seen in the eyes of style historians as characteristics of cinematographic Modernity.' It is also one of the techniques implemented by Cousteau and taken up by Malle; one of the points of agreement between the two filmmakers.

30 Painlevé on *Paysage du silence*, quoted by Barrère 2011: 2. The most emblematic sequences feature Frédéric Dumas, 'god of the water', as he swims alongside posidonia and then plays for a few minutes with an octopus. The choreographic style of this scene prefigures Dumas' game with the grouper that was added to the initial script of *The Silent World*.

31 As if representing an important handover between the two filmmakers, an article in *Science et Vie* that covers the film's shooting prominently features a photograph in which Cousteau shows Malle a device (Vincendon 1956: 87).

32 'Since passing the line [of the equator], it's become a picture book world. Except for a few very beautiful but very cruel episodes of chasing sharks, whales, dolphins, etc. it has been nothing but coconut trees, speaking creole, atolls and lagoons, a sweet living [...]' (Diego, 6 May 1954); 'We have just spent 15 days in a bay underneath of which is the most beautiful natural coral ever seen, to Cousteau's memory. Due to five dives per man per day, we have looted it methodically. [...] All that to make a brightly colored dud' (Mahé, 17 May 1954) (MALLE 1272-B234.).

33 Pierre Billard even indicates that *Station 307* is the result of a request made by Malle: 'Bored from the repetitiveness of core drilling, Louis proposed (and Cousteau accepted) to make a short film in his own way that would condense the key operations of each drilling' (2003: 130). However, I do not agree with the author who seems to find no interest in the film, because in a certain comparative perspective, there are differences that are indeed significant.

34 'Un fait divers de l'Antiquité – une galère engloutie trois siècles avant JC' ('A sensational story from Antiquity – a sunken ship three centuries before Jesus Christ'), eleventh chapter.
35 This is the occasion for Cousteau to pay tribute to his team in a film-report recapitulating fifteen years of exploration for viewers.
36 Letter to his mother, April 1955. Malle Archives 1272-B234.
37 This last note, undated, was found in the folder intended for Jérôme Wybon. Malle Archives 1230-B228. It clearly alludes to an autobiographical film project.
38 Idem.

Bibliography

Barrère, F. (2011) 'Caméra abyssale,' *Eclipses*, http://www.revue-eclipses.com/le-monde-du-silence-oceans/revoir/camera-abyssale-71.html (accessed 10 August 2017).
Bazin, A. (1956) 'Le Monde du Silence', *France-Observateur*, March, 38.
Billard, P. (2003) *Louis Malle. Le rebelle solitaire*. Paris: Plon.
Bringuier, J.-C. (1961) 'Télévision sans frontières,' *Cahiers du cinéma*, 118, 29–38.
Cieutat, M. (2005) 'Souvenirs d'un rite: les sept genres du documentaire et le "petit film",' in D. Blüher et F. Thomas (eds) *Le court métrage français de 1945 à 1968. De l'âge d'or aux contrebandiers*. Rennes: Presses Universitaires de Rennes, 21–8.
French, P. (ed.) (1993) *Malle on Malle*. London: Faber and Faber.
Grégoire, S. (2006) *Louis Malle, un observateur minutieux de la société contemporaine: le 'détour documentaire' et le 'détour américain'*. Unpublished PhD thesis. Université Michel de Montaigne (Bordeaux III).
Jullier, L. '*Le Monde du Silence*, film de Jacques-Yves Cousteau et Louis Malle.' *Encyclopædia Universalis* [online], http://www.universalis.fr/encyclopedie/le-monde-du-silence/ (accessed 10 August 2017).
Machu, F. (2011) *Un cinéaste nommé Cousteau*. Monaco: Edition du Rocher.
Moreau J. (2017) 'Ravageuse et insoumise', *Le Monde*, 2 August, 14.
Painlevé, J. (1947) 'Paysages du silence.' *Ciné-club*, 3.
Soulez, G. (2005) 'Dissoudre le cliché: les documentaires de Bringuier & Knapp. Talk at the conference-debate of the "Lundis de l'Ina."' *L'invention des programmes: la télévision réinvente le documentaire*. Bibliothèque nationale de France.
____ (2015) 'Du cinéma éclaté au levain des médias: rapports de formes,' *MEI*, 39, 239–60.
Vincendon, D. (1956) 'Le premier grand film sous-marin en couleur', *Science et Vie* (March), 84–91.
Violet, B. (1993) *Cousteau, une biographie*. Paris: Fayard.

Archival references

I. Cinémathèque française – Film library.

1/ Malle Archives
MALLE 920-B173 – *Das Silenciozo World* – continuity script without chapters.
MALLE 1210-B218 – IDHEC
MALLE 1230-B228 – Briefing book for the documentary on *Le Monde du Silence* [*Du Silence et des Hommes* by J. Wybon]. It contains the letter-contract dated February 27, 1955 and a chaptered continuity script.
MALLE 1272-B234 – Private correspondence – 'Cousteau years'
2/ Cannes Film Festival Archives
FIFR 155-B19: 1956 Festival – Programmation France
3/ Billard Archives
BILLARD-17-B4 (copies of many documents found in the Malle Archives)

CHAPTER TWO

The Art of Silence: From Documentary to Fiction

Caroline Eades

Louis Malle's first works as a professional filmmaker were met with immediate success: Jacques-Yves Cousteau acknowledged his contribution to *Le Monde du silence* (*The Silent World*, 1956) by listing him as co-director of the film. Soon after, Malle's first fiction films, *Ascenseur pour l'échafaud* (*Elevator to the Gallows*, 1957) and *Les Amants* (*The Lovers*, 1958), were acclaimed by viewers and critics alike. Going straight from a documentary tour de force to accomplished fiction filmmaking was facilitated by Malle's access to adequate financial means and, more importantly, by the intellectual and technical support he found in his entourage.[1] Roger Nimier and Louise de Vilmorin, Robert Bresson, Henri Decae and Leonide Azar respectively contributed to his early and unique mastering of the major components of filmmaking: screenwriting, direction of actors, image composition and editing. This serendipitous transition between documentary and fiction can explain the process that led to Malle's exceptional career henceforth. Several elements appear particularly functional in the switch from one genre to the other, and I propose not so much to look at Malle's debut as a documentary filmmaker before his films on India, the Tour de France, a French automobile factory, and Parisian passers-by, as to locate in his first effort the emergence of another practice, that of fiction film, as attested by *Elevator to the Gallows* and *The Lovers*.

The Silent World was essentially a filmed report on Cousteau's activities on board his research ship, the *Calypso*, which had already been the topic of a book published in 1953. The 1954–55 mission was dedicated to the exploration of tropical and equatorial seas, a few years before Cousteau, a former French officer trained in naval engineering, became the champion of marine life threatened by nuclear testing and human pollution. Malle was added as a camera operator, editor and sound technician, and his first-hand experience of the many instruments used for recording sounds and images on board provided him with a practical realisation of the camera's power to serve both science and art. On one hand, *The Silent World* promoted submarine exploration technology to collect and publicize new scientific knowledge; on the other, the emphasis thus put on technology receded in view of the artistic quality of the film and its acknowledgment as such (it was awarded the Palme d'Or at the 1956 Cannes Film Festival). This experience might, however, account for Malle's persistent interest in technology in his early films as a key feature of a worldview still imbued with classical influence and a conception of cinema infused with a sense of suspicion towards verbal language.

Film as a Craft

The display of man's technical ability in his films reveals Malle's early concern for the mediatisation of vision (see Beattie 2004: 85–8), contrary to his classmates' 'very intellectual approach' (French 1993: 6). His experience on board the *Calypso* right after his unfinished studies at IDHEC provided the young filmmaker with a unique opportunity to explore the technical specifications of all sorts of instruments designed to observe and record. The research ship was by itself a synecdoche of contemporary submarine technology.[2] But, if *The Silent World* exposes the static and indexical nature of pictures produced by the technicians of the *Calypso* in opposition to the film's ability to create moving images and verbal commentary, it also underlines the similarity between the camera as 'an observation post', to use Jean Rouch's definition (2003: 38), and the instruments designed to record accurate traces of real objects and produce a representation of this reality.

For Malle, moving from documentary to fiction was therefore neither a matter of acquiring a certain independence from a scientific approach, nor an attempt at implementing a radical transformation of artistic perception and reception in a culture dominated by industrialisation and technology. Working with Cousteau, an engineer with scientific ambitions, allowed Malle to look at technology as constantly changing and improving, and to remain involved in camera work *per se* with his cinematographers, film after film. His interest in technology was not restricted to innovations in cinematography, film stock and lighting (see French 1993: 12); the short time he spent on the production of Bresson's *Un condamné à mort s'est échappé* (*A Man Escaped*, 1956) provided him with the opportunity to continue filming scenes with a technical content within a narrative framework.

Throughout his career, he has interspersed, in documentary and fiction films, detailed visual descriptions of the minute and precise gestures that characterise human interaction with objects, whether it be unscrewing the doors of an elevator, mixing a cocktail drink, lifting photographs from the developing bath, typesetting the pages of a newspaper or affixing parts of a car on an assembly line. In *Elevator to the Gallows* and *The Lovers* these scenes are properly integrated into the narration, in spite of their quasi-didactic nature, since they contribute to the characters' description (for example, Julien Tavernier as a mercenary trained in survival techniques; Jeanne's husband as a local newspaper director) and the progression of the plot: will Tavernier get out of the elevator in time? Will Jeanne discover her husband's infidelity? In addition to shot

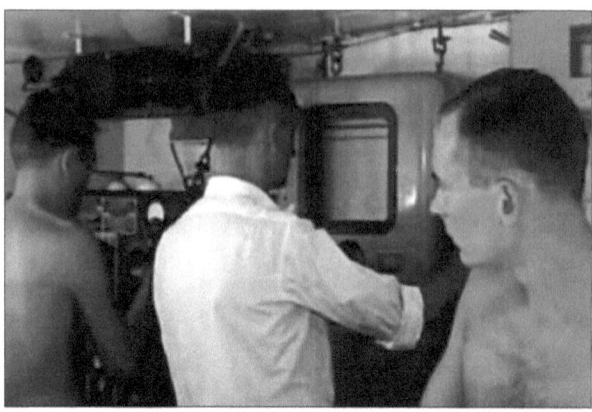

Fig. 1: *The Silent World* (1956): Crew and equipment.

duration, close framing and chronological editing, these scenes draw their informative nature from the emphasis on picture over sound, echoing the style and construction of scenes of submarine exploration in *The Silent World*. The focus on human hands and eyes in search of objects as well as the 'documentary-like attention to even the most mundane details' (Southern 2006: 87)[3] will reappear in *Le Feu follet* (*The Fire Within*, 1963) when Alain Leroy packs his suitcase or proceeds to get dressed, or in *Zazie dans le métro* (1960) with its extensive display of cinematographic techniques. *The Silent World* provides a key to view these shots not simply as explanatory, almost secondary inserts but as episodes that are closely integrated in the narrative of fiction films and play an essential role in defining Malle's mechanistic vision of the world and conception of cinema.

In *The Silent World*, the sonar and the oscillograph constitute the main technical instruments that are used to record the sounds and the images of the seafloor. This data is then presented in the form of audiovisual materials – maps, charts, graphs – that serve to guide eyes and hands in their search of the remains of a sunken ship. The work of the machine must be complemented by human intervention, and instruments are only means to reach a goal whether it is to produce a document or to control the environment. The process that unfolds, from data collection as a preliminary operation to the creation of various iconographic documents, is also described in Malle's first fiction films: maps, blueprints, pictures, photographs are introduced in the narrative to support the characters' actions whether they are criminal lovers covering their tracks, or newspapers' readers looking for a murderer on the run. Just as for the Calypso team, such images prepare characters and viewers to expect and decipher situations that materialise under their eyes after having been literally imagined.

Instead of offering a Bazinian reading of the filmic image as ontologically connected to the real, Malle thus focuses on visual intermediaries supplied by technology to apprehend and understand the world before establishing a direct contact with things and acknowledging their reality. This delayed approach of the real and the function of technology in this process are therefore quite different from the claims then made by Malle's contemporaries and contenders of direct cinema or *cinéma vérité* that new light-weight cameras and portable sound recorders would allow to not only capture reality,⁴ but minimise the contribution of specialists trained in camera work and mise-en-scène. Malle, on the contrary, always defended this double expertise as essential to the art of film since its beginnings,⁵ and put it in practice immediately after his fortuitous documentary filmmaking gig with Cousteau.

Both operations – recording and re-presenting – have a significant part in *Elevator to the Gallows*: the photographic process is not only extensively illustrated, it also plays an important role in the plot by propelling the story towards its conclusion. *The Lovers* provides a brief reference to these operations, first in the opening titles with the *Carte du Tendre (Map of Tendre)*, then in the newspaper printing plant sequence. The *Carte du Tendre* is a drawing representing the various routes a suitor can take to win his beloved's heart, but it is not truly a record of the various stages of human love and was presented by Madeleine de Scudéry as a map to guide the reading of her novel *Clélie* (1654). For Tom Conley, the *Carte du Tendre* in Malle's film takes on the symbolic, reflexive and emblematic value of 'a map (that) helps the lovers in their quest to find new and other spaces but only a tender geography of love intervenes' (2007: 133), which by extension also helps viewers navigate the film's plot.⁶ Similarly, Malle's reference to Dominique Vivant Denon's novella, *Point de Lendemain (No Tomorrow on the Horizon,* 1777), consists in implementing a process of narrative production that follows the same pattern and stems from the same pictorial source as the literary text. Vivant Denon's story is thus a verbal and narrative expansion of an iconographic document, Scudéry's map. Malle's fiction film achieves the same operation by developing a visual narrative based on a pictorial transcription of reality and achieved with an almost mechanical precision.

Malle's emphasis on this preliminary step – to record the movements of the heart on a map or with moving images – suggests an affinity with early modern naturalists who advocated the importance of observation over explanation in their work on human nature. Description of the *'mécanique des corps'* and *'l'homme machine'* in his films, whether documentary or fiction,⁷ is based less on the results of observation *per se* than on its process and the technology needed to present, transcribe and interpret these results. Such choice could have been influenced by the experience on the *Calypso*. In spite of Cousteau's intention to produce 'a very prepared kind of documentary' (French 1993: 75), Malle merely worked to show things as they appeared to the camera and the observer's scrutinous gaze, whether it reflected success or failure. It is therefore not surprising to find in his first fiction films that geological and geographical maps, designed to plan oil drilling in Algeria in *Elevator to the Gallows* or to visit Paris by underground in *Zazie dans le métro*, lead to nowhere and remain useless for the characters: Catala's murder by Tavernier puts an end to his pipeline project in the Sahara; a strike prevents Zazie from travelling by subway. Even the newspapers' pages in the type-room in *The Lovers* can serve as a metonymy for all sorts of texts and pictures, including scenarios, that are meant to be developed and turned into action, but often end up discarded and forgotten. It seems that at the beginning of his career, Malle realised that films could be produced without a 'map' – that is, not without a script, but with a script based on observation with no certain outcome.⁸ Even at the heyday of his career as director of fiction films, his practice remained impervious to the indispensable presence of the written text and pervaded by 'the temptation to go back to the reportage' (Malle 1976), whether through successive returns to documentary filmmaking (in 1962, 1968, 1972 and 1984), or when showcasing seemingly improvised dialogue in *My Dinner with Andre* (1981).

Fiction-Vérité

The opening of three of his first fiction films (*Elevators to the Gallows*, *The Lovers*, *Vie Privée* [*A Very Private Affair*, 1961]) explicitly reflects this emphasis on observation and the visual representation of the observed subject by displaying what Gilles Deleuze has termed the affect-image. At the same time 'reflecting surface[s]' and sites of 'intensive micro-movements' (1986: 88), affect-images are embodied by close-ups of faces that introduce the narrative before turning into action-images as these faces become inscribed in a defined space and time, and contribute to build the psychological, social and relational specificities of each character.[9] Malle's initial dissociation between faces and their contextual environment, possibly influenced by Bergson and Bresson, confers to affect-images a 'quality-power' (ibid.) that sets them apart from conventional narrative openings through establishing shots or *in medias res* exposition. In that sense, Malle seemed to anticipate today's neuroscientists and cognitivists' work on 'facial affect' and its impact on film theory instead of following psychological or sociological approaches favored at the time by film critics such as Jean Mitry and Siegfried Kracauer.[10]

After these first films, Malle continued to use extreme close-ups of faces – and hands – in documentaries and fiction films alike.[11] If *Vive le tour!* (1962) ends with a rather conventional and explicit crosscutting between close-ups of the faces of exhausted cyclists and shots of champions on the victory podium, his 1972 documentary *Humain, trop humain* (*Human, All Too Human*) doesn't provide any clue in the dialogue, the action, or the setting to help viewers decipher the thoughts and feelings of filmed subjects beyond their blank facial expressions and repetitive gestures. In later fiction films, however, Malle's close-up shots served a more conventional narrative function by revealing the characters' personality and progressively solving the suspense they initially contributed to create. More generally speaking, affect-images are used in Malle's work to differentiate fiction from documentary inasmuch as they lead the viewer's gaze from human faces to either a referential space that becomes public, accessible and open to all in documentaries, or a diegetic environment that remains private, subjected to the constraints of the plot, and idiosyncratic to the filmmaker's vision.

The formal quality of this type of openings could also appear as an ode to the beauty of the (mostly female) face, but Malle opposed such aestheticising postures in his next film, *A Very Private Affair*, featuring Brigitte Bardot, where he depicted the illusions and dangers associated with film stars' images, personas and public lives, two years before Godard's similar claim in *Le Mépris*.[12] As Françoise Audé suggests, *The Silent World* had taught Malle to rely on the eye of the documentarist/ethnographer/explorer, attentive to objects, animals and landscapes, to create a work that he intentionally situated 'between the plebeian myth of Bardot and the intellectual summit of Resnais'

(1981: 60).[13] Between exploitative design and contemplative pose, Malle found a middle way that was not unlike that of another documentarist with a penchant for fiction filmmaking: Jean Rouch. In his review of *Moi, un noir* (1958), Godard relayed the enthusiastic response prompted by Rouch's new approach to documentary and the premises of '*cinéma-vérité*' among New Wave critics:

> [although] less perfect than many other contemporary films in terms of cinematography, [Rouch] is foreseeing today that a filmed report gains its worth from being a sort of quest for the Grail that is called mise-en-scène. There are also in *Moi, un noir* some camera movements that Anthony Mann would not disavow. But what is truly beautiful is that they are handmade. (1998: 177)

Malle's experience with *The Silent World* does not necessarily fit the criteria set by Godard to establish a new style and place for documentary filmmaking between news reports and American fiction. As for fictional characters, neither the wanderings of the *grande bourgeoise* Florence Catala in Paris nor the unsavory behaviour of Julien Tavernier can compare with the tribulations and mishaps of Antoine Doisnel, 'Pierrot' le fou, Patricia Franchini and Michel Poiccard. And Malle didn't share the overt and constant preoccupation with politics and social issues that Left Bank filmmakers (Agnès Varda, Chris Marker and Alain Resnais) demonstrated in their documentaries before they too engaged in fiction.[14]

It is therefore in another area that Malle revealed himself as a man of his times. The observational posture, the need to narrativise, and the shift from animals to humans as filmed objects that he had implemented in *The Silent World* suggest that he was interested not so much in the scientific work or environmental mission of the *Calypso* team as in the epistemological issues raised by social sciences in the aftermath of war – a turning-point for thinkers like Morin, Bourdieu, Deleuze, among others – including the question of their relationship with cinema. Both Malle and Rouch addressed almost at the same time and in similar terms what French philosopher and anthropologist François Laplantine summed up as 'the epistemological ethic, which, in cinema as in ethnography, is an ethic of looking and listening' (2007: 101). Rouch's approach as an ethnographer and a filmmaker resembles Malle's own itinerary and can shed a retroactive light on Malle's move from documentary to fiction a couple of years earlier for similar motives:

> I look at the human sciences as poetic sciences in which there is no objectivity, and I see film as not being objective, and cinema as a cinema of lies that depends on the art of telling yourself lies. If you are a good storyteller, then the lie is more true than reality, and if you are a bad one, the truth is worse than a half lie. (1973: 134–5)

After his ethnographic work on initiation and possession rituals in Niger, Rouch co-directed with sociologist Edgar Morin *Chronique d'un été* (*Chronicle of a Summer*), shot in 1960 in Paris. The film was first conceived as a sociological experiment and turned out to be more a fiction film than a scientific demonstration: the final sequence includes a conversation between Rouch and Morin where they acknowledge the performance of their 'actors', their own role as 'directors' and the emotional quality of their film. After *Chronicle of a Summer*, Rouch continued his foray into fiction film before returning to documentary. The comparison between Rouch and Malle can be extended even further. In *Chronicle of a Summer* Rouch returned to Paris to propose a reverse perspective on 'shared anthropology': this time two African students would be in charge of observing the rituals of ordinary people in Western industrialised societies filmed at work, at home and on vacation. The same concern for details and distance from the subject that characterise the ethnographer's camera can be found in *The Lovers* and *The Fire Within*. The scenes when Jeanne dictates the week's menus to her butler or Charlie prepares a Scotch Sour for Alain reveal the presence of an exterior, marginal, unfamiliar observer who focuses on a specific, perhaps unusual practice.

For both Malle and Rouch, filmmaking became an experiment that consisted in leaving exotic, distant and faraway places to come back to well-known environments, local communities and familiar milieus, and try out a new format or genre: social documentary (eventually turning into fiction) for Rouch; fiction film for Malle. Their initial experience in documentary prompted both of them to reflect on the question of realism, truth and objectivity in film. Rouch proposed the concept of '*cinéma vérité*' to avoid the illusion of '*cinéma réalité*' or 'cinéma direct' by purposely showing the camera or the microphone on-screen, putting the observer at the same level as the observed, and turning the ordinary into the extraordinary rather than expecting the extraordinary to emerge from the ordinary.[15] Both Rouch and Malle concluded from their respective filmmaking experiences at the time that the observation of the world did not allow so much for its control by technology as for the revelation of uncertainties, ambiguities and flaws in the use and representation of technology, cinema included, ultimately leading to the emergence of fiction, imagination and art.

The idea that failure deprives technology from adequately serving 'the anthropological machine', to borrow from Giorgio Agamben, and articulating the relation between the human and the animal, contributed to put the emphasis on the figure of the man-machine that would return twice in Malle's documentaries. Whether welded on a bicycle pedal on the Tour de France or clinching a robot's steel arm in an automobile factory, he is clearly shown as the victim of this very technology that makes him 'human, all-too human' – therefore, ultimately fallible. The presence of this disenchanted gaze on a world threatened by technology characterises the key sequences of *Elevator to the Gallows* when Florence wanders in the city streets, Tavernier attempts to escape from the elevator cage, and Louis and Véronique try to recover the pictures proving their presence at the motel with their victims.

The Silent World offers several examples of this shift from nature to man, from distant observation to dramatic narrative, from the illusion of a harmonious world to the realisation of human solitude and despair: on a deserted island, traces in the sand do not lead to the animal searched by the team (a giant sea turtle) but to a local inhabitant. The animal, initially presented as the central focus in the sequence, becomes the conduit for a story of courage, sacrifice and fatalism told by the local man.

In his early fiction films, Malle continued to use animals through dialogues and images for the same purpose: Julien in *Elevator to the Gallows* is shown climbing up and down the elevator cables like a deft but disoriented monkey; Jeanne in *The Lovers* runs away from the dazzling lights of her bourgeois home to meet her lover not unlike the bat once trapped in her dining room; Alain in *The Fire Within* wishes he could disappear in the wall like a rat. These alignments between animals and characters emphasise their feelings of loss and despair associated with situations of control and confinement: objects such as the elevator and vehicles are used not so much to transport characters as to contain them in Malle's first films. Just as Jojo the grouper in *The Silent World*, Louis in *Elevator to the Gallows* enters, leaves, re-enters and hurriedly leaves again the German tourist's car when he realises he might be caught. The fly sequence in *The Lovers* follows the same pattern: trapped in the dining room, the insect will end up smashed by Jeanne, exasperated as she is by the noise of an animal with the same predicament as hers. From animals to humans and back, Malle tells stories of suffering and failing with the eye of an ethnographer turned animal behaviourist to the point that *The Fire Within* might be seen as 'rooted almost entirely in behavioral observation' (Southern 2006: 84).

The representation of technology as the source of a new link between man and his milieu has been a prominent theme in 'city documentaries' from symphony-style documentaries in the 1920s with precursors Walter Ruttmann and Dziga Vertov to 'metaphor[s] for modern urbanistic culture' based on 'lifelike plots' and 'city-narratives' as exemplified by *Zazie dans le métro* (Weihsmann 2011: 38, 39). In *Elevator to the Gallows*, Paris and its suburbs are shown in acute detail, from the bustling atmosphere of the city at night to the objects that connect people with others and their environment: cars, the elevator, the printing press, the photographic laboratory. The movements depicted contribute not so much to suggest a harmonious and unified space/time continuum as to insist on fragmentation and opposition between stasis and movement, horizontal and vertical, feminine and masculine, confinement and wandering, solitude and chance encounters. This is why technology, when it fails, is bound to cause or underline *désassemblage*, or disconnection, which becomes subsequently the modernist trademark of individuals isolated from society and resisting the establishment and the order, including language itself. In *The Lovers* and *A Very Private Affair*, technical settings like the print shop or the photographic studio are explicitly connoted as places of power through the actions of an authority (the newspaper publisher or the filmmaker).[16] In *The Lovers*, road trips are constantly interrupted by breakdowns, extended pauses, unexpected stops. In the same manner as in Raymond Queneau's text with verbal language, *Zazie dans le métro* applies the same metaphor to film language. And indeed in most of his fiction films Malle summoned all the resources of cinema including narrative elements to illustrate the failures of our world, following Deleuze's realisation that 'it is not we who make cinema; it is the world which looks to us like a bad film. [...] The link between man and the world is broken. [...] The cinema must film, not the world, but belief in this world, our only link' (1989: 171–2). And this link is rather loose and fragile.

Cinema as a Land of Silence

For Malle, the move from documentary to fiction resulted in transposing 'le monde du silence' from the marine world to human society in the sense that, although these two environments are not deprived of sounds, their occupants are not always subjected to verbal interaction. The world of silence is an alternative place for Malle's characters when they live like 'loners ... on the margins of society' (Malle 2006): Jeanne and Bernard in *The Lovers*, Alain in *The Fire Within*, Gabriel in *Zazie dans le métro*, Jill in *A Very Private Affair* are 'lost in a land of silence', to use Julien's words at the beginning of *Elevator to the Gallows*.[17] If they deserve to be called '*lâches*' in both meanings of the term in French (coward[18] and loose), it is first because they resist habits and conventions by avoiding any contact with others instead of engaging in arguments and discussions, and also because they experience an unstable, precarious and flexible[19] connection to the world due to their social origin or personal traits. Their silence in Malle's films thus evokes

> the challenge that language poses to the visible, and the ear to the eye, namely, to show that the gesticulatory expanse that makes depth or representation possible, far from being signifiable through words, spreads out on their margins as what enables them to designate, and to show, too, that this expanse is the source of the words' power of expression, and thus accompanies them, shadows them, in one sense terminates them and in another marks their beginning. For one needn't be immersed in language [*langage*] in order to be able to speak. (Lyotard 2011: 8)

Whereas *The Silent World* put the emphasis on the visual and on non-verbal sounds (environmental sounds and music), fiction films use dialogue to reflect the characters' distance from and distrust of verbal language as the main instrument to define individual identity and interpersonal relations, including naming in *William Wilson* and *Elevator to the Gallows*. Dialogues consequently are tainted by absence, misunderstanding and lies in this film: Florence's despair is all the more obvious when viewers cannot hear the sound of her voice, and the accusation against Julien is rendered even more disturbing when pronounced by a little girl. Children's words underline the inadequacy of verbal language when it comes to represent a familiar reality distorted by cultural bias or narrative purposes. Here again, Louis Malle used his experience with *The Silent World* to transfer a common feature in animal documentaries – the use of non-verbal sounds – to his first fiction films. It is therefore not surprising that after Noël Calef's crime novel and Vivant Denon's libertine novella, Malle adapted Queneau's text that offered a playful yet radical criticism of language reduced to a meaningless set of formal elements.

The speech organ itself is used by Malle to convey the distinction we also find in ethnographer André Leroi-Gourhan's work 'between two poles "hand-tool" and "face-language"' (cited in Deleuze and Guattari 1980: 333). The first fiction films illustrate

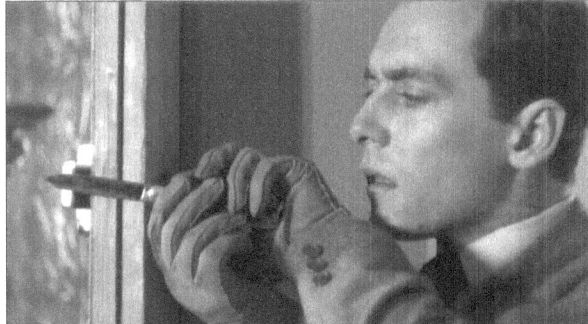

Fig. 2: *Elevator to the Gallows* (1957): 'Hand-tool'.

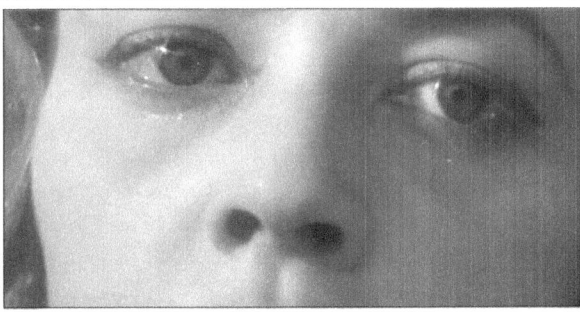

Fig. 3: *Elevator to the Gallows:* 'Face-language'.

this opposition between 'technology' sequences and 'face close-ups' that add to their visual properties specific qualities attached to the voice itself:

> the face with its visual correlates (eyes) concerns painting; the voice with its auditory correlates ... concerns music. Music is a deterritorialisation of the voice, which becomes less and less tied to language, just as painting is a deterritorialization of the face. (Ibid.)

The very first voice heard in *Elevator to the Gallows*, Jeanne Moreau's with her unique intonations and paratactic statements, has a musical quality and yields a sense of defamiliarization that had characterised the islander's voice in *The Silent World*. He speaks creole, a language that can be almost understood by the metropolitan viewer and yet is different enough as to maintain a distance with both the locutor and his discourse. A similar pattern combining extreme close-ups of faces and the use of voice-over is found at the beginning of *The Lovers* and *The Fire Within* to establish the tension between the subject of enunciation as Other and the image as Truth that characterises Malle's conception of cinema as being first and foremost the art of silence, without direct or immediate sound, since it is based on the necessary mediation of recording equipment, musical illustration or defamiliarising voices. With its title, *The Silent World* was inadvertently predicting what would become an essential issue in Malle's œuvre: the inadequacy of verbal language to represent the real in documentaries or to narrate a story in fiction films (see Southern 2006: 16).

In that sense, besides biographical and narrative concerns, the recurrent presence of children in Malle's fiction work[20] can be seen as an offshoot of images of marine animals in the sense that these animals were already 'humanised' by the anthropological machine in *The Silent World*: they were spoken for, muffled and muted by the narrator's commentary, musical accompaniment and the islander's voice. Similarly, children in the first fiction films, although subjected as future adults to education and socialisation by their ability to use verbal language, are shown disconnected from and often misunderstood by elder people in spite of the veracity of their discourse. They play a significant role in the first films since they are everywhere in the city: they play alone like the little girl in front of the Catala building or sit at the *terrasse* of a café with their parents like the Algerian girl in *Elevator to the Gallows*. Zazie is of course the epitome of these children for whom the street, more laboratory than playground, is a place of danger, initiation, experimentation, in-betweenness and growth because it is presented as their 'natural' environment in fiction films equivalent to the ocean in *The Silent World*.

Confronted with adults who are obsessed with the past, their social class, their vulnerable status, whether they are intellectuals, business people or parasites living in a sad, idle and 'dehumanised' world (see French 1993: 16),[21] children are not used in Malle's early fiction films in a conventional manner to represent the future, modernity and hope. Instead, they embody a reality that needs to be 'documented' and give the films a sense of the present forgetful of the past and uninterested in the future. What Malle inherited from his experience in documentary filmmaking led to a much more assertive political discourse in his first fiction films than usually thought. Acknowledging the end of a long-lasting dichotomy in documentary filmmaking between the poetic innocence of Painlevé-style scientific film and the compromises of propagandist films in wartime, Malle seemed to opt for a Bergsonian conception of cinema based on its aptitude to reveal the blind spots of the mind and articulate a world vision through the observation of habit and the multiplicity of the present. *Elevator to the Gallows* reflects the only temporal dimension that mattered in French society at the beginning of the Fifth Republic as a new era of politic stability, economic growth and international prestige, overcoming the traumas of world wars and colonial conflicts. The film contains images that illustrate the ambiguity of a present in the making, almost imaginary (see Malle 2006),[22] and still infused with traces of the past that are characteristic of a world in transition: veterans from Indochina now work in state-of-the-art offices; young people live on the last floor of a Haussmannian building even if their 'consumeristic frenzy' sets them 'ahead of their time' (ibid.); the end of the war allows German people to visit France as tourists. At a time when the generation of filmmakers born in the 1920s, still haunted by the atrocities committed during World War II and the war in Algeria, was searching for 'truth' beyond the images produced by news reports and official documentaries, Malle, Rouch and others (Grierson, Ivens, Sembene, Preloran and Cavalcanti) became chroniclers of the times, to use Barnow's expression. They demonstrated 'an affinity, evidently denied to photography, for the continuum of life or the "flow of life"' (Kracauer 1997: 71), a definition that can be applied to documentary and fiction films alike to exemplify an active concept of history that Malle himself describes as 'a reflection of the particular historical circumstances of the time' (1999: 41).[23]

Malle's first characters live in a world of meaningful silence, forced by history to face not so much its past errors as its current configuration. They embody Malle's own discourse on social constraints and his conception of film as open to flaws as any other technology. After making a scientific film where the visual observation of animal behaviour was enhanced à la Painlevé by Wagner's *Ride of the Valkyries* accompanying a pod of dolphins along the *Calypso* or a voice-over commenting on the tears of a giant turtle laying her eggs in the sand, Malle chose to reverse the process in his first fiction films: this time, human beings, and more precisely the outliers of French society, would be the object of the gaze once set on animals and local inhabitants by white scientists with an agenda (Rouch, Cousteau, Lorenz). Louis Malle strove to describe with accuracy and objectivity the rituals of an industrialised nation: working conditions (in offices and plants), alimentary habits (breakfast in a café, elegant dinners at home), leisure activities (sports and sightseeing) while telling the story of marginal characters (veterans, housewives, criminals), thus sharing with Rouch the idea that film can provide an observation of social practices through the medium of the camera,[24] thus placing a documentary focus at the heart of fiction filmmaking.

Notes

1   See René Prédal (1989: 9–22), Philip French (1993: 1–33) and Hugo Frey (2004: 1–11) on Malle's beginnings as a filmmaker, as well as Louis Malle's 1974 filmed interview on Bresson's influence.
2   André Bazin extends to the whole ship – equipment and crew included – the 'ideal' status of an 'exhaustive place of observation that doesn't modify the aspect and meaning of the object that is being observed' (1994: 40).
3   Another well-known example is the scene in *Les Amants* when Jeanne's hand clutches the pillow, then moves along the bedsheet, before grasping Bernard's back during what François Truffaut described as 'the first night of love ever filmed' (1958: 1).
4   In the sense used by Dziga Vertov to describe the mission of the kino-eye: 'filming life caught unawares' (1984: 40–2), or by Siegfried Kracauer to make 'life in the form of everyday life' (1997: 71–2) the predominant material of film.
5   In 1912, Georges Méliès reminded his audience that cinema's ability 'not to blindly reproduce nature but to offer a spectacular expression of artistic and imaginative conceptions of all sorts contributed to create in fact a real film industry. It is the cinematographic theater indeed that was the cause of the formidable success of the cinematograph, which, without it, would have remained a rather unknown laboratory instrument' (2016: 45).
6   See also T. Jefferson Kline's contribution in this volume.
7   *William Wilson* (1968), Malle's adaptation of Edgar Allan Poe's short story, includes a parody of anatomical lessons that also refers to the mechanist model of the animal-machine based on observation and experimentation (see Mazauric 2009: 135–42, 267–90).

8   This might explain why Malle chose to adapt 'B' novels and short stories 'with interesting concepts yet poor characterization and underdeveloped themes' (Southern 2006: 34).
9   For Deleuze, 'ordinarily, three roles of the face are recognisable: it is individuating (it distinguishes or characterizes each person); it is socialising (it manifests a social role); it is relational or communicating (it ensures not only communication between two people, but also, in a single person, the internal agreement between his character and his role). Now the face, which effectively presents these aspects in the cinema as elsewhere, loses all three in the case of close-up' (1986: 99).
10 See Randal Halle (2009) on the phenomenology of emotion in film.
11 This approach is very different from the traditional function of close-ups in fiction film in terms of plasticity and expression of subjectivity exemplified by Jean Epstein, Germaine Dulac, Abel Gance or Marcel L'Herbier; see Abel 1988: 235–36; Temple and Witt 2007: 87–8.
12 See Sue Harris's contribution in this volume.
13 In that sense, I don't agree with Nathan C. Southern's suggestion that Malle should have 'liberated the film from the trappings of a fictional narrative, perhaps (for instance) directing a documentary on the real-life Bardot' (2006: 74).
14 Contrary to his contemporaries, Malle cultivated paradox in his early filmmaking: not only did he play 'by the rules of temporal and spatial continuity, synchronous sound, and the construction of a first-person perspective' (Southern 2006: 14) in non-fiction films, he also emphasised mise-en-scène in documentaries (sound/picture montage, colour and lighting, camera movements) and graphic and optical effects in fiction films (slow/fast motion in *Zazie dans le métro*, day for night in *The Lovers*, geometric patterns in *Elevator to the Gallows*).
15 See Eric Barnow on the difference between *cinéma vérité* and direct cinema (1983: 254–5). Malle's early fiction films have indeed more in common with Rouch's *cinéma vérité* than his subsequent documentary work which he acknowledged as 'the extreme of *cinéma direct*' (French 1993: 9).
16 Incidentally, they are also places where women are either unwelcome, marginalized, or highly controlled.
17 For a list of other 'socially exiled main characters' in Malle's films, see Southern 2006: 11.
18 Florence blames Julien for being a coward when it comes to love, not unlike Inès accusing Garcin in similar terms in Sartre's *Huis clos* (*No Exit*, 1944).
19 To describe his protagonist in *The Fire Within*, Malle (1975) uses two other synonyms for 'lâche': 'veule,' which is very derogatory, and 'mou' (soft), which refers to a lack of energy in Alain that will turn into indifference and isolation, ultimately driving him to commit suicide.
20 See Ginette Vincendeau on children and women in Malle's films (2011).
21 Triggered by a similar state of mind, the *flânerie* of Varda's protagonist in *Cléo de 5 à 7* leads to a sombre journey across Paris as well, but with a very different outcome; see Mouton 2001; Ungar 2008; Jackson 2010.

22 In his 1975 interview, Louis Malle reckoned that he presented Paris in *Elevator to the Gallows* 'as it would be ten years later' and 'more modern than it really was'.
23 What differentiates his films made in France from the ones he made in America 'whether in drama or in documentary', except for *Elevator to the Gallows*, is, according to Malle, the fact that 'they are set in the past' and include 'a historical perspective, even a slight one' or 'a play on time' (1999: 49).
24 On the 'chain explosion' of documentary films chronicling current history and anthropological fieldwork after World War II, see Barnow 1983: 206–10.

Bibliography

Abel, R. (1988) *French Film Theory and Criticism, 1907–1939* [Volume 1, 1907–1929]. Princeton, NJ: Princeton University Press.
Audé, F. (1981) *Ciné-modèles, Cinéma d'elles. Situations de femmes dans le cinéma français 1956–1979*. Lausanne: L'Age d'homme.
Barnow, E. (1983 [1974]) *Documentary: A History of the Non-Fiction Film*. Oxford: Oxford University Press.
Bazin, A. (1994 [1956]) 'Le Monde du silence', in *Qu'est-ce que le cinéma?* Paris: Cerf, 35–40.
Beattie, K. (2004) *Documentary Screens: Non-Fiction Film and Television*. New York: Palgrave MacMillan.
Conley, T. (2007) 'Michelin *Tendre*', in *Cartographic Cinema*. Minneapolis, MN: University of Minnesota Press, 125–40.
Deleuze, G. (1986 [1983]) *Cinema 1: The Movement-Image*, trans. H. Tomlinson and B. Habberjam. Minneapolis, MN: University of Minnesota Press.
____ (1989 [1985]) *Cinema 2: The Time-Image*, trans. H. Tomlinson and B. Habberjam. Minneapolis, MN: University of Minnesota Press.
Deleuze, G. and F. Guattari (1980) *A Thousand Plateaus: Capitalism and Schizophrenia*, trans. B. Masumi. London: Continuum.
French, P. (1993) *Malle on Malle*. London: Faber and Faber.
Frey, H. (2004) *Louis Malle*. Manchester: Manchester University Press.
Godard, J.-L. (1998 [1959]) 'Etonnant Jean Rouch, *Moi, un noir*,' in *Jean-Luc Godard par Jean-Luc Godard* [vol. 1, 1950–1984]. Paris: Cahiers du cinéma, 177–8.
Halle, R. (2009) 'Toward a Phenomenology of Emotion in Film: Michael Brynntrup and The Face of Gay Shame,' *MLN*, 124/3, 683–707.
Jackson, E. (2010) 'The Eyes of Agnès Varda: Portraiture, Cinécriture and the Filmic Ethnographic Eye', *Feminist Review*, 96, 122–6.
Kracauer, S. (1997 [1960]) *Theory of Film: The Redemption of Physical Reality*. Princeton, NJ: Princeton University Press.
Laplantine, F. (2007) *Leçons de cinéma pour notre époque. Politique du sensible*. Paris: Téraèdre/Murmure.
Lyotard, J.-F. (2011 [1971]) *Discourse, Figure*, trans. A. Hudek and M. Lydon. Minneapolis, MN: University of Minnesota Press.

Malle, L. (1976) Interview by C. Defaye, 'Spécial Cinéma,' RTS. Available at https://youtu.be/bnv_vkRCnY8 (accessed 4 September 2016).
___ (1999 [1987]) '*Au revoir les enfants,*' interview by F. Audé and J.-P. Jeancolas, in *Projections 9: French Film-makers on Film-making*, ed. M. Ciment and N. Herpe, trans. P. Hodgson. London: Faber and Faber/Positif, 33–50.
___ (2006 [1975]) Interview, 'Parlons cinéma,' supplement to *Elevator to the Gallows*. Criterion DVD.
Mazauric, S. (2009) *Histoire des sciences à l'époque moderne*. Paris: Armand Colin.
Méliès, G. (2016 [1912]) *Ecrits et propos. Du cinématographe au cinéma*, ed. J.-F. Hood. Paris: Ombres.
Mouton, J. (2001) 'From Feminine Masquerade to Flâneuse: Agnès Varda's Cléo in the City,' *Cinema Journal*, 40/2, 3–16.
Prédal, R. (1989) *Louis Malle*. Paris: Edilig.
Rouch, J. (1971) 'Interview', by G. R. Levin, in *Documentary Explorations: 15 Interviews with Film-makers*. Garden City, NY: Doubleday, 131–45.
___ (2003 [1973]) 'The Camera and Man', in *Ciné-Ethnography*, ed. and trans. S. Feld. Minneapolis, MN: University of Minnesota Press, 29–46.
Southern, N. C., with J. Weissgerber (2006) *The Films of Louis Malle: A Critical Analysis*. Jefferson, NC: McFarland.
Temple, M. and M. Witt (eds) (2007) *The French Cinema Book*. London: British Film Institute.
Truffaut, F. (1958) 'Louis Malle a filmé la première nuit d'amour au cinéma,' *Arts* 687, 1.
Ungar, S. (2008) *Cléo de 5 à 7*. New York: Palgrave MacMillan/British Film Institute.
Vertov, D. (1984 [1924]) 'The Birth of Kino-Eye', in *Kino-Eye: The Writings of Dziga Vertov*, ed. A. Michelson, trans. K. O'Brien. Berkeley, CA: University of California Press, 40–2.
Vincendeau, G. (2011) 'Girl Trouble,' supplement to *Zazie dans le métro*. Criterion DVD.
Weihsmann, H. (2011) 'Ciné-City Strolls: Imagery, Form, Language and Meaning of the City Film', in F. Penz and A. Lu (eds) *Urban Cinematics. Understanding Urban Phenomena through the Moving Image*. Bristol: Intellect, 23–42.

CHAPTER THREE

No Comment: Direct Cinema in Humain, trop humain and Place de la République

Derek Schilling

When Louis Malle's essays in direct cinema *Humain, trop humain* and *Place de la République* opened in the same week of April 1974, *Lacombe Lucien* was still playing in a half-dozen theatres across Paris and approaching a half-million tickets sold.[1] In the national press, debates continued at fever pitch over Malle and co-screenwriter Patrick Modiano's ambiguous portrayal of a French youth under German Occupation that had broken with the Gaullist myth of a French nation united against Nazi oppression. If *Lacombe Lucien*, with its assertive period style, fueled a backward-looking *mode rétro*, *Humain, trop humain* and *Place de la République* were by contrast trained on the present. Malle's idea of filming assembly work in a French automobile plant dated to the 'États Généraux du Cinéma' of 1968; initially titled 'À la Chaîne', the project was part of a series on industrial society Malle unsuccessfully pitched to the BBC.[2] Shooting took place across six days in July 1972 at Citroën's new assembly facility outside Rennes; the four-person crew reconvened that October at the annual 'Salon de l'Automobile' trade fair. The second, more ambitious, project, *Paris 72*, was intended as a vast neighborhood survey. Although Malle took footage on a half-dozen locations in autumn 1972, the interview segments comprising the ninety-minute *Place de la République* all came from a short stretch of pavement alongside the eponymous square, a landmark in the history of Parisian popular struggle.

Thanks to a paired release that permitted Malle to meet contractual obligations, filmgoers could ponder two approaches to direct cinema side by side, or back-to-back, for those who made the jaunt from the Latin Quarter's Studio Alpha where *Humain, trop humain* opened, to the seemingly predestined Studio-République on the Right Bank. Both works, shot in synchronous sound on rapid colour stocks, rejected the mise-en-scène and editing-room sleight-of-hand associated with *le documentaire reconstitué* of which Malle's *Vive le Tour!* (1962) was one example. Where the factory project pursued the distanced observational style Malle perfected with cameraman Étienne Becker and soundman Jean-Claude Laureux on the streets of *Calcutta* (1969), the neighborhood survey emphasised personal interactions along the lines of *Chronique d'un été* (Rouch and Morin, 1961) or *Le Joli Mai* (Marker and Lhomme, 1962).

Ultimately, the relationship of Malle's mid-career French documentaries to the international history of direct cinema mattered little. For period critics, these were simply new titles from the director of *Lacombe Lucien*. What forms of blindness did that authorial premise create? Both works thwarted expectations in a manner that reveals as much about French politics after 1968 as about the aesthetics of *le cinéma direct*. The aim of this essay is to establish that context, the better to gauge the extent to which Malle's site-specific observation and streetwise interaction runs against the grain of the discourse-centered production of the era. By opting to show but not to comment in one case, and to let women and men comment with minimal input in the other, Malle resolutely positions himself as a filmmaker *à contre-courant*.

* * *

Critic Serge Toubiana clearly penned his double-review for the Leftist daily *Libération* with *Lacombe Lucien* in mind. Likening the man-with-a-camera conceit of *Place de la République* to the 'semi-directed' interviews of market researchers, he accuses Malle of a pernicious 'ideological marketing' that reproduces mass stereotypes (for example, the French are racist, egotistical and worry about sex) in deference to populist rhetoric: 'As in *Lacombe Lucien*, it's about staging a certain image of the middle-class Frenchman. Dupont Jacques or Durand Pierre. An image outside images of struggle.' Inverting, à la *Lacombe Lucien*, two run-of-the-mill French proper names, Toubiana coyly paints Malle as an apologist for reactionary ideology whose subjects are so many Lucien Lacombes in the making. Insofar as it presents the French polity as lacking in historical consciousness and ripe for indoctrination, *Place de la République* stands at odds with the 'enquête militante' that alone can foster transformative struggle.

Humain, trop humain performs a different sort of obfuscation. If it shows in exacting detail the specialised activities required by Taylorist/Fordist organisation, absent are the abuses visited daily upon labourers by factory hierarchy. Toubiana considers the film crew's very presence inside the plant to be suspect:

> At what price did Malle convince Citroen management to let him film human relations inside the factory? At the cost of entirely repressing the dissimulation of the capitalist relations of production, of hierarchy, of factory despotism (how did the camera never catch in the frame, at least once, a low-level manager. At that price, Mr. Citroen was right to let Louis Malle shoot in his factory. (1974)

The critic casts the filmmaker as an objective ally of management who effaces traces of dissent and denies workers the right to speak. Whence *Libération*'s excoriating title linking the two films' parallel containment strategies: 'Let the people speak the better to shut their trap!'

Standing reviewer François Morin of Communist Party organ *L'Humanité* found Malle's civic experiment similarly lacking. Contacts with passersby in *Place de la République* generate reams of anecdote, but few social truths of the kind that emerge in the more capable hands of a Pierre Perrault. Purely informational and external, *Humain, trop humain* leaves workers' living conditions and personal aspirations unexamined, consigning viewers to the same grey zones as *Lacombe Lucien*.

These critical responses present strikingly similar cases of misprision: each film is presumed to want to say something that it does not. The choice of a 'good' documentary object, politically speaking (industrial labour, the people of Paris), assigns the work to a positively connoted socio-cultural space. The chosen content in turn activates a generic horizon of expectations specific to the medium. When the treatment given the 'good' object deviates from discursive norms; when it adopts unorthodox points of view; when it fails to deliver an ideologically 'correct' reading; in short, when core expectations go unmet, the critic then dismisses the work as one-sided and unacceptable. What is singular, and symptomatic, here is that disqualification of Malle's twinned direct films of 1974 doesn't turn primarily on modes of address, texture, form, or even implicit ideology, but on a cheap rhetorical ploy: the argument *ad hominem*. The scandal of *Humain, trop humain* isn't the absence of overseers on the shop floor, no more than the scandal of *Place de la République* is the prevalence of right-leaning populism on the Right Bank. The scandal is that both films are by Louis Malle, author of *Lacombe Lucien* and *grand bourgeois* to boot.

It was characteristically the role of France's premier film journal, *Cahiers du cinéma*, to have the last word in matters of critical import. The present case was no exception. By 1970, the monthly had long put to rest its fabled *politique des auteurs* in favour of semiology (Barthes), post-structuralism (Lacan) and ideology critique (Althusser). Critics were not to judge the aesthetic merits of singular films but to unveil instead the contradictions of the capitalist system and the filmic 'apparatus' that is its spectacular expression. This split with auteurist paradigms notwithstanding, *Cahiers du cinéma* continued to press arguments based on authorship whenever expedient. Thus its May 1974 issue takes to task a handful of 'bourgeois' filmmakers whose features had plundered the twentieth-century totalitarian political imaginary: Jean Yanne, for his big-budget satire *Les Chinois à Paris*; Philippe Clair, who committed the crime of *Le Führer est en folie*; Liliana Cavani for her perverse *Night Porter*; and not least, their presumptive gang leader, Louis Malle. Via a highbrow pun, the three-part dossier 'Fonction critique: histoire d'énoncer' asks *Cahiers du cinéma* readers to consider films as situated utterances in a circuit of exchange (*histoires d'énoncés*) as well as to denounce as illusory both History and the story-form as such (*histoire dénoncée*).

In his lead article, 'Qui dit quoi, mais où et quand?', Serge Daney casts *la mode rétro* as the latest manifestation of bourgeois ideology.[3] Questioning the institutional Left's monopoly on 'positive' messages and heroes, Daney notes that bourgeois filmmakers offer an alternative to those 'sectarian dinosaurs' (Jdanovists, presumably) who demand didactic narratives and conscious characters worthy of emulation. Instead of explicating the real, today's bourgeois filmmakers merely show what was hidden, an operation Daney calls 'décodage'. Spectators become hysterical subjects who fail to see that the taboos purportedly broken onscreen are inconsequential. *Décodage* dresses up bourgeois propaganda as style, and like the revolutionary propaganda it mirrors and inverts, it serves specific class interests. Whence Daney's claim that all films at base are militant: 'c'est l'ensemble des films qui milite' (1974: 39).

Leftist critics can consequently ill accuse European films of the 1970s of neglecting the real. Yet if bourgeois directors increasingly espouse such subjects as sexuality and racism, insists Daney, they nonetheless empty History of its dialectical quality, harnessing the financial power of the system and papering over class contradictions in the name of 'the eternal neither-black-nor-white of "human nature"'. They are, at best, standard-bearers for a de-historicised metaphysics; and at worst, apologists for fascism.

Daney posits complex pragmatic relations among utterance, speaker and the terrain on which utterances are produced, noting that these terms need not align. A 'correct' utterance, politically speaking, can be taken up by a class enemy on foreign terrain. Such is the fate of once-repressed historical utterances that Malle uncovers under the guise of sex in *Le Souffle au cœur* (*Murmur of the Heart*, 1971), history in *Lacombe Lucien*, and work in *Humain, trop humain*. To combat bourgeois hegemony, agents of revolution must make political utterances newly positive for the receiver, without ceding to the naïve mimetics of socialist realism or to the debilitating a-historicity of *décodage*.

Now, Daney may well not have seen *Humain, trop humain*, and from a strictly Marxist-Leninist perspective, it makes little difference whether he did, given that a work signed by a *grand bourgeois* could not but reflect narrow class interests.[4] It is more certain that Thérèse Giraud, whose review '*Attica*/*Humain, trop humain*: deux conceptions du cinéma direct' closes the *Cahiers du cinéma* dossier, had seen it. Like Georg Lukács in his great essays on European novelists, Giraud enacts a confrontation between ideological adversaries. On one hand, *Attica* director Cinda Firestone fosters dialogue with the actor-witnesses of the bloody New York State prison uprisings; through their testimonies, an active camera-eye à la Dziga Vertov 'seeks the communist reality of the world'. On the other, Malle offers a 'passive, ethnological camera-guide' to traverse 'the museum of human mores' (1974: 48). It goes without saying which of these two 'conceptions' is in error. Whereas Firestone allows prisoners to position themselves actively in the history of Black struggle, Malle enforces silent consent, showing assembly-line workers at a moment and in spaces chosen by plant managers. *Humain, trop humain* is for Giraud 'a fictional drama that simply illustrates the agenda of the filmmaker-screenwriter', a 'passive direct cinema' that chimes with capitalist ideology to celebrate the very 'cult' of the automobile it claims to unveil (1974: 50). To view workers passively at work is to assent to passivity oneself, and this attitude any conscious spectator must reject.

To sum up: for Leftist critics of 1974, even when filming the 'right' people on the 'right' terrain, Malle had filmed them at the wrong time and from the wrong perspective. Conversely, when filming the people as bearers of utterances who speak their mind on camera, he had chosen the wrong terrain, a petty-bourgeois Right Bank district where office clerks and retirees outnumber intellectuals and workers. In either case, *Louis Malle had made the wrong film.*

This prompts the question of what sort of film French critics might have wanted to see, say, about autoworkers circa 1970: a film, no doubt, in which historical subjects (youth, preferably) engage in struggle, and where actors speak truth to power and prepare for collective action. For example, we could turn to *British Sounds* (1971), attributed to the Dziga Vertov Collective though manifestly the work of Jean-Luc Godard. Shot in the UK where Godard and his collaborator Jean-Henri Roger gauged conditions for revolution riper that in Gaullist France, the hour-long work opens with a four-minute lateral tracking shot of assembly-line workers at the Cowley plant near Oxford (see MacCabe 2005: 217–18). As bright red Austin MG car bodies move along the belt, quotes are read in voice-over from *The Communist Manifesto*, 'Wage Labor and Capital' and 'The Poverty of Philosophy'. Over wails, screeches, creaks, hammering and machine noise, we learn of the history of the seventeenth-century Levelers. Brechtian title cards and mass-produced images 'detourned' à la Guy Debord and Gil Wolman interpolate the spectator as political subject. Subsequent sequences explore themes of sexual exploitation, right-wing media control, worker self-organisation and the politicisation of art. *British Sounds* is an allegory of class struggle where a bloodied arm reaches not for the Union Jack, but for a red flag raised high against grey skies.

More directly illustrative of *l'enquête militante* are *Les ¾ de la vie* (1971) and *Weekend à Sochaux* (1972), two works shot, performed and 'dreamed' by the Groupes Medvedkine. Here the factory floor is absent. Peugeot's complex at Sochaux is filmed from the outside, its high, prison-like walls surveyed in lengthy tracking shots à la Resnais. Work appears in its causes and its effects. Both the initial black-and-white sketch and the longer colour film employ a canvas for improvisations by non-professionals. A young man to whom a factory recruiter-cum-circus barker has just sold the moon undergoes a battery of motor tests, only to be assigned to a factory shop unrelated to his trade school expertise. Everyday life becomes a litany of hassles, from the fatigue of the swing shift cycle to overpriced groceries at the company store. Billed as a suspect by boorish company informers, the worker is repeatedly expelled from his lodgings. As in Marin Karmitz's contemporaneous *Camarades* (*Comrades*, 1971), his disillusionment yields to political awakening and to activism.

Malle had seen and admired *British Sounds*, and no doubt was familiar with the collectives that pursued the anti-capitalist aims of the Estates General of Cinema. What these works suggest is that factory work was conceivable exclusively from the standpoint of exploitation, alienation and revolt. Its representation was consubstantial with an oppositional Left discourse that after 1968 had become common coin. Asking labourers either to speak about their working conditions or to improvise on a canvas fell within the realm of the acceptable; so too did Brechtian distantiation and Eisensteinian 'montage of attractions'. These themes and techniques had fashioned a clear horizon of expectations for any French film about industrial work.

'A film is not meant to be seen, a film is meant to be read', wrote Daney. Malle's critics of April 1974 seem to have taken this credo to the letter, all but refusing to look. Nor did they seem to listen, deafened perhaps by the stridency of their own rhetoric. For in a cultural moment when film is understood as a vehicle for oppositional discourse, Malle's most radical gesture in *Humain, trop humain* is the decision *not to comment*, whether through written inscriptions or voice-over. Speech is displaced to an inaccessible inner space, while the regimented, machine-disciplined body of the worker is left to express the 'constrained time' that sociologist Henri Lefebvre associates with capitalist organisation.

I now turn to a close reading of that seventy-minute film – the most unrelenting piece of editing in Malle's storied career – to be followed by a brief assessment of *Place de la République*.

* * *

Humain, trop humain mirrors in three parts the structure of modern productivist economies. Part one selectively follows the fabrication of the Citroën model GS, from the cutting of raw sheet metal to rough assembly and finishing, to inspection and transfer of road-ready vehicles to a holding lot. Even as its linear editing reprises the codes of the industrial film, no explicative gloss is present: attention lies squarely on the workers, without whom assembly would grind to a halt. Nearly equivalent in length to the first part at fifteen minutes, part two enters the halls of modern consumption at the Auto Show, where wares are transformed into objects of discourse. As they review each make and model, prospective buyers join sellers in a comical chorus celebrating the latest technical advances. Finally, the forty-minute third part returns to the Citroën factory to scrutinise the minutiae of specialised labour. Assembly-line order is inverted, such that tasks executed last along the belt are shown first. Repeated actions are caught on camera in long takes that expose from multiple angles the pliancy and the rigidity of bodies at work.

In an observational film all but devoid of extradiegetic sound, the opening establishing shot stands out. Halfway into the slow left-to-right pan that situates the Citroën facility next to Breton pastureland, Gregorian chants enter the mix. Stylistically incongruous, these chants justify the hard cut to the interior of an immense, cathedral-like machine shed, its floor littered with spools of sheet metal.[5] Perched at the commands of a gantry crane, a woman directs her portal down the hangar's nave to the spool loader where her cargo will come to rest. The choice of the reel as sacred object, for a filmmaker, could scarcely be more apposite.[6] But it is the auratic, pictorial quality of the crane operator, her arms outstretched in an inverted 'V', that the sequence highlights via reference to the Ascension of the Virgin. Factory work acquires a ritual quality, echoing the 'cult' of the motorcar to be explored in part two, a 'cult' that Roland Barthes had described in his 'mythology' of another Citroën model, the DS.[7] At the same time, however, these initial sequences underscore the secular basis of modern industry. Malle humanises the gantry operator by intercutting wide-angle shots of the hangar with close-ups of her face, arms and hands. Tracking shots taken from the portal connote not transcendence but ordinary human mastery over the material world. Just as the spool must come down to earth, so too must the concerns of a film that everywhere insists upon the 'all too human'.

What immediately follows is a brisk linear presentation of discrete assembly-line tasks. Some of these, such as affixing windshields or installing gearboxes, demand muscular effort and patience; others pose imminent health risks (men wielding spray pistols wear no masks). If the line is mechanised, it is far from automatised, and workers' dexterity

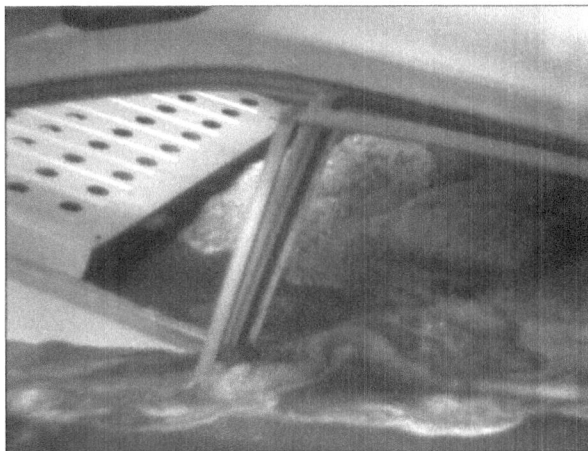

Fig. 1: *Humain, trop humain* (1974): Car body in acid bath.

and attentiveness prove crucial. Malle devotes roughly one minute to each station, introducing the task in long shot or medium shot, then zooming or cutting in, to medium close-up. Though some workers appear oblivious to the camera, others return the gaze to denounce the film crew's complicity with management or simply to draw attention to the muscular and psychological strain that is their hourly lot.

Shooting on 16mm colour stock, Malle and cameraman Étienne Becker revel in the strange beauty of industrial production, its unexpected hues and contrasts. Witness the slow immersion of unpainted car bodies in a bubbling, blue-grey acid bath. *New York Times* critic Vincent Canby saw in this shot a reference to *Psycho*, although given its uncanny aquatic quality a likelier intertext may be Commander Cousteau and Malle's *Le Monde du Silence* (*The Silent World*, 1956).[8] Further down the line, out of a world of steely silver, grey and white, car bodies will emerge a bright *bleu, blanc* or *rouge*, as if to allegorise the transition from black-and-white to colour. Elsewhere a cable-bundling machine recalls nothing so much as an early motion picture apparatus, its peephole aperture making intermittently visible the worker's hand and face. In another composition the interstices of a hydraulic press create an intermittent frame within the frame. These reflexive motifs powerfully conjure up the filmic imaginary even as they describe the task at hand, and the hands on task.

French reviewers had little to say about the 'Salon de l'Auto' sequence, as if the truth of *Humain, trop humain* lay in describing factory work alone. The many candid views of visitors and auto firm representatives roaming the exhibition hall are no less central. On the surface, they provide comic counterpoint. We see the complacency of bourgeois consumers who debate which make and model to purchase next, and the cheery self-assuredness of their children eager to take the wheel. Some obsess over bells and whistles; President of the Republic Georges Pompidou asks worriedly whether a standard model comes with headrests (it does not). Pitches come a mile a minute from salesmen who flatter their clients for their good taste and chide them for thinking that the competition might make a better car. Even those skeptical consumers who lament past design flaws agree that this year's model is an improvement.

Where Godard saw in prostitution to consumer durables a universal analogy for late capitalism, Malle lets women and men speak for themselves, unprompted, uncensored and often unawares. Cramped inside vehicles or milling about, they look by turns curious, elated and indifferent. Malle documents their gestures with an ethnographer's eye: an adolescent tests a brake (smooth) and clutch (stiff); a man probes an oil reservoir with his finger; two men inspect a car body from underneath, as if a cursory glance could replace a road test. The irony of the matter is that not one Salon attendee ever gets to drive. The best one can muster is an imaginary road race, like the young man in a Jaguar convertible whose reverie Malle augments with a drum solo redolent of the highway sequence in *Ascenseur pour l'échafaud* (*Elevator to the Gallows*, 1957).

That same percussive motif where snare and high-hat enter into complex dialogue recurs near the close of part two. Average shot lengths contract, and Salon attendees, shown in close-up, seem to detach themselves progressively from the spectacle. The soundtrack layers together diverse voices, not all locatable in the image or subsequently 'acousmatized', to use Michel Chion's term. If part one aimed tightly to synchronise sound and image, here snatches of conversation and public announcements weave a thick sonic tapestry in which voices blend only to recede in a long fade.

The transition separating the trade fair segment from part three is arguably the conceptual crux of *Humain, trop humain*. Whereas the initial move from factory to Salon took place via a hard cut, editor Suzanne Baron dissimulates the return cut to the factory. It falls in the middle of several medium close-ups of young women examining car doors, their surroundings blurred by the shallow depth of field. In the last shot explicitly tagged to the Salon, a woman tasked with removing fingerprints from car doors mutters, '*J'en ai ras le bol*' ['I can't take it anymore']. We then see a different woman examining a door frame, followed by three similarly composed medium close-ups of young women doing the same. Because Malle bridges the sounds from the Auto Show over these images, only two or three shots in does the spectator realise that the locale has changed: the women are outfitting unfinished windows on the line, not chasing fingerprints on demonstration models. The effect is unsettling due to the lack of hiatus between the worlds of consumption and production, now fantasmatically conjoined.

Up to this point, the film sustains a tragi-comic ritual reading of industrial society. Its final forty minutes will displace the 'cult' of the automobile with another myth, that of the assembly-line worker as modern Sisyphus. By attending to the minutiae of corporeal discipline, this third movement refutes the premises of both the industrial film and the human comedy of the Salon. The worker's body expresses its confiscation in and by the fabrication process, as well as its striving for respite in a controlled space where speech is barred. More than fifteen workstations are covered, and each task is captured multiple times. Standing before a steel mold, the first worker twists a straight wire into a convoluted shape; in an uninterrupted take, she repeats the same series five times, rocking on her sandal-clad feet each time she completes a piece. Another woman feeds sheaves of metal rods rapid-fire into a puncher; over fifty repetitions are shown. We then transition to less specialised tasks reserved for men who wield pneumatic screw guns, soldering irons and blowtorches, but also hammers and mallets. Surveyed

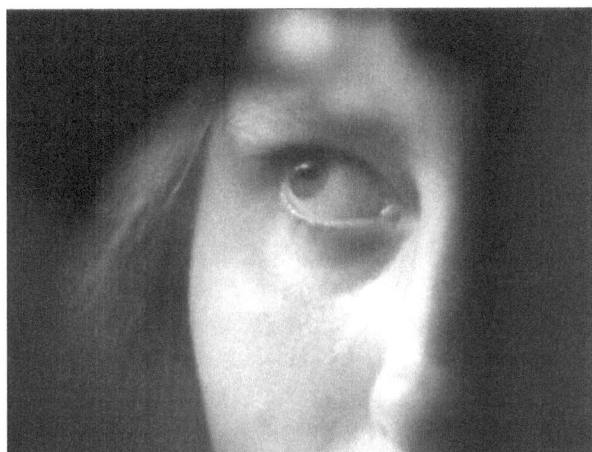

Fig. 2: *Humain, trop humain* (1974): The female worker's gaze.

in long takes, a worker aligns rear hatches and locksets; another mounts a quartet of car doors; another still brazes and files joints.

On the surface, these extended observations are an audio-visual equivalent to the overseers' dreaded *chronométrage*. What prevents *Humain, trop humain* from reproducing management's optimisation strategies, however, is its concern for what ethnographer Marcel Mauss called the 'technics of the body'. What contortions do workstations impose on the human figure? How much room for maneuver does the task afford? How do production rates affect the coordination of eyes, hands and feet? Facial close-ups in telephoto expose the way one worker's gaze, dictated by fixed rhythms, moves incessantly from part to machine and back to part again. These ocular movements show scant variation, such that the rare times the worker looks upward or toward the camera her gaze becomes pregnant with meaning. Views of women stretching upholstery onto metallic frames alternate with shots of their legs and feet: pulled forward by the ceiling-mounted assembly line, the women walk as they work. In the seamstress shop, by contrast, fixity rules. Medium profiles of a worker bending over her sewing machine are intercut with views of her foot pumping the pedal. Since mechanical noise and the spacing of worktables make conversation impossible, Becker's camera correspondingly isolates one seamstress at a time. Workers are also shown at rest, smoking and chatting over coffee or vigorously scrubbing themselves with imbibed rags before leaving the locker room. By design, these moments of respite (rather than release) take up only snatches of running time so as to underscore their integration into factory routine.

Part three's closing sequences unveil in their numbing repetition highly specialised tasks that immobilise the body. A woman wearing a magnetic glove feeds precut sheet metal into a press. Another selects from bins to her left and right metal clips to be placed every few seconds on two rotating spindles. A close-up of the turning cog makes it clear that even the most dexterous worker can't sustain production rates. Indeed, after six or seven turns, the worker fumbles, failing to ready her parts. But this lapse itself may have gone unnoticed by Malle's spectators, their attention now blunted by thirty-five minutes of viewing repeated tasks. It is arguably in this dulling of the senses – brought about, paradoxically, by heightened audiovisual attention – that the formal novelty of Malle's film resides. In lieu of affect and pathos, it creates a discomfort that the immobility of the screening room only aggravates.

The internal movement of *Humain, trop humain* is loosely dialectical. The ritual motif casts consumption as the inverse (negation) of production, with which it entertains nevertheless reciprocity under the Fordist-Taylorist model (workers are the future purchasers of the goods they produce). Part three dispenses with ritualised discourse to register the effects of labour on the working body *in situ*, and the range of bodily responses to that subjugation. In this third, extended moment the viewer undergoes a second-order subjugation of sorts, caught up in the spectacle of production rates yet unable to intervene.

What to make, then, of the final freeze-frame? The arrested image of a young woman worker cannot put a stop to labour *per se*: we know that, despite the strain she endures, she will close out her shift; should she not return the next workday wearing the same red apron, another Breton will flip over car hoods in her place. What the freeze-frame posits is a mental space into which the worker withdraws, her vacant stare left to express the all-too-human truth of daily toil. That mental space is not inviolate for all that: even as the final image suspends movement, the din of the factory floor persists to echo such prior evocations of aural persistence of factory noise as Claire Etcherelli's best-selling *Élise ou la vraie vie* (1967) and its screen adaptation by Michel Drach (*Elise, or Real Life*, 1970).

In *Humain, trop humain* Malle did not make a social comment film about the Taylorist exploitation of workers under capitalism. Nor did he deliver a would-be representative portrait of the French working class. Rather, using footage captured on the shop floor, he and editor Suzanne Baron composed a prescient essay in reverse ethnography focused on human bodies at work. Its loosely dialectical form notwithstanding, Malle's essay in direct cinema proved unreadable in that, contrary to period expectations, it let images speak for themselves, as it were. This failure to conform to discursive expectations set by the anti-establishment Left explains the critical neglect *Humain, trop humain* suffered until resurgent interest in de-industrialisation made its core observational conceit broadly legible.[9]

Following the strikes of May/June 1968, Malle had been nearly alone to receive authorisation to film inside a major French automobile firm. Reflecting on the project in 1987, he noted that in 1972, to shoot at Citroen was de facto a 'political act', albeit in his case one free of explicit ideological aims (Devarrieux and de Navacelle 1988: 27). Camera and tape recorder became precision tools in their own right, and, in the absence of commentary, spectators were left to draw their own conclusions. Interviewed by Gilles Jacob in March 1974, several weeks before the film's release, Malle described *Humain, trop humain* as

> a film that can't easily be coopted: neither a lesson in Marxism nor a moralizing broadside on working-class existence. For me, the film prompts reflection on the fact that a civilization has reached the point of making part of its members

do that. [...] This sort of film requires active participation from the spectator to continue our work. [...] *Humain, trop humain* places viewers ill at ease, simply because they feel for the first time the physical, muscular, and sensorial reality of assembly-line work (noise, for example). (1974: 30)

Malle's self-assessment echoes a report from the 1973 Cannes Film Festival screening that viewers left mid-way, prompting the remark that the average filmgoer 'can't bear for an hour to look at what a worker undergoes for a lifetime' (Lionet 1973: 17). In taking an ethnographic approach to bodies tethered to machines and toolsets, Malle had effectively skirted the watchwords of the day to confound Left and Right alike, furthering an observational mode that other practitioners of *le direct* – principally in France, Raymond Depardon – would adapt to new contexts.

By comparison, *Place de la République* appears the more minor work, one that adopts the recognisable, viewer-ready form of impromptu interviews on a heavily trafficked street corner. Its brief is modest by design: in the credits he reads in voice-over, Malle notes that his objective was simply to make a reportage film about people in the street. Bringing to bear on home turf *Calcutta*'s experiment in urban observation, it insisted on the virtues of dialogue and on drawing city-dwellers out of their anonymity: 'All this talk about non-communication I find wearisome. I'd like in this film for Parisians to express themselves.'[10]

To set Parisians talking, Malle and assistant Ferdinand Moscovitz rely on the material presence of the camera to initiate and mediate spontaneous curbside encounters. Left in full view, the recording equipment allows the interviewer-filmmaker to dispense with the formal introductions typical of subject-driven documentary. His crew pick potential subjects out of the crowd seemingly at random, though the decision to shoot on weekdays limits the age range. Those who stop are generally asked how being on camera makes them feel. Some claim to have been oblivious, like the elderly man in a trench coat whom the crew trails unremarked across several intersections; others half expect to be outed by the cast of *La Caméra cachée*, France's *Candid Camera*. When Malle asks the pale blonde in a powder-blue coat whether the camera bothers her, she exclaims, 'but you're the ones looking!'. Her statement describes in literal terms the moment of shooting and the voyeurism inherent in Malle's conceit while anticipating the imaginary viewing position that future moviegoers occupy vis-à-vis the blonde's own recorded image.

The visible presence of camera and tape recorder – its microphone hidden in plain view, inside Malle's leather pouch – transforms city street into stage: thus a widow-turned-streetwalker, posing against the backdrop of the massive bronze allegory of the Republic, belts out a *chanson réaliste* à la Edith Piaf. Though such bona fide on-camera performances are exceptional, nearly all persons interviewed keep conversation flowing with minimal input. Relaxed in demeanor in his denim jacket, Malle need only add such phatic statements as 'vous croyez?', 'ah bon', 'c'est vrai?', 'vous pensez?'.

Between interview segments, cutaways to the city square or to ubiquitous street traffic ground the experiment in the everyday rhythms and forms of the city life. These interludes are not simply pauses or transitions but point again towards a reverse

Fig. 3: *Place de la République* (1974): A man of the crowd.

ethnography, a trend evident in such contemporaneous literary works as Georges Perec's serial observation piece *Tentative d'épuisement d'un lieu parisien* (*An Attempt at Exhausting a Place in Paris*, 1975). A traffic policeman adjudicates a dispute between two motorists over a parking spot; construction workers try to tame a feeder hose out of control, a 'microevent' (the term is Perec's) reminiscent of the Lumière brothers' *L'Arroseur arrosé*. Malle fully understood the ethnographic value of his *Paris 72* footage, and offered his unedited reels to the French radio and television (ORTF) for creative use in its programming.[11]

What period reviewers retained of *Place de la République* were the sundry portraits of Parisians. Sketched on the fly, these range from two to four minutes apiece. Most interviewees are petit bourgeois shopkeepers, clerks, housewives and retirees. Several men and women are down on their luck: a veteran of the colonies can't find work for his swollen hands; the Guadeloupian whom the film crew takes out for a drink (in the film's sole indoor sequence) evokes chronic bouts of nerves that have landed him in a psychiatric ward. If most topics broached by Malle are mundane and noncontroversial, such as upbringing, work, leisure or fashion, he occasionally asks questions similar to those in *Chronique d'un été* and *Le Joli Mai*: How do you get by? Do you live around here? Are you happy? Are you still working? Do you vote? Though no confessions are forthcoming, some interviewees acknowledge that life hasn't been easy: take the Polish tailor, who need only mention the war years for us to understand that this man is a survivor (ironically, the director, who was preparing *Lucien Lacombe* at the time of the shoot, seems not at first to have understood that the man is Jewish).

As in *Humain, trop humain*, sound is rigorously tethered to the image, and one might argue that Malle's subject is the fact of interacting with strangers, and establishing how much, or how little, individuals volunteer about themselves on camera.[12] The film's energy and playful tone derive in no small part from a scene, roughly three quarters of the way through the picture, where what is exchanged are not just words, but the movie camera itself. When a charismatic Malle asks the thin-faced blonde who had appeared in several prior scenes if she'd like to take charge of the proceedings and shoot the scene herself, she hesitates, then accepts. A moment of strong filmic reflexivity results where Baron's edit conjoins images obtained from the two separate cameras, one wielded by the blonde, the other by Malle's crew, and likely by Malle himself. If this temporary reversal of the camera's gaze doesn't disrupt filmic authority, it nevertheless highlights the ability of the 'equipment' of cinema to transform social relations and perceptions *in situ*.

* * *

Though overshadowed by *Lacombe Lucien*, Malle's French documentaries of 1974 set forth an ethically committed, exploratory mode of cinema that refuses editorialising in the name of open-ended engagement. His distanced observations of factory workers and of those who covet the automobiles they make, as well as his candid interactions with Parisians in their day-to-day ask that we reevaluate the vocation of documentary, a mode that need not espouse a rhetoric of persuasion or didacticism. Each work makes of the film camera and sound recording device tools, by which better to understand the situated aspect of the human, namely how the body interacts with and inhabits a technical and cultural milieu. In this light, *Humain, trop humain* and *Place de la République* are paradoxical works, in the etymological sense: rather than reproduce or challenge frontally the models promulgated by new critical academism of the French Left after 1968, they stand alongside them, adumbrating alternative audio-visual modes of knowledge that in retrospect appear all the more valuable for the fact that dominant critical voices and discourses of the period could not register them in full.

Notes

1. Strong runs in Lyon, Bordeaux and Lille added to this figure another 120,000 spectators (*Le Film Français*, 5 April 1974: 20, 22).
2. Three other projected enquiries dealt with the Amazon River basin, the American Midwest and an undisclosed Arab emirate (see Billard 2003: 328).
3. 'Who says what, but where and when?' The second article is Pascal Bonitzer's 'Histoire de sparadrap', illustrated by a *Lucien Lacombe* production photograph showing a pipe-smoking Louis Malle in front of the detained Resister, his mouth taped shut and decorated with lipstick by Lucien.
4. The authorial fallacy behind this reasoning is patent: *Cahiers du cinéma* erases the collective labour behind Malle's films and assumes that a film author who signed earlier materials will 'sign' subsequent works in a similar way.
5. In a typescript document Malle identifies the interpreters as the Chœur des Moniales de l'Abbaye Notre-Dame d'Argentan. Cinémathèque Française; MALLE 295 B79.
6. In *Bande à part* (*Band of Outsiders*, 1964), Godard frames to similar effect wooden spools of cabling in the suburban stockyard frequented by the trio of Anna Karina, Sami Frey and Claude Brasseur.

7   Homonymous with 'déesse' (goddess). Here is Barthes: 'cars today are the exact equivalent of the great Gothic cathedrals: I mean the supreme creation of an era, conceived with passion by unknown artists, and consumed in image if not in usage by a whole population which appropriates in it a purely magical object' (1972: 88).
8   The car body recalls the submersible 'diving saucer' Denise that Cousteau launched in 1959.
9   Wilhelm Roth dismisses these works as best left undisturbed in the archives (1985: 28), whereas Hatzfield et al. (2009) find them to be exceptional contributions to the history of documentary filmmaking.
10 MALLE 921 B174.
11 Letter from Pierre Schaeffer to Louis Malle, 28 September 1972; MALLE 0294 B79.
12 The one exception is the remark by the nonagenarian violinist, which the soundtrack reprises after he has left the park bench.

Bibliography

Barthes, R. (1972 [1957]) *Mythologies*. Trans. Annette Lavers. New York: Farrar, Straus & Giroux.
Billard, P. (2003) *Louis Malle. Le rebelle solitaire*. Paris: Plon.
Bonitzer, P. (1974) 'Histoire de sparadrap (*Lacombe Lucien*),' *Cahiers du cinéma*, 250 (May), 42–47.
Canby, V. (1975) 'Humain, trop humain,' *The New York Times*, 14 Feb., 28.
Daney, S. (1974) 'Qui dit quoi, mais où et quand?', *Cahiers du cinéma*, 250 (May), 38–42.
Devarrieux, C. and M.-C. de Navacelle (1988) *Cinémas du réel*. Paris: Autrement.
Giraud, T. (1974) '*Attica*/*Humain, trop humain*: deux conceptions du cinéma direct', *Cahiers du cinéma*, 250 (May), 47–51.
Hatzfeld, N., A. P. Michel and G. Rot (2009) 'Représentations filmiques du travail à la chaîne,' in C. Eyraud and G. Lambert (eds) *Filmer le travail/Films et travail: cinéma et sciences sociales*. Aix-en-Provence: Université de Provence, 131–5.
Jacob, G. (1974) 'Entretien avec Louis Malle', *Positif*, 157 (March), 28–35.
Lionet, G. (1973) 'Humain, trop humain', *Jeune cinéma*, 72 (July/August), 17–18.
MacCabe, C. (2005) *Jean-Luc Godard: A Portrait of the Artist at Seventy*. New York: Farrar, Straus & Giroux.
Morin, F. (1974) '*Humain, trop humain* et *Place de la République*', *L'Humanité*, 8 April.
Roth, W. (1985) 'Außen-Ansichten und Einzelheiten: Zu den Dokumentarfilmen,' in P. W. Jansen and W. Schütte (eds) *Louis Malle*. Vienna: Carl Hanser, 23–8.
Toubiana, S. (1974) 'Donner la parole au peuple pour mieux lui clouer le bec!,', *Libération*, 4 April.

CHAPTER FOUR

Louis Malle's Nonfiction: Tradition, Rebellion and Authorial Voice

Alan Williams

For *cinéphiles* with only a limited knowlege of his work, Louis Malle is mainly known as the director of diverse fiction films with a marked penchant for shocking or scandalous subject matter: incest (*Le Souffle au coeur* [*Murmur of the Heart*], 1971), child prostitution (*Pretty Baby*, 1978), a future war between men and women (*Black Moon*, 1975), female *jouissance* (*Les Amants* [*The Lovers*], 1958), transvestism (*Zazie dans le métro*, 1960), to name but a few. But alongside these often controversial fiction films, Malle produced a significant body of less 'sensationalist' nonfiction works: eight or nine major works (depending on how one counts *Vanya on 42nd Street* [1994]) versus eighteen fiction features. This corpus can be approached in a variety of ways, but one convenient and revealing means of beginning an analysis is to compare two nonfiction films on the same subject, one by Malle and one by a French filmmaker of a later generation. In 1986 Malle made *And the Pursuit of Happiness*, about recent immigrants in the United States, their various backgrounds, life trajectories and feelings about their new country. In 2014, Julie Bertucelli made *La Cour de Babel* (*School of Babel*), about mostly but not entirely young immigrants in France in a special school for new arrivals. Both films are highly worthy, well-received works, and the comparisons that follow are not meant to suggest that one or the other is 'better'. A great deal of the dissimilarities between them may be attributed to historical change, not in the politics of immigration in the two countries, but in the history of nonfiction filmmaking.

La Cour de Babel clearly belongs to a comparatively recent tendency in French nonfiction filmmaking, what one might call the 'school of Philibert', after one of France's leading and influential practitioners of documentary filmmaking. Indeed, Nicolas Philibert's *Être et Avoir* (*To Be and to Have*, 2002) hovers in the background of *La Cour de Babel* as cinematic reference point, implicit source of comparisons in subject matter and as the object of a sustained *hommage*. In Bill Nichols' typology, the film belongs to the 'observational' mode, which also covers works by filmmakers such as Richard Leacock and Frederick Wiseman (1991: 32–3 and 38ff.). A more historicising way to describe it would be to invoke the American term 'direct cinema', since Bertucelli's film has relatively little to do with what in France was called *cinéma vérité*, as this label was understood by its initiators: filmmakers of Malle's generation such as Jean Rouch or Chris Marker. Most of the differences between *La Cour de Babel* and a classic *vérité* work such as Rouch and Morin's *Chronique d'un été* (*Chronicle of a Summer*, 1961), however, are quantitative rather than qualitative. Bertucelli's work has been shaped into sequences dominated by what André Bazin called (in 'classic' fiction filmmaking) 'analytical' or 'dramatic' *découpage* (aka 'scene construction') (2009: 96–7). The scenes are constructed to retain the verisimilitude of diegetic space and time, via various kinds of match cuts, such as axial matches, glance-object edits and shot/reverse-shot formations. This is, of course, in one sense all a violation of cinematic 'truth': there is only one camera in this sort of filmmaking, and so there can be no real shot/reverse-shot (true to the original events). As if to acknowledge this, into this classically edited continuity Bertucelli inserts occasional departures: in the opening sequences, for example, there is one interview with quite visible jump cuts, and there are periodic examples of what we might call 'process' edits, in which 'the match is … between actions, but the emphasis is less on spatial continuity than on the concept of a process' (Nichols 1991: 20). These departures from the relatively 'invisible' editing of the classical narrative cinema, however, are comparatively rare, and serve as a kind of *effet de documentaire*, or 'documentary effect'. They periodically acknowledge, without actually threatening it, the artifice of the film's apparent spatio-temporal coherence. In a film like *Chronique d'un été*, or Malle's *And the Pursuit of Happiness*, on the other hand, the proportions are reversed: analytic or dramatic *découpage* can occur fairly often, but in a context where it never seems to dominate.

In fact, few films could be further away from Bertucelli's work, in terms of form and mode of address, than Malle's study of American immigrants, though in terms of subject matter there are striking similarities – particularly striking given the great distance in historical time and in geography between the two works. In Nichols' terms, Malle's work is 'interactive' rather than 'observational': 'the filmmaker's voice could be heard as readily as any other, not subsequently as an organizing voice-over commentary, but on the spot, in face-to-face encounters with others' (1991: 44). In contrast to analytical *découpage*, Malle's preferred type of discourse is the (comparatively) long take, like the ones that open his film. His edits are for the most part very visible. Where he does simulate traditional (fiction film) match cuts, these are ordinarily axial matches. There are few sequences with analytic/dramatic scene construction, though Malle doesn't reject the technique entirely. Curiously (but probably not coincidentally), the most prominent examples of this in *And the Pursuit of Happiness* are the sequences set in various sorts of schools (for adults, for children, even for aspiring actors). Overwhelmingly, however, the cuts correspond not to the dramatic dictates of a scene, but rather to the active presence of the filmmaker, a presence rendered even more salient by his abundant voice-over commentaries and by his (diegetic, but off-screen) voice in the film's numerous interviews. Bertucelli, in *La Cour de Babel*, is absent from the soundtrack, even in sequences that were obviously filmed as interviews. She has, however, a kind of on-screen representative in the form of one of the school's teachers. Most of the time, her subjects ignore the camera – which is to say that the moments when they showed awareness of its presence (mainly due to stress) have been largely edited out – whereas Malle's characters are almost always aware of it.

How to account for Malle's approach to documentary, as opposed to more recent leading French nonfiction filmmakers such as Nicolas Philibert or Raymond Depardon (between whom there are important stylistic differences, but both of whom adopt the same 'observational' approach to their subjects)? The answer is to be found in film history, in the different reactions to the sudden availability of portable synchronised sound machines, most notably the Nagra recording system, in the late 1950s, in the two countries that most thoroughly explored the new technology: France and the United States. American filmmakers enthusiastically embraced 'direct' cinema, with little concern of how their recording of real life would change that life. If they worried about this at all, their standard response was that in moments of intense emotion their subjects would forget the camera and microphone and behave as if they were not present. French filmmakers were not so sure, to say the least, as can be seen most clearly in *Chronique d'un été*. National differences became most public when French national television (ORTF) sponsored a conference on new documentary techniques in Lyon in 1963. American participants claimed that spontaneity and unpredictability of their subjects' behaviour were the guarantors of cinema truth, while the French reaction (much of it post-conference) was intensely skeptical. Jean-Luc Godard wrote two largely critical appraisals of Richard Leacock, who had become something of a test case in France for the American approach, in the pages of *Cahiers du cinéma* (see Winston 1993: 45–8), and Louis Marcorelles argued in another *Cahiers du cinéma* article that although Leacock attempted to reduce authorial commentary to the minimum, it simply crept back in through editing and scene selection (1986: 264–70).

American and French documentary filmmaking therefore had different, yet oddly symmetrical histories. The *nouvelle vague* generation in France favoured reflexivity and overt subjectivity, whereas the Americans favoured transparency, passing ultimately into a kind of stately classicism (think of the slow progress from early Fred Wiseman to late Wiseman.) But the American generations that followed rediscovered, as it were, the French doubts from the 1960s, and leading US documentarians today, such as Eroll Morris or even Michael Moore, are no longer true believers in the power of camera and microphone to convey a direct, all but unmediated truth. In France, on the other hand, the generations that followed Godard, Rouch, Marker and others, rediscovered the power and utility of quasi-objective observation. There, leading filmmakers such as Philibert or Depardon have made Wiseman-like studies of institutions (a very Wisemanian notion) and social processes. Malle belonged to the generation of Godard, Marcorelles, Marker, Varda and many others. This, however, was a generation of proud, self-conscious individuals, each unafraid to reveal and to exploit his or her own personality and taste. Therefore, to say that Malle was a special case as a documentary filmmaker is certainly accurate, but is not to say a great deal: they were all special cases.

***

The principal reason for the national differences in responses to portable sync-sound equipment probably arose from very different cultural and historical contexts. In France, the 1950s had been a veritable golden age of nonfiction filmmaking, with works such as Georges Franju's *Hôtel des Invalides* (*War Museum*, 1951) and Alain Resnais' *Nuit et Brouillard* (*Night and Fog*, 1956). Critical recognition had been abundant: it is no coincidence that Franju, for instance, was named 'The Greatest French Director' in the pages of *Positif*, the left-leaning rival to the center-right *Cahiers du cinéma* (see Demeure and Kyrou 1956). Not to mention there had been an ongoing debate and interrogation surrounding the idea of 'realism', most prominently by the preeminent film critic André Bazin. In perhaps his most influential, reprinted and translated essay, on Italian neorealism, Bazin argued that cinematic realism was not a single, definable entity, but an unstable, potentially contradictory mix of different possibilities of form and subject matter (2009: 230–2). Such considerations could not have failed to impress any filmmaker contemplating a technological leap in apparent realism. In the US, on the other hand, the heyday of documentary had come and gone (in the 1930s), and nonfiction films mostly earned little critical respect or discussion – with the partial exception of the nature documentaries produced by Walt Disney. There was also scant critical debate about the relation of film to reality before the publication of Kracauer's *Theory of Film* in 1960. It thus comes as no surprise that Leacock and his peers leaped in enthusiastically where the French filmmakers expressed doubt.

In this context, it is important to note that Malle, like Varda and Marker, first made nonfiction films in the traditional, pre-Nagra manner by shooting silent footage and later adding a soundtrack typically dominated by music and commentary. While most documentarians used the new technology discretely, if at all, there were two feature-length explorations of the possibilities of the new technology: Rouch and Morin's *Chronique d'un été*, and Marker's *Le Joli Mai* (1962). It took Malle a while to get to the point where he wanted to make his own contributions to *cinéma vérité*, but when he did, it was *Chronique d'un été* which served most clearly as a model. One can argue that Malle was perpetually responding to, and sometimes reworking or even remaking, the subjects and the formal techniques of Morin and Rouch's great, disorderly, sometimes almost incoherent work. Here is a partial list of themes and techniques that Malle takes up again: happiness, work (in an automobile factory, in both Malle and in *Chronique d'un été*), immigration and attendant cultural conflict, war protestors, on-street interviews, having an interview subject subsequently interview other subjects.

But all of this was to come much later. Malle's first engagement with the new equipment came with *Vive le tour!* (filmed 1962; released 1968). This was, clearly, not a film that Malle made in order to use the new portable equipment: sync-sound, on-location interviews take up barely two minutes of the finished film's nineteen-minute running time (it was initially intended to be longer, but commercial reasons dictated its final length). The only other aspect of the film that is artistically or technically new is the relatively large quantity of location-recorded, 'wild' sound. Otherwise, it is an almost entirely classical (pre-Nagra) documentary. It is also a good piece of evidence for why filmmakers like Malle found few pressing reasons to explore new forms or techniques. If the film is, finally, rather traditional, it nonetheless conveys a clear point of view, reflecting Malle's artistic personality – in particular, his respect for tradition accompanied at the same time by his urge to support rebellion *within* tradition (as witness the comments on spectators breaking the rule against helping the cyclists). It is amusing, informative and at times oddly beautiful, the product of what we might call his anarchic conservatism. As a conservative, Malle believes in traditions, with their rules and norms, but he also seems to believe that some rules are to be respected, while others are there for the pleasure of breaking them.

If he was not out to explore the new technology, and if he did not seek to demonstrate his love of bicycle races (his point of view is detached, almost ethnographic), then what exactly motivated him to make *Vive le Tour!*? As with all of his other detours into documentary, the main reason was that he needed a break from fiction filmmaking, generally (as in this case) because his career as a fiction filmmaker took a turn that didn't satisfy him. As he told Philip French, he had been unnerved by the experience of making *Vie privée* (*A Very Private Affair*, 1961), and by that film's generally negative reviews, hence his first 'return to documentary' (French 1993: 36). He returned to it as to a faithful old friend, or perhaps an old lover. It was the first of four times he did so, though in later returns he appears to have needed a stronger dose of mind-clearing nonfiction, and each time subsequently he made two films. It would not be until the second film of his third return, in *Place de la République* (shot 1972; released 1974), that he would embrace *cinéma vérité* of the sort that Rouch and Morin explored in *Chronique d'un été*. In finally making this shift, he was the last of the *nouvelle vague* filmmakers to do so. After that, he would only produce this type of documentary, in his two great 1986 American works, *God's Country* (1985) and *And the Pursuit of Happiness*.

* * *

It wasn't only the form, or 'mode', that changed over the years of Malle's documentary activity, but his attitude toward his subjects as well. In his early works he is a voyager through different parts of society, an ethnographer almost as interested in his own reactions to his subjects as he is in them *per se*. The sea change comes with *Place de la République*, his homage to *Chronique d'un été*. In that film, several of his subjects *talk back*, and ask him questions; he sends one of them out to do interviews on her own (as happens in *Chronique d'un été*). By the time of *And the Pursuit of Happiness*, however, he seems more directly involved in the worlds he observes, at least during the interviews, while his former spirit of detachment remains, in his soundtrack commentaries. He is even willing to show that he often *likes* the people he films, including (as we will see below) when they don't have altogether sympathetic back stories. Perhaps one can say that he ultimately becomes, at least partially, a humanist – in the act of filming, certainly, and mainly in his nonfiction works, this attitude being much rarer in his fiction films, which almost always retain a spirit of authorial detachment. Compare, for example, the warmth of *And the Pursuit of Happiness*, his last nonfiction work, with

Fig. 1: *Vive le Tour!* (1962): Homing pigeon.

the authorial indifference in his last fiction film, *Damage* (1992), which has somewhat the feeling of an autopsy.

Different worlds, different times, even different techniques; is there anything, aside from Malle's personality, that characterises all of this body of work? As a self-conscious member of the New Wave generation Malle was far from reluctant to show his likes and dislikes. The former include (i) anything he finds amusing, or even grotesquely amusing; (ii) marginal figures of all sorts, such as children, the mentally ill, immigrants and refugees; (iii) various types of ambiguities and ambivalences. His main dislike is easy to see almost everywhere in his work: authority and authority figures. All these items he takes up in his nonfiction (for the grotesquely amusing, see the opening sequences of *Vive le Tour!*, particularly the helium-filled advertising balloons), sometimes adding motifs relatively specific to his documentaries, such as the journey. Malle's documentaries are always to some extent *about Malle*, what he likes and dislikes, but also, crucially, how he thinks – and he doesn't want us to forget this. The self-revealingness most obviously surfaces in the voice-over commentaries of films like *God's Country*, but it also can be seen in aspects of film form.

* * *

Formally, the most consistent (and, arguably, the most interesting) element in Malle's films is what I will call the 'contrarian set pieces'. By this I mean first of all a segment of the film set off from the other segments by its length and/or its intensity, and/or the cinematic means employed. This, also, he probably got from *Chronique d'un été*. Said set pieces generally come near the end of the film in which they appear – alone, or in sequences of two or three such distinctive segments. Perhaps the most captivating one comes near the end of *Humain, trop humain*. That film is unique in Malle's work in terms of the lack of the author's presence in one form or another, generally on the soundtrack. Instead, there is an obvious authorial artefact – namely, a clear A B A structure: a brief overview of the workers at the auto assembly plant is followed by first a short visit to a car exposition, then a much longer return to the factory, where various jobs are observed. The film's major 'set piece' comes toward the end, when we see workers assembling, soldering and briefly testing car doors and trunk lids. This segment, unlike all the rest of the film, is conveyed in fluid long takes with abundant camera movement, whereas the workers seen before it are shown in sequences composed of short, repetitive shots. The effect of these long takes, aside from their obvious appeal to the feelings of any admirer of André Bazin, is to make, as the latter would have predicted, the *process* of working much more salient. *Humain, trop humain* is sometimes described as a study of alienated labour, but in these long takes, the work takes on an interest of its own, quite in contrast to the obviously alienating, tedious assembly of electrical cables (shot on much quicker takes) that precedes it.

It is certainly true that every spectator sees his or her own film, based in part on his or her *instrument*, that is, the embodied, lived experience that is brought to film viewing. I can therefore only speak for myself, and my instrument, when I say that I find the set piece of door and trunk assembly riveting, and do not (at least, not immediately) take it as depicting alienated labour. Malle knew in advance that he was going to film this part of the manufacturing process in this manner: 'We're not going to cut [he told his crew] because it must become obsessive.' He added that he wanted the spectator 'to come out of seeing this film exhausted' (French 1993: 162). In my own experience, the rest of the film is indeed exhausting, but not this part. At any rate, Malle certainly intended this sequence to be different from what went before, which leads me to what I consider the most important function of the set pieces in terms of *content*. They typically introduce a twist, or a new perspective on a film's previous subject matter. Whether or not one agrees that soldering the car doors might be perceived as interesting, challenging work, a likely consensus is that the work shown before this set piece is almost the ideal definition of alienated labour. The same small gestures are repeated over and over, in brief, often contextless shots. Although the point is not made explicitly, most of this much less appealing work is done by *women*; in effect, one tacit function of the set piece is to throw into implicit relief the gender hierarchy of the factory. Did Malle intend to comment on gender in the assembly line? This cannot be ascertained, since there is no off-screen voice to explain his intentions, but this would have been something that he relished, as a lover of types of ambiguity.

Sometimes, however, the twist or new perspective given by a set piece is made explicit, as in the first one in episode one of *Phantom India*, where a dead animal is being picked apart, eaten and fought over by dogs and vultures. This scene goes on for an uncomfortably long time, only for Malle's voice to comment: 'When I see this scene again, I realize that we have reacted in terms of the *schémas* of our culture … to us, it was a tragedy, a drama in several acts. For the Indians who accompanied us, it was, on the contrary, an everyday scene, a glimpse of life and death, and their calm alternation. There was nothing to film.'

When we turn to the American nonfiction films, we find the same structure, but to some extent it is less immediately obvious. In *God's Country*, a small farming town is presented for most of the film as a kind of white-bread utopia, and Malle repeatedly mentions how much he likes the people he meets there. The 'set piece with a twist' arrives smoothly, almost naturally, beginning with a brief sequence about the community theatre, then a first portrait of a character who doesn't fit the mold – a perpetual bachelor and member of the theatre group (who may well be a closeted gay) – and on to a woman Malle calls the town's 'free spirit'. The interview with her goes on longer than any other interview (the most basic sign of a set piece), and the questions are more probing, and in a different register. Malle is interested in how a 'free spirit' fits in with such an apparently homogeneous community. The answer seems to be: surprisingly well, though not without some friction.

In *And the Pursuit of Happiness*, we see the same placement of the major set piece very near the end of the film, and Malle quite deliberately makes it a bit of a shock. Most of the film proceeds at an even pace, showing different examples of almost stereotypical legal immigrants. It then comes as a mild surprise that we switch focus away from them to American citizens who deal with 'illegal' (today, 'undocumented') immigrants and, to a lesser extent, with some of those immigrants themselves. Then, in an A B A pattern reminiscent of *Humain, trop humain* (but reversed in running times of the 'A' sections), we return to a story of classical immigration, but with a weird, upper class twist. It's about a family name – Somoza, from Nicaragua. Yes, *that* Somoza, the famous general widely considered responsible for what amounts to widespread, systemic war crimes. Although he is the patriarch of the last family that Malle studies, we don't see that much of him. Malle instead speaks with his sons in several sequences, one of which takes place in the Miami restaurant that the sons have opened to earn a living – and perhaps also to participate in this way of American life and separate from their father (Malle includes some of his questions, and more of their answers, about their rather distant relations with the patriarch).

This part of Malle's film is the longest, most complicated segment; it stands out in running time and in spatio-temporal complexity, and at the end it is this very surprising choice that allows Malle to ask the question that perhaps has been implicit in the entire film, and which certainly at this point is cast retrospectively back in relation to all that has gone before: 'Is it really possible to abolish the past?' Malle answers the question at the end of a sequence where Carlos Somoza helps his children fly a kite: 'Perhaps the dictator's nephew is becoming just another suburban American. I'll drink to that.' The question recalls the similar, implicit enigma that ends *God's Country:* how is it possible for outsiders – a free spirit, a 'perpetual bachelor', and the supportive parents of a notorious antiwar activist – to live within, and at peace with, a white-bread utopia? Malle's questioning of the worlds he films generally comes down not to politics, nor to a study of 'institutions' à la Wiseman or Philibert, but to an examination of the moral situation, and the moral possibilities, of people within a given position in a given society.

Malle's documentary set pieces are designed to surprise, sometimes even to shock the viewer. 'You think you know everything', he seems to say, 'but you *don't*. One way of accounting for this structure in his nonfiction works is that it displaces to the level of society and of the individual's social context an important motif in his fiction films. Perhaps the most striking difference between the director's fiction and nonfiction films lies in their depiction of human nature. In an interview toward the end of

Fig. 2: *And the Pursuit of Happiness* (1986): The Somoza family.

his career, the filmmaker told Melinda Camber Porter: 'In life, people behave incredibly irrationally. But in so-called realism, people eliminate the irrational' (1986: 86). A major goal in many, perhaps most of Malle's fiction films is to give the irrational its due (in *Black Moon*, as well as in *Zazie dans le métro*, *Lacombe Lucien* [1974] and many more) and not to make films based in 'realism'. But in his documentaries, he mainly shows people behaving, if not exactly rationally, then at the very least predictably and *understandably*. It's society as a whole that is, if not irrational, then at the very least paradoxical. Perhaps this was a tension in Louis Malle's artistic mindset that he never resolved, and that becomes evident when one compares his fictional and nonfictional works – between admitting that people cannot really be understood in any logical way, and nonetheless wanting to do exactly that.

Bibliography

Bazin, A. (2009 [1958–62]) *What is Cinema?*, trans. T. Barnard. Montreal: Caboose.
Demeure, J. and A. Kyrou ['J.D. et A.K.'] (1956) 'Le plus grand cinéaste français', *Positif*, 16, 37–41.
French, P. (1993) *Malle on Malle*. London: Faber and Faber.
Marcorelles, L. (1986 [1961]) 'The Leacock Experiment', trans. D. Wilson, in J. Hillier (ed.) *Cahiers du Cinéma: The 1960s. New Wave, New Cinema, Reevaluating Hollywood*. Cambridge, MA: Harvard University Press, 257–63.
Nichols, B. (1991) *Representing Reality*. Bloomington, IN: Indiana University Press.
Porter, M. C. (1986) *Through Parisian Eyes: Reflections on Contemporary French Arts and Culture*. New York and Oxford: Oxford University Press.
Winston, B. (1993) 'The Documentary Film as Scientific Inscription,' in M. Renov (ed.) *Theorizing Documentary*. New York and London: Routledge, 37–57.

CHAPTER FIVE

Louis Malle's 1960s 'Star' Films
Sue Harris

French Cinema and the Star System

In February 1974, with an acclaimed and rich body of work already behind him, Louis Malle published a provocative opinion piece in the trade journal *Le Film Français*: 'Le cinéma français et le star-system.' Malle outlined what he saw as the biggest threat to the future of French cinema: it was in thrall, he argued, to a mediocre and moribund star system that tied the hands of creative filmmakers and had no relevance beyond its own borders. 'It's a catastrophe', he lamented. 'The cinema is populated by the same twenty *Fregolis* who do no more than change costume from one film to another. It's such a shame because most of them are great actors, and they are demeaned by this. They find themselves in parts for which they are ill-suited. It's not them I'm attacking, but the system that locks them into this pattern' (1974: 3).

The domestic industry, as he saw it, had become increasingly narrow and wholly risk-averse. He laid the blame for the state of creative paralysis in which French cinema now found itself firmly at the feet of the nation's overly cautious producers and distributors. They would willingly bankroll screenplays attached to the names of major figures like Catherine Deneuve, Alain Delon and Jeanne Moreau, whatever the interest or quality of the project; but without a star name, a film risked being consigned to invisibility, and along with it, the new generation filmmakers and performers so vital to the health and creative renewal of the industry. Malle's appeal for 'nouveaux talents' to feature in lead roles, and for a wider casting of the net in the French industry, came in the wake of his selection of the unknown and non-professional Pierre Blaise for the titular role in *Lacombe Lucien* (1974). He himself had struggled to convince his backers to invest in a project headed by such an untested figure, but Malle had the advantage of an established career track record. Had he been starting out, he recognised, *Lacombe*

Lucien would have languished in a drawer, perhaps indefinitely. His article was a clarion call for his peers, and a manifesto for a new model of production in France: 'it is time to invest money in the unknowns because that is the only way to get some new blood into our stale cinema … The Malthusianism that the French industry is subject to is unhealthy in every respect, including commercially' (1974: 4).

Malle's intervention was perhaps unexpected considering his own reputation as a star maker, most notably in his work with Jeanne Moreau and Maurice Ronet. Throughout the 1960s he also worked closely with some of France's most established and bankable stars, including Alain Delon and Brigitte Bardot, walking a line between what contemporary critics deemed auteur and commercial cinema. *Vie Privée* (*A Very Private Affair*, 1961) starred Bardot – then the most photographed woman in the world – alongside Marcello Mastroianni, the latter in the ascendant following the international success of *La Dolce Vita* (Federico Fellini, 1960). *Viva Maria!* (1965) was a high-profile pairing of Moreau and Bardot, at the time the two highest paid and most glamorous actresses in France. *Le Voleur* (*The Thief of Paris*, 1967) featured Jean-Paul Belmondo at the height of his fame; and *William Wilson* (1968), one of the short films from the three-part *Histoires Extraordinaires* (*Spirits of the Dead*) portmanteau film (alongside contributions by Roger Vadim and Federico Fellini), starred Delon, France's very own matinée idol, with Bardot in a supporting role. However, in Pierre-Henri Gilbert's documentary *Louis Malle: Le rebelle* (2016), the director reflects on his work in the 1960s and admits that he 'lost ten years' trying to persuade himself that 'great cinema was cinema with great actors'.

Malle's early coronation as an auteur with *Ascenseur pour l'échafaud* (*Elevator to the Gallows*, 1957) and *Les Amants* (*The Lovers*, 1958) had seen him catapulted to fame and able to have his pick of the era's talent. The itinerary he followed in the 1960s certainly testifies to his authority and creative influence in French cinema of the era, and his ability to command the interest and collaboration of its star names. But, with the exception of *Le Voleur*, the star-vehicle films noted above were unhappy experiences for Malle, and he has spoken about them in interviews in terms of their disappointments and frustrations rather than their pleasures. In particular, his efforts to accommodate the star power of his leads seems to have compromised his directorial autonomy, while the films themselves – and their project of testing critical concepts of film stardom and celebrity in narrative and performance – can be seen to distract from, rather than enhance, Malle's artistic profile as an intimist filmmaker focused on personal themes and experiences. What is certain is that the accumulated pressures of these films left him exhausted, disillusioned and, in his own words, in need of a 'dive back into reality'. After the shoot of *William Wilson*, Malle took off for India, and began a new phase in his career, one that prioritised documentary filmmaking, or more experimental work with non-professionals, and that would eventually lead to the critical success of *Lacombe Lucien* and to his departure from France.

The aim of this essay is to consider the extent to which Malle's statements about a 'crisis' in French cinema in the early 1970s might have roots in the practical and personal experiences of the films of the 1960s when, with his artistic reputation and track record, he could have his pick of France's top talent. *Vie privée*, *Viva Maria!* and

William Wilson were all creatively conceived as star vehicles and attracted significant international financing. Each was shot on location outside France, the first two were filmed in the eye of frenzied media storms that threatened to overwhelm the productions. By the early 1970s, however, Malle had fully rejected the star-driven model, turning back to documentary and to complex drama that echoed the style of his earliest films. On his own terms, with *Calcutta* (1969), *L'Inde fantôme* (*Phantom India*, 1969) and *Le Souffle au Coeur* (*Murmur of the Heart*, 1971), Malle embraced the experimentation, novelty and creative risk taking of the kind that had prevailed with such success in France in the late 1950s and early 1960s, and which would motivate his appeal for new faces on French screens in the decade to come.

The Bardot Phenomenon: A Very Private Affair

Following three outstanding successes (*Le Monde du silence* [*The Silent World*, 1956], *Elevator to the Gallows*, *The Lovers*), and one commercial disappointment (*Zazie dans le métro*, 1960), Malle was invited by producer Christine Gouze-Rénal to make a film 'with, or rather, for Bardot' (Southern 2011: 72). Malle's reasons for taking on the project were initially pragmatic: as Nathan C. Southern notes, the director was under pressure following the poor reception and monetary losses of *Zazie dans le métro*, and badly needed a successful follow-up film if he was not to be perceived as a financial liability by the industry. He admitted that his friends tried to prevent him making the film and that he 'should have listened to them': 'I like the end', he added, 'but most of it is lousy' (Crawley 1975: 171). The territory, both narratively and practically, was entirely new for Malle, and amounted to a gamble that he would later come to recognise as 'one of the two "accidents" of [his] film career' (French 1993: 33). Indeed, the experience was so 'unhappy' in his own words, that he decided to take a sabbatical year directly after and spent his time away from France, filming in Algeria (see French 1993: 36).

Released on 31 January 1962, *A Very Private Affair* recounts the story of Jill, a dancer, model and actress who achieves fame and celebrity at a dizzying pace. As her notoriety grows, she suffers a nervous breakdown and seeks refuge with an older cultured lover, Fabio, while he directs an open-air opera of Kleist's *Katherine de Heilbronn* in the Perugian town of Spoleto, Italy. Jill finds herself tracked down and hounded by the press, and dies in the final scene, blinded by a paparazzi photographer's flash as she watches the opera from a high rooftop. The film, which has been overshadowed in cinema history by Godard's magisterial *Le Mépris* (*Contempt*), released only two years later on 20 December 1963, is a quasi-biographical reflection on the life – or more specifically the absence of a private life – of a blonde superstar who simultaneously is and isn't the famed Brigitte Bardot. It was originally conceived as an adaptation of Noel Coward's *Private Lives* (1930), a comedy of manners about the private passions and jealousies of a divorced couple who find they can't live without each other. The screenplay was to be co-written with veteran scenarist Henri Jeanson, and financed by MGM. Very quickly, however, Malle abandoned the original project in favour of an original treatment, co-written with Jean-Paul Rappeneau and Jean Ferry, that was motivated by

Malle's desire to 're-create in the film *the strange social phenomenon* that Brigitte Bardot had become, the sex object who had become an object of scandal' (French 1993: 72; emphasis added). Thus, the opportunity to work with Bardot saw Malle gravitate towards a dramatic fiction with a sociological dimension, one that would expose the shallowness of celebrity by drawing on known biographical elements of Bardot's life. She agreed to collaborate with the writers and co-operated on the screenplay; Crawley claims that Bardot 'dictated much of the scenario herself' as she had done when working with Roger Vadim on *Et Dieu créa la Femme* (*And God Created Woman*, 1956). In his view, it was she, 'more than Malle or Rappeneau [who] developed the story into a monstrous mosaic of a Bardography' (1975: 170).

For a film that proposed a critical reflection on the uncontrollable nature of modern stardom, it was ironic that it was Bardot's star status that proved the biggest obstacle to the smooth running of the project. At the most basic operational level, the timetable for the shoot was determined by her schedule rather than Malle's, and the deadline for completion was fixed by her onward commitments, not his. This had two crucial effects on Malle's ability to stamp his authority and signature on the film. First, there was very little time for casting, resulting in a supporting cast that Malle subsequently described as weak. Second, he was forced to begin shooting before the screenplay was fully finished. Indeed, while on location in Spoleto for the film's final act, he and Rappeneau found themselves writing the script for the next morning's shoot as late as the night before. Malle had reservations from the outset about Mastroianni's suitability for the role of Fabio, and the star, riding high on the success of *La Dolce Vita*, was ill at ease in a role that was clearly more supporting actor than co-star to Bardot. Mastroianni reputedly tried to pull out a week before filming started, and Malle admits that he himself was tempted to do the same. The film's central romantic dynamic never recovered: 'He and Bardot didn't get along at all', Malle told Philip French. 'The film was supposed to have lyrical love scenes between two actors who hardly spoke to each other and behaved like strangers on the set' (1993: 34). Furthermore, Gregor von Rezorri, who played the role of Jill's stepfather, and encountered Bardot again on the set of *Viva Maria!* a few years later, suggests that she was less than fully professional in her commitment to the shoot. Writing of her admirably cooperative attitude and great discipline in Mexico, where the production conditions were harsher and more taxing, Rezzori commended her energy, good humour and collegiality in the following terms:

> If we had been able to predict four years earlier, in Spoleto during the shoot of *A Very Private Affair*, that Brigitte could be asked to travel for an hour, be on set by eight am, and shoot in scorching heat right through till six pm; or that she would sit in costume until her first take at five pm, and all that without throwing a fit? Well, we would just have smiled. We would have been incredulous. (2009: 194)

Bardot's memoirs, however, document the intense press scrutiny she was under while filming on location in Geneva and Spoleto, and the isolation she suffered as a result of this. On a basic psychological level, the project was unusually punishing: 'I was playing myself, without being myself', she recalls. 'I would be overcome with shame when mimicking an episode from my life. It was everything about me that was superficial, already known, everything the newspapers loved to dwell on. There was no depth, no questioning, and none of the instability or despair I felt' (1966: 300)

For all the flaws in its execution, the subject of Malle's film – Bardot as star and cultural phenomenon – could not have been more topical, and the director's ambition to engage critically with both a national icon and contemporary discourses of iconicity and fame was unprecedented in French cinema. Ginette Vincendeau has spoken of the film's hybrid status and the novelty of the approach taken by Malle: 'Neither documentary nor entirely fiction nor conventional biopic, the film is arguably the first of a rare breed, the so-classed 'autobiopic', a film in which the hero/heroine plays him/herself in a fictional film that retraces his/her life' (2000: 100). For Vincendeau, the film succeeds in revealing Bardot's function as the vehicle for contemporary popular culture, placed in opposition to high culture in the form of the operatic *Katherine de Heilbronn*. Geneviève Sellier concurs, and argues that the film 'was not intended to be an homage to a star, but rather a denunciation of the alienating character of that popularity, shown to be typical of the forms taken by modern mass culture: a tabloid press fed by the paparazzi, a "commercial cinema" dependent on the all new and (relative) liberation of sexual behavior, the overflow of the private life of stars into their professional life' (2008: 201). The film in many ways anticipates Jacques Rozier's engrossing short documentary *Paparazzi* (1963), an account of the frenzied intrusion of journalists and fans of Bardot during the *Contempt* shoot in Italy, and gives fictional form to episodes subsequently captured by Rozier, including the star's inability to move through a crowd unhindered, even in a car, or find a quiet space away from prying camera lenses. The scenes of Jill's mother's Geneva home under siege from the paparazzi are particularly well echoed in Rozier's capturing of the surreptitious activities of the paparazzi around the secluded Villa Malaparte where *Contempt* was filmed. More poignantly, given the way in which Jill is hounded to her death, the 'grim topicality' of the subject was all too apparent when it was released in the US merely weeks after the sudden death of Marilyn Monroe.[1]

The film is structured as a classic rise-and-fall narrative, and proposes fame as an isolating and destructive force. It opens on the sweet image of a girlish Bardot dancing alone, clad in a pale blue leotard with her trademark headband in the same colour, and is framed as a fable rather than a morality play: 'Once upon a time…', the male narrator tells us, as Bardot pirouettes balletically across the screen. The three acts of the film trace Jill's early years and rapid rise to stardom, her subsequent breakdown and flight from her professional life, and her tragic demise when cornered into further retreat while in hiding in Spoleto. A series of location shots in Paris testify forcefully to the impact of Bardot on French life in the 1960s: as the star is driven around the city, we see it populated by numerous Bardot-lookalikes, each with blonde bouffant hair attracting their own mob of fans as they go about their business. 'Jill' herself is seen in a towering cartoon-like image reminiscent of Bardot in *And God Created Woman*, a monstrous exaggeration of her physical form that dwarfs the façade of the cinema where her 'latest' film, 'La Garce de Syracuse', is playing. When she retreats from the public arena of the street to the security of her own apartment, she finds herself trapped in a cage-like elevator with a garrulous cleaning lady, who claims not to watch any of her films, but to know everything about this *garce* ('bitch') from the newspapers. The woman's bile at Jill's alleged promiscuity – logical extensions of the type of screen roles we see 'Jill' filming – in the face of young men dying in Algeria conveys more eloquently than any other scene just how far forfeited privacy results in notoriety.[2]

Malle's sympathetic approach in *A Very Private Affair* gives cinematic expression to concepts about Bardot and stardom previously elaborated by philosopher Simone de Beauvoir. An admirer of the young woman, she cautioned in *Brigitte Bardot and the Lolita Syndrome* that

> If we want to understand what Brigitte Bardot represents, it is not important to know what the young woman named Brigitte Bardot is really like. Her admirers and detractors are concerned with the imaginary creature they see on the screen or through a tremendous cloud of ballyhoo. In so far as she is exposed to the public gaze, her legend has been fed by her private life no less than by her film roles. (1960: 8)

Malle's film keeps Bardot unmistakably before us in all her blonde, pouting iconicity; but he emphasises her inaccessibility and unknowability by taking her from the open water of the opening scenes on Lake Geneva, to a series of increasingly small, cramped spaces (mostly bedrooms) which are her only refuge from prying eyes. Beyond those doors, interest in her whereabouts reaches a frenzy and takes on its own momentum: the 'tremendous cloud of ballyhoo' produces 'Jill' as an imaginary concept that overwhelms Jill, the woman.

Jill's rise to stardom in the first act is thus treated in brief episodic fashion, while the latter parts of the film take the time to create a mood of claustrophobia and increased anxiety that coheres with the star's desire for retreat and privacy. By the final sequences in Spoleto, Jill's isolation has become so insupportable that serenity is only achieved in her tragic, but balletic, fall to death; a state that takes her back full circle to the time before she became a commodified spectacle, and is entirely cinematic (within a broadly realist canvas) in its visual echoing of the parachute fall by Dorothy Malone in Douglas Sirk's *The Tarnished Angels* (1957).[3] The strength of this final act seems to lie in its 'unfinished' nature, where the documentary-style shots of Spoleto hint at Malle's ethnographically-inflected artistic interests in place and time, as well as in the final lyrical shots which create a sense of empathy with the solitary, hounded star whose death is rendered as the ultimate slow-motion spectacle.

For all its strengths, subtleties and topical weight, the film failed to gain favour with any of its potential constituencies. For Claude Mauriac, writing in *Le Figaro Littéraire*, the film had a parasitic quality: rather than feed the legend of Bardot, it fed off it, he suggested. Malle lamented that it was criticised as being 'an epic Bardot, but without Bardot alas' (Gilbert 2016: 17:54). MGM deemed the original ending – the

Fig. 1: *A Very Private Affair* (1961): Bardot caught in suspension.

section of the film to which Malle himself was most wedded – to be too prolonged and slow for the American market, and demanded that twenty minutes be cut from the Spoleto section. On release the film made a financial loss of $128,000, and no one involved – not the star, the director, nor the producers – expressed satisfaction with the final cut. For the anonymous critic at *Time* magazine, '*A Very Private Affair* is a very sad affair' (Anon. 1962)

The Dueling Duo: Viva Maria!

The experience of *A Very Private Affair* did not lessen Malle's enthusiasm for another project with Bardot, whom he continued to regard as a remarkable, extraordinary actress (*Grand écran*, broadcast 3 June 1965). In 1965 he began one of the most elaborate projects of his career: a five-month shoot in Mexico of the revolutionary comedy *Viva Maria!* produced by the American studio United Artists with a budget of $2.2 million. The project, starring Bardot and Malle's long-term collaborator Jeanne Moreau, marked a significant shift in tone as well as geography for Malle: the film was to be an homage to and affectionate pastiche of the American western, the genre Malle has described as the 'cherished genre' for his generation. The difference was that Malle saw this as 'an opportunity to put two women in a situation where in Hollywood films it's always two men, two buddies – I think the best example was *Vera Cruz*' (French 1993: 51). Moreover, his idea 'was to put Bardot and Moreau in the place of Gary Cooper and Burt Lancaster'. The film was thus conceived as a double star vehicle, and a female variant on the 'buddy movie' in which women are imbued with classically masculine traits, and assert their gender equality within a generic framework of action and bonding. The film traces the rise of Maria I and Maria II from jobbing showgirls to venerated stars, and on to fully liberated and conscious political agents. In its playful privileging of the apparatus of female objectification (most notably in the scenes where the women 'accidentally invent' the striptease), Malle offers a more optimistic and upbeat reflection on stardom and its attendant pressures than previously: we see the two Marias mobbed by crowds and worshipped in local shrines, their images reproduced and handled like religious relics. As star performers playing ordinary performers who become stars, Maria and Maria's diegetic itinerary echoes that of Jill in *A Very Private Affair*, but here their fame and celebrity are presented as a force for good rather than self-destruction. As they bring their popular revolution to a close, their condition is one of freedom rather than imprisonment, of equality and sorority rather than alienated individualism. It is a sunny, optimistic film, and joyous in its celebration of female complicity and creativity.

In 1965 the two actresses were at the height of their careers and celebrity, with the *auteurist* Moreau acclaimed for her craft and technical range, and the more popular Bardot fêted as an international sex symbol with a gift for instinctive performance. The selling point of the film with the press, public and producers was the casting of Moreau and Bardot as a duo, and a major profile of Moreau in *Time* magazine in March 1965 claimed that her influence in particular was such that 'Malle couldn't get the production financed without her name on the contract' (Anon. 1965).[4] Featured on the front cover of the issue a portrait of Moreau by Mexican artist Rufino Tamayo created a sensation back on the shoot (see Rezzori 2009: 191). The article praised Moreau as one of the era's most important actresses: 'an actress of infinite complexity and conviction, and the only thing wrong with calling her the modern Garbo is that she is so much better an actress than Garbo ever was' (Anon. 1965). Public curiosity about the stars and how they would work together as colleagues was intense and the shoot was under siege by the international press from the very beginning. The *Time* article has little to say about Bardot, but notes that her arrival in Mexico, five days before Moreau, 'had been the real wild-eyed thing – riot police with tear-gas pistols, screams, a fight, grown men fainting' (ibid.). Rezzori notes that on the day when the women shot their first scene together, Malle had to wait patiently for the 'general offensive' of the assembled journalists to come to an end (2009: 155). Somewhat ironically, Malle had found himself caught in the crossfire of a paparazzi mob that all too closely replicated the fictionalised press hounds of *A Very Private Affair*. According to Rezzori's secret diary of the shoot (a diary that was deemed disloyal and partisan on publication), this frenzied fascination with the two stars infected the crew every bit as much as the general public. 'The battle for dominance between two such different life forms', he suggested, 'is a spectacle of such dramatic intensity that the fable of a Latin American revolution in skirts pales in comparison' (2009: 174)

Much of the commentary in the press (in publications across the USA, France, Italy and Germany) about the anticipated rivalry between the two stars had an unapologetically misogynistic undertone. Journalists delighted in speculating that two professional women couldn't work together amicably in a film about female friendship, and it was Malle who had to bear the weight of expectation aroused by their supposed antagonism. Rezzori, in the early days of the shoot, grandly suggested that

> Everyone is waiting for the moment when the sparks will inevitably fly between these two rivals. The French press, which has been full of front line reports, has turned *Viva Maria!* into a national cause. Louis Malle – and with him the whole of French cinema – has made the great leap across the ocean. He has gone into

the American lion's den, and has thrown down the gauntlet with a film whose subject, star power and budget are more American than French. It's not only France, but all of Europe which is lined up here behind him. And we are proud to see the French tricolor flying ahead in the wind. (2009: 62)

With such high stakes, it is perhaps no surprise that when Malle was asked by Philip French 'Was *Viva Maria* as much fun to make as most people think it is to see?' his response was categorical: 'No, it was not.' He explained that 'in terms of the evolution of my work, it was a bit of a regression ... because of all the unfavorable circumstances ... I was not completely in control (1993: 49, 52). This was abundantly clear to his entourage who, according to Rezzori, were agreed that 'something ha[d] shifted with *Viva Maria!* for Louis Malle and his young circle ... To his friends he appear[ed] withdrawn, impatient, impervious to criticism, and sometimes haughty, constantly irritated' (2009: 186).

Clearly, accommodating two of French cinema's biggest stars on an unwieldly and unpredictable foreign shoot was in itself a major undertaking. The scale of the project was unprecedented for all parties; there was an extensive local crew who spoke only Spanish, ten different locations spread over a vast and environmentally inhospitable landscape, crowd scenes featuring up to 1,600 extras, and special effects and stunts to be included. Both Moreau and Bardot had considerable entourages of their own (assistants, hairdressers, costumiers, publicists), who traveled with them *en masse* as they moved about the country, and these gradually gravitated into independent mini-communities. Bardot, from her vantage point in the eye of the storm, described the production as being like a 'plague of locusts' devouring everything in its path as it travelled through rural Mexico (1966: 351). Malle admitted to Philip French that he had some early reservations about the impact of the casting on the project:

> At one point before the shooting, when both actresses and their agents were being very difficult, and I thought I was going to lose them, or one of them, I got fed up and suggested to United Artists, who were financing it, that we switch to the English language and do it with Julie Christie and Sarah Miles. They were really exciting young actresses, and not yet stars. I think it would have worked better but the UA executives didn't want to hear about it. (1993: 53)

But both stars adhered to their contractual obligations and Malle had to deal with the fallout of the press attention, their respective illnesses, the many onward delays to the shooting schedule, accidents (including Moreau's hospitalisation in mid-May after falling on set), and the death of an extra during a battle scene. Malle himself surely added to the tensions of the production when he celebrated his surprise marriage to Anne-Marie Deschodt (on 3 April 1965); Moreau, his former lover, chose to absent herself from the party. Rezzori suggests that by the end of March such a degree of disorder and demoralisation prevailed that the film was already over budget and there was 'practically no more shooting schedule'.[5]

Fig. 2: *Viva Maria!* (1965): Similar and different.

This very checkered production history does not detract from Malle's singular accomplishment in creating one of the great films about female friendship. The revelation of the film is the comic tone and timing that Moreau and Bardot share in all their scenes together, and the sense of complicity that informs the fictional relationship of the two Marias. The stage numbers are light and coy, and when they dance, they are similarly costumed and their gestures carefully mirror each other. In the number in which they 'invent' the striptease, our eye is repeatedly directed to their faces rather than their bodies, and to the moments they lock eyes while smiling, as if they have their own private language that the diegetic audience does not share. When their faces are framed together (on stage, or while captive in Rodriguez's mansion) the close shots emphasise their compatibility (they are equally balanced in the frame; neither is privileged over the other) as well as their individuality (in colouring, shape of facial features). Malle displays a sharp understanding of the screen persona of each of the women, allowing them opportunities to play to their individual brand of stardom. Thus Maria II (Bardot) is seen bruised, disheveled and with tousled hair returning from a torrid night of lovemaking with three men; elsewhere her spontaneous seduction of a lighting operator while a knife-throwing act is taking place on stage results in injury to the performer as the theatre is plunged into darkness. Maria II is a fictional variant of Brigitte Bardot, the screen siren: she performs sexual abandon, amoral promiscuity and dangerous seduction with a careful lightness of touch and a joyful comic edge. Moreau (Maria I) is given more scope for her trademark measured theatricality, notably in the solemn scene of her lover's death in which she parodies Shakespearian tragedy, citing lines from Julius Caesar to the assembled revolutionaries. Earlier, when Florès is chained up in jail in a crucifix-like contraption, she is characteristically sensual, caressing his body with her lips, and bringing a deeply erotic and, within the farcical tone of the film, disconcerting charge to the film. While the villains and secondary characters of the films can only be read as broad caricatures, the two Marias are complex characters who deploy the individual stardom of Bardot and Moreau to dramatic and narrative effect. The film, then, proposes shared female stardom not as a site of tension and antagonism (as per the production history and press coverage), but as a powerful and pleasurable – all the more so given its rarity – screen dynamic.

The Star and His Double: William Wilson

In the 1960s, portmanteau or compilation films were relatively frequent, and Malle's contribution to the format was the forty-minute short *William Wilson*, loosely adapted from the eponymous Edgar Allan Poe short story (1839) by Clement Biddle Wood and French novelist Daniel Boulanger. Malle's film is the second segment in a trilogy of films entitled *Histoires Extraordinaires* bookended by shorts by Roger Vadim and Federico Fellini. Malle agreed to take part in the project, after an initial approach by Alain Delon, who was to play the lead role of Wilson, on the understanding that the other two films would be made by Orson Welles and Luchino Visconti. But by his own admission, he seems to have had little serious investment in it as a creative project; when the directorial line-up was changed, he agreed to remain involved. He later explained that his 'private life was in a shambles' (French 1993: 59) and that he was experiencing a crisis of confidence about the direction his career was taking. 'I was beginning to repeat myself,' he told French (1993: 64). He sought a project that would take him away from Paris and 'shake everything up', and the short film format, with a set script and a defined timetable, seemed a reasonable opportunity to buy some time. Unsurprisingly the film bore the marks of a 'script [that] was so-so' and '[his] direction was completely unfocused' (French 1993: 67). Vincent Canby of the *New York Times* summed it up as a 'simply tedious … pre-Freudian horror story of a man who is driven to the murder of his conscience' (1969).

As a commission by Delon, the film is a different kind of star vehicle from the two already discussed. Delon was a European 'megastar' at this time (see Southern 2011: 336), and the casting of his co-star was key to the project: 'we had to have stars, any stars!' Malle remembers (French 1993: 67), and the producers would not accept an unknown. Malle had proposed Italian newcomer Florinda Bolkan for the part of Giuseppina, the cigar-smoking courtesan whom Wilson cheats at cards; but it was Bardot, who had previously appeared with Delon in an earlier anthology film, *Les Amours célèbres* (*Famous Love Affairs*, Michel Boisrond, 1961), who was imposed by the producers. 'I tried to do what I could – putting her in a dark wig and so on. But it was terrible casting, unforgivable', Malle declared (French 1993: 67). Bardot concurred: 'I was decked out in an enormous jet black wig which sat on me like a helmet: it was like something a Napoleonic soldier would wear, absolutely disastrous! I have always wondered why Louis Malle wanted to disfigure me like that' (1966: 426).

The film is a simple tale, again in three acts, in which a man in a confessional box in a rural church in Bergama, Italy, recounts in flashback what has brought him to a point of existential desperation. In three set pieces, we see William Wilson as a boy, as a medical student and as a military officer, act with sadistic impunity until he is stopped in his tracks and thwarted by the appearance of a *doppelgänger* (also played by Delon) whose good nature prevails over the original's evil intentions. It is an old-fashioned morality tale, in which a cruel bully grows up to be a merciless

Fig. 3: *William Wilson* (1968): Convergence of gazes.

torturer (proposing, for example, to dissect a live woman in front of his medical peers) and takes root as a charismatic parasite in polite society. But when he finally kills his conscience in a duel, he knows he is finished, and must also die. Delon, reputed for his 'cruel beauty' (Vincendeau 2000: 180) and icy performance plays both parts, alternating barely contained violence with calm rationality. The stillness and coldness with which the actor is associated are harnessed to powerful visual effect, but he remains one-dimensional in his construction and actions. The erotic scope of the film, clearly intended by the inclusion of Bardot, who is stripped and whipped by Wilson after the card game, is limited. This scene, as well as the one with the nude woman on the dissection table, arguably have less narrative impact than the first sequence in the school where a boy who has challenged Wilson is lowered into a pit of rats. Tellingly, it is the scenes with the children in a school environment, rather than the scenes of adult sexuality, that are most memorable in the film, and which Malle himself acknowledged as satisfactory (French 1993: 68).

The film was clearly Delon's project more than Malle's, and their relationship quickly soured. 'I had a terrible time with Delon', he told French: '[he was] one of the most difficult actors I have ever worked with – probably *the* most difficult actor I ever worked with' (1993: 66). For the second time in her career, Bardot found him to be an indifferent collaborator: 'Our relationship never advanced beyond professional courtesy. He was far more interested how the light caught his face and his famous blue eyes than in his screen partner. I was just another shadow on the set to him' (1966: 427). Malle's view was that Delon resented being directed and Malle 'had doubts about his sincerity and talent'. But Malle also claimed that this broken relationship was what sustained the film: 'somehow the casting of Delon worked – because the anger he had against me served the character and I made sure I kept him angry all the way through!' (French 1993: 67).

The film is a minor work in the Malle canon, and has received little attention – no doubt with good reason. But the presence of Brigitte Bardot, playing counter to type and image in the dreaded dark wig, is what ultimately gives the film its texture and necessary quality of psychological dislocation. To see the blonde icon so transformed may have seemed a poor choice of costume to Malle, but her altered colouring strikes an uncanny note which allows the short film to claim visual and narrative depth. It is Bardot, now one of Malle's most frequent collaborators, who saves the film from Malle's indifference and Delon's megalomania.

A Prophet in His Own Time

Susan Sarandon has spoken of Louis Malle's discomfort with directing actors and has asserted that he has never been an 'actor's director' (Southern 2011:17). He is always hesitant, she suggests, to offer overt performance-related direction on set. Malle, in his reflections on his casting choices, has claimed that *Le Voleur* and *Milou en mai* (*May Fools*, 1989) are the two films in which he feels the acting strikes exactly the right note. The reason? The time in pre-production devoted to casting. In both cases, he declared, 'I knew enough about actors and what I was looking for to make the right choices. It's one of the things that are most difficult for a director and it takes you a long time to learn how to do it – not directing the actors, but the actual choosing of them, which I think is at least 50 per cent of the final result' (French 1993: 62).

The trouble with Brigitte (and Jeanne and Alain…) was that, as a prominent young filmmaker in the ascendant in France in the 1960s, Malle found himself actively servicing and shoring up what he came to see as the exclusivity and narrowness of the French star system. It was an eclectic decade for him artistically, in which he was still developing his craft and signature. But he was doing so alongside a new generation of increasingly famous stars whose careers were developing in tandem with their directorial peers. As the decade advanced, Malle's ability to assert his directorial autonomy and use his performers counter to their star image and fame seems to have been diluted. He was also dealing with fluctuating critical perceptions of his status as a filmmaker. Was he still a young auteur, or a go-to big-name commercial filmmaker?

Nevertheless, Malle's statements about the industry were in many respects prophetic: 1974 was the year that the French star system was definitively and irreversibly upended by the arrival of a new star caste in the French industry. Bertrand Blier's *Les Valseuses* (1974), the most successful French film of the year with over six million entries, saw a new generation of 'unknowns' called Gérard Depardieu, Patrick Dewaere and Miou-Miou burst onto French screens and bring a daring new naturalist edge to French cinema. This new generation of 'unknowns' would, of course, in turn, come to dominate the industry in the decades that followed. Perhaps it is Louis Malle's critical success with *Lacombe Lucien*, featuring amateur Pierre Blaise in the title role, that was the ultimate valourisation of the position he expressed in *Le Film Français*, and the film which most endures as a testament to what can be achieved when a filmmaker dares to work outside the industry norms.

Notes

1   *A Very Private Affair* was released in the US on 28 September 1962. Monroe was found dead in bed on 5 August 1962.

2   Bardot notes that this episode is based on a real encounter that took place in the Clinique de Passy in Paris: 'At 6am, in an elevator, a cleaning woman armed with brooms and dustpans tried to tear my eyes out when she realised who I was, insulting me, calling me a bitch and a whore' (1966: 300).
3   This point is convincingly made by Lee Russell (1965).
4   The piece was likely penned by Joyce Harber and one other journalist (see von Rezorri 2009: 139–40).
5   The shoot took place in Mexico from 16 January to 15 June 1965, although Moreau and Bardot seem to have stopped filming on or around 24 May.

Bibliography

Anon. (1962) 'Cinema: Sex Tabby,' *Time Magazine*, 26 October.
____ (1965) 'Actresses: Making the Most of Love,' *Time Magazine*, 5 March.
Bardot, B. (1966) *Initiales B.B.: Mémoires*. Paris: Editions Grasset & Fasquelle.
Canby, V. (1969) '3 Unrelated Stories by Poe: 'Spirits of the Dead' at Rivoli and Pacific East', *New York Times*, 4 September.
Crawley, T. (1975) *Bébé: The Films of Brigitte Bardot*. Secaucus, NJ: Citadel Press.
de Beauvoir, S. (1960) *Brigitte Bardot and the Lolita Syndrome*; trans. B. Fretchman. London: André Deutsch.
French, P. (1993) *Malle on Malle*. London: Faber and Faber.
Gilbert, P.-H. (2016) *Louis Malle: Le rebelle*. Ciné+, TV5MONDE, Institut national de l'audiovisuel.
Malle, L. (1974) 'Le cinéma français et le star-system', *Le Film Français*, 8 February.
Russell, L. (1965) 'Louis Malle', *The New Left Review*, 1, 30 (March-April), 73–6.
Sellier, G. (2008 [2005]) *Masculine Singular: French New Wave Cinema*; trans. K. Ross. Durham, NC: Duke University Press.
Southern, N. C., with J. Weissgerber (2006) *The Films of Louis Malle: A Critical Analysis*. Jefferson, NC: McFarland.
Vincendeau, G. (2000) *Stars and Stardom in French Cinema*. London: Continuum.
von Rezzori, G. (2009 [1966]) *Les Morts à leur place: Journal d'un tournage*; trans. J. Lajarrige. Paris: Le Serpent à plumes.

CHAPTER SIX

Experimentation and Automatism in Zazie dans le métro *and* Black Moon

Ian Fleishman

Louis Malle's cinematic oeuvre is nothing if not heterogeneous. Yet among his varied works – both French and American, documentary and fictional – the Oulipian literary adaptation *Zazie dans le métro* (1960) and the surrealist fantasy *Black Moon* (1975) stand out quite distinctly as the most singular of formal experimentations. Twice in his career, asserts Melinda Camber Porter, Malle 'worked from an impossible proposition':

> in *Zazie* ... he attempted to translate the exclusively verbal games of [Raymond] Queneau into cinematic images; [...] in *Black Moon* ... he strove to retain the authentic, primary vision of dreams and the contradictory logic of his unconscious without ... adopting a visual language shared by the public. (1986: 84)

Adaptations from literature in more than the traditional sense, *Zazie dans le métro* and *Black Moon* each attempt an apparently impossible literary ruse: the first in finding cinematic equivalents for Queneau's proto-Oulipian language games and the second in giving filmic form to Surrealist automatic writing.

And yet, the two films come into being at very different moments: the first toward the beginning of Malle's career, against the backdrop of his associations with the *nouvelle vague*, and the second halfway through, just before his move to Hollywood. This presents a sort of paradox, as Georgiana Colvile notes in her treatment of the two efforts: in *Zazie dans le métro* Malle's experimentalism is a mark of juvenilia, whereas in *Black Moon* it testifies to his maturity as a filmmaker (1996: 445). To this extent, the formal stakes of each film mirror its content: like so many of Malle's works, both *Zazie dans le métro* and *Black Moon* are risky, radical and often violent coming-of-age narratives.[1] Although thematically both films trace the fantastic, oneiric education of a young female protagonist, stylistically they could hardly be more different: *Zazie dans le métro* is a schizophrenic, fast-paced, slapstick number whereas *Black Moon* is slow and brooding, patient and profound.

Comparing these two stylistically incomparable films, Susan Sontag insightfully reveals the psychological implications (or perhaps underpinnings) of such aesthetic differences. Her contention is that the adolescent female protagonist of each film, over the course of her on-screen maturation, engages in an opposite way with the world around her, eliciting correspondingly polar viewer responses in the process:

> Zazie arrives in a mad world that she observes and dominates with her glance. We accept that this little girl is at once wise and innocent. In *Black Moon*, on the other hand, the audience is unable to identify with the young girl, unable to see through her eyes. She's the one who drives the plot forward. She isn't innocent, she is part of this world. (1978: 105)

This essay will build upon but also challenge Sontag's improvised argument, bringing her characterisation of the protagonist's development in each of these two trial-and-error coming-of-age narratives to bear on Malle's own stylistic coming of age as a filmmaker.

Close attention to *Zazie dans le métro* and *Black Moon* will reveal that the attitude of each protagonist towards her fantastic cinematic world reflects the *cadre* of Malle's own formal experimentation at key moments in his career. If *Zazie dans le métro* is an exercise in control, a lesson in filmic syntax, *Black Moon* is an attempt at learning to let go. Just as Zazie struggles to exert control over her absurd surroundings, the post-Surrealist, perhaps even anti-Surrealist, Oulipian *exercices de style* Malle undertakes in that film – jump cuts, trick photography, accelerated camera speeds – exert a certain formal violence over the subject matter. In *Black Moon*, much to the contrary, Lily is not, for the most part, an agent of violence but merely its passive witness. Malle's avowed attempt at *écriture automatique* means allowing the film to develop freely at its own pace through an extended series of supple long takes and tracking shots as well as through a frequent use of racking focus that subtly allows the hitherto unconscious elements of Lily's dreamscape to come into view as she discovers them: if Lily does advance the narrative, it is not – *pace* Sontag – because she is part of this world but rather because *it* is part of her. An examination of the two films one beside the other will necessitate a brief reevaluation of the relationship between these Surrealist and Oulipian textual strategies, revealing how Malle negotiates between them in order to come to a mature filmic poetics entirely his own.

Surrealist vs. Oulipian Automatism

As the comments above will have made evident, I am far from the first to compare these two films, despite their very different moments in Malle's career, nor is it entirely uncommon to speak of the filmmaker's connections to the Oulipo or, much more frequently, to Surrealism.[2] While acknowledging the influence of these schools and textual strategies on Malle's work, previous scholarship on the filmmaker has too often – indeed, almost universally – treated Surrealism and Oulipo as more or less interchangeable labels, habitually conflating them under the general rubric of 'surrealism' in the more common (which is to say less technical) sense of the word.[3] But when Queneau published the novel on which *Zazie dans le métro* is based, his first major popular success, in 1959, his break with Surrealism proper was already three-decades-old news. And while the publication predates the official inauguration of the 'Ouvroir de littérature potentielle' by somewhat more than a year, the premiere of Malle's cinematic adaptation coincides very closely chronologically with the launching of the literary movement. Malle's film was in fact released in the final days of October 1960, and the 'Séminaire de littérature expérimentale' (abbreviated to SLE or Sélitexte and renamed Oulipo on the occasion of their second meeting) was first convened as a subcommittee of the ever-playful absurdist 'Collège de 'Pataphysique' in late November of the same year.

More pointedly, it seems fair to suspect that the institution of the Oulipo, which was first conceived at a colloquium on Queneau's work, was motivated, or at the very least encouraged, by the unprecedented and unexpected popular success of the author's belated breakthrough novel and the additional attention paid to it following Malle's adaptation, as has been convincingly argued (see Boschetti 2010: 25). Malle's film is thus intimately linked to the origins of the movement, and it makes sense to think of both the novel and its adaptation as what Gérard Genette, in his critique of Oulipian poetics, designates as autonomous *oulipisms*, which follow self-imposed proto-Oulipian formal constraints although they predate official Oulipian theorisation of such procedures (1997: 39).

As it will not be possible here to give comprehensive treatment to either the Oulipo or Surrealism, it might prove most fruitful to focus, as has recent scholarship, on the question of their differing attitudes towards automatism – included by André Breton, in the original *Surrealist Manifesto* (1924), as the very first word of the very definition of his movement:

> SURREALISM, *n*. Psychic automatism in its pure state, by which one proposes to express – verbally, by means of the written word, or in any other manner – the actual functioning of thought. Dictated by thought, in the absence of any control exercised by reason, exempt from any aesthetic or moral concern. (1969: 26)

Surrealist automatism, in this canonical account, is less a procedure, let alone a method, than it is the lack of one: an attempt to circumvent whatever conscious, rational control would obstruct a direct, unmediated transcription of the workings of the unconscious mind. This, precisely, is the procedure known as automatic writing and one of Raymond Queneau's, and by extension the Oulipo's, main points of contention with Surrealism. As Queneau insists in an interview with Georges Charbonnier:

> What we do isn't surrealism; it may appear surrealist, but the method isn't, which is a very important distinction. [...] [I]t's an automatism, but it's an

automatism that has absolutely nothing to do with what used to be called surrealist automatic writing. (1962: 147–8)

The distinction is, to a certain degree, less a matter of form than of intent: Surrealist automatic writing and related strategies seek to transcribe unconscious mental activity, whereas an Oulipian automatism of this sort instead aspires, if only implicitly, to foreground the *structure of the automatism* itself.

Phrased differently, the philosophical dispute highlighted by these two programmatic declarations can be distilled into a question of *mediation*: where Surrealism seeks to suspend the influence (or rather interference) of the signifier, the Oulipo delights in it; whereas Surrealist automatism is an attempt at allowing the unconscious to express itself unconstrained, Oulipian *contraintes*, as implied by the term itself, are intended to impose clearly defined limitations on that expression. As Alison James summarises: 'The distinction lies in the Oulipo's insistence on the *conscious* use of rules, whereas Surrealist automatism is that of unimpeded unconscious production. Rather than expressing "le fonctionnement réel de la pensée" ['the actual functioning of thought'] ... Oulipian automatism unveils the functioning of *language*, in order to better exploit its possibilities' (2006: 113; emphasis in original). By reversing this literary history and filming the quasi-Oulipian *Zazie dans le métro* fifteen years before the surrealist *Black Moon*, Malle provides an intuitive archeology of such literary automatism.

This is in keeping with the filmmaker's own description of each work. In an oft-cited passage from his interviews with Philip French, for instance, Malle describes *Zazie dans le mértro* as a learning experience, as an attempt to translate Queneau's experiment with literary language into a cinematic one (1993: 26).[4] *Zazie dans le métro*, as Malle describes it, is a self-aware and metafilmic game – an inventory of prior cinematic strategies intended as an exercise in mastering them.[5] Nothing could be further from his discussion of *Black Moon* with Sontag, where he insists on the attempted *realism* of the dreamscapes depicted: 'I meticulously abstained from any temptation toward "dreamlike" writing: distortions, slow motion, bizarre camera angles and lighting. Instead I wanted it to be more like a documentary of an invented world' (1978: 103). *Black Moon*, to Malle's mind, is stylistically blank, empty of the flashy technical tricks to which *Zazie dans le métro* is devoted.

And yet, even absent obvious automatisms in the plural, *Black Moon*, as a self-conscious *récit de rêve* and an explicit attempt at *écriture automatique*, is very much a film invested in *automatism* as a general strategy. Malle does not so much take sides in the debate described above between Surrealism and the Oulipo as he dialectically synthesises their approaches, first consciously endeavoring to parse and to manipulate filmic grammar before attempting to exploit its full potential more organically. He thus offers two different methods of transcribing the inner workings of the mind in film: one, in *Zazie dans le métro*, which foregrounds its own techniques of representation, and the other, in *Black Moon*, which chooses to obscure them. Taken together, these efforts instruct us that automatism cannot be reduced beyond its material constraints, that mediation must be mastered rather than suspended. The formal concerns of these two filmic essays – *films d'apprentissage* for both their protagonists and their director

– are mirrored in their plot and content: both can and ought to be interpreted as allegories of precisely this evolving poetics.

'Contraintes' in Zazie dans le métro

Considering the radically dreamlike nature of both film narratives, it will not be necessary to provide extensive plot summaries here. Suffice to say that each film, as Malle describes *Black Moon*, depicts a strange voyage: Zazie's brief stay in Paris in the first and, in the second, Lily's sojourn in a peculiar and secluded country estate caught in the no man's land of a civil war between the sexes. Accordingly, both films begin in motion, and a comparison of their opening sequences will demonstrate how each instructs its viewer in the distinct varieties of automatism employed.

Zazie dans le métro, for instance, starts out with its compendium of cinematic tropes and strategies even before it begins directly translating Queneau's verbal gags into filmic ones. This is just the first stage of Malle's literary-filmic apprenticeship: his acquisition of a fuller cinematic vocabulary. The film begins outside of Paris, looking forward from the front of a train as it approaches the city. What seems at first blush a fairly straightforward and traditional establishing shot, can, upon closer inspection, be interpreted as an elaborate, self-reflective in-joke. Not only does the railway trope recall the Lumières' archetypal *Arrivée d'un train en gare de La Ciotat* (1895) and other iconic filmic antecedents, but Malle also signals his film, as is made obvious in the original *découpage*, as a parody of a western (1970: 10). Strictly speaking, this is, of course, a tracking shot, but only as a *spoof* on a tracking shot: focusing ahead on the railroad track itself, rather than moving laterally alongside what is being filmed, Malle draws direct attention to the mechanism of the technique. Passing through drab, beige-coloured suburbs, confined to a rather claustrophobic aspect ratio of 1.33:1 and ineluctably following the straight path of the rails into the horizon, the perspective here is quite literally *constrained*. One would expect the shot to be continuous, but it instead jumps forward periodically through four apparently unmotivated and slightly disorienting cuts. (Contemporary audiences may have associated these with Godard's *À bout de souffle*, which premiered earlier the same year; to the modern viewer the effect feels like a poorly buffered YouTube video.) These jump cuts are not used to any discernible dramaturgical effect but instead emphasise the film's constructedness, the abbreviated and arbitrary nature of the framing device. Subtly, then, even before any of the characters or plotlines have been introduced and before the experimental nature of the film has become apparent, *Zazie dans le métro* has already set out to inventory its own cinematic techniques as they are deployed.

Not only does this embedded critique of filmic language become much more obvious as the plot progresses, it is increasingly the eponymous protagonist herself who exercises control over these procedures. Zazie first enters the film through an act of unseen violence. The towering Philippe Noiret, who plays her Tonton Gabriel, stands tightly framed from a slight low angle in a medium close-up, only his head and shoulders visible, when he suddenly lets out a yelp of pain. As he glances down to the apparent source of the discomfort, we hear a young girl's voice introduce itself from off screen. Gabriel obligingly bends down, momentarily leaving the frame entirely empty save the blurred background of the ceiling of the Gare de l'Est, in order to lift Zazie into the image. This will not be the last time she asserts herself this way: the ruse is repeated in reverse mere minutes later when the camera tilts up to adult height again to focus on Gabriel's discussion with his friend Charles in front of the taxi and Zazie takes advantage of her brief absence from the image to stage her first escape. By literalising what is seen and unseen, Malle makes otherwise entirely orthodox conventions of framing into an estrangement technique: it is almost as if the film's diegesis were confined to the audience's field of vision. In fact, *whenever* Zazie is out of the frame she is also unaccounted for, and much of what follows is focused on gradually training the camera downwards to the child's level – placing the manipulations of the image increasingly under her control.

Once in the cab, Zazie is treated to a confused and comic sightseeing tour of Paris. Passing by the Église Saint-Vincent-de-Paul, Gabriel makes a sweeping gesture and directs his niece's attention to the impressive edifice, which he, perhaps in jest, mistakes for the Panthéon. A debate ensues as Charles insists it is not the Panthéon but maybe the Madeleine. Not only is the geography false, the eyeline is mismatched: Zazie is clearly looking out the window on the left side of the car, whereas the church in question is on the right. When, moments later, through another trick of continuity editing, the same building, now on the left, is declared Les Invalides, Zazie begins to lose her patience. As the dialogue continues – the church once again returned to the right side of the vehicle which appeared to have been driving in an uninterrupted straight line – Zazie stops traffic and sets the taxi meter in fast forward with her outburst: 'If you're trying to make fun of me, then let me tell you that you're just a couple of old jerks!' Followed by a well-known metacinematic quip delivered by Noiret ('What can I say, it's the New Wave!'), the car continues onwards, the sequence concluding with the trio headed directly for the Église Saint-Vincent-de-Paul. 'And that', asks Zazie, 'what's that? That', replies her uncle, 'dunno'. Through this bit of humour Malle celebrates his ability to continue to create a visually coherent filmic space even after the underlying constraint has repeatedly been pointed out.

I highlight this geographic confusion and the temper tantrum that ensues to demonstrate that Zazie's ultimate aim – as is evident from her obstinate desire to ride the métro – is freedom of movement. Within the universe of the cinematic experiment that bears her name, this means exerting control over formal filmic restrictions, and it is in this manner that Zazie's trajectory mirrors her creator's. There are moments where she fully realises this wish. The apogee of her mastery over cinematic mechanics – editing, in particular – is also Malle's greatest accomplishment in the film: the iconic slapstick chase sequence where Zazie uses every trick in the Road Runner's book to evade capture – accelerated or reverse motion, split frames where she appears in duplicate, jump cuts that place her suddenly behind her pursuer, even a stick and then a ball of dynamite followed by cartoon explosions. When Zazie, delivered to her departing train through a more traditional (although still accelerated) tracking shot, concludes the film by breaking the fourth wall and declaring directly to the camera that she has matured ('J'ai vieilli'), we have good reason to read the assertion, in this context, as Malle's own. There is indeed an Oulipian aim to this particular variety of metacinematic awareness: a self-conscious adherence to otherwise implicit filmic conceits and concealed constraints. As Peter Consenstein summarises an essential Oulipian dictum: 'if an author does not define his or her constraint, the constraint will in turn define their work for them. In other words, all literature is built upon constraints, either consciously or unconsciously. Building consciousness through the use of constraints is the group Oulipo's greatest achievement' (2002: 17). In *Black Moon* Malle will use the skills he has acquired in the earlier experiment to achieve a fuller measure of artistic freedom. Having become conscious of the cinematic codes that will govern his work, the filmmaker is now at liberty to exploit them in his quest for a cinema of the unconscious.

Écriture Automatique in Black Moon

If *Zazie dans le métro* begins with an arrival, *Black Moon* starts out, rather, in flight. 'The culmination is in *Black Moon*', writes Gilles Deleuze, describing the dreamwork of Malle's cinema, 'it is by running away from the initial images of violence that the heroine moves from one world to the other' (1989: 60; also quoted in Frey 2004: 50). The camera, fixed on a badger sniffing around an empty country road at night, is stationary. Lily, like her predecessor, is introduced acoustically and through another act of (this time unintended) violence: we hear her car approaching as the camera pans

Fig. 1: *Zazie dans le métro* (1960): Passenger in a driverless car.

Fig. 2: *Black Moon* (1975): Leaning and gazing out.

left to reveal it speeding towards us from the distance in a slow, single take that lasts almost exactly as long as the opening credits of *Zazie dans le métro* (around eighty seconds in both cases) with their four seemingly superfluous cuts. *Black Moon* is as smooth and associative as *Zazie dans le métro* is discontinuous and willfully contrived. This first long take is followed by a match-on-action to a close-up of the animal as Lily runs it over, and then another, so quick as to appear nearly seamless, as the camera, now panning right, continues to follow the car as it brakes to a sudden stop. This is classic continuity editing, as realistic and conventional in its presentation of the material as any of Malle's American films to come. A cut-in to an extended close-up of Lily's countenance registers her reaction after she has gotten out to inspect the damage; the camera lingers there with an almost uncomfortable unhurriedness until it finally follows her gaze back to the left, panning very slowly toward the origin of the sound of distant explosions. From off-screen we hear her car door slam and the engine whir as she drives off.

While this might initially appear to recall Zazie's disappearances while she is out of the frame, it is in fact the final moment in the entire film that is not clearly oriented by Lily's perspective. The remainder of the narrative is focused on her psyche to the extent that even within its marvelous diegesis, replete with talking animals and bizarre imagery, it becomes difficult to distinguish between her dreams and reality – true to Breton's original definition of Surrealism as the reconciliation of these two states. We rejoin Lily in the car as she drives on, and the camera attentively follows her actions: a close-up on her face pans to her hand as she adjusts the radio dial and then back up to her face before cutting to a pov-shot of the road in front of her. If Zazie struggles for control of cinematic focus throughout that film, in *Black Moon*, Lily guides attention from the outset. Ultimately, Sontag is mistaken to assert that we see the first film through Zazie's eyes but cannot see the second through Lily's. Zazie finds herself in a foreign world that she learns to navigate; Lily's world, as real as it may be, is one of her own imagining.

Malle's description of *Black Moon* as a reportage is not, however, wholly inaccurate: when Lily, in the shots that follow, comes across a barricade, where a group of women soldiers are being executed by machine gun, Malle films the scene with the sobriety and patience of a war documentary. (There is a brief moment of excitement, more like an action film, as Lily escapes the situation under gunfire, followed by another pov-shot, this time from the side of the car, near the tire, as she drives off through a field of tall grass.) If *Zazie dans le métro* is all about the editing, *Black Moon* is an exercise in cinematography. As Lily continues her journey she encounters a hanged shepherd swaying above his flock, a snake when clearing stones out of the path, and another group of female soldiers torturing a prisoner before she flees on foot through the woods (followed by an extended tracking shot). She later pauses to examine a millipede and a grasshopper shot in extreme close-up just inches from her face – all through a series of long takes and slow pans. It is less that Lily discovers the world around her than she brings it into view, constitutes it through her observation.

When listed as a plot summary these images might sound disjointed, but what characterises the film is, in fact, its even continuity. Despite the variety of shots and techniques employed, the progression feels organic, natural, as if the full film were a single take and the editing were incidental – again recalling Breton on the structure of the dream:

> Within the limits where they operate (or are thought to operate) dreams give every evidence of being continuous and show signs of organization. Memory alone arrogates to itself the right to excerpt from dreams, to ignore the transitions, and to depict for us rather a series of dreams than the *dream itself*. (1969: 11; emphasis in original)

This extended sequence concludes with Lily's discovery of what will be the key elements of the meandering narrative: a black unicorn (her desideratum equivalent to Zazie's métro), which exits frame right just as the first of a set of twins enters on horseback, and, ultimately, the country home, Malle's own, where the remainder of the film will be set. This house is twice introduced in racking focus: the first time just after Lily has, uncharacteristically, briefly stepped outside the frame, as if to reveal to the audience what she has not yet noticed, and the second, moments later, over her shoulder from behind as she turns her attention to it. Malle once again exploits what is in focus and what is not as a means of raising consciousness, but here Lily's unconscious is subjected to none of the workings of the waking mind. It is the discovery of this estate that marks the definitive passage into a private world of Lily's fantasies, which are of course Malle's own; the filmmaker has veritably invited us into his home, where he attempts, as he insists, a filmic transcription of his dreams.

This opening is, despite the divergent styles, comparable to the geographic manipulations Malle plays with at the beginning of *Zazie dans le métro*: what he discovers there, a lesson that he takes to heart in *Black Moon*, is that narrative cinema itself is a matter of rendering irreality in a realistic fashion. If Zazie's filmic journey is the story of her maturation, in Lily's trajectory we can recognise a certain romantic regression. To quote one final time from Breton's foundational manifesto: 'The mind which plunges into Surrealism relives with glowing excitement the best part of its childhood. […] It is perhaps childhood that comes closest to one's 'real life' […] childhood where everything … conspires to bring about the effective … possession of' (Breton 1969: 39, 40). If *Zazie dans le métro* aspires to move from Malle's own cinematic infancy into a new awareness and maturity, what *Black Moon* attempts, instead, is an ecstatic (if terrifying) return to childhood.

Conclusion

The obvious irony is that in order to achieve an effect of realistic, seamless narrative continuity in *Black Moon*, Malle must take recourse to an arsenal of techniques every bit as sophisticated as the ostentatious inventory of cinematic strategies to which *Zazie dans le métro* is dedicated – only that here these work to efface rather than to emphasise the traces of their own construction. *Black Moon* has nothing of the willfully disjointed montage of *Un Chien andalou* (1928) or comparable efforts at Surrealist filmmaking.

What would be for Lily automatic writing, as she investigates the unconsidered logic of her dreams, requires, from the filmmaker, meticulous planning and an acquired ease. That much of the movie was 'improvised' – Malle claims to have mapped scenes out *ad hoc* each morning and shot them in the afternoon – does not detract from this carefulness but rather testifies to his hard-won mastery of his art: through experiments like *Zazie dans le métro*, Malle has gained a comfort in his filmmaking that allows him skillfully to render realistic spaces and timelines even extemporaneously.

Reassessing the relationship between Surrealism and the Oulipo, Alain Chevrier cautions that 'surrealism and formal constraints find themselves at opposite ends of the literary spectrum, but there are constraints in surrealism and surrealism in Oulipian constraints' (2007: 16). As provocative as this claim may appear, it is not a new idea. In another programmatic essay, seven years after his break with Queneau, Breton subtly, perhaps unwittingly, revises his position on Surrealist automatism:

> The path which surrealism proposes to take would be insufficiently defined if we were content to state only its direction and the ground it covers. The nature of the activating motive also must be made clear. We must search, therefore, for a link common to the various modes of perception, enumerated above, from which surrealism proceeds and of which it claims to be the sum total. We have been anxious to demonstrate that this link exists. This link – this constant or motive – is *automatism*. (1978: 155; emphasis in original)

The accent has shifted: now, speaking in the past tense, automatism is no longer an anti-method of Surrealism that allows the unconscious mind to come into view. Instead, Breton proclaims it the very goal of Surrealism not merely to reveal pure unmediated thought, but rather to reveal *automatism itself*, since

> An appeal to automatism in all its forms is our only chance of resolving … the antinomies … of being awake and sleeping (of reality and dream), of reason and madness, of objectivity and subjectivity, of perception and representation, of past and future, of the collective sense and individual love; even of life and death. (Ibid.)

It is precisely this suspension of such binary opposition that Malle hopes to achieve in his attempt at automatic writing and the realistic representation of dream states in *Black Moon*.

Ultimately, then, perhaps we are not wrong to speak of Surrealism – even if we choose to write it large, even in a strictly literary-historical sense – in the Oulipian exercises of *Zazie dans le métro*. Perhaps, implicitly, Malle instructs us to reconsider the relationship between these methods dialectically, as complementary attempts to open up the text to all the aleatory of the unconscious. While *Black Moon* might well be its consummation, this passage into an unfettered dream state had in fact begun fifteen years earlier with *Zazie dans le métro*. Quoting Queneau's Tonton Gabriel in various interviews, Malle describes both films as a *songe d'un rêve*: transpositions of one dream, be it written or unwritten, into a cinematic one. And such a dream is none other than Malle's own – a dream of a pure cinema of the unconscious.

Notes

1. Commentary on both films has often underscored the undeniable (and intentional, if mostly only very general) similarities to Lewis Carroll's *Alice in Wonderland*, not lastly the visual appearance of the English actress Cathryn Harrison, who was reportedly chosen in part for her resemblance to Sir John Tenniel's iconic illustrations. An examination of the press clippings archived by the Département des Arts du Spectacle at the Bibliothèque Nationale de France reveals that a fascination with the sixteen-year-old Harrison (granddaughter of Rex Harrison) and the parallels to Lewis Carroll dominated the contemporary reception of the film. While agreeing that *Alice in Wonderland* is an apt intertext for the Queneau adaptation, Susan Sontag, whose interpretation is my point of departure here, cautions against both this comparison, seeing it as superficial, and the Surrealist association of a *récit de rêve* in the case of *Black Moon* (1978: 104). Instead, in Sontag's reading, it's in part due to its distinction from *Alice in Wonderland* that *Black Moon* differs from *Zazie dans le métro* as well: she calls *Black Moon* 'the anti-Alice, or even the anti-Zazie' (1978: 105).
2. While the link between the Queneau adaptation and the origins of the Oulipo are occasionally acknowledged, I have only ever seen Malle's film itself described as Oulipian once, in passing, in a volume on another filmmaker entirely: '*Zazie*'s cinematic revelry distinctively displays an Oulipo aesthetic dream and reformulation of logic' (Gerstner and Nahmias 2015: 142). In his monograph, Hugo Frey inventories the director's personal historical associations to Surrealism, coming to the conclusion that *Zazie dans le métro* and *Black Moon* can both be considered of a piece with the French *avant garde*: 'These connections alone indicate how it is difficult to understand Malle without addressing the wider *avant garde* tradition in general, and surrealism in particular. In retrospect, the synthesis of commercial classicism and experimental surrealism might seem an impossible *rendez-vous* but bringing contradictions together was often the way Malle worked. In some films – like *Zazie dans le métro* or *Black Moon* – the experimental side won out and was the dominant mode' (2004: 61).
3. Comparing *Zazie dans le métro* and *Black Moon*, for instance, Georgiana Colvile insists that 'What makes them similar is, doubtless, the influence of surrealism, relatively spontaneous in *Zazie* and more consciously elaborated in *Black Moon*' (1996: 445). But as this phrasing ('relatively spontaneous') insinuates, while both films are *surreal*, one ought to be cautious of too readily associating the Queneau adaptation with Surrealism writ large. Even more problematic, historically speaking, is Colvile's assessment that *Zazie dans le métro* was filmed at a moment when Queneau still frequented the Surrealists and that the film therefore is coeval with the final years of the movement (1996: 445–6). While it can be difficult to

date the precise endpoint of Surrealism proper, Queneau's break, at least, explicitly occurs in 1930 with his contribution to the anti-Breton pamphlet, *Un Cadavre* [*A Corpse*]. Frey, too, in his otherwise exacting monograph, quite accurately describes the author of Malle's source text for *Zazie dans le métro* as an 'ex-surrealist' in the very same paragraph where he asserts that 'The first signs of the importance of surrealism in his oeuvre were demonstrated in Malle's decision in the late 1950s to adapt Raymond Queneau's *Zazie dans le métro*' (2004: 49). Inez Hedges also associates the film with Surrealism on the basis of avant-garde characteristics like its metafilmic awareness, the association with Queneau and its thematic emphasis on childhood and dreams: 'the sub-code of dream logic makes Malle as close as Queneau to the Surrealists and to the … transgression of the linguistic code by the adoption of the logic of dreams' (1984: 233).

4   As has been noted, scholarship on the film tends to focus on this aspect of adaptation (which itself inherently resembles Oulipian strategies of translation or transformation): 'Analyses of the film to date have mainly focused on this challenge of cinematic language taken on by Malle' (Blin-Rolland 2014: 48). And, as Johanne Bénard has insisted, this reception of the film is, admittedly, largely influenced by Malle's own account (1994: 137).

5   This variety of pastiche has been identified as Malle's 'major innovation in adapting Queneau's novel': 'Just as Queneau shifts registers, combining spoken French with the *passé simple* [simple past], neologisms, and recherché vocabulary, Malle's style is a mixture of genres. […] In this too, Malle rejoins the encyclopedism of Queneau's work, which often reads like a compendium of literary antecedents, scientific fact and *français argotique*' (Hedges 1984: 230).

Bibliography

Bénard, J. (1994) 'Un cinéma zazique?', *Cinémas: revue d'études cinématographiques*, 4, 3, 135–52.
Bibliothèque Nationale de France. Département des Arts du Spectacle. *Black Moon* (Document d'archives): film de Louis Malle. Cote: 4-sw-9046–1975.
Blin-Rolland, A. (2014) 'Cinematic Voices in Louis Malle's Adaptation of Raymond Queneau's *Zazie dans le métro*', *Studies in French Cinema*, 14, 1, 48–60.
Boschetti, A. (2010) 'La Notion de manifeste', *Francofonia*, 59 (Autumn), 13–29.
Breton, A. (1969 [1924]) 'Manifesto of Surrealism (1924)', *Manifestos of Surrealism*; trans. R. Seaver and H. R. Lane. Ann Arbor, MI: University of Michigan Press, 1–48.
____ (1978) 'Limits Not Frontiers of Surrealism,' in F. Rosemont (ed.) *What is Surrealism? Selected Writings*. New York: Monad Press. Part Two: 1930s, 150–59.
Chevrier, A. (2007) 'Liminaire', in H. Béhar and A. Chevrier (eds) *Les Actes du Colloque: 'Surréalisme et Contraintes Formelles'*. Paris: Noésis/Reflet des Lettres, 11–15.
Colvile, G. (1996) 'Malle surréaliste: *Black Moon*', *The French Review*, 69, 3 (February), 445–52.

Consenstein, P. (2002) *Literary Memory, Consciousness, and the Group Oulipo*. Amsterdam: Rodopi.
Deleuze, G. (1989) *Cinema 2: The Time-Image*, trans. H. Tomlinson and R. Galeta. Minneapolis, MN: University of Minnesota Press.
French, P. (1993) *Malle on Malle*. London: Faber and Faber.
Frey, H. (2004) *Louis Malle*. Manchester: Manchester University Press.
Genette, G. (1997 [1982]) *Palimpsests: Literature in the Second Degree*. Trans. C. Newman and C. Doubinsky. Lincoln, NE: University of Nebraska Press.
Gerstner, D. A. and J. Nahmias (2015) *Christophe Honoré: A Critical Introduction*. Detroit, MI: Wayne State University Press.
Hedges, I. (1984) 'Form and Meaning in the French Film, IV: Language', *The French Review*, 58, 2 (December), 223–35.
James, A. (2006) 'Automatism, Arbitrariness and the Oulipian Author', *French Forum*, 31, 2, 111–25.
Malle, L. (1970) '*Zazie dans le métro*: Ça c'est du … cinéma!', *L'Avant-scène*, 104, 10–70.
Porter, M. C. (1986) *Through Parisian Eyes: Reflections on Contemporary French Art and Culture*. Oxford: Oxford University Press.
Queneau, R. (1959) *Zazie dans le métro*. Paris: Gallimard.
____ (1962) *Entretiens avec Georges Charbonnier*. Paris: Gallimard.
Sontag, S. (1978) '"Black Moon": Conversation avec Louis Malle', in J. Mallecot (ed.) *Louis Malle par Louis Malle*. Paris: Éditions de l'Athanor, 103–7.

CHAPTER SEVEN

Louis Malle and 'His' Writers
(Drieu La Rochelle, Nimier, Modiano)

Michel Ciment

The 'New Wave' phenomenon that began in the late 1950s has been interpreted in various ways. The 1957 release of Louis Malle's first feature film, *Ascenseur pour l'échafaud* (*Elevator to the Gallows*), was unquestionably a harbinger of the emergence of new talents in French cinema. One of the salient features of this new generation was the assumption that the director was to be the sole writer (or co-writer) of the script, with one notable exception: Alain Resnais who never wrote his screenplays but, like Alfred Hitchcock, directed the screenwriters. In the past, such a concern existed among filmmakers but never to that extent. Unsurprisingly the 'new kids on the block' all had a marked interest in literature, whether classical (Balzac, Stendhal, Conrad, Dostoyevsky) or contemporary. The first group came from *Cahiers du cinéma* where they wrote film criticism. If the founders of the journal, André Bazin and Jacques Doniol-Valcroze, were left-wing intellectuals, the young Turks (Truffaut, Godard, Chabrol) had obvious right-wing, if not extreme-right, tendencies with the support of their elder, Eric Rohmer. The latter was a monarchist and, under his birth name, wrote a review of *Tabu* (1931), a film directed by F. W. Murnau (and co-written with Robert Flaherty), entitled 'La revanche de l'Occident' where he praised the purity of the race in the South Seas natives. Truffaut was close to Lucien Rebatet, a novelist and essayist who had published *Les Décombres*, a virulently anti-Semitic pamphlet, during the Occupation, and was later condemned to prison for several years. Truffaut welcomed him when he got out of jail and offered him a trip on the Seine River. He would subsequently publish a conversation in four instalments with Rebatet in an extreme right-wing Sunday publication. Claude Chabrol, a friend of Jean-Marie Le Pen (later founder of the National Front) was close to the writer Paul Gégauff, an outspoken supporter of extreme right-wing ideas while Godard flirted with these same ideas. They all wrote in politically conservative papers like *Arts* and *La Parisienne* under the leadership of Jacques Laurent, a strong anti-Gaullist pamphleteer, and an activist for French Algeria. Theirs was a reaction to the prevailing influence at the time of the Communist and existentialist writers (Sartre, Camus) on the French intellectual scene. They were dandies who extolled an individualistic view of life, praised style over political and social content.

At the opposite end of the spectrum were the directors of the Left Bank as defined by critic Richard Roud, an Englishman who founded the New York Film Festival. 'Left Bank' because they lived there (whereas the headquarters of the *Cahiers du cinéma* group were on the Champs-Élysées, on the right bank) and because of their political commitments. Alain Resnais, Chris Marker, Agnès Varda, William Klein, Georges Franju, Jacques Baratier were older and part of the film industry, directing some of the best short documentaries ever filmed. They collaborated with each other on the writing, the directing and the editing of their films and, except for Varda, a forerunner (*La Pointe courte*, 1955), directed their first features in the wake of their younger colleagues (*Hiroshima, mon amour* [Resnais, 1959], *La Tête contre les murs* [*Head Against the Wall*, Franju, 1959], *Le Joli Mai* [Marker, 1962], *Goha* [Baratier, 1959]). In a similar way, the third group, led by Louis Malle, was tightly knit. Jean-Paul Rappeneau collaborated on the scripts of Alain Cavalier's first film, *Le Combat dans l'île* (1961), and of Louis Malle's *Zazie dans le métro* (1960) and *Vie privée* (*A Very Private Affair*, 1962). Claude Sautet, the eldest of the group, and Alain Cavalier co-scripted with Rappeneau the latter's first feature, *La Vie de château* (*A Matter of Resistance*, 1965). If Malle wrote several original screenplays, he often adapted classical and modern writers, from Vivant Denon (*Les Amants* [1958]) and Raymond Queneau (*Zazie dans le métro*) to Georges Darien (*Le Voleur* [*The Thief of Paris*, 1967]) and Anton Chekhov (*Vanya on 42nd Street* [1994]).

I would like to concentrate on three of Malle's major films that share a common ambiguity and a pessimistic world-view: *Elevator to the Gallows*, *The Fire Within* (*Le Feu follet*, 1963) and *Lacombe Lucien* (1974), two adaptations and one original screenplay. *Elevator to the Gallows* was adapted by Malle and novelist Roger Nimier from a whodunit by Noël Calef; *The Fire Within* was written by Malle from a novel by Drieu La Rochelle; and *Lacombe Lucien* was written by Malle with the then young novelist (and future Nobel Prize winner) Patrick Modiano, whose screenplay was his first.

For his fiction debut (*Elevator to the Gallows*), Malle picked up a same-titled crime novel by Noël Calef, who had previously penned a short story that had inspired Joseph Losey for *Stranger on the Prowl/Imbarco a mezzanotte* (1952/53*)*. The noir genre was very popular among French artists after the war both in literature and cinema; many Hollywood directors (from John Huston to Nicholas Ray) likewise chose a criminal story for their first film. Malle asked Nimier (whom he had met for the first time a few months prior) to co-script with him. Nimier was highly considered as a novelist, starting with his first novel, *Les Épées* (1948), followed, among others, by *Le Hussard bleu* (1950), *Les Enfants tristes* (1951) and *Histoire d'un amour* (1952), until he stopped writing fiction at the early age of 28. He was part of a group of right-wing writers (Antoine Blondin, Michel Déon, Jacques Laurent) whom Bernard

Frank in an article in *Les Temps modernes* had dubbed 'Les Hussards'. Their admiration went to Céline, Drieu La Rochelle, Paul Morand and Jacques Chardonne who had all been collaborationists during the Nazi Occupation. Malle shared with Nimier a disenchanted lucidity, an ironic elegance as well as a verve and a sense of humour.[1] In a novel like *Les Enfants tristes*, Nimier had anticipated Françoise Sagan's first novel, *Bonjour Tristesse* (1954), with its secret bitterness, a certain carelessness and a search for a new kind of happiness which were also all part of Malle's psychological framework. Even if he had worked on a script with Antonioni for *I Vinti* (1952), Nimier was not particularly fond of cinema, literature being his true passion. He later refused to join the OAS, the terrorist organisation fighting to keep Algeria French, but nonetheless signed the Vincennes Manifesto, an answer from the extreme right to the Manifesto of the 121, which supported the young men refusing to fight in North Africa. When *Elevator to the Gallows* was awarded the famous Delluc Prize for the best French film of the year, there were criticisms in some quarters that it was honouring an extreme right-wing writer.

At first blush, *Elevator to the Gallows* recalls a James Cain story like *Double Indemnity* (1943). A married woman has an affair with her husband's employee, the latter ending up killing the former. Both the structure (the wife is never seen with her lover who is stuck in an elevator) and the various developments of the plot make it, however, an original piece of cinema. Julien Tavernier (Maurice Ronet), the murderer, is a former paratrooper, a 'lost' soldier from the First Indochina War which had ended three years before with a French defeat. When he is confronted by his boss Carala, Julien tells him to 'have some respect for war': 'It's your family heirloom'. Carala obviously sells weapons. Malle and Nimier pit the young idealist against the corrupt bourgeois with his fraudulent deals which have enriched him. Carala sarcastically tells Julien 'a paratrooper is an angel'. *Elevator to the Gallows* is one of the first screen illustrations of the myth of the paratrooper which in turn encapsulates the myth of the French Foreign Legion. Nimier was presumably sensitive to this side of the character. During the 1950s, there was a feeling of unease in France towards those who had fought in Indochina, not unlike the American sentiment towards the Vietnam veterans who had fought for nothing and whose many friends had died there. They were ill-considered, embarrassing witnesses of an absurd and lost war. A second development of the plot is the parallel story of two youngsters who steal Julien's car and kill a German tourist couple after having taken Julien's identity papers. Louis and Véronique, the pitiful teenagers, prefigure the young protagonists of *À bout de souffle* (*Breathless*, 1959) and other late 1950s French films. Their love of driving cars also echoes Malle and Nimier's automobile passion. Nimier had an Aston Martin, Malle a Jaguar. Driving fast reflects a certain romanticism, a new way of life where speed has no limits and Nimier himself would end his life tragically in a car accident on a highway at age 36. A third aspect of the film is the nightlife embodied by Jeanne Moreau who walks through Paris, a Paris filmed with a hidden camera very much in the manner of Godard two years later for *À bout de souffle* and on the same Champs-Élysées, but four years after René Clément shot the city of London for *Monsieur Ripois* (*Knave of Hearts*, 1953) in a similar fashion. Antonioni was possibly inspired by those sequences when he offered

Fig. 1: *Elevator to the Gallows* (1957): A melancholy *flâneuse*.

Jeanne Moreau the role of Lidia in *La Notte* (1961). Malle and Nimier shared the same passion for these long wanderings by car or on foot through the streets of Paris. Malle has confessed that, at the time, he lived mostly at night, except during the shooting, and would occasionally go directly from night club 'Chez Castel' to the set. Nimier and Malle considered themselves as people on the fringe, solitary, despising the Stalinist and bourgeois intelligentsias of the time. The rift between them came later as Nimier increasingly became a staunch supporter of French Algeria.

A fourth modern aspect of *Elevator to the Gallows* is the 18-minute soundtrack of Miles Davis which was recorded in one single session. The use of the jazz quintet, which predates Otto Preminger's *Anatomy of a Murder* and Robert Wise's *Odds Against Tomorrow*, both released in 1959, reflected the passion of French artists and intellectuals alike, whether on the right or on the left, for this music. It was Malle's decision, but Nimier certainly agreed. The choice of Henri Decae as cinematographer may have come from his work on Jean-Pierre Melville's *Bob le flambeur* (1955), a film noir shot on real locations. Malle depicts characters in search of an identity, solitary and forlorn, describes a society – that of the 4th Republic at the end of its tether – and locates the action in a futuristic Paris. There were only four or five steel-and-glass buildings such as the one in which Carala's consortium is locked, the motel where the German tourists are staying was the only one existing in France, and the young couple anticipates the consumer society that would take shape in the next decade. Malle admitted that he would have thought of Nimier to co-adapt Drieu La Rochelle's *Le Feu follet*, his fifth film after *The Lovers*, *Zazie dans le métro* and *A Very Private Affair*, had he not died a year before. Nimier admired Drieu wholeheartedly even if he did not share his anti-Semitism or his passion for Nazism. Drieu, who committed suicide in the last days of World War II rather than face trial for his ardent collaboration with the enemy, had been inspired to write his novel (published in 1931) by the suicide of his friend

Jacques Rigaut, a writer close to the Surrealists, with whom Drieu rubbed shoulders in his youth, particularly through his friendship with Louis Aragon who turned communist. Suicide was favoured by a number of artists close to the movement led by André Breton, like Jacques Vaché and René Crevel. *The Fire Within*, one of Malle's masterpieces, was written single-handedly by the director who confessed that the best way to avoid committing suicide was perhaps to direct a film about it. There are similarities between *Elevator to the Gallows* and *The Fire Within*, even if the former film is made up of opposite influences, Hitchcock for its suspense and Bresson (for whom Malle worked as an assistant on *Un condamné à mort s'est échappé* [*A Man Escaped*, 1956]) with its spare style. *The Fire Within* reveals a permanent trait in Malle's psychology: his fear of failure, his refusal to congratulate himself or, as Pierre Billard states in his important biography, his identification with Sisyphus 'rolling his rock to the top of the mountain and starting all over again' (2003: 87). In *The Fire Within*, the nocturnal existence, the human solitude, a temptation to escape the world, a certain melancholy are once more seen as part of Malle's personality at the time. He generally brought more tenderness towards Alain, his protagonist, than could be found in the original novel. More specifically, he added a short scene at the Café de Flore where Alain is confronted by two OAS militants who had been his colleagues during the military service. He refuses to join them because he realises that he could not find in their action a reason not to kill himself. This sequence is a way for Malle to distance himself from the extreme right. The film, like the novel, like Drieu's life itself, is the story of a failure. Before he kills himself, Alain reads *The Great Gatsby*, and on his desk lies a copy of *Babylon Revisited*, which inspired Malle for the episode of the barman. Malle, who admired F. Scott Fitzgerald, admitted that the character of Alain could have been invented by the American novelist.

Fig. 2: *The Fire Within* (1963): Outside the Café de Flore.

The narrative of *The Fire Within* marks the end of a decadent society which knows it is condemned and prefers death to mediocrity. It echoes films like *La Dolce Vita* and *La Notte* of a few years before, where Fellini and Antonioni portray a doomed lifestyle. Maurice Ronet embodies a Marcello Mastroianni type, harboring a profound ennui, sick of making love and drowning his despair in alcohol. This is a kind of romantic self-destruction akin to Drieu La Rochelle's source novel published in 1931, just after the Great Crash and the end of the Roaring Twenties. Alain lives in a kind of post-adolescence which considers that not killing oneself would be an act of cowardice. He admits that he drinks because he does not make love well; his spleen reveals an identity crisis. While the film is not a self-portrait, Malle had himself somehow always been on the margins, be it of his own wealthy family, of the New Wave, of France, or through the dream of living in another place (India or North America). In a 1986 interview with Jean-Claude Carrière for the French television programme 'Face à Face', Malle revealed that he was turning thirty when shooting the film and had found it difficult to cross the line between adolescence and adulthood: 'I had the impression that thirty years old was the age of retirement. I had always been the youngest everywhere and it was no longer true. I wondered what I could do with all my life, if it was not time to become an adult, that is to accept the world as it is, which I have always refused to do' (Billard 2003: 231). Before he dies, Alain meets with his former friends, trying to find a reason to stay alive. The recent death of Nimier with whom he shared so many things made Malle feel, for the first time, the presence of death. It was also for him the end of a way of life. The *Gymnopédies* music of Erik Satie – a companion of the Surrealists – as the leitmotif of the film expresses the protagonist's dark humour. As a child, Malle had found *Le Feu follet* in his conservative parents' personal library. Unlike them he disagreed with the moral and political ideas of the book, but shared its melancholy, its romantic spleen.

The film continues the portrait of Paris begun with *Elevator to the Gallows* and *Zazie dans le métro*. Alain's wanderings in contemporary Paris during half a day and half a night from Versailles and back to Versailles take place mostly on the Left Bank (contrary to the novel), from the hotel at Quai Voltaire to the Luxembourg Garden, from the Boulevard Saint-Michel to the Odéon Theater, with the exception of the Lavaud apartment on the Place des Vosges and the Champs-Élysées. This precise itinerary is familiar to the films of the New Wave, the most important forerunner being Agnès Varda's *Cléo de 5 à 7* (1962) where a woman walks through Paris waiting for the results of a cancer test. To make the story even more personal, Malle gave Ronet his own shirts, trousers, tie and jacket. He fully identified with Alain Leroy.

A decade later, Malle directed *Lacombe Lucien*, another peak of his career and one of his favourite films with *The Fire Within* and *Au revoir les enfants* (1987). In the preceding years, Malle had witnessed historical events which were food for his thoughts. In 1962, during the Algerian war, he heard the confession of a pro-OAS officer who had tortured native Arabs. In 1966, he read an *Esquire* article about a young Marine who had slaughtered civilians in a Vietnamese village. In 1971, in Mexico, he met young unemployed men from the Lumpenproletariat who were hired to attack students rebelling against the government. It was, however, a story happening near his country house in the Lot that prompted him to shoot a film reminiscent of the Harkis, those Algerians who fought on the French side. Lacombe Lucien is a young peasant who worked with the Gestapo during the Occupation, infiltrated the *maquis* and had twenty members of the Resistance arrested. Malle asked Patrick Modiano, a young writer who had only published two novels, to collaborate on the script. Modiano had won the Roger Nimier Prize in 1968 for his first book, *La Place de l'Étoile*, one of whose characters, Jean-François des Essarts, is based on Nimier: 'He had precious qualities: tact, generosity, a great sensibility, a biting irony.' He advises Raphael, the protagonist, to read Cardinal de Retz's *Mémoires*, Maurice Scève's *Délie* and the comedies of Corneille, three favourite writers of Nimier's. The latter's father was always absent, unreachable; Modiano's was both endearing and villainous. Nimier and Modiano both shared an interest for shady characters. Modiano had found in the period of the Occupation a time that fitted his inclination for ambiguous situations and moral dilemmas. In his first novel, *Les Épées* (1948), Nimier anticipated the retro fashion of the 1970s with collaborationists, instead of *Résistants*, as main fictional protagonists. *La Ronde de nuit* (1969), Modiano's second novel, recalls *Les Épées* with the same fascination for the image of the traitor who, without knowing it, is on both sides of the fence. When, in *La Place de l'Étoile*, Modiano imagines an anti-Semitic and collaborationist Jew (inspired by Maurice Sachs) and a Resistance militant man, he almost parodies Nimier and Drieu La Rochelle. At that time in his career, including his third novel *Les Boulevards de ceinture* (1972), it could be said that Modiano in a sense was an heir to Nimier. After the experience of *Lacombe Lucien*, however, he adopted a style with almost no literary flourish, a kind of blank and neutral prose that became distinctive. The Nimier page had been turned. His contribution to *Lacombe Lucien* was important particularly with the portrayal of the Jewish family and the love story between Lucien and their young daughter.

Fig. 3: *Lacombe Lucien* (1974): Scandalous rapprochement.

Like Marcel Ophuls' documentary, *Le Chagrin et la pitié* (*The Sorrow and the Pity*, 1971), *Lacombe Lucien* was unjustly attacked for providing a more complex view of France during the Occupation. In the film, there is no ambiguity about the Gestapo, which is the place where horror is happening. In his book with Jacques Mallecot, *Louis Malle par Louis Malle*, the director commented indirectly on both his affinities and differences with the writers who inspired him:

> Malraux once wrote: 'A man of action who is also a pessimist is, or will become, a fascist unless he has a loyalty behind him.' I am active and a pessimist but I know also to what I am faithful. It was this morning of January 1944 when I saw that young Jewish classmate stand up, when the Gestapo came in, and shake our hands one after the other, looking at us straight in the eyes. (1978: 72)

This episode told by Malle became a film ten years later, *Au revoir les enfants*, a story of his own life, a solo effort as a screenwriter and adapted from no book.

Note

1   On Malle's relationships with Nimier and the 'Hussards' group, see his interview with Marc Dambre (2006) and Hugo Frey's essay (2006).

Bibliography

Billard, P. (2003) *Louis Malle. Le rebelle solitaire*. Paris: Plon.
Dambre, M. (2006 [1988]) '*Ascenseur pour l'échafaud* (*Elevator to the Gallows*, 1957): An Exclusive Interview with Louis Malle', trans. H. Frey, *South Central Review*, 23, 2 (Summer), 12–21.
Frey, H. (2006) 'Louis Malle and the 1950s: Ambiguities, Friendships and Legacies', *South Central Review*, 23, 2 (Summer), 22–35.
Mallecot, J. (1978) *Louis Malle par Louis Malle*. Paris: Editions de l'Athanor.
Schérer, M. [E. Rohmer] (1953) 'La revanche de l'Occident', *Les Cahiers du cinéma*, 21 (March), 46–8.

CHAPTER EIGHT

A Gendered Geography of Death: Louis Malle's Orphic Voyage

T. Jefferson Kline

In an essay published many years ago (Kline 1992), I attempted to read the image of *La Carte de Tendre,* displayed behind the opening title and credits of Louis Malle's *Les Amants* (*The Lovers*, 1958)*,* in the light of Joan de Jean's excellent analysis of that map as a kind of utopia of gender relations in the seventeenth century. In her essay, she had interpreted *La Carte de Tendre* as symbolically depicting the salons as

> an alternative space … a sort of alternate court, a new center of power, a place where power was exercised through conversation. […] The salons were a world presided over by women … *Préciosité* thus began as a feminist movement … and the *précieuses* made demands for women that would today be termed control over their bodies. (1989: 299)

In yet another context, Claude Filteau had added that

> the *carte* aimed ultimately at giving women as much to gain from friendship as men. Thus, the map itself signifies an egalitarian project couched in geometric and discursive terms. Its code, in fact, is meant to imitate another code: that of 'la conversation spirituelle' and the essence of the code can be learned by men only by a sort of *devenir femme*. (1979: 42)

Their brilliant contextualisation of this map led me to read Malle's film as a woman's successful quest for an identity, free of the constraints of marriage and motherhood. In the light of these readings of the Carte, *The Lovers* appeared to be a wonderfully openended quest, launched by a brave couple, daring to venture into the unknown territory of a new kind of love. When, however, Malle himself jocularly referred to his last film,

Damage (1992 [French title: *Fatale*]) as *Les Amants II,* I realised that there was another, equally compelling interpretation of Malle's 1958 work that needed to be explored.

Damage, made thirty-four years after *The Lovers,* was based on a novel that Josephine Hart had sent to Malle in 1991. Curiously, Hart had transmuted her own narrative voice to that of a British man in his late fifties, who begins by telling us that 'There is an internal landscape, a geography of the soul; we search for its outlines all our lives' (1991: 3). This notion of geography is immediately problematised by being penned by a woman, yet spoken by a man. In addition, it is a geography of the *inaccessible.* The narrator notes: 'I know the bridge that connects me to my former self, but the other side has disappeared, like some piece of land that the sea has overtaken' (1991: 22). When Stephen Fleming seems to regain some sense of connection to his own geography through his explosive encounter with Anna Barton, he also ironically encounters his own death. Indeed, Anna does not *connect* him to anything immediately map-able! As he thinks of meeting her, he says, 'I was like a traveler lost in a foreign land…' (1991: 27), and adds, 'I was uprooted by a storm of such force that even if there were a dim possibility of survival, I would be permanently damaged, permanently weakened' (1991: 32). When, almost immediately after entering her apartment, they make love, he says: 'I thought of Christ, still nailed to the cross, which had been laid on the earth' (1991: 33). Then: 'Around every meeting with her spun a ribbon of certainty that my life *had already ended*. It had ended in the split second of my first sight of her. It was time out of life. Like an acid it ran through all the years behind me, burning and destroying' (1991: 40) and: 'I was colluding in some needed, longed-for destruction … some great machine of fate' (1991: 48). There can be no doubt that Stephen's attraction to Anna is a manifestation of a powerful death-wish. It is not she he wants; it is, as Hamlet puts it – since Stephen begins by talking about geography – a visit to 'The undiscover'd country, from whose bourn / No traveller returns…'

We have here a confluence of personae: Orpheus and Hamlet. This fascination with death signals how thoroughly Hart's and Malle's ventures collude in the desire to descend into a fatal realm, lured there by the promise of finding a woman at its centre (Eurydice, Ophelia or his mother?).

To bring her back or to get her back? That is the question. And perhaps Anna Barton's initials, AB, give us a clue: this is Stephen's moment of *ab*-reaction which is defined as the release of emotional tension achieved through recalling a repressed traumatic experience. Nor can we fail to notice that both the English title and the French title (*Dame*-age/*Femme*-Fatale) suggest, by implication, a woman, only slightly disguised – a screen memory. Moreover, we become aware that virtually every erotic scene in *Damage* is a theatre of violence and, indeed, that one of them is borrowed directly from Bernardo Bertolucci's *Last Tango in Paris* (1972) – a film I have elsewhere shown (with Bertolucci's entire endorsement) to be a retelling of the Orpheus legend.[1] Of these erotic scenes Malle mentioned that

> a friend reminded [him] that Baudelaire once said: 'The supreme and unique sensual pleasure of love lies in the certainty of inflicting pain.' There is in these scenes *a kind of core of darkness, a weight, a sense of grief and tension that are the*

components of passion. The actors certainly did not seek ... their inspiration from life [...] Anna is unquestionably a figure of death' (Tranchant 1992: 12)

Now the Orpheus legend is founded, as Michel Serres has noted, on the fact that the very name of Orpheus has the same root as the words for hell and/or orphan (a status to which we know Malle aspired as a way of freeing himself from his conservative, bourgeois origins):

> The myth focuses on the most primitive aspects of our nature, since Orpheus's art is music [...] well before language, the pure signal, deprived of specific meaning ... which first emerges from the hell of disorder, and whose name can be deciphered as a kind of double mirror. In this sense it would no longer be a question of an artifact or a canvass hidden by the cleverness of the author, but of a secret invariant, integral to stories of eros and of the death instinct. (1974: 255)

Jean Normand, for his part, has observed:

> Orpheus is that which has no name, no face, no expression, that which is hidden, unknown, that which in man is foreign to man. [...] The truth of Orpheus is the eternal struggle of Eros against Thanatos. Orpheus is, like other men, split between the creative and the destructive drives. (1980: 76, 77)

In speaking of his own *Orphée* (*Orpheus*, 1950), Cocteau has repeatedly insisted on the relation of primary narcissism to death: mirrors are doors through which Death enters our soul, and through which Orpheus enters the kingdom of Death. And he has purportedly asserted, making clear the connection between film and mirroring: cinema is about capturing death at work (*Faire du cinéma, c'est saisir la mort au travail.*)

From this perspective, Malle's work would appear to be an extended meditation on, and mise-en-scène of, these darker aspects of the Orpheus myth. The Orpheus legend suggests paradoxically that what is central to the poet's journey is *not* the woman who awaits him in Death – she is, as Cocteau made clear in his film, merely the pretext and a figure of ambivalence, for he may love her but cannot help but be angry with her for her infidelity. Getting her back becomes an ambivalent gesture, and that ambivalence will be fronted when, though told he must not turn around to look at her during the journey back, he does precisely that. Here again, in Cocteau's version, Orpheus has become so disaffected with Eurydice that he angrily looks at her in his rear-view mirror and actively casts her back into the utter darkness. The real attraction of death is the excitement of Death herself (who can't help looking a bit maternal). How telling, then, that Malle should have said, 'The cinema is all about looks, and I tried to have that be the focus of this film. Destiny depends on looks exchanged. [...] We might say it's the equivalent of the severe constraints of classical tragedy' (Tranchant 1992: 12).

What becomes central to Orpheus's project is not the return of Eurydice but the *fame* that accrues to anyone who can successfully make the round trip. The chances (and success rate) of such a return are, of course, normally minimal. So how does Orpheus succeed? Through his art. And what is so uncanny here (in relation to Malle's entire oeuvre) is that, having proved that his art can 'charm the Gods', he is then free to *reel around* and (continuously) transform Eurydice into *an image that signifies her absent presence*. She thus becomes the emblem of the art shared by Cocteau and Louis Malle: the cinema, which, as Bazin made clear in 'The Ontology of the Photographic Image', is based on 'the objective character of photography': 'only photography derives an advantage from [man's] absence. [...] The photographic image is the object itself, the object freed from the conditions of time and space that govern it' (1967: 13, 14). This definition affirms the existence of some thing or person that, when looked at on the screen, will no longer be present: Eurydice. It is precisely Malle's Orphic ability to evoke her *absent presence* that seems gradually to emerge, like a photograph in the developer's fluid, as the pretext and genius of his art. We are thus looking at a structure which is defined as a piece of geography but that exists simultaneously as the locus of a woman – or women – and death; that place from which no one but the most talented artist can return. We may think here of Malle miraculously returning from the bottom of the sea (*la mer*) with that other Cocteau – Cousteau. Louis becomes known, among his generation, as he who risks traveling to remote (and, at times, submerged) geographies.

When we take another look at *The Lovers* in the light of both these Orphic themes and Malle's observation that *Damage* was a kind of *The Lovers redux*, we notice that the director's own statements about *La Carte de Tendre* were, in fact, quite despairing: 'There's something very pessimistic in the ending of *The Lovers*', he says, before adding:

> *La Carte du tendre* is like a map, but the names of the villages and towns are Passion, Remords, Jalousie [...] – it's very bizarre actually, it's a geographic representation of all the variations around the theme of love. (French 1993: 24)

There could not be a more radical departure from de Jean's reading: to move from 'the establishment of *nouvelle amitié*' to 'Passion, Remorse, Jealousy'. This conversion effectively turns a prescription for vital liberation into a deadly poison. Indeed, Pierre Billard reminds us that all of the first versions of *The Lovers* end with a statement that Jeanne speaks off screen, after being abandoned by Bernard along the road: 'These adieux have never ceased, and I've never loved anyone again, never understood what happened.' The film, Pierre Billard comments, 'introduces us to two major registers in Louis Malle's œuvre: ambiguity and disenchantment' (2003: 180).

This retrospective transformation of the map's potential for love and identity into separation and despair has the potential effect of transforming all of the film's images, beginning with the map, into a place of loss. In this light, we see the name Jeanne Moreau on the map as the sign that she is the symbolic locus of the film, her very ontology darkly defined by Malle's re-reading of the map as tracing a river that passes through jealousy to empty (necessarily) into a deadly sea (*la mer dangereuse*) and from thence, on to lands beyond labeled *terrae incognitae*. In the light of Hamlet's previously quoted soliloquy we suddenly realise that what we might initially have understood to be a positive direction on the Carte toward a discovery of the power of the feminine, may instead, or also, be a descent down a river to a point of no return.

We therefore see Jeanne as already lost before the image of Jeanne Moreau can even represent her – a version of the irrecoverable Eurydice, a 'found' woman, discarded along the road like road kill, whom Bernard (Malle's alter ego) sees initially as simply one among the dead objects of his archeological search: a withering interest, which includes the Vase de Vix, an immense funerary urn, and other finds that he wishes to share with his teacher. *His* journey is of a purely archeological order; it thereby so thoroughly denies Jeanne's presence that, to escape from it, she inadvertently drives his 2CV into the river – as if trying to cross the Styx to get out of (or into?) her predicament. She becomes an always-already dead object in this version of Malle's mise-en-scene. Stealing her away at night suddenly feels as though it's a story of grave-robbing… Or, a re-transcription of the myth of Orpheus.

Such a re-telling is 'certified' by another series of hints at Cocteau's Orpheus: Jeanne Moreau's some fifteen glances in mirrors, that, in a more positive context, might be interpreted as an effort to establish her identity, become, instead, in the light of Malle's view of *La Carte de Tendre,* merely an insistent series of allusions to *Orph*ée in which, as already noted, mirrors are the doors by which death enters us. Ironically, her husband also treats her as already dead when he says to her at dinner: 'You don't need to have style [*un genre*] since you have a husband.' She acquiesces by admitting she is 'nobody'. What's more, she drives a Peugeot 203, whose number evokes the French dictum 'Jamais deux sans trois' ('All things comes in threes'). Two lovers will lead to one more, all of whom are 'accidents' that have her pass like an object from hand to hand of a series of upper-class men, all of whom resemble each other. Clearly, both from the apothegm and from the unraveling of the film, bad luck does come in threes: Raoul rides a polo horse, Bernard drives a '2 chevaux' and the *third* horse will be the white horse standing saddleless on the road at the end – a final symbol of death. In other words, Malle's Orpheus may enjoy visiting Eurydice in that dangerous place from which other travelers may not return, but he ends up being more interested in the route than in his companion. Notice, by the way, that as they drive away together, she cries, 'Don't look at me!' But it was always already too late for such a plea…

Despite the original intent of the map, and particularly despite the centrality of Jeanne Moreau's name (and symbolically her body)[2] on the map, Billard notes that:

> Spontaneously, *fatally,* since it's no doubt partly unconsciously, Louis reclaims [Louise's] story as his own, with his own world, his own values, and his own feelings. His hero, Bernard, resembles him more and more… (2003: 176)

No wonder Louise de Vilmorin wanted nothing to do with this film once Malle took it over. In an article titled 'Louis Malle, un homme qui m'est inconnu' ['Louis Malle, a man I no longer know'], she would fulminate:

> The story he tells [in *The Lovers*] … has nothing in common with the story that originally attracted his attention. […] Stubborn and authoritarian, he leads

Fig. 1: *The Lovers* (1958): '2 chevaux' and one horse.

his characters wherever he pleases. […] I believe he has a much too tyrannical notion of what pleases him, what displeases him, and what he wants to show, to allow anyone else to influence him. (Billard 2003: 176)

For Louise, like Jeanne, is only a vehicle for the director's 'trip'.

To refer to *Damage* as *Les Amants II*, i.e. as a remake of his earlier film, is to make it clear that Malle 'bookended' (even if his debut feature was *Elevator to the Gallows* rather than *The Lovers*) his career with two films that suggest that to pursue a woman in his world is to lose oneself in the fatality of her space, to make the geography of death present and habitable, rather than to free *her* from *her* hell – two geographies of hell coded as a feminine space that it is the artist's special privilege/talent/science to attain, but not linger in. If Charles Mauron's psycho-critical theory about obsessive metaphors dictated by an author's personal myth is correct, we should expect to see traces of this Orphic theme in them, as well.

Like *Damage*, *The Fire Within* is a film about approaching ever nearer to death: the main character's decision to kill himself is arrived at 'not because my friends didn't love me enough, but because I didn't love them enough'. One could not allude more certainly to Orpheus here, for the Ovid's traveler didn't love Eurydice enough to bring her all the way back, but he did get very excited about the journey. Malle's biographer notes that 'anyone who knows Louis well will immediately recognize him as the subject of the film' (Billard 2003: 234) and, as the filming continued, that 'Louis slipped more and more into his character' (2003: 236). So much so, indeed, that when Philip French observed to Malle that he and Maurice Ronet 'look like brothers', the filmmaker responded:

> Well, we were very close, extremely close ... My collaboration with him in the making of the film was far more intimate than I'd ever experienced with any other actor or actress before. There is a scene where he gets dressed in his room at the clinic and everything in the closet was mine. I'd put everything from my apartment in suitcases and taken them to the set ... Even the gun was mine. I almost resented the fact that he was playing the part. I think I was very hard on him – he kept saying, 'Louis, let me play the part.' Yes, there was a strange osmosis between the two of us. (1993: 43)[3]

Elsewhere, Malle noted: 'It's a very pessimistic, very dark film, but I think for me it was completely liberating' (1993: 42). How wonderful to be able to commit suicide but not die… We see an imitation of Orpheus's desire to use his art to visit Hades at every turn in this film. *Damage* presents an even more ironic and tragic version of this same pattern. While Stephen runs toward Anna as though he's heading full-tilt toward death, the film doesn't end with *his* death, but instead, like Malle surviving his own suicide in *The Fire Within,* his son's death. In the end, he sits, naked, holding the dead body of his son, who has died *for him.* Indeed, Malle himself confesses that

> When I read *Damage*, there were themes, visual moments and characters that really intrigued me; I was very compelled. [...] Reading it I thought immediately of *Les Amants.* It's the same kind of milieu; it's about somebody discovering that his life (or, in the case of *Les Amants,* her life) is very empty; something happens which brings about the collapse of the conventional world in which he lives. It seemed interesting for me to revisit this theme… (French 1993: 200, 201)[4]

The film ends with Martyn's (Stephen Fleming's son) horrifying glimpse of a hell inhabited by a Eurydice figure, whose presence now causes him to lurch *backwards* and fall to his death. Once again, we have an obsessive structure in which the world inhabited by the central female becomes a space of death. The death, however, is not that of the narrator, who, like Orpheus, survives his descent into hell, but, like Ronet standing in for Malle in *The Fire Within,* that of a double, who allows the 'storyteller' to commit suicide (visit the underworld) without dying.

To return to *The Fire Within,* there is one detail that feels even more uncanny in terms of the Orpheus/Eurydice connection. We remember that what we have called the 'gendered geography of hell' is, in both *The Lovers* and *Damage,* gendered female. Billard, in discussing the shooting locales of *The Fire Within,* notes that '[in] the only breath of oxygen in the film, an unusual movement of the camera accidentally frames a strange building with a set of columns': 'the Temple of Friendship', also known as 'the Temple of Lesbos' (2003: 238). We must recognise that this 'unusual' moment of the film's mise-en-scene can – nay, because of its deliberate displacement and introjection into the otherwise quotidian landscape, *must* – be read as Malle's anticipation of *La Carte de Tendre* in *The Lovers.* It essentially labels this particular geography of death as feminine.

And is *Elevator to the Gallows* so different? We already see Maurice Ronet in the role of a man seeking to find his way into death. At the centre of this hell stands Jeanne Moreau (preparing for her role in *The Lovers,* so to speak), deadened by her enslavement to her industrialist husband, Carala. Like Orpheus, Ronet moves along a vertical axis to accede to the centre of this inferno (as the film operates almost more on the vertical plane than it does on the horizontal one) where he gets to *enact a suicide without dying* – by finding himself *entombed* in an elevator car (for three-quarters of the film). While so trapped, he is accused and about to be condemned and executed for a heinous crime he didn't even commit (and whose architects commit suicide but don't die), but then the image of his Eurydice emerges in the form of a developing photograph sent to her lover. One look at this image will condemn *her* but not *him* to the equivalent of death. Orpheus and Eurydice thus find their way back into Malle's work. I believe it is this insistent and compulsive act of repetition that ends up making Louis Malle one of the most appropriate exemplars of Bazin's theory of the ontology of the filmic image: the absent presence.

Notes

1   See Kline 1976. Jeremy Irons noted the intertextual nature of the love scenes in *Damage*, stating: 'Louis Malle fell into all the traps that this difficult story of adaptation laid for him, not the least in the way he shot the love scenes' (Capretti 1994: 28). Indeed, the way Malle shot the love scenes was unquestionably by allusion. The first 'space' they visit is a re-visitation of the Rue Jules Verne apartment in Bertoluccci's film, which is a re-working of Cocteau's scenes of mirroring and death in *Orpheus*. And, as if to emphasise the continuity of this theme in Malle's own work, this particular scene from *Damage* also recreates a scene from *The Lovers*. As Irons and Binoche sit in the position of Brando and Schneider in *Last Tango in Paris*, each covers the other's eyes – a gesture that recaptures the scene from *The Lovers* in which the lovers cover each other's faces with a towel.

Fig. 2: *Damage* (1992): Blind man's buff?

Fig. 3: *Last Tango in Paris* (1972): Looking into each other's eyes.

2 In a contemporary reading of the map (i.e., in the twentieth century) one can discern the outlines of the fallopian tubes and ovaries in the design of the river and the sea above it. Joan de Jean has argued that this anatomical knowledge was not available at the time of the map's composition, but it was at the time of Malle's choosing the map on which to display the film's credits.
3 See also: '[The film] is completely personal, deliberately personal, incredibly close to me … I'd reached a point where I was really myself' (French 1993: 40).
4 See also: '*Damage* brings back many things I've covered during my lifetime and in my work' (French 1993: 202).

Bibliography

Bazin, A. (1967) *What Is Cinema?* Trans. H. Gray. Berkeley, CA: University of California Press.
Billard, P. (2003) *Louis Malle. Le rebelle solitaire*. Paris: Plon.
Capretti, L. (1994) 'Not Just Butch, but Jeremy', *Fascino*, 5, 4 (April–June), 23–31.
De Jean, J. (1989) 'The Salons, 'Preciosity' and the Sphere of Women's Influence', in D. Hollier (ed.) *A New History of French Literature*. Cambridge, MA: Harvard University Press, 297–303.
Filteau, C. (1979) 'Le Pays de Tendre: l'enjeu d'une carte', *Littérature*, 36 (December), 38–44.
French, P. (1993) *Malle on Malle*. London: Faber and Faber.
Hart, J. (1991) *Damage*. New York: Alfred A. Knopf.
Kline, T. J. (1976) 'Orpheus Transcending: Bertolucci's *Last Tango in Paris*,' *The International Review of Psycho-Analysis*, vol. 3, 85–95.
____ (1992) 'Remapping Tenderness: Louis Malle's *Lovers* with No Tomorrow', in *Screening the Text*. Baltimore, MD: Johns Hopkins University Press, 24–53.
Mauron, C. (1963) *Des métaphores obsédantes au mythe personnel. Introduction à la psychocritique*. José Corti.
Normand, J. (1980) 'Le Poète, image de l'étranger: L'Orphée de Tennessee Williams', *French American Review*, 4, 2 (Fall), 73–9.
Serres, M. (1974) *Jouvences sur Jules Verne*. Paris: Les Editions de Minuit.
Tranchant, M.-N. (1992) '*Fatale*: Louis Malle, Parfum de Scandale,' *Le Figaro*, 9 December.

CHAPTER NINE

The Figure of the Mother in May Fools, Au revoir les enfants *and* Murmur of the Heart

Justine Malle

'If I dared, I'd say my mother may be the most important person of my life.'
– Louis Malle, *Parlez-moi d'elle*

Though it may have occupied a very important place in Louis Malle's work as well as in his life, the figure of the mother has not been explored critically. Is it one of those themes that are so obvious one no longer sees them? Is it that it weaves together the author's life and his work in too mechanical a way? A radio interview Malle gave in 1993 about his mother prompted me to investigate the way he represents her in three of his 'autobiographical' films where the figure in question plays a central part: *Milou en mai* (*May Fools*, 1989), *Le Souffle au cœur* (*Murmur of the Heart*, 1971) and *Au revoir les enfants* (1987). I discovered that there was a real opposition between the director's real mother, Françoise Malle, who was very much attached to a system of values that her son rejected early on, and the way she is portrayed in these films. In all three of them, even when she seems like a typical bourgeoise (in *Au revoir les enfants*, for instance), she is still, at heart, a child. Why such a hiatus between the 'biographical' mother and the paradigm of anti-conformism the mother incarnates in these films?

Three Autobiographical Works

Unlike *May Fools*, which its author never claimed to be a reflection of his personal life (despite some strong confessional elements), *Murmur of the Heart* and *Au revoir les enfants* clearly belong to an autobiographical vein.

The situation depicted in *Au revoir les enfants* is strictly the one Malle experienced at the time: in 1944, his father was living in the German-occupied north of France taking care of the family sugar factory, while his mother was in Paris expecting, at 44, her last child. Louis, who had lived with his parents until then, was sent to the same boarding school as his brothers, near Fontainebleau. The headmaster was Père Jacques, a charismatic and spiritually demanding Carmelite who hid Jewish children and men fleeing compulsory work service in Germany. Père Jacques' radical sermon (censuring the wealthy as unfit to enter the kingdom of Heaven) in the presence of the visiting bourgeois parents is a reportedly exact transcription of the one he delivered at the time (see Billard 2003: 473). Malle represents with documentary precision the social group (*la grande bourgeoisie*) that sent their children to this kind of religious institution, the intensity of the cold, the (relative) lack of food, the rigours of the order. Julien Quentin, the main character, is a faithful portrait of the boy Malle himself was: sensitive, smart, curious and feisty. Julien's older brother also has the nonchalance, humour and sense of provocation shared by Malle's two elders, Bernard and Jean-François. Another important biographical element is the class opposition between Joseph, the young servant who is fired because of his black market shenanigans and ends up denouncing the Jewish children to the Gestapo, and the upper-class school kids with whom he deals. The last scene (Père Jacques and the three kids being taken away by the Gestapo) is also rigorously faithful to reality, as asserted in the last sentence of the film ('Forty years later, I can still remember every detail of that January morning'). What is completely fictional, however, in *Au revoir les enfants*, is the increasingly close bond between Julien Quentin and Jean Bonnet, as Malle himself always made clear. In real life, the director observed his new classmate from afar: they were much more rivals than friends.

As for the connection between the story of *Murmur of the Heart* and Malle's life, an anecdote says it all: at the end of the film's screening, his mother famously ran up to him, opening her arms wide and crying out: 'My dear Louis, this brings back so many memories!' which on a film about incest, was, to say the least, malapropos… The premise of the film is meticulously autobiographical: in 1946, when Malle was thirteen (in the film Laurent is fifteen), he started to suffer from a murmur of the heart due to scarlet fever and had to be home-schooled. His mother later spent a month with him at a spa in Burgundy, exactly as in the film. Pierre Billard emphasises the precision with which the family atmosphere and mores are reconstituted (2003: 65–7 and *passim*). Though Paris becomes Dijon, World War II the Indochina War and the sugar dynasty a more modest middle-class milieu (the father is a gynecologist), the film's family is very much like the director's; two provocative siblings who drive their Jesuit teachers crazy and initiate their younger brother into various forms of transgression; an absent, less-than-warm father who is completely outshined by the mother; an Italian nanny. The episode during which the brothers pretend to destroy the family's Corot painting (which they have replaced with a fake) is a true story, except that in Malle's case, it was a Cézanne that his brothers had asked a friend (Ghislain Uhry, painter and artistic consultant on many of Malle's films) to reproduce. Even the reference to Dien Bien Phu is close to home: a Malle cousin had almost died there and it had been a huge shock (see French 1993: 89). Like Julien Quentin, Laurent Chevalier has many traits of the young Louis: a passion for jazz (here Charlie Parker), an intellectual curiosity, an interest in the question of suicide, an apparent perfection (altar boy, boy scout, brilliant student) hiding intense inner rebellion (he masturbates constantly, reads forbidden books, hates priests and religion in general). What is not autobiographical, of course, is the mother. In *Malle on Malle,* the filmmaker confides that he could not use his mother as an inspiration, as it did not seem very plausible to him for a woman of the upper Catholic French bourgeoisie in the 1940s to have a sexual relationship with her son (French 1993: 84–6). Instead, he used as a model the mother of a friend, a free, sensual Brazilian woman he would have loved his mother to be like. The incest theme came, not from his memories (as his mother's exclamation at the screening might lead us to believe), but from a Georges Bataille novel, *Ma mère* (1966; published posthumously), which he was trying to adapt. But as he was working on the adaptation, the memories of his stay at the spa in the same room as his mother came flooding back. He abandoned Bataille's radical and dark eroticism, and integrated the incest theme into his own biography.

In contrast *May Fools* is not generally considered one of Malle's autobiographical films, since it is a more or less explicit variation on a Chekhov play, *The Cherry Orchard* (1903), which he had wanted to direct for the stage a couple of years earlier. Moreover, the film's sociological frame (a ruined provincial bourgeoisie) is quite different from Malle's upper-class industrial family. Co-scriptwriter Jean-Claude Carrière has repeatedly asserted that most of the inheritance traditions and rules in the film were inspired by his own southern, provincial, petit bourgeoisie background. Personal references are nonetheless numerous in a film that was shot about six years after the director's mother's death, which, as it does in *May Fools'* Vieuzac tribe, spurred quarrels and resentment about the inheritance as well as the sale of the family house, Thumeries, where the Malle children had almost all been born and spent their childhood. In addition to what each member of the family must have felt individually, Françoise's demise signaled, for Louis if not all of them, the possible end of the family circle as such, Françoise Malle having been its core. In a posthumous letter, she begs her children to always stay close to each other (Billard 2003: 426–7). One finds an echo of this in the film when Milou protests: 'We can't sell the house, this house is what unites us, without it we're nothing, we're gypsies.' There is also a physical resemblance between the mother here played by Paulette Dubost and Françoise Malle: in *Parlez-moi d'elle,* Malle points out that this actress is the one – as opposed to the maternal figures in *Au revoir les enfants* and *Murmur of the Heart* – who physically reminds him the most of his own mother. Last but not least, a kinship between Milou and Malle is hard to miss, from a certain informal elegance to a way of being silent while observing things around him, and a huge sympathy for May '68 (which, if too 'old' to be an active participant in it, Malle was immensely curious and excited about).

Portrait of the Mother as a Child

As has been often stated, the distinction between the adult world, with its conformism, lack of imagination and hypocrisy, and a realm in which fantasy and playfulness rule is a *topos* of Malle's films. It is obvious in *Zazie dans le métro* (1960), where the fantasy comes to an end when the little girl returns home with her mother; in *The Fire Within* (1963), where Alain Leroy cannot face reality and kills himself; or in *Lacombe Lucien* (1974), whose dream-like ending (with Lucien and France playing like children in nature) is brutally cut off by the spelling-out on screen of his sentence to death. Similarly in *Pretty Baby* (1978), where Violet lives a scandalously unorthodox life in a brothel with her prostitute mother before entering an orderly, bourgeois life with her now-married progenitor, or in *Vanya on 42nd Street* (1994), whose titular character must face a dreary daily life after Yelena's departure (putting an end to the mix of elation and despair her presence used to call forth), the movement invariably goes from fun, chaos and extravagance to the termination of all that, more commonly named 'end of innocence'. This division is very present in our three autobiographical films.

The end of innocence is the very subject of *Au revoir les enfants* whose title can self-evidently be read as a farewell to childhood itself. The inscribed coda refers not only to the tragedy that is taking place but also to a break in time. All that occurs between the Gestapo's arrival in the school and the farewell in the courtyard marks Julien's transition from childhood to adulthood. He is acquiring a sense not only of the injustice and absurdity of the world, but also, more subtly, of its complexity: the priests, whom he despises and considers part of the establishment, are those who risk their lives to help his Jewish classmates; the young man who is on the victims' side (Joseph) is the one who denounces them. The director of *Lacombe Lucien* suddenly starts to realise the impossibility, not of distinguishing right from wrong (as has so often been said about him), but of considering oneself on the right side, in a morally comfortable position.

Murmur of the Heart is entirely based on the notion of the end of innocence. The film's running gag, so to speak, is Laurent's continually interrupted sexual initiation: the first attempt, with the prostitute, is a disaster; when he starts to kiss a girl at a party, he is disgusted when she uses her tongue; a young woman he brings up to his hotel room will not have sex because she wants to wait for the right one. All this builds up to the incest scene which marks Laurent's first real sexual experience. Before that point, he is constantly being referred to as a child – by the nanny, the hotel's clients, the father, or the brothers, and even more so by the mother. In contrast to *Au revoir les enfants*, the ending is not brutal but solemn and beautiful, despite an air of melancholy, as exemplified by the mother/son conversation after the incest which can be read as a mutual goodbye: 'I don't want you to be unhappy, to be ashamed or even sorry about this. We will remember it as a very beautiful, very poignant moment which will never take place again.' The passage from childhood to adulthood is also made explicit by the last scene in which Laurent comes back to his mother's room, after spending the rest of the night with a girl his own age, and finds his whole family there waiting for him. One by one they all break into peals of laughter. The flippant and gratified manner in which the men in the family greet him is indicative of his new status as a legitimate member of society. Interestingly, in a previous draft of the script, after having sex with his mother, Laurent committed suicide in the bath, which was meant to represent an act of shame, but could also be seen, not unlike in *The Fire Within*, as a refusal to enter that other realm, a desire to remain a child.

For Milou, a sixty-year-old unpragmatic 'child' living with his mother who has never earned a cent and is only happy in a natural environment, it is obvious that his mother's death and the prospect of selling the family house constitute a traumatic break with this state of infancy, the passage from a life ruled by nature and poetry to a confrontation with solitude and bitter reality. 'I will not be deprived of my childhood', he insists. The house is not the mere repository of his childhood memories, but the metonymy of childhood itself. Its sale therefore entails the end of this state of withdrawal from the 'serious' world (personified by solicitors, doctors, and the like). Thanks to May '68, though, this passage from one realm to the other is momentarily postponed. With its famous slogan, *l'imagination au pouvoir* ('all power to the imagination'), May '68 refers to a state of childhood or utopia: no more rules, class divisions or 'strangers' (everyone talks to everyone else in the streets). This frame of mind contaminates the family itself: these very matter-of-fact bourgeois start dreaming of transforming the house into a commune with hundreds of people, of producing their own food, of free love. And then, suddenly, everything falls back into place: De Gaulle returns, family dissensions (about who will get the mother's jewelry) and money issues crop up again. This abrupt ending to a beautiful parenthesis is indicated by two typical administrative operations: the burial of the mother in the family vault (rather than on the property itself) and the sale of the house, followed by the family's dispersion. Each member of the family, except Milou, goes back to his life; the children leave. It's the end of the holidays, a theme very central to Malle's world. One of the films that galvanised his directorial ambitions was Roger Leenhardt's *Les Dernières vacances* (*The Last Vacation*, 1948), which depicts the last summer a family spends in their ancestral home and the way the children try to prevent the sale of the house (see Billard 2003: 76–7). Whenever the end of the holidays arrived in our house in the southwest of France, not far from where *May Fools* was shot, my father would become deeply melancholic. I remember him once murmuring to himself as he looked out the kitchen window: 'The end of the holidays, the end of the day, the end of life.' Such a sentiment is perfectly encapsulated by the eponymous protagonist at the very end of *Zazie dans le métro* when she tells her mother, after a crazy weekend in Paris with her uncle Gabriel: *J'ai vieilli* ('I've aged / grown older'). The party's over.

The Fictional Mother Belongs to the Realm of Childhood

Murmur of the Heart is the most obvious example of this. In the way she speaks, moves, touches people, Clara offers a stark contrast with her heavy, serious bourgeois environment. She is free, spontaneous, childlike – the polar opposite of her husband, who is reserved, critical, endlessly discussing politics and repeating what he's read in the newspaper. While Laurent despises his father (at the end he asks his mother if he really is his son) and loathes Jesuit hypocrisy or repression, he admires his mother's freedom and sensuality. For Laurent (and the spectator), Clara is on the side of simplicity, nature and childhood. Mother and son are on the same side against the adult world. As Clara says in the scene where Laurent is sick and the nanny storms off because she doesn't want him to get too excited listening to his mother sing to him in Italian: 'You see,

I always get scolded because of you, always.' The mother character in *Murmur of the Heart* thus has an entirely different set of values than the ones that govern her milieu: she is seductive (at the spa she is always letting herself be chatted up by Laurent's friends); she has a lover and cannot bear it when he becomes too possessive ('like a husband'); she walks around half-naked in the hotel room she shares with her son. At one point she leaves him at the hotel to spend a couple of days with her lover, which is instantly noted by all the clients at the spa who take pity on the young boy for having such a promiscuous mother. Laurent (whose surname, Chevalier, means 'knight' in French) takes her side. When a very respectable lady calls him 'my poor little boy', he replies: 'I'm neither poor, nor particularly little, and I'm certainly not yours.' Mother and son are together and alone in this rejection of social conventions. After she comes back from her escapade, there is a beautiful moment, before the incest scene, where she shares her feelings, her broken heart and her frustrations with him. They are no longer mother and son, but equals and friends.

In *Au revoir les enfants*, the mother is no longer a sensual Italian expatriate but a devoutly Catholic, upper-class bourgeoise. It is remarkable, however, that every time she appears on screen, she has a softness and a dreamlike quality that transform her, like her *Murmur of the Heart* counterpart, into an incarnation of youth. As opposed to the harshness of this world of young boys and priests, where survival of the fittest is the rule, the mother represents warmth, playfulness and charm. In the very first scene, at the train station, before Julien goes off to school, the humour, the complicity, the innocence which are an integral part of her character clearly stand out in opposition to the brutal and austere environment of the school Julien is heading towards ('What about me? Have you thought of me? I miss you every second. I'd like to dress up as a boy and go with you to your school. We could see each other every day. It would be our secret.') Another scene shows how the mother, in *Au revoir les enfants*, as much as the one in *Murmur of the Heart*, is always set apart from the rest of her milieu, even as she completely takes part in it, and more generally from the adult world, its seriousness and dread. In the restaurant scene, the mother's general attitude (towards Bonnet, the young Jewish boy whom she has invited to join them and whose relatives she thinks she knows because the bourgeoisie always thinks everyone is related; towards

Fig. 1: *Au revoir les enfants* (1987): Mother and son.

Fig. 2: *May Fools* (1989): Dying with her dolls.

Julien; even towards the Germans) is so naïve and playful that it becomes unexpectedly charming and innocent. Bonnet looks at her as if she were from another planet, not only because he is not from that social class at all, but because she is so vivid and lively, with her quick pattern of speech and her spontaneity. Even Julien, at one point, says tenderly: 'My mother? She's nuts.'

In *May Fools*, the mother's childlike quality is most obviously expressed by her physique: she is petite, has huge expressive eyes and a dreamy smile. It is probably not a coincidence that the actress who plays the role, Paulette Dubost, is most particularly remembered for playing Lisette, the adorable wide-eyed, innocent and mischievous maid in Jean Renoir's *La Règle du jeu* (*The Rules of the Game*, 1939). The scene, at the very beginning of *May Fools*, where the mother suffers a heart attack, is also a wonderful evocation of her undramatic, light-hearted reaction to approaching death. As she slowly walks up the stairs, trying to catch her breath, she sings a very gay, old-fashioned children's song. Typically, she dies looking into the eyes of a group of dolls. Though she does not appear explicitly in one of the most beautiful scenes of the film, her presence permeates it. It takes place just after her death, the same night. Milou is in bed and starts crying like a little boy. We hear an owl cry and then all of a sudden the nocturnal bird is there, on the windowsill, looking at him. The mother has come back to see him, reincarnated into this beautiful, otherworldly creature. The supernatural quality of the scene is, if not underlined, palpably there, like a scene out of the surrealistic *Black Moon* (1975). During the film, the mother's ghost returns twice. First, when Leonce, the property's jack-of-all-trades, is digging her grave in the garden at night. It is no coincidence that she would appear to him, who, just as much as she, represents, with his regional accent, his ancestral-looking face, his attachment to his dog and his bees, and to nature in general, the childlike, rebellious grace of this area of France Malle so loved for its permanence. And then, of course, there is the final scene. Everyone has left, including Françoise, Milou's ten-year-old granddaughter and the only person in the family he has a real rapport with. Milou enters the empty house. We hear music wafting from one of the rooms in the back: it is the mother playing a very vibrant ragtime and joining Milou for a dance. Again, the maternal figure is associated with fantasy and gaiety, a whole dimension of life that the sale of the house will force Milou to leave behind.

A Key to the Unconscious

Though loving, kind and extremely intelligent, the 'real' Françoise Malle was a far cry from a carefree 'soixante-huitarde'. She was, for one, very much a product of her class and milieu. Heiress of the Beghin sugar empire, one of the big late-nineteenth-century industrial fortunes, she was part of what Malle, in *Parlez moi d'elle*, describes as an 'aristocracy', with the arrogance that goes with it, in a way which, he adds, his father – also from a very bourgeois background – was not. As such, she had certain standards for her children. She was the one in charge of their education and counseling them on their future.[1] She wrote innumerable and beautiful letters to Louis' older brother, Bernard, about his calling as a writer. Admittedly, she could also be quite unsentimental and tyrannical with her children.[2] When Jean-François, her eldest, joined the Leclerc division in 1945, which was a very perilous enterprise, Françoise sent him a letter telling him that it would perhaps knock some sense into him, or more disturbingly in the original French: *lui mettre du plomb dans la tête*, ('put some lead into his head').[3] She had perfectly mapped out Louis' future as first a prestigious 'Polytechnicien' and then future head of the Beghin factory, as she considered that he was the one who was the most like Henri, her father, the one who had brought the factory to its international level.[4] Malle claims the slap she gave him when he told her he wanted to make films determined his vocation. A letter she sent to his brother Bernard shows how pragmatic and direct she was where her children are concerned:

> I completely agree with what you say about Louis [he was thirteen at the time]. He thinks he is the center of the world. I hope he will soon get rid of this

Fig. 3: Françoise Malle, the matriarch.

unpleasant trait and discover how sterile it is to be constantly contemplating one's feelings. For the moment his mood is rather unstable. Every time he talks to someone new, he decides on a new career. His latest hobby is movies. We will not oppose this systematically, I mean writing scripts and directing, as he really doesn't have the looks to become a star, this said without any judgement on his anatomy. In any case, children are a source of great distress and parents will surely become more and more scarce, discouraged as they will surely become by the job's difficulty.[5]

Unlike the somewhat irresponsible and 'out of it' mothers in *Au revoir les enfants* and *Murmur of the Heart,* Françoise Malle was definitely the one in charge in her marriage. Her husband, Pierre Malle, is famous for having stated: 'I take care of my wife and my wife takes care of the rest of the world.'

She also seems to have been less close to her children, and in particular to Louis himself, than what she is portrayed to be in these films. In *Parlez moi d'elle*, Malle says it is precisely because she was otherwise 'never there' that he remembers his murmur of the heart period, the year during which she took him out of boarding school and devoted herself to him, so intensely. Normally Françoise was taken in a whirlwind of activities: charity work, political duties, mass attendance, social activities, manifold artistic interests, the education of seven children and an intense relationship with her husband, Pierre, which lasted throughout their whole life (as attested by a correspondence spanning over more than sixty years).[6]

Why, then, such a discrepancy between fact and fiction in works that purport to be autobiographical? My hypothesis is that what Malle understands by autobiography has less to do with biographical data than with an attempt to map out his own psyche and to explore the world of unconscious fantasies underlying his experience.

Diving into the Unconscious

It is important to note that Malle's very first film, *Crazéologie* (1953), made while he was still at the Institute for Advanced Cinematographic Studies (IDHEC), is very much influenced by surrealism and by Ionesco (Malle even helped to finance the first production at the Parisian theatre La Huchette, famous for playing Ionesco's *The Lesson/The Bald Soprano* in permanent repertory since 1957 [see Billard 2003: 112–15]), and that his last project, based on Maria Riva's book on her mother, Marlene Dietrich, which was in production when Malle became terminally ill, was to be a sort of frantic dance, a funny but threatening libido-driven spectacle. Though Malle is sometimes considered as a filmmaker who, while denouncing the bourgeoisie, films in a bourgeois, classical manner, one can safely say that his work constantly refers to a realm which neither logic nor reason have access to, in an attempt to liberate the unconscious fantasies that civilisation represses. His interest in India stems from the possibility his trip there offered him to put Western principles and taboos into perspective. The importance, for him, of a movement like May '68 also has to do with the questioning of bourgeois values, including the Western view of the family.

Black Moon is perhaps his most radical attempt at expressing his deepest unconscious fantasies.

In the case of the three films I have examined, it seems difficult to speak of such a hardcore endeavor. *Murmur of the Heart* and *May Fools* are relatively light-hearted comedies, and *Au revoir les enfants* is a classical evocation of one of the darkest pages of European history. Yet the process of creating these films seems, at least in the case of *Murmur of the Heart* and *Au revoir les enfants*, to have involved a good deal of unconscious elements. Right after he abandoned the idea of adapting Bataille's *Ma mère*, Malle wrote in a very short period of time a long treatment, which was the basis for the script of *Murmur of the Heart*. Discussing this process with Philip French, he evokes the famous 'automatic writing' of the Surrealists, something emerging from him as if it were being dictated to him (1993: 107). In his personal notes, he writes: '*Murmur*: this film, I didn't do it on purpose. So I can't talk about it (and yet !!!).'[7] It is interesting that this first draft of the film was written shortly after a ten-page text entitled 'The Mind as concentration camp', in which, in the summer of 1971, under the influence of some potent drug, Malle reflects at length on the reasons why Westerners chose to 'close the lid' on their unconscious processes, at the price of their relationship to the world around them.[8]

About *Au revoir les enfants*, Malle confesses that it is only when he saw the film on television that he realised how important the place of the mother was in it – as if it had emerged on its own, unconsciously.[9] While *May Fools* is arguably a more deliberate case, it was written with Jean-Claude Carrière, co-writer of many of Luis Buñuel's scripts, which is no coincidence given the early ambition to give the film a bizarre, oneiric quality.

If we look at these three films from the angle of the representation of the mother, it is obvious that all three, and not only *Murmur of the Heart*, stage a transgression of the most fundamental taboo of all: incest, which Malle always harbored a deep interest in. In *Parlez-moi d'elle*, he contrasts the 'primitive' nature of the father/daughter incestuous relationship with the tender, delicate mother/son fusion, which he calls, provocatively, 'the ideal relationship'. All three films, in their own way, enact the fantasy of such a rapport. In all three mother and son are, in a way, in a conjugal relationship, with a father who is either physically present but uncharismatic and not interested in the mother (*Murmur of the Heart*), barely mentioned (as a rival – *papa, je le déteste!*) but physically absent (*Au revoir les enfants*), or never mentioned at all (*May Fools*). In *Murmur of the Heart*, mother and son sleep in the same hotel room. She undresses in front of him and bathes with the door open. She mockingly calls him 'my little husband' and, when she comes back from an unhappy escapade with her lover, Laurent is the one who finds the right words to console her. The fact that this 'ideal relationship' is consumed sexually is almost secondary, a natural consequence of their mutual tenderness (these are the words Malle uses in *Parlez-moi d'elle* to describe their relationship in that film). In *Au revoir les enfants*, we have the same type of exclusive bond between Julien and his mother. They are apart from the rest, whispering to each other, hugging each other (Julien's older brother calls them 'lovebirds'). In the letters Mme Quentin sends Julien as well as in the words she says to him in the first scene, there is a tenderness that always borders on sensuality (see the lipstick trace she leaves on his cheek after kissing him). In *May Fools*, Milou and his mother *are* a couple, in a way, since the father has died and Milou lives with her in the same house. He is the last person she calls before dying, and, when all the rest of the family go back to their life, she and Milou are finally left alone together.

In an interview with Jacques Chancel,[10] Malle said: 'I don't really know what I'm looking for but I'm looking for it tirelessly.' To me, it is this very search that made him exceptional as a man and as a filmmaker. In his work, he did try, tirelessly, to go deeper and deeper into his emotions, deeper than where words could ever bring him (which is why, in the same interview, he mentioned he would have loved, above all, to be a musician). Through the 'paradox' of the figure of the mother in these three autobiographical films, we see that, far from aiming for a simple, documentary-like reconstitution of the world of his childhood and of the experience of his mother's death, Malle attempted to dive into himself and to open the lid of his own psyche.

Notes

1   See her correspondence with the Jesuit fathers about Louis in the Malle archives at the Bibliothèque du Film/Cinémathèque Française.
2   See *Parlez-moi d'elle*.
3   Ibid.
4   Ibid.
5   Private Malle family archives.
6   Ibid.
7   Bibliothèque du Film/Cinémathèque Française MALLE 0376B94.
8   MALLE 0390 B96.
9   *Parlez-moi d'elle*.
10 Radioscopie cinéma, 'Jacques Chancel reçoit Louis Malle', France Inter 1972.

Bibliography

Billard, P. (2003) *Louis Malle. Le rebelle solitaire*. Paris: Plon.
Bredin, J.-D. and B. C. Bastide (2016) *Parlez-moi d'elle*. Editions Radio France/INA.
French, P. (ed.) (1993) *Malle on Malle*. London: Faber and Faber.

CHAPTER TEN

Jazz as Counterpoint in Elevator to the Gallows, Murmur of the Heart *and* Pretty Baby

Jean-Louis Pautrot

Throughout his career, Louis Malle paid great attention to sound, evaluating film scenes that he shot by how they sounded (see Billard 2003: 317).[1] The care and trust extended to music, which Malle always used meaningfully. Among his musical choices, jazz held a special place and was indeed one of his lifelong interests. As a director, he included this music genre in the soundtracks of almost a third of his films (seven out of 25 commercial full-length releases). *Lacombe Lucien* (1974), set in 1944 during the German occupation, used seminal period tracks by Django Reinhardt, Stéphane Grappelli and the Quintette du Hot Club de France. *Milou en mai* (*May Fools, 1989*) featured a virtuosic Grappelli score as background to an exuberant social comedy set in May 1968. In *Au revoir les enfants* (1987), the Jewish and Gentile youngsters, Jean and Julien, cement their bond by playing a four-hand boogie-woogie on the piano. *Alamo Bay* (1985) resorts to Ry Cooder's distinctive southwestern mix of Chicano, Tejano and blues influences. Malle's last film, *Vanya on 42nd Street* (1994), features, in an echo to his first, the music of a young, upcoming jazz musician, Joshua Redman. This chapter will, however, focus on three other Malle films where the use of jazz is at once diverse and particularly meaningful, for biographical and artistic reasons: *Ascenseur pour l'échafaud* (*Elevator to the Gallows, 1957*), *Le Souffle au cœur* (*Murmur of the Heart, 1971*) and *Pretty Baby* (*1978*).

In a groundbreaking essay Michel Chion identifies three main functions of film music: as a structural element, as a window to the world and as a topic or a metaphor (1995: 187–292). Following Roland Barthes' *L'Obvie et l'obtus*, Véronique Campan lists three types of listening to film music: listening for clues, listening for meaning and listening for desire (1999: 9–11). Rearranging these categories somewhat, I propose to apply to Malle's films three reading codes: music as a cultural marker, music as an affective emotional marker and music as an ontological marker – all of which contribute to the films' aesthetic configurations as structural elements.

What broadly defines each film seems self-evident: in *Pretty Baby*, jazz serves as a cultural, historical marker of the 1917 period in New Orleans; in *Murmur of the Heart*, it acts as an affective, autobiographical marker; the mesmerising yet detached jazz of *Elevator to the Gallows* is first and foremost an ontological marker. Upon closer scrutiny, however, lines start to blur. To take but one example, *Murmur of the Heart* also uses jazz as a cultural marker, while Charlie Parker's stunning and unpredictable musical phrases also serve at the ontological level. These categories will nevertheless provide a convenient tool for analysis, but not until we first examine how Malle's approach to jazz interrelates to other traits of his artistic *ethos*: rebellion against Western society, *bourgeois* values and 'taste'; a drive to show what has never been seen; a detached, non-judgemental, documentary-like outlook at the world that signals an endless curiosity;[2] and a lasting influence of the absurd as theorised by Albert Camus among others, and as represented by the Theater of the Absurd in the 1950s.

A Lifelong Relationship

In 1992, Malle's first words to Philip French depict his early love of music, before literature and, later, cinema: 'Music was (a great passion). I went very quickly from Beethoven to Louis Armstrong to Charlie Parker at the age of fourteen, fifteen and sixteen [i.e. 1946–1948]' (1993: 1). This was no mere passing teenage infatuation. In an essay on film music penned for the magazine *Jazz Hot*, he was more explicit about his youth and the evolution of his taste, making it clear that the passion carried into adulthood:

> Although I am not very old, I can say that I am an old fan of jazz. When I was 10 or 11, I was forced to learn piano and developed a real aversion to music, and it was through jazz that I returned to appreciating classical music. Today, I am an avid music listener, and have arrived at a certain equilibrium between jazz and classical music. I remember a time when each month I would buy every 78 rpm that appeared. Louis Armstrong was of course my first idol … [now] Miles Davis is probably my favorite jazz soloist (1960: 14)

The passion bloomed in 1948–49, when Malle found himself in Paris, relatively unsupervised, studying without enthusiasm and entertaining a busy social agenda. He collected jazz records, some bought in stores; typical of a true, obsessive jazz fan, those unavailable in France he obtained from stationed American troops. He almost certainly was a regular reader of *Jazz Hot*, the only jazz magazine that not only provided news, but also, with André Hodeir as Editor-in-Chief, proposed articulate, almost scholarly analysis, and considered jazz a true art form.

It was at that time that Malle realised that, following the example of Jacques Becker's *Rendez-vous de juillet* (*Rendezvous in July*, 1949), cinema and jazz could be used jointly to great effect. In May 1949 he also attended the International Jazz Festival in Paris (Salle Pleyel), organised by Charles Delaunay, President of the Hot Club de France and owner of *Jazz Hot*. While Charlie Parker and Sidney Bechet were the headliners (see Tournès 1999: 128), Miles Davis was being featured for the first time in France.[3] In his journal Malle enthusiastically praised the latter's 'round, polished, velvety and so musical sound' (cited by Billard 2003: 88), which led, several years later, to his approaching Miles for *Elevator to the Gallows*. The festival program reflected the on-going battle of the Ancients and the Moderns, pitting the 'moldy figs' who remained true to a traditional, pre-war jazz against the 'sour grapes' who advocated be-bop, the new style that incubated during World War II and appeared on records in 1946.[4] Malle was aware of the quarrel, as it filled the columns of *Jazz Hot* and made for animated discussions among his friends. His journal entries on the festival testify that if he loved Davis's and Parker's ground-breaking playing, he was also ecstatic at Bechet's New Orleans-tinged, more sedate style (see Billard 2003: 88).[5] Years later, the contrastive tension was to make its way into *Murmur of the Heart*, with Parker's and Bechet's respective music styles.

If, from 1951 to 1953, Malle studied cinema at the Institut Des Hautes Études Cinématographiques (IDHEC), jazz remained a focus. Alain Cavalier listed the 'heroes' of his group of friends as Charlie Parker, Eugène Ionesco and Robert Bresson. Around that time, Malle also started a friendship with Boris Vian, whose literary genius and taste for Alfred Jarry and surrealism impressed him (see Billard 2003: 112–13), but whose vast knowledge of jazz history and personal acquaintance with African-American jazz creators must also have been attractive. Another indicator of Malle's sustained fascination with jazz while at IDHEC is the short student film he made in January 1953, titled *Crazéologie*, a transposition of Parker's 'Crazeology'.[6] As for its subtitle, 'Essai de rendu cinématographique de l'absurde théâtral ou littéraire', it refers to Ionesco as much as Buñuel, and betrays affinities with Queneau. In a dramatic climax reminiscent of Ionesco's play *La Leçon* (*The Lesson*, 1951), the Parker record is repeatedly broken and replaced. Besides Louis' older brother, Bernard, the actors were Nicolas Bataille and Pierre Frag, two Ionesco regulars at La Huchette theatre. Jazz's 'craziness' was thus tied to the developing absurdist movement,[7] and *Crazéologie* constitutes an 'important revelator of his outlook on the world', where comedy and tragedy merge in an emotionally bland and amoral manner (see Billard 2003: 114–18).

The desire to make a film set in New Orleans and documenting the infancy of jazz also seems to date back to the formative early 1950s:

> The reason that I decided to go [to the US] is that one of my long-term projects [was] to make a film about the beginnings of jazz. I've always been fascinated by the jazz pianist Jelly Roll Morton. [Alan Lomax] recorded Morton talking and playing the piano – a sort of interview with music. Jelly Roll tells his version of the beginning of jazz… (French 1993: 117)

Indeed, when Polly Platt, who was to co-write *Pretty Baby*'s screenplay, asked in 1976 what interested him about America, Malle replied: 'The music that came from New

Orleans, in the early 1900s' (Southern 2006: 173). He may also have mentioned one of his unfinished projects, a 1967 script titled 'Jelly Roll', co-written with American playwright Jack Gelber, that was to be a biopic of Morton, adapted from Lomax's biography (Southern 2006: 343). Pierre Billard traces Malle's interest in the Morton project even further back, to 1964, probably because the translation into French (by Henri Parisot) of Lomax's book appeared that year. There is actually evidence that Malle reflected on the project before 1964. In the above-mentioned 1960 *Jazz Hot* article, he writes: 'I have always dreamed of starting from the remarkable Jelly Roll Morton recordings for the Library of Congress, because I think it would make for an extraordinary film' (1960: 15). The obvious conclusion is that Malle had read the book in English by 1960. It so happens that Boris Vian owned a copy of the original (1950) edition.[8] It is thus not unreasonable to surmise that Vian either recommended the book or even let Malle borrow it from him.

All of this anchors Malle's later determination to use jazz in all three films in the years prior to his becoming a filmmaker, and thus speaks to the profound, lasting impact that jazz had on his life and career. It has been rightly pointed out that jazz served Malle's cinema vocation as much as travels, readings and his outlook on the world (Billard 2003: 93–4). Like books, jazz is an intellectual venture; like traveling, it is a cultural experience. It is also rebellion turned into art, a medium where form is crucial in conveying a different perspective, an existential manner of being that challenges established values, one of the first aesthetic attacks on Eurocentrism.

Elevator to the Gallows

The musical soundtrack to *Elevator to the Gallows* has become as famous as the film. To jazzologists, it marked a turning point in Miles Davis's composing and playing, as it betrayed an emerging evolution from a harmony-based, tonal and chromatic style to a new modal language that he would fully develop on later albums. From a film history perspective, it is groundbreaking as the first feature-length experiment in a live-recorded jazz soundtrack, conducted with a true musical innovator. Malle considered it 'one of the biggest opportunities in [his] career' (1960: 14).[9]

Accounts vary on how the venture originated, but it has been ascertained that François Leterrier (Malle's assistant), Marcel Romano (Davis's impresario in Europe), and Boris Vian (then A&R director for Phillips Records) were instrumental in the meeting of musician and director, as well as the recording session and subsequent release of the disc. Malle recalled : '[I]t is uncanny [...] as I listened to Miles Davis records exclusively during the filming; [...] as I imagined, without much hope, that he could provide the music, suddenly Miles was landing in Paris' (1960: 14, 15). Romano approached Davis on Malle's behalf upon the trumpeter's arrival for a European tour and subsequent tenure at the Club St. Germain. As Davis 'hadn't done anything like it before, he asked to see the film and … if he liked it, he would gladly give it a try' (1960: 14; see also Davis 1990: 217). The recording was completed in one night on 4/5 December 1957, at the Poste Parisien radio studio.[10] As shown in a short promotional film released at the time,[11] the band played along to selected scenes, screened in loops in front of them. This meant that tracks had to be short, and Urtreger's recollection of the evening is that of a repeated 'coitus interruptus' (quoted by Desarthe 2016: 140); 26 minutes and 16 seconds of recorded music appear on the soundtrack album (Pejrolo 2001: 74), but only '18 maximum' were used in the 92-minute film (French 1993: 19), which makes for sparse use of film music.

Malle met Davis days before, showed him the edited film 'only twice', and they 'agreed on the parts where [they] felt music was needed' (French 1993: 19). Davis had a piano brought to his hotel room (see Perchard 2015: 124), and took ideas to the Club St. Germain to try out with the band: 'Miles had prepared chord sequences, simple chords based on modes' (Urtreger quoted by Pejrolo 2001: 233). Davis thus chose ahead of time what harmonic, modal and possibly melodic material to use. At 'rehearsals' and in the studio, Davis gave further instructions: he showed Urtreger specific piano voicings of clustered notes in the low register; some musicians were excused from certain tracks for specific effect (see Pejrolo 2001: 234). Malle, who supervised the recording session, helped orient the playing by explaining what each scene was about, then asking for something that 'underlined' and 'emphasized' the images (Michelot quoted by Pejrolo 2001: 233), sometimes voicing the need for a musical 'counterpoint' (Michelot quoted by Perchard 2015: 125). It should also be noted that Malle added significant postproduction to the recorded music: he 'used certain takes for sequences other than the ones they were recorded for' and, in the crucial scenes when Florence wanders in the streets at night, added reverberation to Davis's trumpet (see Perchard 2015: 125, 129).

If, then, the band improvised their parts on the spot, as Pierre Michelot and Kenny Clarke describe it (see Pejrolo 2001: 233), they did so not only within pre-charted musical territory and pre-assigned filmic boundaries, but with precise prompting from the director. *Elevator to the Gallows*' score is neither 'completely improvised', as Malle later claimed (French 1993: 19), nor the child of one or several musicians, but a collaborative creation between a determined young director, an extraordinary frontman, and a well-honed modern jazz band. Malle judiciously remarked that, when listened to independently from the film, the music 'remains rather shapeless', and conversely that the film would be sorely lacking without the soundtrack (1960: 14).

What exactly does jazz music bring to *Elevator to the Gallows*? We have Malle's own, enlightening analysis to ponder regarding Davis's contribution which, I contend, critics have overlooked or misinterpreted, missing key elements. 'I showed a Paris not of the future but at least a modern city, a world already dehumanized', said Malle (quoted by Rafferty 2006). Jazz in the film may indeed be construed as partaking in such modernisation and moral detachment, not to say emotional numbness, and in that respect it acts as a cultural marker of Americanness. It would, however, be wrong to think it merely reflects the *zeitgeist* 'of postwar, existentialist "caves" in Paris, as it does in a number of other films of the period. *Elevator to the Gallows*' music is groundbreaking, powerful and efficient enough to function beyond the role of realistic 'sonic background' (Chion 1995: 135). This has not escaped some scholars, who describe it as 'discreet but haunting' (Prédal 1989: 16), as 'gloomy, dark, mysterious, but not tragic' (Pejrolo 2001: 119), or as giving the film 'its tone and its tension', a sort of 'muted anxiety' (Billard 2003: 166). It is so intense and carefully placed that it colours the whole film, and 'transcends its force and modernity' (Mouëllic 2000: 84).

In his essay on film music, Malle begins by stating his dislikes in the matter, explaining that '99 times out of a 100, [film and music] do not agree, or agree too much' (1960: 14), as not enough attention is paid to their interaction. He criticises, on one hand, the pleonastic use of music that simply mimics or amplifies the images – a practice known as 'mickey-mousing' – and, at the other extreme, the artificially synchronous 'pasting' on images of music conceived separately and with a different artistic logic in mind. Malle also theorises further what he encouraged the musicians to do in the studio: 'a successful film music must be the complement, the contrary and the commentary of images' (1960: 14). *Elevator to the Gallows*' music achieved that goal because Malle sensed beforehand that 'there was an undeniable relation between [Davis's artistic] sensibility and what the film tried to express' (ibid.). He resorts repeatedly, as he did in the studio, to a key word, describing Davis's contribution as 'a sort of natural counterpoint' to images, then adding that he planned the shooting script so that, in specific scenes, music was to be an 'essential counterpoint' without which these scenes 'could not exist' (ibid.). One can hardly miss the opposition drawn here between 'essence' and 'existence', so central to Sartre's existentialism, and the role assigned to music of functioning at the 'essential', or ontological, level. To Malle, music here reveals an otherwise inaccessible truth about the world represented in the film. The filmmaker varied little from this analysis and reiterated in 1992 that 'the soundtrack of *Elevator* "wasn't like a lot of film music": "it was a counterpoint, it was elegiac … somewhat detached", and it eventually "helped the film "t[ake] off"' (French 1993: 19).

The terms that Malle chose, years apart, are charged with meaning and history. Using sound or music as *counterpoint* is a notion as old as sound cinema. At the advent of sound, in 1928, Soviet filmmakers S. M. Eisenstein, V. I. Pudovkin and G.V. Alexandrov published 'A Statement' calling for a creative, non-redundant use of sound-image relationship, and advocating 'an orchestral counterpoint of visual and aural images' (1985: 84). A year later, Pudovkin published his essay 'Asynchronism as a Principle of Sound Film', describing the role of sound as 'much more significant than slavish imitation of naturalism'; its first function was 'to augment the potential expressiveness of the film's content' (1985: 86). Avoidance of redundancy, contrasting separate messages that combine to reach a complex, enhanced meaning, these notions resonate with Malle's remarks almost word for word. As a former IDHEC student, Malle was undoubtedly familiar with the Soviet directors' theories, and probably borrowed the term from them, as evidenced by his mention of Eisenstein's experiments in his *Jazz Hot* essay:

> One of the few notable filmmakers who became interested in this problem was Eisenstein. In his last two films, he pushed an experiment to the limit, a manner of approaching film music quasi mathematically. Prokofiev's music is written as a systematic counterpoint to the image. (1960: 15)

Malle may also have been familiar with Theodor W. Adorno and Hanns Eisler's *Composing for the Films*, in which they discuss Eisentein's experiments. They advocate a use of music in opposition to what is usually expected – not as an expression of inner feelings, but as a 'distanciation' (Adorno and Eisler 1951: 10), which recalls Malle's depiction of Davis's work as 'detached'. Moreover, they specify that music 'should not be introduced at all costs' (1951: 121), especially not to fabricate an ambiance or fill a void, which is consonant with its spare use in *Elevator to the Gallows*. Finally, they call for music that combines with the film 'to create a productive tension and a global meaning (images, dialogues, and music)' (1972: 122), which is what the director alluded to when he described the film as 'taking off', as providing a wider perspective. Malle is therefore speaking as someone knowledgeable in music history and theory, whose reflection centres on the idea of counterpoint.

How does that counterpoint theory translate into *Elevator to the Gallows*' jazz soundtrack? Michel Chion points out that 'the absence or quasi-absence of music' in a film is never meaningless (1995: 241). Malle's precise plans for *Elevator to the Gallows*' music prove that he wanted some scenes 'highlighted', in a film that otherwise contains much silence and a relative scarcity of dialogues. Music is then, first and foremost, part of a tri-partite aural experience, and its function depends on the other two elements. Of the ten musical occurrences in *Elevator to the Gallows*, one belongs to what Chion calls 'screen music' (1985: 153), meaning that its source is clearly located in the diegetic action and within the frame: the track titled 'Au bar du petit bac', meant to be coming out of a jukebox as Florence enters the bar, looking for Julien, during her endless, nocturnal perambulation. This specific use points to a cultural marking, as one of several 'US cultural signifiers' (Perchard 2015: 119), like Julien's American convertible and his gun, that are meant to show a mutating French culture. The other nine tracks are 'pit' or 'acousmatic' music (Chion 1985: 154), the source of which cannot be located anywhere on screen, thus acquiring a more complex structural role. It has been remarked that some of the acousmatic tracks are 'empathic' music, destined to inform about the characters or maximise the suspense: 'Sur l'autoroute', 'Julien dans l'ascenceur', and 'Visite du vigile' are part of those 'moments when music and event are tied' with a view to heighten drama. Such tracks clearly act as emotional markers, but 'play a minor role' (Perchard 2015: 127) and are not the most memorable.

Most significant in the film are the few tracks that accompany Florence's search for Julien at night in the Paris streets ('Florence sur les Champs Élysées', announced by the stunning credit music, 'Générique'), all revolving around similar harmonic sequences and melodic lines and thus echoing each other. They give the soundtrack its mesmerising quality, the film its tone and unity, and are the truly transformative agent.

Most critics consider them also 'empathic' music (Chion 1985: 123). For Colin Nettelbeck, 'Davis's jazz translates and echoes' the plot's climate of existential desolation, 'tapping into emotional anxieties', and 'amplifying what we get from images' (2004: 169): it thereby 'clarifies and liberates what is latent' (2004: 170). For Tom Perchard, the indirect, bluesy music generates 'a sense of cool languor' and empathises with Florence – to the point of sounding like a female voice – with the added reverb imparting a mental-space quality. Davis' trumpet is then Florence's inner voice, a 'projection of the character's psychological state' (2015: 129), prompting the spectator to identify with her (2015: 138). In short, commentators tend to see these tracks as affective markers.

Such conclusions may underestimate how cool jazz, of which Davis was a major proponent, actually operated, less as an expressive commentary than as a mirror:

> Neither appealing to the listener nor ignoring him, the cool performer speaks to him from inside the listener's head. ... Cool fascinates, but not the way inwardness fascinates, the listener is not the observer but the observed. (Eisenberg 1987: 157)

What Davis's trumpet suggests may then be less about Florence's pathos than about a shared experience between character, director, musician and spectator. My contention is that it does not function as empathic translation, but as anempathic 'didactic counterpoint' (Chion 1985: 123) – which is how Malle saw it.

Approaches reading music as reinforcement of psychological realism may also misread Malle's very notion of realism. Malle's noted use in *Elevator to the Gallows* of documentary techniques, influenced by Bresson, Rossellini and others, as well as his own experience filming *Le Monde du silence* (*The Silent World*, 1956) for Cousteau, may not signal increased psychological verisimilitude, but instead, the stating of an enigma. Florence's music does not so much take us deeper into the action as it takes us out of it. The strange phrases and tone of Davis's trumpet places us, in those instances, in front of what Lacan called the 'Real', that dimension of reality excluded from language and other symbolic representations: the World in all its thick, anempathic, foreign otherness. It is no coincidence that Malle liked this quote from Camus' *The Myth of Sisyphus*: 'The absurd is born of this confrontation between the human need ("*l'appel humain*") and the unreasonable silence of the world' (quoted by Billard 2003: 234). The irrational, the human nostalgia – Malle's 'elegiac' – and the absurd that springs from their face-to-face, Camus continues, are the three characters of the human drama. If 'unreasonable silence' in *Elevator to the Gallows* is materially present in the soundtrack, we may infer that the 'human call' is too – in the form of the trumpet call that perpetually tries to make sense of it.

Fig. 1: *Elevator to the Gallows* (1957): Florence (Jeanne Moreau) immersed in her thoughts and in music.

In a sense, Davis's playing exemplifies a unique, privileged function of music, i.e. 'to evoke the deepest mystery of being in existence' in 'a relation of pure otherness' (Rosset 1979: 65) with the rest of reality, or here, of the film. In brief, not an expression of, but a 'counterpoint' to any psychological or diegetic time and state (see Rosset 1979: 69). This is why Malle could describe the film as 'taking off' as soon as music was added: the latter gave the former the extra, heterogeneous dimension, the virtual 'depth of field' necessary to turn an ordinary murder story and study of mores into the sudden relativisation of petty, Parisian, bourgeois society by the World. In that sense, music contains the film, and not the other way around. Gilles Deleuze alone, to my knowledge, sensed that dimension in *Elevator to the Gallows* and other films by Malle: 'one movement of the World replaces the stalled movement of the character' (1985: 80). The rest of the Mallean *oeuvre* confirms that intuition: its one subject is the World, of which it endeavors to make sense without any presupposition. *Elevator to the Gallows*' music, when at its most potent and detached, is, beyond words and dialogues, the human call reverberating amid universal silence, not an answer to the viewer's search for meaning but a question directed at reality – and thus back at us, an unmistakably ontological marker, planned as such by the director, and beautifully articulated by Miles Davis and his musicians.

Murmur of the Heart and Pretty Baby

If both films thematically establish a connection between music and sexuality, *Murmur of the Heart* and *Pretty Baby* are, musically speaking, less innovative than *Elevator to the Gallows*, as they use mostly pre-existing music or recordings. Largely autobiographical (except for the incest), *Murmur of the Heart* is a story of sexual awakening and tumultuous adolescence: 'My passion for jazz, my curiosity about literature, the tyranny of my two elder brothers, how they introduced me to sex – this is pretty close to me' (French 1993: 83).

Jazz represents a crucial part of the experience. Malle's previously noted enthusiasm for Jelly Roll Morton is reflected in the first scene, as part of a discussion on the merits of the Ancients vs. the Moderns that elicits this conclusion from Laurent, the fourteen-year-old protagonist: 'I don't like old jazz. It's always the same

Fig. 2: *Murmur of the Heart* (1971): Reading Boris Vian and listening to Charlie Parker.

thing.' His room is plastered with photos of jazzmen like Louis Armstrong or Sidney Bechet. One recognizes Boris Vian (who was also a trumpeter) and Albert Camus as well, suggesting Laurent's literary tastes while signaling where the director's own influences lie. At one point, Laurent locks himself up in his room to masturbate while reading Vian's *J'irai cracher sur vos tombes* (*I Spit on Your Graves*, 1946) and listening to Charlie Parker.

Murmur of the Heart's music, then, is primarily jazz, although some 'screen music' at the brothel is rhythm 'n' blues, and, at the spa ball near the end, violin and accordion dance music. Credits list the music as being by Sidney Bechet, Charlie Parker, Gaston Frèche and Henri Renaud (the latter two for documentation and incidental music). Two 1949 songs by Bechet are used as 'screen music' to which boys and girls dance and kiss during a surprise-party thrown by Laurent's brothers in their parents' absence: 'Les oignons' and 'Sobbin' and Cryin'', both very popular in this context in 1950s France. The eight Parker numbers are more difficult to identify, as they are never played in entirety, and excerpts heard are fragments of dizzying solos, sometimes from the same number. Strikingly, they always function acousmatically and accompany Laurent, five of them occurring during sexual scenes: Laurent masturbating, sleeping with a prostitute, manipulating his mother's lingerie, having sex with teenage Daphné after the incest. The rest amplify some particular scenes' ebullience: at the record shop, arriving at the spa and sharing a final laugh with the family.

As mentioned above, it seems clear that jazz functions essentially in *Murmur of the Heart* as an emotional, autobiographical marker, through which Malle inoculates his own adolescent enthusiasm, arousal and frenetic energy into the story, as part of the same effort of recreation as other autobiographical details. Yet it also functions as historical marker, providing an external frame to the story timeline, together with the on-going Dien Bien Phu debacle in Indochina, and the sports events listened to on the radio. While this is indeed period music typical of the social milieu in the spring of 1954 (see Billard 2003: 357), there is one major exception: Charlie Parker's music. Compared to the rest of *Murmur of the Heart*'s soundtrack, the Parker excerpts are so complex, so unpredictably driven, so nearly demented, so adult also, that a young provincial *lycéen* would have been unlikely to listen to them (Malle was already seventeen and living in Paris when he saw Parker in concert in 1949). Something here exceeds historical marking and, besides affective marking, points to the ontological level.

For postwar French youth, jazz, especially be-bop, epitomised a form of intellectual revolt and modernity that concentrated crucial traits – 'new-worldness', ideological and moral freedom, physical liberation, an alternative to stuffy 'classical music' (Malle's hated piano lessons), approachable without (too much) musical education. What Parker additionally brought was the notion that vertiginous, telluric forces were at work, impossible to contain, sometimes so furiously overflowing that they turned destructive – and Parker's own demise is a case in point. His 'spark of lunacy' was similar to what compelled contemporary avant-gardes to question Western civilisation (see Hodeir 1954: 212).

What Parker's music brings to the film may be the fundamental confrontation of culture and nature, Apollo vs. Dionysus, rational forces of containment vs. seminal forces of chaos and creation. Such bursting out of nature through cultural customs is as transgressive as incest.

For *Pretty Baby*, Malle used existing music but not original recordings as in *Murmur of the Heart*, because the story set in 1917 New Orleans documents pieces that were not put on records until much later. The music was recorded on location, with obvious care for authenticity. Produced by Jerry Wexler, it included Bob Greene (piano) and a slew of instrumentalists steeped in early jazz tradition, like John Robichaux (drums) whose uncle was a legendary Orleanian bandleader at the turn of the twentieth century. The soundtrack sequence provides a digest of jazz evolution from the origins to the 1920s: ragtimes by Scott Joplin and Louis Chauvin; church-hymn tinged compositions; quadrilles turned into rags; sentimental songs; suggestive double-entendre or downright sexual songs or blues; and five Jelly Roll Morton favourites (out of a total of nineteen). Also included in the film, not on the record, are several songs: in particular, the traditional 'Careless Love' sung by a prostitute during a brothel 'break', famously part of Buddy Bolden's repertoire, and 'Mademoiselle from Armentières' sung by Navy men, a song popular during World War I for its bawdy lyrics.

The compilation, meticulously framing a period when all pieces could be heard in Storyville, indicates that music in the film is foremost intended as a historical, cultural marker, in a long-planned homage to the creators of jazz (the end credits are preceded by the mention: 'With our gratitude to the priceless music of Jelly Roll Morton').

We saw that Malle became interested in early jazz – probably thanks to Boris Vian – through Alan Lomax's biography of Jelly Roll Morton, which includes Morton's memories as recorded for the Library of Congress in 1938, as well as testimonies by a number of musicians who knew him when he played piano in Storyville whorehouses. What probably fascinated Malle, apart from the birth of a new art form, was its connection to the 'District' that facilitated its emergence and where prostitution was permitted by municipal ordinance. Lomax's collection of narratives offers precious, at times documentary, insight into the daily lives of musicians in Storyville, of which creole Morton became a staple (not to mention his illicit activities 'on the hustling side' [1973: 122]), and into a social ranking based on skin colour. Two other books provided the rest of the documentary inspiration that would nurture the writing of *Pretty Baby*:

> I'd read [a book] on early jazz in New Orleans. It was a history of the red-light district, Storyville, and contained a lot of documents, a lot of photographs, and interviews with witnesses from the period. ... [Then] a friend sent me a recently published book of photographs by [E. J.] Bellocq that had been rediscovered ... and published by the Museum of Modern Art in New York. Not only were they remarkable photos, but they were very close to my story [on Morton] because Bellocq's photos were of Storyville prostitutes ... I wrote a twenty-page synopsis putting those two characters together: Bellocq meets Violet and falls in love with both her and her mother. (French 1993: 117)

The MoMA catalog of Bellocq photos directly informed the script and the film visuals, but most of the authentic material included into the script comes from Al Rose's *Story-*

ville, New Orleans, which already contained a dozen of Bellocq's photos of prostitutes, and a description of his activity in the District, praising his 'sensibility' and the respect with which he treated his subjects 'that elevated his photographs to the level of art' (1974: 59). In Rose's book, Malle found a description of the economic system that made Storyville possible and greatly profited from it (1974: 30); a portrait of Jelly Roll Morton that complemented Lomax's (1974: 55); a study of how jazz was used as an incitement to sex, and the role of the brothel pianist;[12] a precise description of racial segregation in the district (1974: 67); and the title of his film, since 'Pretty Baby' was a song by pianist Tony Jackson, much admired by Morton, a successful 'ditty', with lyrics so suggestive of pedophilia that they had to be revised by famous lyricist Gus Kahn before they could be published (1974: 111). Polly Platt recalls hearing Morton's own version, with 'very sexually explicit lyrics' and thinking it would make 'a perfect title for the movie' (quoted by Southern 2006: 174).

Moreover, Malle and Platt found in Rose the central character of the story. Chapter nine, titled 'Some anonymous survivors of Storyville' (1974: 147–66), contains testimonies, frank and informative narratives provided years later by former actors of prostitution: pimp, madam, wealthy customer, poor customer, working girl, 'crib woman' (self-employed). The most gripping account comes from 'Violet', a 'trick baby', whose mother was a whore. Violet performed sexual acts as a child in Emma Johnson's infamously depraved sex show, was made to auction her deflowering at thirteen, became a prostitute afterwards, and yet grew up to become a normal, well-adjusted woman and mother of four. Malle was so impressed by her account, and the fact that she 'never felt sexually abused' (Southern 2006: 179), that he kept the name for the character. With Platt, he centered the script on her coming of age in the claustrophobic and nefarious environment of a whorehouse and on her relationship with Bellocq, whom she marries, still under-age, only to be whisked away at the end by her mother who has married in St. Louis and become a 'respectable' woman.

Fig. 3: *Pretty Baby* (1978): the 'Professor'.

In this context, the imbrication of music and sex is pushed even further than in *Murmur of the Heart*, to the extent that, in addition to music's function as historical marker, the other uses are also at play. Violet's exuberance and rebellion are echoed in the music, much like Laurent's. Even though, unlike in *Murmur of the Heart*, it is not made to be the foremost guiding principle, music still acts as an emotional marker. Furthermore, Violet's platonic friendship with the 'Professor' constitutes an important element of her psychological resilience. The close shot on the pianist's face, at the moment of Violet's 'virgin auction', makes it clear that he deeply resents the situation, but does not voice his revulsion and sticks to cheerful and compelling music playing. More generally, the fact that music can also serve as a shield (against the crushing feelings that prostitution generates in women and men) is perceptible in the switch from exclusive piano 'screen music' in the first half of the film to acousmatic ensemble music in the second half, when Violet has found relative relief from turmoil in the paternal care and love of Bellocq (despite the fact that the latter's relationship with Violet is also sexual). The effect then is less jumpy and titillating, more lyrical and carefree, and signifies peace and protection.

This points to an ontological dimension of music in *Pretty Baby* and closely resonates with Lomax's book as well as 'Big Eye' Louis Nelson Delisle's reflections on the secrets of his art:

> Don't play like no funeral. Keep a lively tempo but 'shove in crying whenever you get the chance'. Then your listeners can dance and feel the tears behind. This is the master formula of jazz – mulatto knowingness ripened by black sorrow. (1973: 93)

This is essentially the portrait of Violet, who goes through adolescence craving for parental presence, hiding her wounds behind a front of bravery, cheerfulness and defiance. This may also have been the essence of what attracted Malle to the early jazz of Jelly Roll Morton and others: an intensely exquisite, sensual experience that belied pain preserved at its core, a way of being multi-dimensionally human.

Conclusion

Malle used the three types of markers in the three films examined with varying proportions and focus, which testifies to his art as a filmmaker. He also seems to have identified with jazz creators inasmuch as he shared their outlook: a refusal of conventions, a desire to impart his own reading on reality, a curiosity about what lies behind accepted limits, the spirit of a perpetual outsider. In closing, it is meaningful to cite remarks that he made years apart and that bring into focus what his artistic maturation owed to music – to jazz, in particular:

> In *Le Monde du silence* … there is a lot of music. For one of the scenes … we did a sort of collective improvisation. … That prompted me to reflect on the idea of improvisation. I am probably more interested in problems raised by

film music than my fellow-directors, and probably because I would have liked to become a musician. (1960: 15)

In 1972, Malle admitted in a radio interview:

Looking back, I realize that I have always lived steeped in music, because music is not an intellectual perception (as opposed to language that offers only 'degraded' communication), it really speaks to something a lot more profound, to the senses. If I had to do it all over again, I think I would have preferred to be a musician. (Chancel 2017: 122)

The emphasis on improvisation and on sensual communication makes it probable that Malle meant in both cases that he would have liked to be a jazz musician.

Notes

1. Candice Bergen confirmed that, especially after his transformative 1968 trip to India, Malle 'learned to rely on sound as his key reference on determining which take to use' (Southern 2006: 16). See also John Guare's final observations in his interview with Philippe Met in this volume.
2. 'Curiosity pushes me forward … I do not like to repeat myself. It is more than a mere behavior; it is an ethics' (Malle quoted by Prédal 1989: 169).
3. Miles Davis's band included Kenny Clarke (drums), who would perform on *Elevator to the Gallows*' soundtrack. That first Parisian stay made an impression on Davis, as he met Sartre, Picasso and Juliette Greco. He also met writer and musician Boris Vian, the most notorious advocate of American jazz in postwar Paris, who would facilitate his working with Malle in 1957 (see Davis 1990: 126).
4. In France, the first article on be-bop was authored by André Hodeir in 1946. The ensuing controversy led to a schism within the Hot Club de France (see Tournès 1999: 106–10). The 'jazz war' lasted several years.
5. In a report on the festival for *Combat* (10 May 1949), Boris Vian confirms that the high points were indeed the Parker, Davis and Bechet performances (1981: 342–3). Here, as in other cases, Malle seems to have concurred with Vian's opinions on jazz.
6. Composed by Bennie Harris, it appears on tracks that Parker recorded for the Dial label in 1946–47.
7. Ionesco's *La Cantatrice chauve* (*The Bald Soprano*) premiered in May 1950, *The Lesson* in February 1951. Beckett's *Waiting for Godot* premiered on 3 January 1953.
8. Alan Lomax's 1950 edition of the book appears in a listing of Vian's musicology library that contains a number of English titles on jazz (15 out of 36). The list was communicated to me in 2000 by Nicole Bertold, curator of the *Fond'action Boris Vian* at Cité Véron (Paris 18è) that holds the books.

9   Some earlier attempts at short improvised soundtracks had been done by Django Reinhardt, and some experiments in modal jazz by André Hodeir (see Pejrolo 2001: 235).
10 The band consisted of Davis's unit for most of the European tour and Paris stay: seminal be-bop drummer Kenny Clarke, and French musicians René Urtreger (piano), Pierre Michelot (bass), Barney Wilen (tenor saxophone).
11 Included in the 2006 Criterion Collection DVD release.
12 'In most of the better houses the music was supplied by a live pianist, the "professor" [...] It was to be expected that sex in all its permutations would be a dominant theme in the songs that came into being in or around the District. Jelly Roll Morton was famous for his limitless repertoire of dirty variations on standards' (Rose 1974: 103, 105).

Bibliography

Adorno, T. W. and H. Eisler (1951) *Composing for the Films*. London: Dennis Dobson.
Barthes, R. (1982) *L'Obvie et l'obtus. Essais critiques III*. Paris: Seuil.
Billard, P. (2003) *Louis Malle. Le rebelle solitaire*. Paris: Plon.
Campan, V. (1999) *L'Écoute filmique. Écho du son en images*. Saint-Denis: Presses Universitaires de Vincennes.
Chancel, J. (2017) 'Louis Malle,' in *Entretiens avec Jacques Chancel*. Paris: La Table Ronde/France Inter/INA, 113–139.
Chion, M. (1985) *Le Son au cinéma*. Paris: Cahiers du Cinéma/Éditions de l'Étoile.
____ (1995) *La Musique au cinéma*. Paris: Fayard.
Davis, M., with Q. Troupe (1990) *Miles: The Autobiography*. New York: Touchstone.
Deleuze, G. (1985) *L'Image-temps. Cinéma 2*. Paris: Minuit.
Desarthe, A. (2016) *René Urtreger, le roi René*. Paris: Odile Jacob.
Eisenberg, E. (1987) *The Recording Angel: The Experience of Music from Aristotle to Zappa*. New York: Penguin.
Eisenstein, S. M., V. I. Pudovkin and G. V. Alexandrov (1985 [1928]) 'A Statement,' in E. Weis and J. Belton (eds) *Film Sound: Theory and Practice*. New York: Columbia University Press, 83–5.
French, P. (1993) *Malle on Malle*. London: Faber & Faber.
Hodeir, A. (1946) 'Vers un renouveau de la musique de jazz?,' *Jazz Hot*, 4/5, 7.
____ (1954) *Hommes et problèmes du jazz*. Paris: Le Portulan.
Lomax, A. (1973 [1950]) *Mister Jelly Roll: The Fortunes of Jelly Roll Morton, New Orleans Creole and 'Inventor of Jazz.'* Berkeley, CA: University of California Press.
Malle, L. (1960) 'Le problème de la musique de film', *Jazz Hot*, 155, 14–15.
Mouëllic, G. (2000) *Jazz et cinéma*. Paris: Cahiers du Cinéma.
Nettelbeck, C. (2004) *Dancing with de Beauvoir: Jazz and the French*. Melbourne: Melbourne University Press.
Pejrolo, A. (2001) 'The Origins of Modal Jazz in the Music of Miles Davis: A Complete Transcription and a Linear/Harmonic Analysis of *Ascenceur pour l'échafaud*, 1957'. Unpublished PhD thesis, New York University.

Perchard, T. (2015) *After Django: Making Jazz in Postwar France*. Ann Arbor, MI: University of Michigan Press.
Prédal, R. (1989) *Louis Malle*. Paris: Edilig.
Pudovkin, V. I. (1985 [1929]) 'Asynchronism as a Principle of Sound', in E. Weis and J. Belton (eds) *Film Sound: Theory and Practice*. New York: Columbia University Press, 86–91.
Rafferty, T. (2006) 'Louis Malle on the ground floor,' DVD notes to *Elevator to the Gallows*. Criterion Collection.
Rose, A. (1974) *Storyville, New Orleans: Being an Authentic, Illustrated Account of the Notorious Red Light District*. Tuscaloosa, AL: University of Alabama Press.
Rosset, C. (1979) *L'Objet singulier*. Paris: Minuit.
Southern, N. C., with J. Weissberger (2006) *The Films of Louis Malle: A Critical Analysis*. Jefferson, NC: McFarland.
Tournès, L. (1999) *New Orleans sur Seine. Histoire du jazz en France*. Paris: Fayard.
Vian, B. (1981) *Autres écrits sur le jazz*. Tome 1. Paris: Christian Bourgois.

MONOGRAPHIC ESSAYS

CHAPTER ELEVEN

The Fire Within: *Touching*
Elisabeth Cardonne-Arlyck

At the start of Louis Malle's *Le Feu follet* (*The Fire Within*, 1963), an anonymous narrator articulates neatly, in voice-over, the incipit of Pierre Drieu La Rochelle's novel from which the film was adapted: 'At that moment, Alain was looking at Lydia relentlessly [*avec acharnement*]' (1966: 5).¹ The intense act of looking that the narrators of both novel and film describe binds the male protagonist, Alain, to his partner of the moment, Lydia. But this is not your run-of-the-mill sexualised gaze. At the etymological root of Alain's *acharnement* is the word *chair* ('flesh'). To train a dog or a falcon

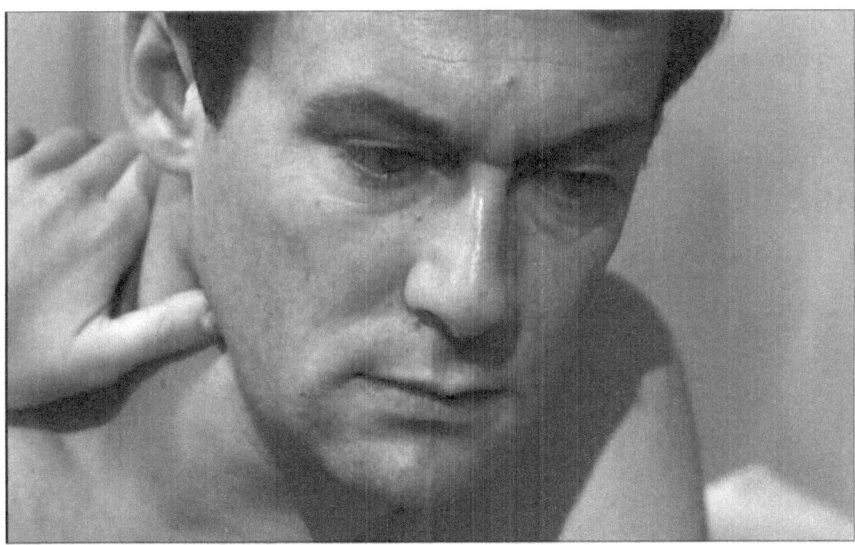

Fig. 1: *The Fire Within* (1963): Alain's (Maurice Ronet) 'relentless' gaze.

to seek flesh is called *acharner* the animal. A sense of vital urgency is thus implicitly attached to this *acharnement*, a need to touch the other viscerally, to get hold of her in the flesh, so to speak. Clearly, this has nothing to do with erotic cannibalism as in Claire Denis' *Trouble Every Day* (2001). What the very first shot of the film shows – the object of Alain's (Maurice Ronet) scrutiny – is Lydia's (Lena Skerla) calm supine face, in a sustained close-up. The length and tightness of the shot enables us to observe the texture of the actress's face, with its neat eyebrows, dark eye make-up, beauty marks and fine lines: detailed, tactile flesh. But Lydia's steady upward gaze dominates the shot, calling for a reverse-shot of Alain watching her: a lengthy close-up, equally tight, equally detailed and tactile, which focuses on the face of Maurice Ronet, intently looking down. His sombre, even mournful, expression and the shadows on his face belie any erotic pleasure that might linger in this post-coitum moment. Although Lydia's hand rests on Alain's naked neck, there are no gestures and little skin contact, little concerted touching in this introductory exchange of looks.

Pathos of Time

Nine close-ups on the lovers' silent faces compose the film's striking initial sequence, shifting from shot/reverse-shot to two-shots. This shift would suggest an increased closeness, which small gestures seem to confirm: Alain lightly kisses Lydia's shoulder, they faintly smile at one another. But over the images the narration, taken from Drieu's novel, comments on the characters' separate sensations: 'Lydia turned her head away and, lowering her eyelids, she lost herself. In what? in herself? Was it her contented rage that swelled her neck and belly? This sensation that emanated nothing, but was so clear?'[2] Heard over Alain's unrelenting gaze, the free indirect speech that folds Lydia unto herself opens a gap between the image and the narration – between Alain's looking and Lydia's feeling. The gap widens as the narration turns to Alain: 'Once again the feeling had eluded him, like a snake between stones.' Not just circumscribed: vanished. Looking and feeling are at odds; the more insistent the gaze, the more fleeting the sensation. Although Lydia will assert a little later that 'it was fine', Alain's attempt to reach some vital principle, some incitement to survive through touching Lydia's body has failed. Thus, a triple disconnect separates the actors' heads, framed in close-ups, from their bodies; the image from the voice-over; and looking from feeling and touching. It translates in filmic terms the terse, distanced stance of the novel's narrator towards its characters. But Alain's *acharnement* in looking is not the same on paper and on screen. The sheer length of the shot pushes Alain's fixed gaze to an uncomfortable edge; it adds to it the pathos of time.

In *Louis Malle par Louis Malle*, the director comments on Maurice Ronet's characterisation of the protagonist: 'There is in the character something pitiable, that was neither in the novel nor in the script' (Mallecot 1978: 25). This affecting quality is not solely due, I would argue, to Ronet's performance, but to the very act of performing. As it is visually acted out, Alain's *acharnement* in looking is, literally, *fleshed out*: embodied in time – hence, movingly vulnerable. Little happens in *The Fire Within* up to the last second, when Alain aims his gun at his heart. The mise-en-scène of small gestures, the performance of muted emotions, the unspoken language of bodies, the interaction of touching and looking, and Erik Satie's bittersweet music form the texture of the film. It is this deliberate pacing of restricted dramatic means that holds our attention and elicits our empathy.

To be sure, Alain and Lydia do touch one another in the course of their reunion, from the hotel room to the gate of the clinic where he has been undergoing detox treatment. Alain kisses Lydia's naked shoulder when she bends over him, fetching her pearl necklace; he leans his head on her arm in close-up, as he thanks her, with restrained effusiveness, for coming. She, in turn, wraps her arms around his neck, like a noose, while telling him that his estranged wife, Dorothy, is not the right woman for him: he needs a rich spouse who will cleave to him; otherwise, he'll get sad and act erratically. Conversely, Alain puts his arm around Lydia's shoulder when he informs her that he can't accompany her to the airport. These gestures of easy, affectionate intimacy display none of the *acharnement* that characterised Alain's gaze. The only pressing gesture occurs in the taxi, when Alain clutches Lydia's hand in close-up, begging her not to leave: 'It's serious' (*C'est grave*). Like the other friends he visits later, she perceives the urgency of his plea, but postpones acting on it. During this interval, Alain will kill himself. The pathos of time that his prolonged gaze introduces from the start is therefore contradictory: as Alain's stare insists, his reasons to survive dissipate: he will not join Lydia in New York, his friend Dubourg in Egypt, Eva in her opium den, nor Solange and Cyrille Lavaux in their mansion. In the last close-up shot, after Alain has pulled the trigger, his fixed stare, straight to the camera, is the final step of his *acharnement*, turned towards the void.

Things

The film's circular structure, from initial to final gaze, emphasises the poignancy of a death foretold. As Alain paces around his room at the clinic, his movements within the frame meet repeatedly the date of 23 July, written large on the mirror. In the novel, Drieu launches the description of the room with the classical device of the protagonist's point of view: 'He lit a cigarette and looked round' (1966: 22). Similarly in the film, close-ups of Alain looking around after he has shut the door alternate with reverse-shots that reveal his surroundings. In the film as in the novel, however, looking at objects is tightly linked to touching them. 'Instead of human beings who vanished as soon as [Alain] left them', Drieu writes, 'these objects gave him the illusion of touching something outside himself' (1966: 23). Two contradictory artefacts exemplify 'the absurd objects which his short-lived, sardonic whims elected' (ibid.): a sophisticated chronometer and an ugly, vulgar statuette. The mixture of refinement and kitsch that, for Drieu, defines Alain's decadent contempt for any hierarchy of value translates in the film into a different juxtaposition of objects.[3] Whereas the novelist can choose two objects to illustrate the character's attitude towards the world, the filmmaker must build an environment – in this instance the room in which Alain stays after leaving Lydia. Therefore, in addition to the highbrow/lowbrow contrast that, in the film as in the novel, divides Alain's private objects, Malle and Bernard Evein, his production designer, created (with characteristic precision) a second contrast between these objects and the room to which they are juxtaposed. The detailed accuracy of the decor highlights the importance of touch.

As Alain looks around, we see the continuity of furniture and objects that fill the room. All surfaces are covered with things that, like the ostentatious façade of the clinic, connote a prosperous bourgeoisie: on the marble fireplace, an elaborate Art Nouveau clock is flanked by matching candlesticks and sconces as well as a pair of Chinese vases; on a long narrow table covered with a brocade cloth in front of a wide mirror, a pair of lamps with decorated globes is next to the oval portrait of a young woman and a Sèvres figurine; on the chest of drawers, a lavish cup and a dictionary (*Petit Larousse illustré*); around the window, thick flowery draperies. Behind the bed covered with velvet cushions, a large tapestry evoking some complicated antique decor further crowds the set, blurring the distinction between things and their representation. Superimposed, as it were, on these tokens of solid (inherited or acquired) wealth and status are Alain's light and ephemeral objects, mocking the décor's plush sturdiness: a contact sheet of Dorothy's photographs is taped over the tapestry; other pictures of Dorothy, with Alain or Lydia, line the mirror, along with newspapers clippings of deadly incidents; empty cigarette packs are strewn over the table. Next to them, however, are a row of books, including Scott Fitzgerald's *Babylon Revisited and Other Stories* and a list of works by Erik Satie, whose first *Gymnopédie* and first three *Gnossiennes* punctuate the soundtrack of *The Fire Within*: modernist works that refer both to the diegesis and to the film itself.[4] The room's objects thus weave several opposing threads: accumulated possessions versus wasted money; lasting artefacts versus ephemera; tradition versus modernity; the past preserved versus the future pressing on. As the clock strikes the hour, Alain moves the hand forward: 'Life flows too slowly in me', he will later say, holding his gun; 'So I speed it up.' Hastening the course of life is the flip side of looking lengthily, *avec acharnement*. They are two interrelated faces of the pathos of time – of Alain's anguished sense of the evanescence of people and things: 'I'd have liked to captivate people', he confides towards the end of the film, 'hold on to them, bind them close. So that things would stay still around me. But it always went to hell.'[5]

The objects – his own – that Alain manipulates all participate in the pathos of time. Some measure it and have a dramatic function: the fountain pen with which Alain writes a diary that he will tear up later on; the gun he unwraps in this first room sequence and fires in the last; *The Great Gatsby*, which he calmly finishes reading before shooting himself. Others participate in the *cérémonie des adieux* that punctuates Alain's final day and confirms his decision to die: the shirts, ties, cuff-links, suits, among which he carefully composes his persona of understated dandy before making the rounds of his old friends in Paris.[6] But more tinged with pathos are the objects devoid of practical function that Alain touches while moving aimlessly around his room, marking time. The complex mise-en-scène and camera work of this whole sequence follow Alain's minute gestures in close-up: he leans over the mantelpiece to straighten one of Dorothy's photographs behind the Art Nouveau candlesticks and traces her features, humming along with Satie's music (a discreet conflation of narrative and diegesis); he blows on a miniature American flag inserted into an Art Deco figurine and switches it to the companion piece. This playfulness turns sardonic as Alain clips, still humming and smiling slightly, a headline from *Le Parisien,* which he posts on the large mirror: 'Shocking! Jean-Jacques (age 5) tries to fly but hangs himself on curtain cord.' Needless to say, this tabloid version of the fall of Icarus is not without connection to the demise of a *petit bourgeois* who lacks the means to fly high and live the only, affluent, life he desires.

Reflections

As in Cocteau's film *Orpheus* the mirror shifts shapes and engulfs the hero. Alain catches his own reflection in medium close-up, narrowly framed by objects: Jean-Jacques' and other newspaper clippings, the protruding angle of an ornate picture frame, a cut-out photograph of Dorothy and Lydia seem to wedge him in on all sides. As if suddenly self-aware, he rubs his face, hides behind the posted clippings, emerges again with an anguished expression. Reminiscent of Freud's *fort/da* game, the presence/absence alternative enacted by Alain's peek-a-boo pertains to the decision he faces to stay or to leave. Those are the terms in which his decision is cast throughout the film: 'I'm going', he warns; 'You will come back, won't you?' respond his friends, eager to be reassured. But Alain's vanishing is also enacted by the mise en-scène itself. As he paces back and forth in front of the mirror, softly repeating Dorothy's name like a mantra, his image splits between himself and his reflection: Alain and his double seem to be pursuing one another in front and behind the circled date of '23 juillet' (23 July). Filling the frame, the date marks the invisible screen that separates Alain's presence from his absence. The uncanny effect of this evasive doubling is furthered

Fig. 2: *The Fire Within* (1963): Self-scrutiny in a busy mirror.

by the camera's soft focus and by the moving shadows cast by Ronet's body. Hardly distinguishable from his blurred reflection and whispering his wife's name obsessively, Alain becomes a ghost, like the poet in Robert Desnos' famous lines from *Corps et biens* ('J'ai tant rêvé de toi', 1926):

> I have dreamed of you so much, walked so much, spoken/and lain with your phantom that perhaps nothing more is left me/than to be a phantom among phantoms and a hundred times more shadow/than the shadow which walks and will joyfully walk/on the sundial of your life. (1972: 17)

Whereas Alain seems to lose substance, his things, shown in medium close-ups, are vividly distinctive: the diminutive bowler hat he moves from his nose to his eye to the top of the lamp, the little wooden head he ejects from its support, the empty cigarette packs he piles up in a tower. Useless and worthless, they are marginal to the market economy, as is Alain in his refusal to mature and work. (The fact that he packs all his miniature objects in his suitcase before firing the gun underlines their emotional and symbolic significance.) Moving from one object to the other and touching them, Alain *kills time*. But he also rehearses the round of visits he will pay to his friends the following day and the emotional touching he will test.

Money

The last object that Alain encounters as he paces along the mirror is the check for 4,500 francs that Lydia gave him before she left. 'Money, money', he repeats in close-up and puts the check on the mirror next to a photograph of Dorothy and Lydia, humming a popular song: 'Money … It slips right through your fingers.' 'Money', writes Drieu, 'he always had it and he never had any. Always a little, never much. It was a furtive and fluid credit which flowed permanently through his fingers but would never settle there.' (1966: 25) Devoid of any worth or cachet but solid and personal, the trinkets that Alain manipulates are the opposite of the money that he cannot hold on to. The junction of Lydia's check to the photograph of the two beautiful and rich women who might have saved him echoes Drieu's blunt description of the triangular relation that binds Alain to money and women: 'For years, it had been his dream to get himself a woman; it meant money, shelter, the end of all the difficulties that made him cringe' (1966: 8). Not only does Drieu's phrase, *mettre la main sur une femme*, which denotes physical possession, connect unpleasantly with the misogyny that pervades the novel; it also connects directly with the notion of touch in all the contradictory complexity that Malle's film explores.

When Alain leaves the Versailles clinic, his first stop in Paris is at a bank, to cash Lydia's check. This scene, absent from the novel, dramatises the crucial importance of money and its close relation to touch, through the underlying French expressions *toucher un chèque* and *toucher de l'argent*. The scene is entirely built on the circulation of gaze and touch around money. A tense montage of close-ups in shot/reverse-shot alternates repeatedly the face of the cashier and that of Alain, as they look up at one another across the window and down at the 100-franc bills that the cashier counts (all forty-five of them!) with professional speed, and which Alain takes at the end. Ordinary conversations can be faintly heard in the background, but the sound that dominates the totally wordless sequence is that of the crisp bills moving swiftly between the cashier's fingers. His bulging eyes emphasise watchfulness, as he looks at Alain while counting the money, and follows him with his gaze, smiling faintly, when Alain leaves. Stone-faced, uncivil and framed by the cashier's window, Alain exhibits none of the *gentillesse*, the pleasant manners that characterise him throughout the film. He appears on the defensive, as if, under the cashier's gaze, cashing Lydia's check – *toucher son chèque* – might be suspect. A whiff of film noir – and the venality central to the genre – thus hovers over the scene, accentuated by the black and white stock. It discreetly evokes the somewhat unsavory relation between getting hold of a woman (*mettre la main sur elle*) and receiving her money (*toucher son argent*). Contrary to the novel, which is very explicit in its description of Alain's parasitism, the film attenuates the trait. Judgement only appears fleetingly in the cashier's insistent gaze and slight smirk, and in Alain's challenging expression.

Whereas touching personal objects (the gun, the pen, the clothes, the figurines) relates Alain solely to himself, and only indirectly (the photographs) to others, money implies direct transactions with people and the feelings attached to them: Lydia writes the check for Alain as a way to bind him to her; he hands a 100-franc bill to a taxi driver who comments with contempt 'What a dope!' Cyrille, fearing Alain's despair, asks him whether he needs money, etc. The bank scene, unfolding in real time, marks the point, roughly in the middle of the film, when, as in the opening scene, touching becomes inextricably physical and emotional. The motif of the window that separates Alain from the cashier (and the idle man from the worker) is developed in a later scene when Alain visits his friend Eva (Jeanne Moreau) in her art gallery. When she notices Alain behind the window, Eva comes close and, while telling him that he looks like a corpse, she flashes a luminous Jeanne Moreau smile and pretends playfully to scratch his nose through the glass. In their affectionate banter across the windowpane, closeness and separation are conjoined, two contradictory faces – already alluded to in the initial scene – of Alain's agreeable yet hopeless relations to others. The mise-en-scène, the dialogue, and Ronet's performance enact this contradiction in the complex interplay between touching and looking, most spectacularly in the antepenultimate sequence, at Cyrille's and Solange's dinner party.

A Dance of Touch

This sequence is the next-to-last loop in Alain's downward spiral. It is marked by his relapse into alcohol after he has, seemingly on an impulse, emptied out the drink left by a client at the café de Flore, where he had met the Minville brothers, out of prison for right-wing activism. Sick and drenched, Alain is in a piteous state when he arrives at the Lavaux's mansion; they let him rest. In this decisive sequence, the last of his visits to old partying companions, Alain is no longer confronted with a series of individuals from various social backgrounds, but with a worldly set of people who possess what he lacks: wealth, power, purpose, fame. 'The peace of mind of these people', he remarks, surveying the invitation cards that line the Lavaux's bathroom mirror and the toiletries and other personal things strewn about. As in his room at the clinic, in Dubourg's study, and in Eva's studio, Alain is surrounded with things that belong to other people's lives, estranged from his. His reflections in the two bathroom mirrors emphasise his alienation amidst objects that seem to hem him in. Once he has joined the other guests, however, objects, albeit opulent, recede somewhat in the background and people hold him in a mesh of gestures and looks.

In an elegant mise-en-scène that evokes Renoir's *The Rules of the Game* (*La Règle du jeu*, 1939), the rituals of after-dinner conviviality are orchestrated in a ballet of touch. While coffee, cigars and spirits are being passed around, the same light gestures circulate, like coded dance movements, smoothly joining the guests and pulling them apart. But upper-class ritual and anodyne dance of touch serve to envelop Alain in a web of fleeting but conflicting interactions. Thus, as the guests pair up to leave the table for the sitting room, Mignac, 'a model Parisian', puts his hand on Alain's shoulder to tell him he has heard rumours of his divorce: 'Mental cruelty?', he adds ironically. When Solange (Alexandra Stewart) offers Alain a cup of coffee, he makes the gesture, looking distraught, of retaining her; but Cyrille (Jacques Seyres) intervenes with cigars and pulls her away. Maria (Claude Deschamp), in turn, holding a sugar bowl, puts her hand on Alain's shoulder to tell him she's glad to see him; he caresses her neck gently when she confides she has found 'le grand amour'. The very same gesture is used by Brancion (Tony Taffin) with Solange, whom he's wooing, after he has remarked sarcastically, looking at Alain across the room: 'So that's the fabulous, legendary, irresistible Alain Leroy…' A glass of cognac and an arm around the shoulder are Cyrille's tactic again to pull Alain away from a young woman flirting with him and to talk about Brancion: 'He's irritating, but he's someone.' Touch is essential to the social game; it's an instant connector, enabling conversation; but it's also an instrument of control, as Cyrille's interventions show. At the level of the narrative, it is essential to the mise-en-scène, connecting characters and enabling the director to modulate the affects that circulate between them. Cyrille, who maneuvers and watches, can be seen as his implicit stand-in.

I Can't Touch

Contrary to the scene in Alain's room, where looking and touching are extensions of one another, in this dinner-party sequence, they seem increasingly at odds. Friendly touch and chitchat fade away when Alain confronts Brancion and breaks the rules of social decorum. This, stylistically, translates into breaking the rules of continuity editing. Whereas touching softens social exchanges, looking stiffens them. Thus, the fluid mise-en-scène of effortless civility gives way to the abrupt editing of awkward outbursts against a stand-offish gaze. In fact, from the start of the scene at the diningroom table, looking does not initiate connection, but blocks it. Both Alain and Cyrille watch Brancion monopolise Solange's attention. Cyrille interrupts him by telling, with gusto, the 'famous' story of a drunk discovered asleep on the tomb of the Unknown Soldier as if in his own bed. 'Who was the hero of our tale?', Brancion asks icily. In mock accusation, Solange points to Alain. A shot/reverse-shot opposes Brancion's hard and confident stare to Alain's mortified look.

This conflict of looks governs the subsequent exchanges – or lack thereof – between the two characters. It translates into a disruption of space. Thus, when, in a two-shot medium close-up, Alain tries to regain some dignity in Brancion's eyes by denouncing his youthful drunken joke, the camera jumps the line to register Brancion's rebuke in medium close-up: 'Forgive me. I never get drunk, and I hate stories about drunks.' A new spatial disconnect follows, as Alain exits right and unexpectedly reenters left, turns while emptying his glass, and faces Brancion on the right again: 'We drunks are poor cousins … and we know it' – and he smashes his glass against a table. In the novel, Drieu backs Alain's self-abasement with Brancion's rejection: 'He put forward his trembling hand and looked at Brancion, seeking a moment's attention. But Brancion had heard, once and for all, the call of the crowd, and his ears were closed to this recital of vagrants, of street-corner quacks, of sentimental thieves' (1966: 116). Only Alain's suicide will retrospectively contradict the contempt of a man whom the narrator defines as a charismatic adventurer, rumored to have stolen and killed, and connoisseur of Asia (à la Malraux?). In Malle's film, however, Brancion is defined rather vaguely by Cyrille as 'a somebody', by Alain as 'a real Martian', and by Solange as a 'force of nature' – the opposite of Alain. The character's strength resides essentially in his silent posture and stare.

Tony Taffin's performance thus opposes Brancion's erect, motionless bearing and fixed gaze to Maurice Ronet's movements, frequent leaning on objects, and distraught looks. Yet, Ronet's grace, as he moves around, performing Alain's drunken state, and his facial expressiveness caught in close-up counterbalance Brancion's authority with the poignant power of what Jean Epstein termed *photogeny*: the attribute of filmic movement on which such performers as Buster Keaton and Charlie Chaplin based their creations. Moreover, it is Alain's very loss of dignity and self-control that brings forth the figurative dimensions of touching in Malle's film. Part of Alain's desperate address to Brancion comes verbatim from the novel: 'As it happens, I'm a man. But I've never had money or women. Yet I'm very active … The thing is … I can't reach out with my hands. I can't touch things. And when I do touch things, I feel nothing.'[7] Mise-en-scène and editing foreground Ronet's performance of Alain's *anguish of touch* against Brancion's *noli me tangere*, his forbidding mien: Alain cannot, in any way, touch Brancion. Although they are framed together in two-shots, their shared space appears discontinuous: while Alain addresses Brancion, the camera crosses the axis three times, so that, in medium close-ups, the focus stays on Alain's mobile face, whilst Brancion remains immobile, silent, and almost faceless: a wall. Alain makes his inability to touch palpable, as it were, by bringing his hand close to Brancion's shoulder and stopping. Brancion's total lack of response to the gesture and to Alain's obvious distress points to his own inability to be touched. He leaves the frame without a word, while the camera remains focused on Alain's face.

Immediately after, when Maria introduces her lover, Frédéric (Henri Serre), Alain asks him whether he believes in his own acts.[8] As Frédéric dodges the question, Alain pursues: 'You believe in Maria? … You have a woman. I have nothing.' A network of

Fig. 3: *The Fire Within* (1963): Inability to watch.

connections unravels then, as if interrelated strands of experience, all issuing from touch, were pulling one another into total emptiness. In a brilliant montage by Suzanne Baron of medium close-ups and jump cuts, Alain paces and turns, seemingly trapped in the web of lack and incapacity that he spins out with a string of negative statements: 'You don't know what it's like, being unable to touch anything. I'm incapable of wanting. I can't even desire. The women here tonight … I can't desire them. They scare me. Scare me! Scare me!' Alain's expanding dispossession (of believing-touching-having-wanting-desiring) leads him to implore Solange in a two-shot close-up: 'You're life itself. Yes, life. But I can't touch you. It's horrible.' As Alain goes to sit on a chair and Solange joins him, sitting on the table, he occupies the lower position of a child or a supplicant: 'To leave without having touched anything. Beauty. Goodness. All their lies. You can work miracles. Touch the leper', he begs in a high angle close-up, advancing his hands towards Solange, in the traditional gesture of supplication. 'A real entreaty can contain a great deal of power', writes Drieu (1966: 119). It reverses the *touching-getting hold of-having* sequence (that defines in terms of dispossession Alain's relationship to women) into its opposite: request and gift. But these belong to religious, moral or emotional realms foreign to ordinary worldly interactions. 'It's a matter of timing between a man and a woman', replies Solange, unwittingly echoing Alain's warnings – 'I have to go', 'I'm late' – that have sustained the pathos of time throughout the film. Brancion, standing by the door and staring hard when Alain leaves, looks like a figure of death from Cocteau's cinema.

From the Heart

'Touch the leper', and its Christic connotations lead to the last loop in Alain's downward spiral. Walking in the dark streets of Paris with Milou (Bernard Tiphaine), his younger alter ego, in the midst of night life and traffic, Alain delves further into his failure to touch: 'You must make people feel you want them and that you'll hold on to them … I don't love them. I never could love them.' In close-up he adds: 'I can't touch. I can't take. It has to come from the heart.' These remarks, borrowed from Drieu's novel, seem to pick up again the 'want-touch-take-hold' thread that grounds relationships in will and action; but, in a sort of brusque revelation, Alain finds in love, which belongs to sentiment, a deeper foundation for touch. Will and action, as exemplified by Brancion, pertain to a notion of virility that Drieu shared with other contemporary writers like Montherlant and Malraux. Stating that the ability to touch and to take comes from the heart complicates the notion; it undercuts the opposition between action and sensitivity that runs through the film. It also ties together the physical and the emotional dimensions of touch, as act and as feeling, by anchoring them both in love. 'You really love people that much?', asks Milou. 'I wanted so much to be loved', responds Alain, 'that I feel I do love.' The screen fades to black.

In this final statement, which marks the end of Alain's tour of his friends, love is desperately circular, a tragic infolding. This connects to Alain's early reflections in his bedroom mirror, next to the photographs of Dorothy and Lydia, and to the vanishing of his body into his own image. To touch, to be touched or touching are, for Alain, deprived of the ability to grasp and retain; they graze, evanescent, the surface of people and things. But the despair contained in this statement and expressed by Maurice Ronet's face cast in shadow also refers back to the protagonist's *acharnement* at the start of the film, as he stared at Lydia's face. He would have wanted so much to touch Lydia intimately, to be deeply loved, but sexual touch had no lasting resonance for either of them. In Malle's film as in Drieu's novel (albeit less insistently), men need not only money to hold on to women, but erotic know-how. Since Cyrille has both, says Milou, Brancion does not have much of a chance with Solange. Alain has neither: 'I'm awkward', he confides to Milou, 'inept.' The fear of women that underlies his good looks may be related to this sense of inadequacy. It is yet another ring in the negative chain of touch.

The mise-en-scène of Alain's suicide, however, invalidates the negativity attached to touch. It opposes Alain's purposeful handling of things to the idle manipulation of the first room sequence. After shaving and packing his belongings in his suitcases, he finishes reading *The Great Gatsby* and closes it, removes his glasses and puts them on the book, seizes the gun, searches for his heart, and pulls the trigger. The pace of the mise-en-scène, Maurice Ronet's clean, deliberate gestures and calm expression all contribute to turn Alain's desperate gesture into an intentional, clear-eyed act which nullifies the opposition between heart and action that has run through the film, and that Solange reiterates shortly before Alain kills himself.[9] The concluding address, superimposed on the last still shot of Alain's face, confirms the intention: 'I'm killing myself because you didn't love me, because I didn't love you. Because our ties were loose, I'm killing myself to tighten them. I leave you with an indelible stain.' The lack of love that prevented Alain from touching others is reversed into a permanent bond. It's our turn to be touched.

Acharnement Revisited

The *acharnement* that defines Alain's looking at Lydia at the very start can, more broadly, characterise his relentless exploration, throughout *The Fire Within*, of reasons not to live. Such relentlessness, linked to touch, marks other characters in Malle's subsequent films. Most particularly, Georges Randal in *Le Voleur* (*The Thief of Paris*, 1967) and Dr. Stephen Fleming and Anna Barton in *Damage* (1992). The violence that is etymologically implicit in *acharnement* (and turned by Alain against himself) is explicit in the thief's willful devastation of the houses he burglarises in *Le Voleur* and in the lovers' fatal sexual passion in *Damage*.

The circular structure that Alain's return to his room and manipulation of the same objects creates in *The Fire Within*, is emphasised in *Le Voleur* by the flashback governing the whole film. The first and the last scenes mark the beginning and the end of the same burglary, starting at 11pm when Georges (Jean-Paul Belmondo) climbs over the wall of a suburban villa and ending at 6am when he climbs out (a distant clock, conveniently, strikes the hours). Within the temporal framework of a full night, acts initiated in the first scene are completed in the last, so that the whole film is framed by George's cool ruthlessness, his *acharnement*. As in other robbery films, such as Jules Dassin's *Du rififi chez les hommes* (*Rififi*, 1955) or Jean-Pierre Melville's *Le Cercle rouge* (*The Red Circle*, 1970), the emphasis is on the coordination of gaze and touch, in real time. But, contrary to these films, Georges uses his skills to attack a bourgeois opulence that Jacques Saulnier's luxurious design and Henri Decaë's gorgeous cinematography magnify. Led by a light that brushes walls, antique furniture and works of art, Georges inspects room after room, thing after thing, before choosing a beautiful rosewood writing desk, which he dismantles and explores methodically: 'Some thieves', he remarks in voice-over, 'take lots of precautions not to damage furniture. I don't. Others put everything back in order at the end of their visit. I never do. I have a filthy job, but I have an excuse: I do it filthily.' Like Alain, he piles negative on negative. Like him, he is hollowed out by his relentlessness and driven to a stark moral vacuity. The return to the initial burglary at the end of *Le Voleur* underlines the process. Before Georges leaves at dawn, the camera grazes over objects that the lamp illuminated briefly when he arrived; he grabs several statuettes in a cabinet, shatters the glass of a display case and chooses some coins, cuts out with a razor the painting of a young woman, surveys the ravaged space; in a last, compulsive gesture, he breaks into a chest, and finds nothing. Its emptiness matches the blank expression on Georges' face. As he confides to his beloved cousin Charlotte (Geneviève Bujold), his first burglary was a revelation, uniting sight and touch: 'I saw the jewels glitter in the dark; I felt their weight in my hand … All of a sudden, I grasped happiness. I was alive.' When the action is over, he is no longer anything and awaits the next occasion. 'I need you, Charlotte, he adds, you're the only one I can tell that I'm alone.'[10]

Acharnement and dispossession also define the arc of *Damage*, produced almost thirty years after *The Fire Within* and twenty-five years after *Le Voleur*. As in these two films, a relentless desire to take hold (of a woman, of jewels) leads to emotional bareness. As in them, looking and touching are tightly interconnected by interdiction. But, whereas Alain's impediment is emotional and Georges' is exclusively social, Stephen's (Jeremy Irons) is moral as well as social: the object of his sexual passion, Anna (Juliette Binoche), is the fiancée of his son, Martyn (Rupert Graves). Looking and touching are dramatically interlocked from the very first encounter, when Stephen and Anna have sex right after exchanging looks for the first time. But looking and touching are also at odds, because of the illicitness of the affair and the spatial closeness of family life. The tension between look and touch runs through the film, carried by Jeremy Irons' forceful looks, and Juliette Binoche's opaque gaze.

Obsessive and unbridled eroticism puts the flesh inscribed in *acharnement* at the centre of the film. The lovers' bodies are gradually denuded as the narrative progresses from one fervid sex scene to the next, until the last one, when Stephen and Anna are shown fully naked and making kinetic love in long shot. When Martyn discovers them and, stumbling back, falls down the staircase to his death, the long naked body of Irons hurtling down the stairs exposes the flesh in all its vulnerability. Stephen's bare nakedness, oblivious of propriety, initiates his shedding of all that constituted his privileged British life: political position, wife, family, possessions. The final sequence opens on a shot of sandaled feet walking on a paved street, next to a dangling net bag. 'It takes a remarkably short time to withdraw from the world', Stephen comments in voice-over. 'I traveled until I arrived at a life of my own. What really makes us is beyond grasping. It's way beyond knowing. We give in to love because it gives us some sense of what is unknowable. Nothing else matters, not in the end.' Arrived at his sparse room in the medieval village of Caylus in the South-West of France,[11] Stephen unwraps a slab of cheese in close-up, folds the paper carefully and adds it to a pile of similar sheets, turns the cheese around just so, and cuts two slices. The precise, meticulous gestures, which could be those of a Franciscan monk, connect to Stephen's previous confession to Martyn: 'I thought you could control life' – a belief that his turbulent affair with Anna has shattered. But they also hark back to Alain's deliberate gestures before he kills himself: they are the gestures of a character who has renounced worldly conflicts and faces the unknowable.

Towards the end of each of these three films the protagonist, either in dialogue or in voice-over, enunciates some truth about himself. In each case, this truth has been reached through a form of destructive relentlessness, in the pursuit of acts of touch that are either unattainable (Alain) or prohibited (Georges and Stephen). In the arc of dispossession that shapes each of the films, the three characters are, in all their differences, figures of Job. Each of them, at the end, turns, like Job, towards the very source of love that initiated his dispossession: Alain towards the friends and lovers whose insufficient bond led to his suicide, which will, retroactively, tighten the bond; Georges towards Charlotte whose betrothal led to his first burglary, but whose presence he needs; Stephen towards Anna, whose attempt to love both father and son caused Martyn's death, but in whose enlarged photograph he contemplates the only thing that matters, the unknowable. For Job, the unknowable is God; for Malle's irreligious characters, it is life and personal destiny.

Notes

1   The subtitles on the Criterion DVD release read: 'At that moment, Alain studied Lydia's face relentlessly.'
2   As per Criterion subtitles (used thereafter).
3   Contrary to Hugo Frey (2004: 68–71), I don't believe that Malle shared Drieu's notion of decadence, which was anchored in the political and economic situation of the *entre-deux-guerres* in Europe.
4   Charlie Hayes, in Fitzgerald's 'Babylon Revisited' (1931), led the high life in Paris during the Roaring Twenties, before losing his wife and money. Now sober and working in Prague, he's returned to Paris to regain custody of his young daughter and tours, disenchanted, the old haunts. The parallels with Malle's film are clear.
5   Malle has acknowledged his empathy with Drieu's character: 'I *was* Alain Leroy.' It was shared by Maurice Ronet: 'There was a very deep connection between him and the character; he was incredibly moving in that part' (French 1993: 39, 40).
6   This ritual is all the more significant since it does not usually feature men – contrary to women – in cinema. Malle has recounted that Alain's things actually belonged to him: 'everything in the closet was mine' (French 1993: 43).
7   'Just imagine that I am a man; well, I have never managed to have any money or any women. Yet I am very vigorous and very virile. But there it is, I can't stretch out my hand, I can't touch things. And when I do touch things, I don't feel anything' (1966: 116).
8   The fact that Alain leans on a sculpture as he addresses Frédéric, played by the tall, upright Henri Serre, suggests that the opposition between bent and erect is part of Alain's characterisation: a feature of his *gentillesse*, his desire to please, as opposed to power.
9   Calling Alain to remind him of their lunch engagement, Solange tells him that she likes him a lot; he has 'heart', she says, whereas Brancion is 'a force of nature'. 'I don't understand any of this', responds Alain, who hangs up and concludes that Solange has answered for Dorothy.
10 See also chapter twelve in this volume for a more extensive analysis of the film.
11 Malle had a house in that village (French 1993: 205).

Bibliography

Desnos, R. (1972) *The Voice: Selected Poems of Robert Desnos*; trans. W. Kulik with C. Frankel. New York: Grossman.
Drieu La Rochelle, P. (1966 [1931]) *Will O' the Wisp (Le Feu follet)*; trans. M. Robinson. New York: Marion Boyars.
French, P. (1993) *Malle on Malle*. London: Faber and Faber.
Frey, H. (2004) *Louis Malle*. Manchester: Manchester University Press.
Mallecot, J. (1978) *Louis Malle par Louis Malle*. Paris: Editions de l'Athanor.

CHAPTER TWELVE

Le Voleur: (Self-)Portrait of the Filmmaker as a Thief

Philippe Met

Upon its initial release in 1967, *Le Voleur* – or *The Thief of Paris*, as it is usually, albeit misleadingly retitled in English (given the titular hero's incessant travels between several European capitals – Paris, but also London or Brussels – as well as through provincial France – Valenciennes and Dieppe, in particular)[1] – was disappointingly received in both commercial and critical terms. As Louis Malle later surmised, this might have been due to the pre-May 1968, Maoist-inflected *zeitgeist* iconised by Jean-Luc Godard's *La Chinoise* (1967) and largely at odds with *Le Voleur*'s classical aesthetics and *fin-de-siècle* setting, even if the latter, with the onset of anarchist terrorism, could now be contextually read as a 'foreshadowing' of the major societal upheaval to come. Be that as it may, it remains to this day, over a half-century later, one of the least – if not *the* least among his French-language features – commented upon of all of Malle's opuses. Could it be that the accuracy and impeccability of its mise-en-scène defies or invalidates all exegesis? As his biographer puts it, perhaps hyperbolically, 'it's hard to imagine the film could have been shot any other way' (Billard 2003: 270). And yet, counter to most critics, including his detractors, who readily elect *The Fire Within* (*Le Feu follet*, 1963) as his very best film, the director has consistently ranked *Le Voleur* as potentially his favourite and most successful accomplishment, despite its being the story or, better still, the 'confession' 'of a *defeat*',[2] so that it concomitantly constituted an acme, a turning-point and even an endpoint. All of the latter evidently called for a fundamental paradigm shift that the journey to India was soon to initiate, via self-questioning and the discovery of Otherness, and that, to a lesser extent, the switch to original scriptwriting and away from literary adaptation would signal in its own right.[3] It is arguably no accident that while Malle himself labeled it his 'last classical film',[4] Pierre Billard discusses it in a chapter of his monograph aptly titled 'Fin de partie' (or a Beckettian *endgame*), and a young Gilles Jacob, later to become Cannes Film Festival

Director extraordinaire, wrote an equally laudatory and perspicacious review under the compelling heading: 'Louis Malle au pied du mur' (1967). A Louis Malle perhaps less pushed to the wall or hitting a wall than standing at a crossroads or facing a watershed moment.

Even more importantly perhaps, the director never made any secret of the deeply personal underpinnings of *Le Voleur*, even going so far as to identify it, continuing in the vein of superlatives, as 'the most autobiographical film [he] ever shot',[5] in a filmography that is hardly lacking in strong contenders for the distinction, starting with *The Fire Within* and the protagonist played by Maurice Ronet as Malle's alter ego in transparent (self-)disguise. 'I *was* Alain Leroy', the cineaste stated outright (French 1993: 39), adding that he could have refrained from releasing the film altogether: 'I'd made it mostly for myself' (1993: 43).[6] 'Georges Randal, c'est moi', Malle might as well have exclaimed (the way Flaubert once thunderously (re)appropriated his fictional Madame Bovary's identity), and even more convincingly, especially in light of the character arc (notwithstanding the time gap – end of the nineteenth century vs. the 1960s):

> We [Randal and Malle] both came from a conventional, affluent background and broke with it out of rebellion, anger, and the desire to take revenge and shatter it. Of course, then follows an adventurous romantic life, lots of women, success, money. The society you rejected acclaims you, and you find yourself back where you started. (French 1993: 55–6)[7]

Or could it be that the hero is but a screen for (yet not exactly a foil to) another type of authorial doppelgänger, namely abbé La Margelle? An equivocal Janus figure himself (is he a priest moonlighting as a thief or a thief moonlighting as a priest?), La Margelle, after all, not only shares his initials with Louis Malle's name (several pages of the densely annotated shooting script bear the mention 'LM' in the director's own handwriting and in reference to the abbot character),[8] but is also the philosophising voice of 'moral' guidance in thievery for Randal…

In an ironic coincidence, the question of authorship as well as the confusion between writer and protagonist are thematised in and exacerbated by the very source material. Malle's film is very loosely based on a same-titled novel published in 1897 by Belle Époque anarchist sympathiser Georges Darien, who was also an often censored and mostly unpopular playwright, a virulent polemicist and a failed (Georgist) politician. Although appreciated by the likes of Alfred Jarry, Alphonse Allais and André Breton, he died in complete oblivion in 1921. It took over three decades before his oeuvre was somewhat 'rediscovered' with the reprint of *Le Voleur* and *Bas les cœurs!* (1889) in the mid-1950s by maverick publisher Jean-Jacques Pauvert, who happened to be a personal friend of Jean-Claude Carrière. Carrière ended up co-scripting the Darien-based film and rapidly made a name for himself in the industry as a leading screenwriter.[9] It is around the time of the book's re-release that Malle perused it with great fascination (see French 1993: 54) and presumably first toyed with the idea of bringing it to the screen. Tellingly, he seems to adhere to, or relay, a widespread – although not necessarily erroneous – biographical reading of the novel (as if this were, for instance, albeit in a very different vein, a precursor to *The Thief's Journal*),[10] fueled not only by a shared first name and the realistic precision in the description of a thief's way of life, but also by the writer's dearth of documented earnings and his unexplained 'disappearance' during a six-year period that immediately preceded the publication of *Le Voleur*: 'I think the central character is very close to the author, Georges Darien, whose life is mysterious' (French 1993: 54). Such a conflation is, on the one hand, prompted by the self-narrative or 'memoirs' format (with a first-person protagonist narrator) in Darien's book, to which Malle's film will substitute not so much a day-in-the-life narrative as a night-encapsulating-a-lifetime structure, or what he terms, looking forward to the biopic-of-Marlene-Dietrich-in-one-day project that was ready to go into production at the time of his demise, 'both the story of a night and of a life' (MALLE 149-B33).[11] On the other, it is subverted by a peculiar bookending of the novel that precisely operates a ludic distancing or feigned denial of authorship via a found manuscript trope that was even more popular in seventeenth- and eighteenth-century European literature. A foreword, signed 'Georges Darien' with the mention 'London, 1896', thus effectuates or confirms by anticipation, as it were, what the coda will prophesise (with the narrator eventually relinquishing in one go his dual thieving/writing career, i.e. leaving his memoirs behind for the taking, and expecting the purloining process to come full vicious circle since 'one is always robbed by someone' [Darien 1987: 480]): 'The book you are about to read, and bearing my name, I did not author. […] I stole it. I confess my crime' (1987: 27). The author pilfering from – or preying on, or masquerading as – his character: might this not be an 'advance' metaphor for another turn of the screw, with Malle appropriating Darien's Randal as his own double, using him for the vicarious purpose of cinematic self-portraiture?

Even in the presence of archival documents, the adaptational trajectory is inevitably arduous to reconstruct, and genetic criticism-oriented approaches are too often thwarted by insurmountable hurdles in the search for definite conclusions. An added difficulty in the specific case of *Le Voleur* is the fact that none of the genetic materials, including the various screenplay versions (synopsis, treatment, continuity drafts, shooting script), collected in the 'Fonds Louis Malle' at Bibliothèque du Film/Cinémathèque Française are dated, which unavoidably muddles the chronology or renders it uncertain. The main thrust of the process can nonetheless be delineated with some ease and clarity, and might be generically summarised as a shift from picaresque to classical. Georges Darien's novel is particularly dense and profuse, if not wordy and ratiocinating at times; its plot layered, if not overladen with the criss-crossing of a multitude of characters. A number of initial attempts on Malle's part are shown to pursue many of the narrative threads in the original text as well as to explore more or less tangential potentialities. Examples would include Georges raising their daughter alone after Charlotte's death and grooming her into a full-fledged *voleuse* despite her receiving an excellent education at a British school; his being led by circumstances to kill with his own hands; his witnessing and barely escaping a deadly anarchist bombing perpetrated by Canonnier's daughter and her husband; his being unsuccessful (despite Roger Voisin *aka* Roger-La-Honte's assistance) at breaking Canonnier out of the Île de Ré citadel. One palpable orientation of the overall scriptwriting effort is, however, a progressive trimming or streamlining of the source material, a push toward narrative-discursive condensation, economy and efficacy. This called, first and foremost, for the elimination or amalgamation of several characters: Issacar, an engineer and Randal's first mentor and associate; Paternoster, a disreputable moneychanger; Hélène, Canonnier's daughter; Balon, the psychologist-anarchist; etc. Accordingly in order as well were the jettisoning of most of the lengthy political disquisitions and philosophical digressions, and the reinforcement of the titular protagonist as the almost exclusive focal point and/or point-of-view, with the choice of the voice-over narration technique being established early on in the writing process before being fully implemented, formalised and systematised.

After a protracted opening sequence that – perhaps under the influence of such classic caper or heist films as John Huston's *The Asphalt Jungle* (1950) and Jules Dassin's *Rififi* (1955) with their dramatically silent extended centerpieces – is devoid of both dialogue and score (while the former is far from sparse in the rest of the film, the latter will be deliberately non-existent throughout), the *voix off* kicks in just shy of seven minutes into the film. It is a carefully calculated effect, as the shooting script makes clear (even if the actual edited scene does not follow the intention to the letter): 'George's face, concentrated in his effort. All of a sudden, his voice is heard, without any perceptible lip movement. His words are "placed" in the intervals between his efforts, as if Georges truly spoke and addressed us at that precise moment' (MALLE 143-B32; f. [4]). Assuming for the most part a transitional and contextualizing function, or contributing to fill in the blanks and 'cover' narrative ellipses, the device can at times be used for overlapping, bridging or suturing purposes, as with a continuing voice-over when the camera cuts from Georges and Roger narrowly escaping from a perilous situation after a failed burglary to Georges and Charlotte relaxed and smiling aboard a train (1:31:20–1:31:40). At other junctures, an ironic, contrastive or contrapuntal result is privileged, as when we cut from uncle Urbain's streak of luck at the casino table to a telegram calling Georges and Charlotte to his deathbed (1:32:40–1:33:10). Whichever the case, the *voix off* is an unmistakable linkage agent and the indispensable vehicle for the retrospective-recapitulative narration. It might also be said to be akin to a mix of mise en scène and montage, as it seemingly drives or controls both the framing and the unfolding of the diegetic events. Briefly stated, in his role as voice-over narrator, Georges-the-thief appears to be a half-veiled stand-in for Louis-the-director, especially if one takes into additional account a visual equivalent of this aural technique: the shaft of light emanating from Randal's lantern as early as the opening sequence, after our hero has broken into a benighted *hôtel particulier* and starts finding his bearings through the deserted rooms and hallways. Significantly, the title page of a treatment bears several evidently disconnected and non-contextualised handwritten mentions, including one that reads *coups de pinceau dans la nuit* – literally, 'paintbrush strokes in(to) the night'. If this analogy is clearly of a pictorial rather than cinematic nature, one may surmise that it points in the direction of theft as a creative act that 'illuminates' reality, if only for a moment as fleeting as a flash of lightning, and with epiphanic potential. Georges's lantern is, indeed, a *magic lantern* lighting the scene, dictating frame composition.[12] Sweeping across the ubiquitous artwork (paintings,

Fig.1: *Le Voleur* (1967): Georges Randal's (Jean-Paul Belmondo) 'magic lantern'.

sculptures, tapestries, furniture) and resting briefly on a few items, the lantern-camera eventually captures the burglar-filmmaker's own reflection in the glass pane of a door (5:35) leading to the room where the protagonist will begin his 'dirty work'. For a split second he peers intently at the self-portrait his light device has unexpectedly conjured up out of the gloom. Such a doppelgänger moment – a potentially monstrous, decidedly enigmatic double image of the self – cannot but herald Malle's next (troubled) project, the *William Wilson* segment of the horror omnibus piece based on Edgar Allan Poe, *Histoires extraordinaires* (*Spirits of the Dead*, 1968), where marked overtones of schizophrenia and autoscopy will logically prevail.

In *Le Voleur*, a sense of scopophilia is more specifically attached to the eponymous character with renewed metafilmic implications. During his inaugural burglary stint with Roger, as the pair find their way to the in-house safe, Georges stops to peek through the bedroom keyhole at the mustachioed Belgian industrialist blithely snoring away with his wife by his side (35:20). Left uncommented (either in voice-over or in the dialogue) in the released film, the quietly precursory libidinal investment, as it were, of such a glimpse had been made explicit in the various script stages, referring for instance to the 'delightfully guilty impression of prying [*indiscrétion*] that one experiences when stepping upon someone else's privacy [*intimité*]' (MALLE 149-B33; f. [3]). Ironically enough, after another, much later break-in (when he is no longer a novice but an accomplished gentleman-burglar), spiced up by an on-site, impromptu tryst with Geneviève Delpich (who turns out to be captivated and aroused by the *intimate* proximity of a safecracker at work), Georges stumbles upon a public spectacle testing the limits of his scopic drive and all but sending him off the deep end: a guillotine execution on a town square (1:00:35–1:01:15). From his inscrutable look – at once mesmerised and repulsed, forlorn and appalled – among a crowd of anonymous gawkers, we swiftly segue into a rare display of anger and frustration when Randal debates with La Margelle the ideological quandary of wanting to 'blow the whole thing up' at the risk of 'bit[ing] the hand that feeds you' (1:01:20–1:01:50). Strikingly indicative of Randal's dogged nonconformism and fierce anti-gregariousness (in congruence with Darien's apologia for individualism against a 'civilization of faceless, irresponsible, unconscious and ruthless despotism' [Darien 1987: 478]) within a pervasive public vs. private tension are not only his increasing propensity to work solo,[13] but his visually irreducible isolation when he stealthily exits from the burglary premises at the crack of dawn and gets re-immersed into *mainstream* society. Literally and spectacularly so in the execution scene, as walking down the street he finds himself caught from all sides in a human *flow* – an anonymous throng of silent plebeians and bourgeois rushing to the scaffold site. In a more subdued but equally glum mode, the epilogue reveals an irremediably lonesome Randal, largely divested of his former imposing presence and self-confidence as he leaves the scene of his larceny. He seems to have inordinately aged and grown weary over the course of the night: his features are drawn, his jaw is shadowed by early morning stubble, and he has dark circles under vacant eyes. A sustained lateral tracking shot follows him as he walks, with two heavy bags in hand, along grey ashen property walls where a 'Post No Bills' (*Défense d'afficher*) inscription is a discreet final reminder of societal interdictions. Before reaching the train station Randal looks back once but without any noticeable sign of apprehension, unlike the ending proposed in the shooting script where sudden panic at hearing dogs bark or seeing two cyclists looking like policemen in the distance causes him to break into a cold sweat and breathe heavily, 'as if he were haunted by a secret angst' (MALLE 143-B32; f. [157]). The previously mentioned three-page synopsis precisely ends on a perpetuation of such a cycle on the job, as it were (aging and fatigue; solitude; dread), with the full knowledge of an inescapable capture, whether imminent or distant.

In an earlier version that also heightens the protagonist's *embourgeoisement* (as symbolised by the Legion of Honor ribbon in his buttonhole), an explicit mention[14] had capped the transparently and continuously sexualised tenor of the hero's burglarizing activities: breaking and entering, picking strongboxes or drilling through safes, prying open secretaires and commodes, or shattering glass display cases with a phallic crowbar. First verbalised by La Margelle as an irresistible, indomitable, all-consuming force ('It'll take your days, your dreams, your sorrows and you'll neither get profit nor notoriety in return' [30:53–31:00]), this erotic possession or addiction is echoed near the conclusion when Georges intimates to Charlotte (who, subsequent to the misappropriation of her late father's estate, already contemplates a cushy *rentier's* existence for the two of them) that he has no intention of mending his ways. Eloquent is his description of the impulse (stronger than himself – nay, 'stronger than anything') and the experience (bringing a sense of plenitude [*plein, lourd*]) of the thieving act:

> At night, in an unknown house, when all is quiet and I arrive, and all those things are there for the taking. I feel as if I were reborn. [...] Then? I go home. Once again, I feel worthless, waiting for the next time. I wait for the whole thing to begin again. (1:49:32–1:50:10)[15]

Among the various script variants, alternate dénouements oscillate between relatively tame classicism and unbridled *romanesque* imagination, between suspended closure and crepuscular mood. Thus, on the one hand, a final – at once definitive and self-questioning – summation-cum-retrospection in voice-over narration borrowing heavily from the original novel (see Darien 1987: 479–80);[16] on the other, one last

Fig.2: *Le Voleur* (1967): Georges as 'picture thief'.

coup d'éclat with Randal letting himself be drafted at the onset of World War I and sent to the front line before deserting in the midst of bloodshed and carnage – 'his closing gesture as a free man' (MALLE 149-B33; f. [25]). He is promptly arrested, tried and … executed! 'He dies without regret, if not without sadness, and leaves a world that is going to disappear with him. He was an individual. The last one, perhaps' (f. [26]). The hero's personal plight coincides with – or is inscribed within – a macro-level, epochal sense of an ending, and a bleak one at that: 'the age of the Assassins'[17] is fast replacing the era of 'thieves acting on moral conviction…' (f. [25]). Regardless, and in the vein of nineteenth-century dramas, a coda has the young Hélène Randal (who might as well be an avatar of Canonnier's daughter, also named Hélène and similarly vengeful…) bring flowers to her father's grave weekly, swearing under her breath to take revenge for him (f. [26]).

In a sense, the thief's ontological status is equally, if not quite correspondingly, fluctuating and labile. Is Randal an outlaw – dare I say, in the name of onomastic homophony, a *vandal*? – relishingly ransacking the beautiful and the antique? *Confer*, towards the film's conclusion, the near-sadistic emphasis on the 'messy' cutting out of oil canvases and taking apart of picture frames, both gestures referring us back, at least approximately, to the cinematic syntax and practice – *découpage* and *deframing*. Is the protagonist then not a both literal and figurative *voleur d'images* (picture thief), a savage desecrator and a deeply melancholy aesthete rolled into one, so to speak – at any rate, a vicarious iconoclastic figure, however *prima facie* improbable, for and of the director himself (with, here again, a desinential echo between their two surnames)? More largely, the thief seems to be undecidedly positioned between predestination and necessity, integration and marginality, foundation and election (or exception). Given to paradoxical witticisms, La Margelle defines *le voleur* indissociably as society's 'safety valve' and 'safeguard' (MALLE 149-B33; f. [5]). He is thus, on one hand, 'the most sociable of men' (MALLE 138-B32; f. [16]) or 'a pillar of bourgeois society' (MALLE 139-B32; f. [15]), not to mention *homo faber* par excellence (MALLE 139-B32; f. [37]); on the other, a defiant maverick (MALLE 149-B33; f. [5]) strictly out of step with the rest of mankind,[18] or, in the priest's words in the film, 'special, completely apart' and, as 'the face they cannot show', 'bound to be misunderstood by the mediocre' (31:08–31:18). Relayed by Roger Voisin, La Margelle puts it even more poetically and gnomically: 'The thief is like moonlight to the honest man' (32:36). Similarly, Malle's film can hardly be defined, even in a subversive or perverted way, as the cinematic equivalent of a *Bildungsroman*, if only owing to the conspicuous ellipsis of the titular character's *coming of age* ('behind bars', as he himself sees his fourteen years spent in boarding school and in the army) – unlike, say, literary exemplars in the art of (self-)portraiture like James Joyce's *A Portrait of the Artist as a Young Man* (1916) or Dylan Thomas's *Portrait of the Artist as a Young Dog* (1940). It could still be seen as akin to a *Künstlerroman*, provided that one considers burglary as a form of (anti-) artistic expression or (anti-)aesthetic performance, intrinsically in conflict with – or in transgression of – the upper classes' values of the hero's time.

Irrespective of such a degree of confusion and contradiction, Bressonian inflections and overtones are easily discernible through the various traits and facets of the Mallean *voleur*. It is worth reminding that a young Louis Malle briefly assisted Robert Bresson on the set of *Un Condamné à mort s'est échappé* (*A Man Escaped*, 1956), before writing a laudatory and hyperbolic review of *Pickpocket* (1959) upon its release which he described as no less than 'one of the four or five great dates in the history of cinema': 'if you deny this film', he further asseverated, 'it is cinema itself as an autonomous art that you call into question' (2011: 731). If Malle assuredly intersected the former opus (and experience) with the Hitchcockian thriller format to create and shape his debut (fiction) film, *Ascenseur pour l'échafaud* (*Elevator to the Gallows*, 1958), *Le Voleur*'s filiation – borrowing, let alone pilfering!, would be overstating the case – lies more patently, *mutatis mutandis*, with *Pickpocket*. Just as much as Michel in the latter film, Randal is meticulously and painstakingly portrayed as 'an individual in the morose fulfillment of his solitary vice' (Billard 2003: 269), even if Michel's is a mostly unmotivated drive, gesturing more toward a Dostoevskyan gratuitous act. Which is not to say, of course, that his sleight of hand, more delicate than intrusive compared to his Mallean counterpart's housebreaking forays, is entirely devoid of erotic subtext.[19] Additional points of commonality would include the internal focalisation (first-person confession in monotone voice-over), the alternation between team work, or *esprit de corps*, and professed elitist individualism (whereby certain *hommes supérieurs*, 'set … apart … by their conscience', 'should be free to disobey laws in some cases', as *Pickpocket*'s protagonist argues), or the tension between chronological continuity and episodic fragmentation. The last of these components is marked by much greater ellipsis in Bresson, as exemplified by Michel's two-year exile in London summarised in one sentence: 'I lost most of my earnings at cards or wasted them on women.' This stands in stark contrast to the merry-go-round of 'fugitive female figures' mentioned in an early treatment of *Le Voleur*, 'successively met, loved and left' by Georges Randal, all caught in a 'whirlwind' perhaps not dissimilar to the signature song (*Le Tourbillon de la vie*) of Truffaut's *Jules et Jim* (1962), 'full of charms, surprises and, very rarely, regrets' (MALLE 149-B33; f. [4]),[20] as well as, for that matter, to old lecherous Urbain's *petites femmes*. Nevertheless, Michel and Georges both have a subterraneously unwavering romantic anchor point in their lives, and Randal might conceivably appropriate Michel's final words in *Pickpocket*, substituting Charlotte for Jeanne: 'Oh, Jeanne, to reach you at last … what strange path I had to take.' In Georges' case, the actual reunion with his childhood love is, despite a lesser diegetic delay and a lack of spiritual dimension, just as circuitous and unexpected.

Literally as well symbolically, Georges Randal's story is precisely that of a *stolen* childhood. The flashback narration unsurprisingly starts with a state(ment) of orphanhood, immediately associated with a prediction of compensatory wealth. Such concerns can surely be apprehended in, but not easily reduced to, materialistic or psychoanalytic terms only: rebellious or illegal greed of gain coming full circle with re-assimilation into – and by – bourgeois society; 'addiction to stealing as [a] psychological response to a childhood trauma', not to mention as a possible authorial reflection of 'a repeated dramatic struggle for freedom from guilt' (Frey 2004: 131, 132). If there is a quest for retribution and reparation it is in fact pursued and attained via the self-chronicling process, in the original novel, as the protagonist is able to rewrite his childhood or 'steal' a new existence through writing. In the film, the emphasis is on the now self-evident and untroubled, now covert and onerous perpetuation of childhood, since theft is not unlike one of the fine arts,[21] or more fittingly perhaps, *l'enfance de l'art*, as the French idiom has it: the infancy of art (the previously-discussed lantern as pre- or primitive cinema) as well as child's play. Concomitantly an impulsive *coup d'essai* (first attempt) and a successful *coup de maître* (master stroke), Randal's debut, as La Margelle describes it, 'showed great dash, and an almost *childish* boldness' (29:53–29:56; emphasis added). Were it not for the melancholy frame and the glum bookending of the retrospective narrative (start: the visit to the grave of Georges' parents, and uncle Urbain's smug, sanctimonious observations; end: Georges confessing his kleptomaniac enslavement and his existential solitude to Charlotte), the guiding thread of 'the green paradise of youthful loves', *aka* 'the sinless paradise of *stolen* joys' ('Mœsta et errabunda,' Baudelaire 1993: 131; emphasis added), would loop the film back on itself. A paradise (and a love) lived, lost and resurrected:[22] from playing ball on the lawn as children (8:57–9:09) – or, much later in life but with renewed childish complicity,[23] pass-(or hide)-the-parcel (i.e. the pouch of purloined jewels) under Urbain's nose (21:25–23:20), after the engagement has been called off – to their reuniting in Georges' London apartment and playful frolicking in the bathroom (1:26:10–1:26:59),[24] and on to what appears on the screen, after the rewriting of Urbain's will by Randal and the 'All's well that ends well' pronounced by the executor, as a slightly toned-down version of the 'childlike, amorous saraband' slowly danced by Charlotte and Georges (1:48:05–1:48:28), as per the description of the shooting script (MALLE 143-B32; f. [153]). While the circular motion (again rendered by the idea of *tourbillonner* – 'whirling around') that thus concludes the fragmented flashback story allegorises the film's overall dynamic, the valorisation of childhood nonetheless knows one (early) exception that takes the form of an outwardly immaterial incident at the reception for the engagement of Armand de Montareuil to Charlotte. A plainly senile Monsieur de Montareuil *père* is reprimanded by his own son for stealing matches from the mantelpiece and sheepishly escorted to bed: 'a peer of France threatened to be strapped', as La Margelle bitingly remarks. In lieu of the willing continuation of, or reconnection with, the idyllic love(s) from early youth what is here witnessed is

Fig.3: *Le Voleur* (1967): The imperceptible 'wrinkle of time.'

passive infantilisation as loss of power or castration, a lapse into a doddering second childhood.

And yet, however discreet it might be, the very notion of aging – of time catching up with the characters – is far from being insignificant or ancillary. Even in such an elated, light-hearted moment as the above-mentioned bathtub scene, Charlotte cannot help but notice Georges' presumed loss of weight or, more tellingly, an imperceptible wrinkle under his left eye (although neither observation is visually corroborated). A certain crepuscular ambience has already been noted earlier which is perhaps less a legacy from decadentist themes permeating the source material (nature vs. culture; order vs. disorder; a moribund society retreating into its shell; a fragmented subject; etc.) than a more or less melancholic rendition of the end of an era, of a page being turned, with the self-protecting bourgeoisie and the repressive authorities making the days of burglar cats and anarchists alike acutely difficult and perilous. This is, in a sense, where author and protagonist part ways. For Malle, such a watershed reflected a deeply felt need for a personal change of direction, for a rejuvenating *ressourcement* that would presently take the dual form of an ethno-cultural 'escape' (even if it turned out to be an illusion and only brought him back to himself in the end) and a return to (his) documentary roots, with *Phantom India* (1969). For Randal – who has 'always dreamed of that which [he] know[s] to be impossible' (1:45:31), as he confesses, by way of farewell, to La Margelle who himself has just expressed a sense of weariness and disgust in an increasing glacial, maniacal world – the waning of the heyday of thievery inversely coincides with his constitutive incapacity to put away the jimmy, so to speak, unlike Roger-La-Honte who makes good on his decision to retire once and for all. A few years later, in the more controversial contexts of the red light district of New Orleans, ca. 1917, in *Pretty Baby* (1978) or of French collaboration during the German Occupation in *Lacombe Lucien* (1974), a *huis clos* setting will be foregrounded, smacking again of decadence, in terms of both sexual dissolution and epochal nadir, or historico-moral exhaustion. In the words of a stupefied john in *Pretty Baby*, as the Storyville brothels are being closed down and their occupants evicted, 'In Rome ... times like these ... barbarians came ... oh, did they. It goes on and on.' In *Le Voleur*, right-wing populist politician Courbassol, haranguing his followers, gives his own ideologically hateful version of a morally corrupt nation whose traditional noble pillars ('family, virtue, property, patriotism') are supposedly 'undermined by these strange insects ... the Jews, the Masons, and hordes of bleating Socialists' (1:19:05–1:19:25).

If fin-de-siècle *Le Voleur* might not be historically on a par with either of the above films there exists something of an inverted symmetry between the characters of Georges and twelve-year-old Violet, in particular, with their indefinable blend of *gravitas* and childishness, melancholia and endurance, showing through the surface – a tension between precocious (forced) maturation and resistance to growing old. More crucial, perhaps, than the sense of a precipitous fall or a sharp tectonic shift is the insidious, but no less insistent suggestion, in *Le Voleur*, of an irreversible erosion at play as well as a polarisation between a period piece (i.e. the reconstruction of a historical subject, era or event) and the notion of cinematography 'as death at work', to use an oft-quoted Cocteau phrase (later reprised by Godard) that somehow finds a chilling concretisation in the creaking noise emitted by the body of a freshly dead woman (1:15:50).[25] If, counter to John Donne's admonition, one were to ask, or 'send to know', for whom the bell tolls in *Le Voleur*, the answer would have to be not 'for thee' – since, after all, nothing could be further from Darien's individualistic anarchism than the metaphysical poet's social and spiritual interconnectedness of humanity – but for Georges Randal. In point of fact, the faint sound of a distant church bell can be heard at both ends of the encompassing narrative, when the protagonist respectively enters (eleven strokes, for 11pm) and leaves (six strokes, for 6am) the targeted estate. While definitely contributing to what might be termed the film's 'quietly tragic', or 'tragically untragic' structure, the strict and tight temporal frame does not preclude a form of manipulation (as early as the opening sequence, which almost seems to have been shot day for night, although there are no indications to that effect in the archival material, including the shooting script) or a touch of irony (the film ends at dawn, despite the contextual sense of a 'twilight' or decline).

The abrupt, visible aging process affecting George's body in the epilogue, as previously noted (that wrinkle below the eye), extends to other characters as well, chief amongst whom is uncle Urbain whose spectacular physical decrepitude lamentably accompanies his descent into moral turpitude. In a brief burial scene that comes between Urbain's death and the opening of the forged will at the *notaire*'s office in the shooting script, but was somehow either never shot or edited out of the film version (might it be because this belated 'return' to the beginning's cemetery was eventually deemed an all-too-obvious closing of the loop?), Renée, the exuberant and fickle socialite who used to act as paid informant for the ring of burglars, is said to have 'aged a bit'. She looks 'less dapper than before' and seems to have lost her gaiety (MALLE 143-B32; f. [151]). In an already-mentioned treatment that presents a much more convoluted, meandering and eventful plot, the criss-crossing of characters and incidents is thusly commented: 'It's a small world, and the same faces, a bit drawn, a bit aged, keep reappearing' (MALLE 149-B33; f. [20]). If such small touches – even smaller in the finished product – are only remotely reminiscent of the famous 'Bal de têtes' episode (a grotesque costume ball) at the Guermantes' matinee toward the end of the monumental *In Search of Lost Time*, if already in the last chapters of the Darien novel the reader crosses paths with most of the characters again and finds out what fate has in store for each of them, the Proustian substratum – previously glimpsed in connection with the magic lantern,[26] but possibly resonating as well in the bell as bookending device[27] – is nonetheless subtly indubitable in Malle's work. The director's notebooks,[28] not to mention other personal documents, are peppered with references to Proust, but more profoundly his films, *Le Voleur* par excellence, illustrate both the ontological essence of the seventh art and the ultimate truth of the Proustian inquiry, namely: 'Time embodied' (Proust 1993: 529). A time at once layered and out of joint, be it prospective (e.g. the dystopian *Black Moon* [1975]), retroactive (exemplarily, *Lacombe Lucien* and *Au revoir les enfants* [1987]), parenthetical (*May Fools*), or transitional (*Atlantic City* [1980]), etc. In the *Recherche*, the final narratorial gesture or intent is simultaneously and indissolubly the greatest authorial achievement: stamping the seal of Time on one's oeuvre. It might not be excessive to state that, notwithstanding *spatial* restlessness being an apparently more immediate, defining trait for both him and his *voleur*, this is precisely what Louis Malle, in his own medium, managed to not only approximate but embrace and effectuate: a self-portrait within a portrait of time – and vice-versa.

Notes

1. I will therefore retain the original title throughout. In Gilles Jacob's striking words, the protagonist is 'a traveling salesman on the common market of thievery' (1967: 56), hence a quintessential modern criminal. If there is one sedentary anchoring point in the narrative one may find it in the King Solomon Hotel, an unsuspected hub or resort of thieves, in Brussels.
2. Interview with Yvonne Baby (*Le Monde* 24 February 1967, quoted in Billard 2003: 271; emphasis added).
3. This is admittedly only relative, since the filmmaker kept dreaming of adapting a number of (mostly classic) novels or novellas to the screen throughout his life, as is amply demonstrated by the screenplay 'The Loner' published for the first time in this volume and discussed in the Introduction. That said, after *Le Voleur* Malle never based any of his films on literary works, with the sole exception of *Damage* (1992) at the opposite end of his career.
4. Interview with Yvonne Baby (Billard 2003: 271); see also: 'For me it was the end of this first period in my film career' (French 1993: 59).
5. Interview with Yvonne Baby. Billard concurs in his description of *Le Voleur*, calling it 'the most secret(ive) [*secret*] of Malle's films to this day' (2003: 270)
6. On the multiple ties between *The Fire Within* and *Le Voleur*, see chapter eleven in this volume.
7. See also: '*Le Voleur* is a film about a disillusioned character shot by a disillusioned director, the only difference being that I had the sense of becoming mainstream [*m'embourgeoiser*], not socially – I've always been a bourgeois – but intellectually' (Mallecot 1978: 27). The spectre of disenchantment generated by a sense of facile skillfulness periodically rears its head in Malle's life and career.

8   MALLE 143-B32 (Louis Malle Archives, Bibliothèque du Film/Cinémathèque Française). In the original novel the priest's name is spelled 'Lamargelle,' rather than 'La Margelle'. A *margelle* is commonly used in French to designate the coping of a well, but also evokes *marge(s)* or margin(s), suggesting the peripheral, and yet decisive, role and influence of the unorthodox man of the cloth (even Georges Randal admits in voice-over never finding out whether La Margelle was a genuine priest) as initiator and protector in the titular thief's trajectory.
9   His other collaborations with Malle include *Viva Maria!* (1965) and *Milou en mai* (*May Fools*, 1990).
10 *Journal du Voleur* (1949), a novel by Jean Genet, whom Malle met with when he was in the early stages of writing the script of *Lacombe Lucien* (see Billard 2003: 337).
11 This description is featured at the start of an undated, typewritten three-page synopsis. In the same archival folder, it is accompanied by the following cursory note that equally captures the gist of the film: 'Dramatic comedy – Autobiography of a criminal. A thief narrates his joys and his adventures, his worries and his loves.'
12 I am here using the term less in connection with Ingmar Bergman's (in his autobiography titled *Laterna magica*) than with Proust's (see the incipit of *Swann's Way*) childhood reminiscences. Coincidentally, in Darien's novel, Georges calls Geneviève Delpich 'Geneviève de Brabant' (chapter XVI) in reference to a famous medieval legend, a key scene of which was featured in the magic lantern that so entranced the Proustian narrator when he was a youngster.
13 Roger revealingly finds it suspicious: '… you're a lone wolf now. It's not my cup of tea. There's something dirty about it' (52:59). The sexual (contextually, onanistic) subtext is even more palpable in the original French with the adjective *vicieux*. From a bilingual perspective, the English 'dirty' does connect, however, Roger's stance to the protagonist's initial self-description of his occupation: 'It's a dirty [*sale*] business I'm in. But there's a reason [*j'ai une excuse*]. I do it dirtily [*salement*]' [07:10]. This direct quote from Darien (1987: 208) is later echoed by Mme Delpich ('It's a very dirty [*vilain*] business you're in, Monsieur' [56:53]).
14 'Before making his way out, as if emerging from a long night of passion [*comme au sortir d'une longue nuit d'amour*], he straightens his untidy clothes, puts his morning coat back on, lights a small cigar and drinks a glass of water' (MALLE 138-B32; f. [25]).
15 In the original monologue, *cette chose à éventrer*, or to be ripped apart (for 'things … for the taking'), reverberates with overtones of violent sexuality. A parenthetical indication in the shooting script clearly equates the end of the looting with postcoital deflation (*subitement dégonflé comme après l'amour*) (MALLE 143-B32; f. [155]). More largely, the paronomastic proximity of *vol* (theft) and *viol* (rape/violation) in French might have been at the back of the director's mind, as well as a term like *jouissance* referring both to property ownership and sexual climax.
16 'I have recounted the story of my life, following the example of so many great men. My existence is over and I am only slightly older than thirty. I have done far

more than I wanted to do, and far less. What shall I do with my heart? What shall I do with my energy? What shall I do with my strength?' (MALLE 139-B32; f. [106]). Juxtaposed to an existential sense of dejection and (self-)disgust, the first interrogation is reprised, by l'abbé La Margelle rather than by the eponymous character, in the shooting script (MALLE 143-B32; f. [148]) and in the film itself.

17 The syntagm is borrowed from a poem by Rimbaud ('Matinée d'ivresse', *Les Illuminations*) and had already served a decade earlier as the title of Julien Duvivier's gloomy crime film, *Voici le temps des assassins* (*Deadlier Than the Male*, 1956).

18 'We went against the tide [à contre-pied du monde]. Summers, far from the beaches. Winters, far from the cities' (voice-over; 44:05–44:10).

19 In his review of the film, Malle notes: 'Not so paradoxically, *Pickpocket* is "also" an erotic film, pickpocketing obviously being but the barely veiled symbol of the sins of the flesh (example: the spasm the first robbery provokes in the hero)' (2011: 734).

20 A list of characters on a loose folio of the MALLE 139-B32 script version bears testimony to the importance of women as *actants* alongside three other categories: 'Thieves / Sympathizers / Others'.

21 Needless to say I am here 'rewording' the title of a well-known 1827 essay by Thomas de Quincey (*On Murder Considered as One of the Fine Arts*), which coincidentally had been adapted to the screen (albeit never theatrically released) by Maurice Boutel two years prior to *Le Voleur: De l'assassinat considéré comme un des beaux-arts* (1964).

22 Interestingly, Billard describes the early Cousteau peregrinations aboard the *Calypso*, in particular in the Seychelles archipelago, as a half-Rousseauist, half-Baudelairean beginning-of-the-world experience before a primordial and pristine nature, the nostalgia of which will soon turn Malle into a 'director of *lost paradises*' (2013: 131; emphasis added).

23 An indication on the shooting script evokes 'a tender, childlike scene that becomes sensual' (MALLE 143-B32; f. [23]).

24 The shooting script refers to those bathtub moments as full of 'very natural gestures', as if Charlotte and Georges found themselves 'falling back into childhood habits' (MALLE 143-B32; f. [126]).

25 'She's not quite dead, though she has stopped living', as arch-anarchist Canonnier – who soon after advocates the dissection of the old bourgeoisie's carcass (*désosser la vieille carcasse bourgeoise*) (1:17:35) – quietly explains.

26 It is revealing that Raúl Ruiz emphatically inserts this determinative episode from the first pages of Proust's saga into his screen version of *Time Regained* (*Le Temps retrouvé*, 1999) when the final tome in fact barely returns to it (except *in fine* in the guise of the magic lantern of Time). One may add that Volker Schlöndorff, who provides a vibrant remembrance of his close ties to Malle in this volume's Foreword, also adapted Proust in *Swann in Love* (*Un Amour de Swann*, 1984), based on the initial book.

27 See 'the noise of the garden bell at Combray – that far-distant noise which nevertheless was in me' (Proust 1993: 530), which, at the end of *Time Regained*, takes narrator and reader right back to the very beginning of *Swann's Way*.

28 See, for instance, Billard 2003: 408–9.

Bibliography

Baudelaire, C. (1993) *The Flowers of Evil*. [*Les Fleurs du Mal* (1857)] Trans. J. McGowan. Oxford : Oxford University Press.
Billard, P. (2003) *Louis Malle. Le rebelle solitaire*. Paris: Plon.
Darien, G. (1987 [1897]) *Le Voleur*. Paris: Gallimard.
French, P. (1993) *Malle on Malle*. London: Faber and Faber.
Frey, H. (2004) *Louis Malle*. Manchester: Manchester University Press.
Jacob, G. (1967) 'Louis Malle au pied du mur', *Cinéma*, 67, 52–62.
Malle, L. (2011 [1959]) 'With *Pickpocket* Bresson Has Found', in J. Quandt (ed.) *Robert Bresson Revised*. Toronto: TIFF Cinematheque, 731–4.
Mallecot, J. (1978) *Louis Malle par Louis Malle*. Paris: Editions de l'Athanor.
Proust, M. (1993 [1927]) *In Search of Lost Time*. [*À la recherche du temps perdu* (1913–1927)] Vol. VI *Time Regained* [*Le Temps retrouvé*]; trans. A. Mayor and T. Kilmartin, revis. D. J. Enright. New York: The Modern Library.

CHAPTER THIRTEEN

Absorption and Reflexivity in Phantom India
Ludovic Cortade

In the autumn of 1967, Louis Malle is invited to present eight of his films in India. Fascinated by what he discovers, he decides to stay on site to undertake a documentary project that he would begin filming at the start of the following year (see Grélier 2005: 11–23). Composed of seven episodes, *Phantom India* (*L'Inde fantôme: Réflexions sur un voyage*, 1969) is an ensemble film lasting nearly six hours in which Malle expresses an interest in the experience of foreignness and the concept of cultural relativity. A complex relationship with India informs Malle's ambivalent rapport with the substance of the images in his film. On one hand, the director allows for free rein of his camera, creating a feeling that the documentary is recording reality, as if it were the mirror image of the facts, a posture that resembles that of Jean Epstein's while shooting his Breton cycle forty years earlier.[1] On the other, *Phantom India* is haunted by the shape-shifting spectre of subjectivity that includes the awareness that the camera modifies the reality which it is supposed to capture, perpetuating a risk of ethnocentrism, as well as the difficulty the director faces in uniting himself with the object of his gaze. Should Malle yield to the belief in the objectivity of the moving image, the documentary can only be understood as a mirage: the voice-over undermines the 'ineffable joy of being one with the universe' on the basis of reflexivity and social criticism.

'*The Impossible Camera*'

Cognisant of the cultural gap which separates him from the Indian subcontinent and sensitive to the inherent difficulties in communication due in part to his lack of knowledge of the local languages, the director introduces his documentary series with caution: 'Words are useless between us. The image is our only connection' ('The

Impossible Camera' [7:12]). He is immediately conscious of his Western point of view; in his notes throughout the production of *Phantom India*, Malle paraphrases Montesquieu's famous inquiry: 'How can one be a filmmaker?'[2] In response to the risk of ethnocentrism to which he exposes himself on his journey, the filmmaker makes his intentions known in the first episode, 'The Impossible Camera': 'Gradually we discovered the simple joy of not planning ahead, of deciding neither what we shoot nor its meaning. We follow the camera. It guides us. We're not filming to defend an idea, or demonstrate one' [11:40]. In 1979, Malle describes his method for *Phantom India* as follows: 'Total improvisation, no pre-conceived judgments, just a camera, a tape recorder and my acute curiosity' (Grégoire 2006: 198). At the same time, Malle is skeptical about the supposed powers of the camera to capture reality as it is. Far from the Bazinian ontology of the photographic image (see Bazin 2002: 9–17), Malle holds that, in a documentary, man is not absent from the image. He thus warns the viewer: 'The gestures, the attitudes, the ceremony, everything happens in the present tense, in the indicative mode, in reality. Once the film has been finished, edited and projected, it can be seen as folklore but it's you and I who make it so' [24:34]. Rather than capture reality the camera serves to dissociate reality from the screen by creating a divide between the subject and the object of the gaze. The making of *Phantom India* rests on the paradox that an attempt at escape through contemplation and absorption actually results in a return to the self towards the end of the series: 'One does not escape oneself by shooting a film' [12:59]. Evoking the disillusion of young Western tourists that he meets on a beach, Malle comments: 'They have come here, like me, to find something else. But none of us can escape our civilization. I'm afraid they're dreaming India, like I am' [40:01]. As such, he suggests a conception of documentary cinema inspired by a literary tradition spanning from Joseph Conrad to Michel Leiris, author of *L'Afrique fantôme* (1934) (see Malle 2005: 21; Ravindranathan 2009).[3] Malle asks the viewer to remain attentive, since the discovery of India and the difficulty of understanding the country inherently invites traces of ethnocentrism (see Cooper 2014).

In *Phantom India*, the perception of cultural difference is often dismantled by a projection of a frame of references which betray a Western point of view. When he discovers dancers, Malle considers the films of Fellini ('The Impossible Camera' [15:34]). The unusual scene of a man peddling a sewing machine along the side of a road is an inevitable echo of Surrealism ('Dream and Reality' [12:00]).[4] When the camera records dogs and birds of prey feeding on a cow's remains, the director experiences the import of his own culture. What appears to be a tragic death for him is, for his companion, but the banal succession of the circles of life and death in a coldly indifferent landscape:

> When I see this scene again today, I realize we reacted in terms of our culture. Around us, the landscape reminded us of Greece, bathed in some austere grandeur that lent an air of mysterious sacrifice. To us, it was a tragedy, a drama in several acts. For our Indian companion, it was an everyday scene, a glimpse of life and death and their calm alternation. There was nothing worth filming, nothing extraordinary. ('The Impossible Camera' [18:00])

Even though Malle states that he and his crew 'follow the camera' and that 'the camera guides us', he eventually projects his own culture and his '*musée imaginaire*' as a Western subject (2005: 8). This strangeness is brought forth not only by an inability to communicate, stemming from a lack of knowledge relative to the country, but also by the presence of the apparatus that is necessary for the production of the film. The camera reveals nothing if not the distance between the observer and the observed. The former modifies the latter by its very presence: 'I think of Levi-Strauss who noted that among ethnographers, the great problem is that the presence of the observer always subtly changes the behavior of those whom he observes' (2005: 204).

The close-up notably illustrates how the presence of the camera creates the facts it is supposed to record. In the presence of the apparatus that is deployed by foreigners, the filmed faces respond with a fixed gaze which escapes from all interpretation and reminds the director of his intrusion: 'We came to see them, but they're the ones looking at us' ('The Impossible Camera' [7:55]).[5] The director remembers the reaction of Etienne Becker, the cameraman for *Phantom India*, whose response is symptomatic of the temptation to render the device invisible and to procure the illusion of transparency while engaging, as Erika Balsom points out, 'in what Oudart calls a "syntagmatic paralysis"' (2009: 128; see Oudart 1969: 61):

> And Etienne said, 'But they're all looking at me, it's not right, tell them not to look.' I said, 'Why should I tell them not to look at us since we're intruders. First, I don't speak their language; just a few of them speak a little English.

Fig. 1: *Phantom India* (1969): Direct cinema, or gazing into the camera.

We're the intruders, disturbing them. They don't know what we're doing, so it's perfectly normal that they look at us. To tell them to not look at us, it's the beginning of mise-en-scène.' It's what I resent about so many documentaries where filmmakers arrive from somewhere and start by telling the people, 'Pretend we are not here.' It is the basic lie of most documentaries, this naïve mise-en-scène, the beginning of distortion of the truth. Very quickly I realized that these looks at the camera were both disturbing and true, and we should never pretend we weren't intruders. So we kept working that way. (French 1993: 71)

It is not surprising that Malle distances himself from the ostensible *cinéma-vérité* that he rejects in favour of *cinéma direct*. The former is 'cinéma mensonge' whereas the latter is based on instinct and improvisation: 'It seems to me that *cinéma direct* is the best way to describe what I was trying to do in India or the documentaries I did in France in 1972, or those American documentaries I did later on' (French 1993: 155). It is therefore not about pretending to conceal the presence of the director in order to reveal the ontology of reality. Rather, it is about placing the director's presence at the forefront so as to communicate the only possible reality to the spectator: the heuristic of a self-reflexive filmmaker. Malle indirectly rejects the conception of a documentary relying on the dramatisation of filmed facts when those same facts claim to be a representation of reality as in *The Silent World* (*Le Monde du silence*, 1956) (see French 1993: 9; Grélier 2005: 26–7).

In *Phantom India*, the distance between the camera and reality imposes itself: 'If the film should be subjective, it is without a doubt that which should be filmed, a team of filmmakers arriving in a village enveloped by the crowd, and all that they film is but an act, short of reinventing reality themselves, another kind of act' (Malle 2005: 143). The act of filming India lies in a transformation of reality which is the product of the history of the gaze and its metamorphoses in the West. Commenting on the statues in a temple in the third episode, 'The Indians and the Sacred', the director notes: 'The statues are regularly repainted in vivid colours, to the great indignation of Western tourists who forget that Greek temples and medieval cathedrals were brightly painted in their heyday too.' [23:40]. In that sense, contemplation is a cultural statement. He expounds on this critical moment of Western art history whereby an aestheticising stance discredits the value of sacred forms: a religious statue is no longer worshipped, but simply admired. Cinema is thus 'the synthesis of a deteriorated esthetic and westernization'.[6] Malle alludes to a problematic dear to André Malraux, that of the disenchantment of the Western gaze which has substituted the cult value of art with its own cultural value, thereby resulting in a bitter statement: 'The West is no longer in harmony with the world.'[7]

Malle holds that religious dances in India should be considered the expression of a cult that engages its witnesses and participants in a collective ritual. With the 'deteriorated aesthetic' perceived by a gaze that is driven by art appreciation, the director opposes the idea that Indian rituals are an ensemble of cultural collective practices: 'Crowds of believers and throngs of priests, countless rituals and intense spiritual life, it reminds us of medieval Christianity when it was a living religion, when the house of God was the house of men, a refuge, a place of rest, a free zone. Atheism does not really exist in India.' ('The Indian and the Sacred' [30:00]). The religious rituals to which Malle bears witness are a reflection of the director's questioning about the evolution of Western art and cinema. Malle's voice-over here reconnects with the *topos* of film criticism of the first half of the twentieth century: that of viewers experiencing a sense of collectivity and belonging in front of a screen. When he speaks of sacred possession and religious enthusiasm in India, Malle references an era when cinema had not yet entered into the dialogue around the disenchantment of critical distance. Inscribed in his commentary appears a conception of art and of cinema that is forged by first-generation film critics such as Elie Faure, for whom the seventh art was an avatar of religious architecture (see Faure 1964). For Malle, the experience of religious rites constitutes a tipping point in *Phantom India*. While the documentary begins with the notion of the 'impossible camera', the director performs a shift that instead leads him on a quest for harmony with his surroundings and the 'ineffable joy of being one with the universe' [21:30].

The Temptation of Absorption

In 'Dream and Reality', the fourth episode of the series, Malle is one with the elements. He and his team travel India 'with no other goal but to lose (themselves) in the vastness of Indian villages' [2:00]. The anxiety generated by fleeting time dissolves into a posture which privileges instant experience over its artistic evocation. In many ways, Malle follows in the footsteps of eighteenth-century aesthetic of absorption (see Fried 1998). He seems to echo Rousseau who, in his *Confessions*, makes mention of moments during his journey between France and Switzerland where he abstained from writing to savour the present moment: 'We'd spend entire days without filming, as if it was no longer what mattered. Freed from my habitual anxiety and dissatisfaction, I lived in the present moment' [3:08].[8] The filmmaker radically distances himself from his initial disclaimer. The distinction between subject and object allows for self-abandonment and the body's absorption into nature:

> We wanted to experience things, not understand them. For instance, these priests officiating on the beach near a temple use gestures that we don't understand. But that no longer matters. We may not understand those people, but we're instinctively connected to them, sharing their link with nature. Letting ourselves go in their presence, we feel as we've rediscovered something we've lost. [3:49]

The film then unfolds in silence for four long minutes while the viewer observes farmers working the land on screen. The voice-over resumes:

> Nothing shocked me anymore, for I'd accepted another perspective on the world. It's not about explaining or dominating the world, but being part of it,

Fig. 2: *Phantom India*: Contemplative absorption.

fitting into it. [...] If happiness is defined as a sense of balance and bliss, being in harmony with one's surroundings, interior peace, then these Indian peasants are happier than us, who've destroyed nature and do battle with time in the absurd pursuit of material well-being in the end sharing only our loneliness. 'Man must lose himself in the universe, like an elephant in the forest, a fish in the sea, a bird in the sky', says one of their texts. [6:50]

During these contemplative sequences, Malle substitutes the close-ups with a more inclusive framing scale to situate the priests' and the farmers' gestures within their environment. At this time, as the voice-over vanishes, Malle conveys that the film is shot in real time. He seems to be calling back to the second episode of Rossellini's RAI television miniseries, *India: Matri Bhumi* (*L'India vista da Rossellini*, 1959), in which the narrator articulates his thoughts regarding religious cremation: 'Maybe it's beautiful to dissolve into nature' (see Rosenbaum 2009: 57). In this way, the director dissolves

Fig. 3: *Phantom India*: Harmony in space.

his subjectivity into the object he contemplates. The consciousness of the subject and his self-imposed limits of observation disappear to make way for the fantasy of the '*bon sauvage*': 'In the Nilgiri mountains at an altitude of 8,000 feet, we found the ideal society: the Toda tribe. Today there are only 800 Todas. For untold centuries they've lived in these isolated mountains, where their solitude was undisturbed until the arrival of the English' ('On the Fringes of Indian Society' [40:30]).

Even if Malle suspends the voice-over for extended periods of time to fabricate an illusion of perfect harmony with reality, he winds up resisting this temptation in order to revive the consciousness of the relationship between the filmmaker and the person filmed, as had been established in 'The Impossible Camera'. The gaze cannot be completely dissolved into the object of its contemplation: 'The danger of this business is losing the subjective aspect, the reality on which I work being so complicated, so absorbent' (Malle 2005: 140). The desire to be a part of the universe is but a vain attempt: the yearning for absorption is a ghost. It is the role of the link between sound and image to bring to light the director's presence in the work: 'The Semitic tradition says, 'In the beginning was the Word', and the Hindu respond that the Absolute is sound' ('The Indians and the Sacred' [17:20]).[9] In *Phantom India*, the sound/image connection is never superfluous. As such, Malle's work is placed under the auspices of Robert Bresson. During his training, the filmmaker-apprentice delighted in *Les Dames du bois de Boulogne*, then *The Diary of a Country Priest*, a film which he went on to include in the oral exam portion of his entrance exam at the French national film school IDHEC (see Billard 2003: 93, 101). Furthermore, Malle participated in *A Man Escaped*, a co-production between his brother Jean-François and Robert Bresson. This experience was, however, curtailed by Malle's involvement in shooting *The Silent World*. It is probable that Bresson's film influenced Maurice Ronet's meticulous gestures in *Elevator to the Gallows* (*Ascenseur pour l'échafaud*, 1958) (see Billard 2003: 151–3). Malle subsequently devoted an article to the subject upon the release of *Pickpocket* (1959). In his *Notes on the Cinematographer*, written between 1950 and 1974, Bresson hollows out the apparent substance of images: 'Cinematography, the art, with images, of *representing* nothing' (1997: 116). Sound is used to refrain from indulging in what Bresson calls *cartepostalisme*, or the aesthetic of the postcard.

Malle's archives document the filmmaker's hesitation with regard to the function of the commentary in *Phantom India*. He had first envisioned an ensemble of quotes and personal comments that would place his 'Indian experience' within the context of world events and the history of mankind. The voice-over would have assembled a montage of various texts by André Malraux, the anthropologist Louis Dumont and Nehru; blurbs from Indian media; and reflections on the film itself. Malle ultimately rejected this layout, deeming it 'artificial and complicated'.[10] He also considered an 'editing journal' (*journal de montage*) based on a dialogue with his editor, an option which he ended up viewing as 'pretentious [and] uselessly chatty'.[11] His goal was also to remind the spectator of the relative failure and frustration of his documentary insomuch as it did not show what Malle wanted to 'truly film'.[12] While Malle considered different voice-over options, he settled on one objective: sound should be conceived as a reflective practice, serving as a way to undermine the viewer's absorption in the moving image, thus allowing him or her to grasp the extent to which reality has been transformed due to the implicit biases of the Westerner who holds the camera. Malle aims at bringing the marks of enunciation to light as well as the performative presence of the Indians who are in front of the camera: 'We were often tempted to direct them. Very basic direction, like trying to get this woman not to look at the camera, to act as if it weren't there. The woman gets involved. She watches her child, she watches herself. It becomes a kind of performance in which she plays herself, a spinner' ('A Look at the Castes' [8:32]). Upon seeing the camera, the villagers take out musical instruments which they have not used in years, thinking they are playing their role by offering a picturesque image of themselves: 'They're having a great time reconstructing this scene' [10:30]. In this way, Malle does not film individuals whose ethnographic interest could be captured by the camera; instead, he films people who play the role they believe they should play in the face of Westerners.

It is thus impossible to untangle the survival of traditional cultures specific to India from the acculturation they endure, but by its inferred reflexivity, the voice-over allows for a critical distance. Cultural aspects that look to be authentic are described as the manifestation of Western tastes. Malle emphasises: 'Strangely enough, the wave of interest in yoga in the West led to a somewhat spurious revival in its country of origin. There's a new nostalgia for the past. Bombay's bourgeois will discuss the evils of consumerism with you' ('Bombay' [22:18]). Malle's voice-over casts a light on how the Indian people's body and language espouse Western norms. He establishes a contrast between an Indian woman who speaks like a technocrat and the inhabitants of an Indian village who ignore that colonialism had ended [42:20]. In the penultimate section of *Phantom India*, the director questions the members of the 'ashram', a religious community. Initially, he allows his interlocutors to explain their project and their metaphysics. They are working on the edification of an ideal city in which different ethnicities and beliefs would come together for a movement of internal peace. The idea would be embodied by a monument containing dirt from all the continents. The director concludes by superimposing his own ironic comments to expose the theatricality of his interlocutors: 'They're annoying, this rich Indian businessman who found his road to Damascus, and this pompous French man. To my mind, all mystical experience is accompanied by a certain anguish, or at least anxiety' ('On the Fringes of Indian Society' [37:30]). If India is a ghost, it is above all because meeting the Other comes from an illusion, in the same way that the body can be absorbed into a holistic vision of the universe. Malle's voice-over questions the legitimacy of the image. The critical function of the director's voice depends at once on the illustration of the performativity of Indian people as well as a commentary about social and economic realities that weaken Westerners' imagined fantasies about India. If in the third and fourth episodes of the series Malle was fascinated with an organic unity strengthened by common beliefs, in the last episodes he eventually demystifies the illusion of cohesion produced by the images of a traditional village with an economic analysis and social criticism: 'An idyllic vision of agricultural communism where everyone's needs are met, which, even if it did once exist, is lost to the villagers today. These water carriers are no longer linked to the community but to the landowners who pay their salary. Today, the division of labour looks more like one person exploiting another' ('A Look at the Castes' [31:20]). The temptation of absorption makes way for social criticism. In the same way, Malle explains that the Indian caste system offers the individual a compensation for the rule imposed on him: 'Living interdependently, in relation to everyone else, he's part of a whole, shielded from solitude' [29:33]. However, he opposes social reality: 'castes are becoming rigid, autonomous blocks that are no longer interdependent, but rivals and competitors. The hierarchy subsists but, stripped of its traditional framework, it's become a plain and simple form of economic oppression' [38:18].

Among the films that he directed, *Phantom India* was the one which made Malle most proud (see French 1993: 224). The documentary series takes on a particular importance in the director's filmography in the sense that it clearly lays out the terms of ambivalence fundamental to the director: tempted by the 'ineffable joy of being one with the universe', Malle is reminded of his own subjectivity which he ends up cultivating in the name of reflexivity and social criticism. Several films of his bear the same ambivalence. If the underwater depths of *The Silent World* constitute the prime example of absorption, Malle subsequently critiqued the film for conveying a questionable impression of truth and transparency. *Lacombe Lucien*'s (1974) final bucolic sequence, which borrows a part of the soundtrack from *L'Inde fantôme*, is a reminder of the main character's special relationship with nature that was troubled by his war collaboration activities. As in *Phantom India*, the residents of Minnesota who appear in *And the Pursuit of Happiness* (1986) produce an impression of immutable joy and content for which the reward is a social conformism that Malle deems intolerable. *May Fools* (*Milou en mai*, 1989) outlines the satirical portrait of the upper class in the French countryside: the harmony between family members takes shape in a bucolic setting, but it cracks when the events of May 1968 precipitate their escape to a forest which reveals itself to be as hostile as imaginary hordes of raging protesters. Malle's works present us with an ambivalent relationship to the world that rests on the temptation of absorption and self-reflexivity. In that sense, and despite the fraught rapport with the New Wave, Malle's work is sharing a common ground with Jean-Luc Godard (see Cortade 2014). On the one hand, beauty is unfolding in space and time. On the other, the beholder's self-reflexivity eventually undermines absorption. Like Javal speaking to Camille in *Contempt* (*Le Mépris*, 1963), Malle might well whisper to India: "I love you totally, tenderly, tragically."

Notes

1. Regarding *Finnis Terrae*, Epstein wrote: 'Leaving the Ouessant archipelago, I felt I was taking with me not a film but a fact. And once this fact had been transported to Paris, something of the material and spiritual reality of the island life would henceforth be missing. An occult business' (Abel 1988: 424).
2. MALLE 0223 B55 1/5. Archives held at the Bibliothèque du Film (Cinémathèque Française, Paris).

3   'I like to be in exile, to be displaced. I always was a total fan of Conrad, I like the literary tradition of people who are displaced in another country, be it that they speak of their own country while somewhere else or that they observe a society that is not their own, but about which they have adequate knowledge' (Malle 1987: 38–9).
4   Malle alludes to Lautréamont's phrase in *Les Chants de Maldoror* (chant VI, 1): 'As beautiful as the chance encounter of a sewing machine and an umbrella on the dissection table' (1938: 256). The quotation is considered a catchphrase for Surrealism. Dali drew a gouache painting: *Sewing machine with umbrellas in a Surrealist landscape* (1941).
5   It would be difficult to find a posture more opposite to Epstein's conception of the close-up: 'The close-up modifies the drama by the impact of proximity. Pain is within reach. If I stretch out my arm I touch you, and that is intimacy. [...] It's not even true that there is air between us; I consume it. It is in me like a sacrament. Maximal visual acuity' (Abel 1988: 239).
6   MALLE 0223 B55 1/5.
7   MALLE 1281 B236 3/6.
8   See *Confessions* IV: 'Ah! If only they could have seen the works of my first youth, those I conceived during my journeys, those I composed and I never wrote down … but why, you will ask, did you not write them down? And why, I reply, should I have done so? Why deprive myself of present joys simply in order to tell others that I have enjoyed them? What did I care for readers, a public, or all the world, so long as I was soaring on high?' (Rousseau 2000: 158).
9   Sound is of particular importance in Malle's filmography. See in this volume 'Truth and Poetry. An Interview with John Guare,' where the *Atlantic City* co-screenwriter reminisces about the care with which Malle judged the quality of a take with regard to its rhythm and musicality.
10 MALLE 0223 B55 1/5.
11 Ibid.
12 Ibid.

Bibliography

Abel, R. (1988) *French Film Theory and Criticism: A History/Anthology, 1907–1939* [Vol. 1: 1907–1929]. Princeton, NJ: Princeton University Press.
Balsom, E. (2009) 'Haunted by Impossibility: Louis Malle's *Phantom India*,' in S. Jhaveri (ed.) *Outsider Films on India 1950–1990*. Mumbai: Shoestring, 124–47.
Bazin, A. (2002 [1945]) 'Ontologie de l'image photographique', in *Qu'est-ce que le cinéma?* Paris: Les Editions du Cerf, 12–13.
Billard, P. (2003) *Louis Malle, le rebelle solitaire*. Paris: Plon.
Bresson, R. (1997) *Notes on the Cinematographer*; trans. J. Griffin. Copenhagen and Los Angeles: Green Integer.
Cooper, D. (2014) 'Louis Malle's "Jana Gana Mana" in Three Episodes from *Phantom India*', *Journal of Commonwealth and Postcolonial Studies*, 2, 2, 19–26.

Cortade, L. (2014) '*Le Mépris*: Landscape as Tragedy,' in T. Conley and T. J. Kline (eds.) *A Companion to Jean-Luc Godard*. Hoboken: Wiley-Blackwell, 156–70.
Faure, E. (1964) *Fonction du cinéma. De la cinéplastique à son destin social*. Paris: Denoël/Gonthier.
French, P. (1993) *Malle on Malle*. London: Faber and Faber.
Fried, M. (1988) *Absorption and Theatricality: Painting and Beholder in the Age of Diderot*. Chicago, IL: University of Chicago Press.
Grégoire, S. (2006) 'Louis Malle, un observateur minutieux de la société contemporaine: le "détour documentaire" et le "détour américain",' unpublished Ph.D. thesis, Université Michel de Montaigne (Bordeaux III).
Grélier, R. (2005) 'L'Inde vue de profil', in L. Malle, *L'Inde Fantôme. Carnet de voyage*. Paris: Gallimard, 11–29.
Lautréamont [I. L. Ducasse] (1938) 'Les Chants de Maldoror', in *Œuvres complètes*. Paris: GLM.
Malle, L. (1987) Interviewed by F. Audé and J.-P. Jeancolas, *Positif*, 320, 32–9.
____ (2005) *L'Inde fantôme. Carnet de voyage*. Paris: Gallimard.
Oudart, J.-P. (1969) 'Les trajets et les lieux', *Cahiers du cinéma*, 213, 61.
Ravindranathan, T. (2009) 'Le regard en miroir: *L'Afrique Fantôme* et *L'Inde fantôme*', *Cahiers Michel Leiris*, 2, 148–77.
Rosenbaum, J. (2009) 'The creation of the world: Rossellini's *India: Matri Bhumi*', in S. Jhaveri (ed.) *Outsider Films on India 1950–1990*. Mumbai: Shoestring, 48–75.
Rousseau, J.-J. (2000 [1782/1789]) *Confessions*; trans. A. Scholar. Oxford: Oxford University Press.

CHAPTER FOURTEEN

Fog of War: Lacombe Lucien *and Its Afterlives*

Steven Ungar

'War is the realm of uncertainty; three quarters of the factors on which action in war is based are wrapped in a fog of greater or lesser uncertainty.'

– Carl von Clausewitz

Questions

When, in 1945, Jean-Paul Sartre asked 'What is a Collaborator?' he went beyond abstract definition by situating his answer in the immediate aftermath of the 1940–44 German Occupation.[1] *Situer* and *situations* were Sartre's preferred terms for the mandate to historicise he would soon formulate in *What is Literature?* (1948) as a priority for the committed writer (*écrivain engagé*). Neither 'who is a collaborator?' nor 'who collaborated?' but instead something closer to what constituted the collaborator as a specific type of individual or subject. A year later, Sartre wrote a book-length essay, *Réflexions sur la question juive* – literally *Reflections on the Jewish Question*, but more often translated as *Anti-Semite and Jew* – in which he asserted that a Jew was, at least in part, someone whom non-Jews designated as a Jew. The assertion – provocative, to say the least – arguably extended to collaborators for whom the term was likewise imposed from outside. Which suggested that few among the 30,000 French men and women who carried out policies of the German military and its puppet regime at Vichy would have identified themselves as collaborators. Where many among them likely saw themselves as patriots of a true France, others dismissed them outright as *collabos* or, more crudely, *salauds* (bastards).[2]

This reconsideration of Louis Malle and Patrick Modiano's 1974 feature film, *Lacombe Lucien*, begins with Sartre in 1945–46 because the questions he raised at the time – 'what is a collaborator?' and 'what is a Jew?' – persist in ongoing enquiry surrounding the Occupation. The questions were subject to debate in 1945–46 and in 1974. They remain so today. I argue below that the film's portrait of a seventeen-year-old who joins the German Gestapo in June 1944 overlays the collaborator question in a strict sense – that is, what is/was a collaborator in 1944 France? – with a sense of what this 1974 film can tell us today about the period in question. What follows is an essay in two parts: a recap with commentary, followed by remarks on how the evolving reception of Malle and Modiano's film continues to recast the questions 'what is a collaborator?' and 'what is a Jew?' into a concomitant *Lacombe Lucien* question. I conclude with remarks on Modiano's role in the film's genesis and production.

More Questions

When, at an early point in *Lacombe Lucien*, the film's adolescent protagonist asks 'what is a Free Mason?' – and not, as at least one scholar has suggested 'what is a Jew?' – he does so out of ignorance (see Hewitt 2000: 86).[3] This sets him apart from the intellectual collaborators Pierre Drieu La Rochelle, Marcel Déat, Abel Bonnard, Henri Béraud and Robert Brasillach named by Sartre and others. Lucien utters the word 'Jew' midway through the film when he says to the fugitive Albert Horn, 'So, it's true … you're a Jew?' before adding that Monsieur Faure, one of Lucien's new cronies, had described Jews as the enemies of France. Horn was until recently a high-end tailor in Paris. He is hiding with his mother, Bella, and his teenage daughter, France. All three are waiting to cross over to Spain to escape arrest and deportation. Earlier in the film, Jean-Bertrand de Voisins, another of Lucien's Gestapo cronies, had described Horn as a rich and miserly Jew (see Malle and Modiano 1975: 36).[4]

Both sequences suggest that Lucien has had little or no prior contact with Jews. In this, he resembles the man in Sartre's *L'Être et le néant* (*Being and Nothingness*, 1943) who learns how to become a waiter by pretending to be a waiter. Lucien assumes the role of 'Gestapo bully boy' (Pauline Kael's expression) by imitating the words and prejudices of those whom he meets at the Hôtel des Grottes. But exactly when does playacting become real? At what point does Lucien become a real rather than a pretend collaborator? What is a collaborator? (see Kael 1974: 94).[5]

Loose Plot Recap, With Commentary

Lacombe Lucien is set in Southwestern France between June and October 1944. Malle and cinematographer Tonino delli Colli filmed in and near the town of Figeac, about seventy kilometers east of Cahors. The film's plot duration coincides roughly with the 6 June D-Day landings in Normandy and the aftermath of the August liberation of Paris. Lacombe is first seen as an orderly mopping the floor and emptying bedpans in a Catholic hospice. When he returns on work leave to his family farm in a nearby village, he discovers that his mother has taken up with a local farmer, Laborit, who has moved in to direct farm operations after Lucien's father was sent to Germany as a prisoner of war (see Billard 2003: 340).[6] Laborit informs Lucien that his 'good for nothing' (*feignant*) older brother, Joseph, has joined the resistance underground (*maquis*). He adds that Lucien should have forewarned his mother that he was coming to the farm. Bored with his menial job and feeling unwelcome at home, Lucien approaches his former school teacher, M. Peyssac, about joining the local resistance underground. Peyssac turns him down as not ready for serious business. When the rear tire of Lucien's bicycle blows out on his way back to town, he walks the rest of the way. It is mid-June and nightfall occurs after 10pm. Lucien is unaware that he is violating a curfew.

The sequences of Lucien bicycling to and from his family farm provide contrasting treatments of how he occupies his spatial environment. The first sequence [2:54–6:06], which also serves as a credit sequence, is a montage of long, medium-long and medium shots from the left and front. Tracking shots and pans occasionally turn the vegetation into a green blur. Gypsy jazz (*jazz manouche*) by guitarist Django Reinhardt and the Quintette du Hot Club de France enhances the exhilaration exuded by shots of Lucien coasting and pedaling. The music is extra-diegetic: Lacombe does not hear it. The only word spoken is that of a young shepherdess who calls out to Lucien as he nears the farm house. By contrast, Malle and Delli Colli set Lucien's departure from the farm [17:38–18:45] beneath a glaring sun, with minimal shadow. The grass and trees are yellowish-green, with ambient sounds of crickets and the crunch of Lucien walking his bike after the blowout. There is no music and no speech except for Lucien's expletive – *merde* – when the tire blows out.[7]

Back in the town at dusk, Lucien watches noisy revelers (*fêtards*) pull a sporty convertible into the courtyard of a hotel. He sticks his head inside the entrance just as a man accuses him of spying and pushes him ahead. He will need to explain himself. Once inside the hotel, Lucien is awed by the music, dancing, liquor and gaiety at odds with the sober day-to-day life he leads. He does not yet realise that he has walked into the local headquarters of the German police (Gestapo) staffed by local French sympathisers. Lucien fails to see that these men and women are collaborators.

One of the men, a former bicycle racer named Aubert whom Lucien remembers seeing in a race five years earlier, offers him an apéritif to loosen him up and ply him for information. Unaccustomed to being the object of attention and to the effects of the drinks that keep coming his way, Lucien names Peyssac – codename *le lieutenant Voltaire* – as a contact for the local underground. He wakes up the next morning in the hotel just before Peyssac is brought in for questioning. Lucien does not realise that he has denounced the man with whom Aubert and his comrades are preparing to have 'a little chat' (*on va bavarder*). Adopted as a new recruit by the local Gestapo without really knowing who they are or what they do, Lucien thrives on the attention of people who seem ready to treat him as one of their own. Much like Edward G. Robinson's Enrico ('Rico') Bondello in *Little Caesar* (Mervyn LeRoy, 1931), Lucien sees an opportunity to be somebody.

Later that day, Aubert tests Lucien's skills with a pistol by asking him to shoot for the left nostril of an elderly man photographed in close-up on a large poster inside the hotel. Malle heightened the incongruity of the situation by placing the poster only a few feet from where a man and woman are playing ping pong. Was this a way for Malle to suggest the rapidity of Lucien's turn from the Resistance (ping) to the German

Fig. 1: *Lacombe Lucien* (1974): Marshall Pétain's moustache.

Gestapo (pong)? Lucien misses the nostril, but shoots off part of the man's right moustache. He seems not to recognise the man in the poster as Field Marshall Philippe Pétain, the World War I hero and figurehead of the Vichy regime. A portrait of Pétain on a bedside table also appears in the opening hospice sequence. A rosary draped over the photo suggests a shared devotion toward the Catholic Church and the État Français. Might this devotion extend to collusion? The association is reinforced when a nun turns on the radio to listen to Vichy propagandist and Minister of Information Philippe Henriot. An outspoken anti-Communist and anti-Semite sometimes called 'the French Goebbels', Henriot was assassinated in his ministry office in Paris by resistance members disguised as members of the paramilitary pro-Vichy *milice* (militia). The assassination occurred on 28 June 1944, only days after the broadcast heard in the opening sequence. The period detail inscribes the fictional sequence within a historical moment whose short-term outcome at least some of the film's spectators in 1974 – but not Lucien in 1944 – would know.

The target practice sequence seems by design a provocation. Shooting at a poster of a government leader whose portrait is displayed throughout France makes Lucien into a literal iconoclast. By implication, *Lacombe Lucien* is a myth-breaking (mythoclastic) film that takes figurative potshots at accounts of a unified resistance among Gaullists and Communists. In 1974, debates surrounding wartime and postwar France were still under the sway of what historian Henry Rousso would refer to a decade later as Resistancialist myths of an occupied France united in opposition to a tiny minority loyal to the État Français. Lucien's unawareness concerning the man at whose image he was shooting suggests his political ignorance and/or indifference. It is also an instance of dramatic irony that belittles Lucien for not knowing what spectators of the film would likely know about the man in the poster.

By 1974, the release of Marcel Ophüls' documentary, *Le Chagrin et la pitié* (*The Sorrow and the Pity*) in 1969 and the publication of Robert O. Paxton's *Vichy France* three years later had challenged received accounts of the Occupation. Ophüls and Paxton could be dismissed, at least momentarily, as foreigners. Malle was French, and so perceptions of the betrayal attributed to what he and Modiano had done in *Lacombe Lucien* were less forgiving. Moreover, the film's portrait of an unthinking and boorish collaborator did little to ease Malle's complex relations with the 'Young Turk'

Cahiers du cinéma critics turned New Wave filmmakers. Ginette Vincendeau writes that Malle's early filmmaking placed him in an odd position vis-à-vis the New Wave: 'He is a precursor to it with *Ascenseur pour l'échafaud* (1957) ... and already marginal to it in *Zazie dans le métro* (1960)' (1996: 60). Michel Marie points out that Malle never worked as a critic and that he came to filmmaking after studying at France's national film school (2003: 58).

Interviewed in *Cahiers du cinéma*, Michel Foucault inscribed his remarks on the eroticisation of power in *Lacombe Lucien* within a broader consideration of popular memory (see Bonitzer and Toubiana 1974: 7–8). In *Les Temps modernes*, Christian Zimmer wrote that what was at stake in the film went beyond wartime collaboration toward the politics of the present day. The *mode rétro*, he argued, was not a morbid attraction to a sinister period of France's recent past, but the expression of a political tendency (*courant*) associated with the decline of Gaullism (1974: 2495). A decade later, the historian Pascal Ory's smug look back at the *mode rétro* peppered accounts of films and books dealing with the Occupation since 1971 with *ad hominem* swipes at writers and filmmakers. *Lacombe Lucien*, he wrote, was an upsetting dream (*chimère troublante*) in which Malle's proverbial coldness combined for better or worse with Modiano's passion for recounting the escapades of a kind of black Percival; Lucien, Ory wrote, was 'this wild youth, swept by history into a radical amorality [who] entered the Gestapo rather than the Resistance because he killed chickens with his hands and because his bicycle tire blew out at the wrong moment' (1981: 113).

Writing in the *Nouvelle Revue Française*, Michel Mohrt argued that the film's major weakness was the mediocrity of its principal character whose lack of self-awareness he found atypical: 'Is he good? Is he cruel? Neither one nor the other: he is stupid' (1974: 116).[8] More interesting for Mohrt was Albert Horn whose acute sense of his absurd situation resembled those of characters in novels by Patrick Modiano. Most of those who attacked *Lacombe Lucien* saw themselves as guardians of a historical truth under threat (see Austin 1996: 28). This was especially the case among Gaullists and Communists for whom the portrait of an apolitical Lucien insulted the memory of the Resistance. Among notable exceptions, Jean-Louis Bory described *Lacombe Lucien* as the first true film about the Occupation because it drew on the temporal gap of some twenty-nine years from the events it depicted (1974: 56). Likewise on target was Jill Forbes who identified the significance of *Lacombe Lucien* in its valorisation of history as an individual rather than a collective experience. Lucien, Forbes wrote, is presented as a loner, not part of any collectivity and thus carrying no mark of exemplarity: 'He is almost the anti-Brechtian hero par excellence, moving through a war, even camp-following like Mother Courage, but unlike Brecht's character, unable either to understand, or to teach us about, the collective processes at work' (1993: 244).

Many who mistook the adjective *rétro* as an abbreviation of 'retrograde' rather than 'retrospective' dismissed Lucien and the Horns as invented characters with no grounding in the historical past. Yet Malle recounted as early as 1974 that when he described the character of Lucien to a garage owner in the village of Limogne near Malle's country house, the man told him about a certain Hercule, an eighteen-year-old whom the Gestapo in Cahors had sent to infiltrate a resistance group in the area:

> He was very active. He denounced a lot of people. Thanks to him there was a raid by the Gestapo and the German army in Figeac and they deported a hundred people from the town. Eventually Hercule was arrested and executed immediately after the war. So the garage owner said, 'You're telling the story of Hercule.' (Greene 1995: 89)[9]

Malle and Modiano's cinematic portrait of Lucien was indeed that of a collaborator, but of a collaborator type whose remove from the one Sartre had portrayed in 1945 confused many viewers of the film. It is thus all the more important that archival research has documented the existence of collaborator-types similar to Lucien in regional police and judicial records of rank-and-file youths who aided the Germans or who actively supported Hitler's regime (see Ott 2009: 290).

When De Voisins decides that Lucien needs a new suit to match his new identity, they visit a tailor to whom De Voisins' father had introduced him as a little boy. The cosmopolitan Albert Horn (Holger Löwenadler) is accustomed to being treated with deference. He is visibly upset by the humiliations his fugitive status imposes on him, his mother, and his daughter. Horn is further disheartened by the attention Lucien soon pays to France (Aurore Clément), who seems alternately amused by and wary of this young Frenchman from a world other than her own. Difference stimulates attraction, as much for France as for Lucien.

Belle Juive, France Juive, Sale Juive

The decision to name Horn's daughter France was first and foremost a provocation. And this because it drew on the sexual aura attributed to Jewish women whose taboo status among non-Jews – and especially among anti-Semites – cast them as simultaneously repulsive and desirable. Jean-Bernard tells Lucien that some female Jews are so incredibly beautiful that compared to them, other women look like mares.[10] This beauty can prompt jealousy, as in the case of the Hôtel des Grottes maid, Marie, who lashes out at France by calling her 'sale Juive' (dirty Jew). The expression *belle Juive* is never explicitly associated with the character of France Horn. Yet the statements by De Voisins and Marie register what Maurice Samuels has described as the complex affective ambivalence directed toward figures of the Jew in literature and other discourses (2006: 170).[11] This ambivalence is evident not only in the Baudelaire poem cited above, but also in the character of Rachel in Fromenthal Halévy and Eugène Scribe's 1835 grand opera, *La Juive* (*The Jewess*). By extension it conjures up the 1886 book *La France juive*, in which Edouard Drumont argued for an anti-Semitism grounded in differences of race, finance and religion. France Horn is an object of curiosity for Lucien not only because she is a Jew, but also because she is a cultured urbanite (*citadine*) whom her father describes rather subjectively as *une vraie Française* (a real French woman). In sum, she is literally and figuratively a *France juive* (a Jewish France) whose identity hovers between assimilation and exclusion. Following the confrontation with Marie, France breaks into tears as she tells Lucien, 'I'm so tired I can't stand it anymore… I'm so tired of being a Jew…' (Malle and Modiano 1975: 83).[12]

Fig. 2: *Lacombe Lucien*: France (Aurore Clément) as Botticellian Venus.

Lucien's behaviour toward the Horn family alternates between boorishness, generosity and thuggery. Sensing that he is not their equal in terms of education and sophistication, Lucien offers gifts of champagne, a watch, and flowers as tokens of the power and material wealth his new identity affords him. When the Horns' landlord tries to exploit their fugitive status by raising their rent, Lucien humiliates him by demanding to see his papers before dropping them to the floor. A later sequence with a naked France lying in her bed suggests that Lucien has raped her. Yet at another point, Albert Horn confesses that he is unable to loathe Lucien completely (Malle and Modiano 1975: 88). Horn eventually buckles under the strains of his life in hiding. He dresses in fine clothing and goes to the Gestapo headquarters, ostensibly to talk man-to-man with Lucien. Going to the Hôtel des Grottes is Horn's way of committing suicide. He prefers to die by asserting who he is/was rather than continue the shady existence he and his family endure as fugitives.[13] When Lucien accompanies an SS officer sent to arrest France and her grandmother, he shoots the soldier. Tellingly, he does this less out of a desire to help France and Bella than because the soldier had pocketed the (stolen) watch Lucien had offered to Albert Horn. Throughout the film, Malle and Modiano show Lucien's actions to be motivated less by ideology than by the advantages his new identity as 'German police' affords him.

Lucien, France and Bella leave by car for the Spanish border. When the car breaks down, they retreat to an isolated forest area where Lucien's skills as a hunter enable them to undertake a temporary break from the war. Cinematically, the sequence takes shape as an extended montage. As France bathes in a spring, Malle and Delli Colli film her in shallow depth-of-field close-up with the facial features and colouring of Venus in Alessandro Botticelli's *Nascita di Venere* (*The Birth of Venus*, mid-1480s). Even so, France's look of uncertainty darkens the radiance she exudes. The final minutes of the film feature segments of Lucien and France in sexual play as well as others that suggest insurmountable differences. At one point, France calls out to Lucien whom she fails to see perched on a tree branch directly above her. As with the shepherdess who had called out to him earlier in the film, Lucien does not reply. Soon after, France holds a large rock as she stands over a dozing Lucien. Will she attack him or is this merely a passing thought? The film's closing shot is a medium close-up of Lucien from the left, lying supine on the ground with a pensive expression on his face. White letters

Fig. 3: *Lacombe Lucien*: The end of an 'idyll'.

superimposed on the shot read: 'Lucien Lacombe was arrested on October 12, 1944. He was tried by a military court of the Resistance, sentenced to death and executed' (Criterion DVD subtitles).

The final shot and caption resituate the brief idyll in its historical moment. Yet the closure they provide is less than complete. For Lucien, the final shot recasts the idyll as a figurative parenthesis; for France and Bella, it is closer to an ellipsis. Equally meaningful is the fact that the superimposed caption reinstates the patronymic designation – Lucien Lacombe – that Lucien had dropped when he first introduced himself to France. Use of the *passé simple* tense likewise anchors the assertion's finality. In the end, death and history return the self-styled Lacombe Lucien to the patronymic order from which he had sought to escape.

Malle and Modiano intended from the start to portray Lacombe as a collaborator, but an ordinary collaborator rather than one with a high public profile.[14] As early as 1974, Malle described in detail how he had wanted to tell the story of a young peasant from southwest France who joined the Gestapo under circumstances that included rejection from a local Resistance contact and a bicycle tire blowout that led him inadvertently to violate a curfew imposed by occupying forces. In the same interview, Malle stated that the genesis of the film drew on an early 1970s stay in Mexico City during which he learned of adolescent delinquents whom the police had recruited as informants in place of serving jail time (see Jacob 1974: 29). Known in Spanish as *halcones* (falcons), the delinquents infiltrated groups of student demonstrators, resulting in denunciations, arrests and deaths.

Another working project drew on collaboration among indigenous Algerian *harkis* who sided with the French colonisers and military against the Front de libération nationale (National Liberation Front, or FLN). Malle dropped this approach when he realised that the events resulting in the end of French Algeria in 1962 were still too close in time to engage without controversy. Elsewhere, Malle stated that in 1954 he spent several evenings at the home of Jacques-Yves Cousteau's father, Daniel, where he met the younger Cousteau's brother, Pierre, a one-time editor-in-chief of the anti-Semitic weekly *Je suis partout* and Pierre's friend, the journalist-writer Lucien Rebatet.[15] This encounter might explain Malle's inclusion of a shot in *Lacombe Lucien* in which the rightwing ideologue Faure brandishes an issue of *Je suis partout*.

As with the portrait of Pétain earlier in the film, it was unlikely that Lucien knew what *Je suis partout* was and what it stood for. Accordingly, its visible presence was directed to spectators in 1974 for whom Faure's choice of reading matter would be something more than a period detail. Less than a decade later, Malle and Volker Schlöndorff accompanied a journalist friend at *Paris-Match* to Algeria where they visited a mountain-based army fortress of paramilitary fascist *colons* (colonisers) and witnessed incidents of violence inflicted on local populations. Documentary footage shot during the visit was never used. Finally, Malle cited the impact of reading a 1969 *Esquire* magazine article on Lt. William Calley, Jr. and the March 1968 My Lai massacre as marking another possible dimension of the unformed collaboration project (see Southern 2006: 151).

Any serious discussion of *Lacombe Lucien*'s genesis and production needs to address Malle's recollections of his wartime childhood, which included ideological as well as generational divides among pro-Resistance and pro-Vichy family members. Of special relevance is Malle's memory of the Gestapo's arrest and deportation of a Jewish student granted haven by priests at the Jesuit boarding school to which Malle's parents had sent him to keep him safe away from Paris. Richard Golsan has noted that Malle did not exorcise his personal ghosts of the Occupation until the 1987 release of *Au revoir les enfants* (*Goodbye, Children*), a film whose box-office popularity and positive critical reception built in part on the absence of the ambiguities in *Lacombe Lucien* that had infuriated critics a decade earlier (1996: 145). But what if *Lacombe Lucien* and *Au revoir les enfants* staged Malle's efforts to work through his wartime memories in a two-phase process? If so, their ordering suggests that *Lacombe Lucien* staged the ambiguities whose residual effects Malle needed to disclose before confronting the boarding school incident. This would make *Lacombe Lucien* a screen account that disclosed only in part Malle's recollections of the Occupation period to which he would return a decade later. Lynn Higgins writes that Malle's awareness of the contagious nature of guilt in collaboration and his attempt to take responsibility for it are discernible in differences of structure and narrative technique in the two films (1992: 205–6). For H. R. Kedward, the character of Lucien can be understood better if one imagines *Au revoir les enfants* already made (2001: 231). The prospect is tempting, but only if one excludes the notion that Malle needed to confront the difficult truths staged in *Lacombe Lucien* before addressing the incident he had experienced as a child in 1944.

Fog of war

The release of *Lacombe Lucien* a decade before *Au revoir les enfants* raises questions concerning Malle's turn to fiction as a means of testing historical facts and their traces. And this as a way of contending with multiple types and degrees of ambiguity affecting strategic, operational and tactical practices of war. Usage of the expression 'fog of war' in conjunction with military simulations as well as video games can extend to literary and cinematic representation. *Lacombe Lucien* has retained its timeliness through the verification of details that critics of the 1970s and 1980s had condemned as invented or inaccurate. I want to pursue this line of thought in conjunction with ongoing scholarship before concluding with considerations of the *mode rétro* and the role of screenplay co-author Patrick Modiano. In so doing, I take my cue from Malle's statement to Gilles Jacob that the backward gaze fifteen years after the fact is a freer and sharper gaze that often brings us back to the present and to current reality (Jacob 1974: 30).

Writing in 1991, historian Paul Jankowski assessed evolving receptions of *Lacombe Lucien*. He started by citing Sartre's twin claims in 'What is a Collaborator?' that: (i) all workers and almost all peasants were resisters; and (ii) most collaborators came from the bourgeoisie, before linking Malle with novelists who had replaced historical mythology and social geometry with human portraits, 'and so had started to print the story that *Lacombe Lucien* would continue on film' (1991: 458). Placing Malle and Modiano's film alongside clandestine texts by Louis Parrot, Marcel Aymé, Jean-Louis Curtis and Jean-Louis Bory going back as far as 1943, Jankowski argued that all had jettisoned the Manichean lexicon of civil war in order to treat collaborators in psychological, sexual or pathological terms. Seventeen years after *Lacombe Lucien*'s release, Jankowski documented how resistance and collaboration groups had exploited fear of deportation to Germany under the aegis of the Vichy regime's *Service du Travail Obligatoire* (Service of Obligatory/Forced Labor) to attract new recruits. Far from releasing Lucien from responsibility for his actions, Jankowski concluded that Lucien's punctured bicycle tire explained the situation that led him to the local Gestapo headquarters, but not its consequences (*dénouement*) (1991: 466).

More recently, Sandra Ott has drawn on trial dossiers she characterised as providing 'a rich ethnographic resource' with which to test conclusions that historians have drawn about rank-and-file adolescents and youths in southwest France who aided the Germans or who actively supported Hitler's regime (2011: 290). Ott based her remarks on the dossiers related to accused collaborators Johan de Chappotin and Henri Lasserre, noting that she did this less to draw parallels with Malle's cinematic portrait of Lucien than to challenge perceptions that youths such as Lucien responded to wartime conditions in France naïvely and apolitically. Taking Jankowski and Ott's research into account counters earlier allegations that the collaborator portrayed in *Lacombe Lucien* was an invention with no grounding in the historical record. This deferred reply to critical response in the 1970s holds true. And this in large part because of Ott's documentation concerning young collaborators, even when the latter's motivations were more openly political than those of Lucien.

The evolving status of *Lacombe Lucien* among ongoing debates is best understood in conjunction with cinematic treatments of Occupation-era France at least as far back as *Le Silence de la mer* (*The Silence of the Sea*, Jean-Pierre Melville, 1949) and *Nuit et brouillard* (*Night and Fog*, Alain Resnais, 1956). Much depends on the moment of release. Comparing two films directed by Claude Berri – *Le Vieil Homme et l'enfant* (*The Two of Us*, 1967) and *Uranus* (1991) – discloses differences in visual treatment and period detail inflected by historical perspective and the respective star qualities of male leads Michel Simon and Gérard Depardieu. For the 1970s, productive comparisons with *Il Conformista* (*The Conformist*, Bernardo Bertolucci, 1970), *Il Portiere di notte* (*The Night Porter*, Liliana Cavani, 1974) and *Monsieur Klein* (Joseph Losey, 1976) coincide with a period of obsessional scrutiny concerning the Occupation.

Reducing *Lacombe Lucien, The Night Porter* and *Monsieur Klein* to examples of a *mode rétro* grounded in period detail seems in retrospect a shortsighted response in contrast to the revised understanding associated with the Vichy syndrome paradigm that Rousso and others would champion starting in the 1980s. Released only months after *Lacombe Lucien,* Resnais' *Stavisky* (1974) featured period details including a musical score by Stephen Sondheim and costumes by Yves Saint-Laurent. Presumably subject to the same allegations as *Lacombe Lucien, Stavisky*'s mixed reviews fell far short of the vituperative reception prompted by Malle and Modiano's film. *Stavisky* is also relevant with reference to Modiano, for whom Alexandre Stavisky had been a childhood hero embodying all the ghosts he sought to exorcise: 'Stavisky is the father, the Jewish father ... the crook-acrobat ... whose fate announces that of the real father around whom the same climate of spinelessness and corruption develops during the Occupation' (Nettelbeck and Hueston 1986: 49).

Alexandre Stavisky was a Russian Jew born in 1888 in present-day Ukraine. In the late 1920s, he was a small-time crook who emerged from prison in France as a self-styled financier named Serge Alexandre. In December 1933, revelations concerning the collapse of Stavisky/Alexander's junk bond schemes implicated members of Camille Chautemps' Radical party government. On 8 January 1934, Stavisky was found dead in a chalet near Chamonix. The official cause of death was suicide, but press coverage suggested that he may have been 'suicided' (see Andrew and Ungar 2005). A month later, allegations of a government cover-up of Stavisky's death precipitated demonstrations on the Place de la Concorde and threats of a right-wing putsch. The fact that Serge Alexandre was the name Modiano chose for the narrator of his third novel, *Les Boulevards de ceinture* (*Ring Roads*, 1972), attests to the fusion – and often deliberate confusion – of autobiography and fiction across Modiano's opus (Nettelbeck 2006: 36). Such fusions and confusions already abound in Modiano's first novel, *La Place de l'Étoile* (1968), whose protagonist, the self-described *Juif antisémite* Raphaël Schlemilovitch, goes to the movies with Robert Brasillach.

Different kinds of fusion and confusion extend in *Lacombe Lucien* to the interactions between Malle and Modiano across three versions of a four-handed screenplay (*scénario à quatre mains*). Aurélie Feste-Guidon (2012) notes in her close reading of a sequence involving Lucien, France and Albert how the versions disclose a progressive elimination of explicit violence that adds, in particular, to the complex portrait of France Horn. Alain Kleinberger reaches a similar conclusion when he argues that while Modiano's contribution to the evolving screenplay does not inflect Malle's original project, the final screenplay displays a chasteness more typical of Modiano's fiction than Malle's films (2010: 463). In both instances, access to archival materials adds to what I have referred to above as a *Lacombe Lucien* question that continues to make Malle and Modiano's film a timely measure of enquiry and debate surrounding the Occupation. *Lacombe Lucien* is thus a striking instance of revised perspectives associated with accounts of the Occupation in literary and cinematic fictions. I am thinking here of how reception and debate surrounding Irène Némirovsky's *Suite française* (2004) and Jonathan Littell's *Les Bienveillantes* (*The Kindly Ones*, 2006) have renewed understanding of the same questions – what is a collaborator?' 'what is a Jew?' – raised by Sartre in 1945 and some three decades later by Malle and Modiano (see Golsan and Watts 2012). Close to a half-century after the fact, there is more to learn about the past and the present by questioning *Lacombe Lucien* and its afterlives.

Notes

1. First published in *La République Française*, 8 and 9 (August and September 1945).
2. Concerning the figure of 30,000, see Singerman 2005. On Sartre's *Réflexions*, see Suleiman 1995 and 1999. Philippe Carrard cites *Lacombe Lucien* in conjunction with the contingency of choosing between the resistance and collaboration among adolescents and young adults in 1944 (Carrard 2010: 150).
3. Leah Hewitt corrects Naomi Greene when she writes that it is Julien in Malle's *Au revoir les enfants* (1987) – rather than Lucien in *Lacombe Lucien* – who asks the meaning of the derogatory term *youpin* ('Yid'); see Malle 1987: 85–6. The Criterion DVD shows the passage at 47:14.
4. Lucien is a quick learner. When Albert Horn objects after Lucien invites France to a party at the Hôtel des Grottes, Lucien threatens to take him instead: 'There are some people down there who aren't fond of Jews, Monsieur Horn' (Malle and Modiano 1975: 76).
5. Kael's review displays a keen sense of what Malle wanted to achieve cinematically when she asserts that the movie is the boy's face, especially when the failure of his face to register emotion forecloses any minor urge for spectators to identify with Pierre Blaise's Lucien.
6. The name Laborit is a homonym of Pierre Laborie (1936–2017), a Professor of Modern History at the University of Toulouse whom Malle consulted throughout the production. Pierre Billard alerts readers to this connection, but he spells the professor's name as Laborit.
7. The sequences recall the flashback sequence in *Hiroshima mon amour* (Alain Resnais, 1959) during which the disgraced female protagonist (Emmanuelle Riva) leaves wartime Nevers by bicycle for Paris. In Bertrand Tavernier's *Laissez-passer* (*Safe Conduct*, 2002), the male lead Jean Devaivre (Jacques Gamblin) likewise pedals roundtrip between occupied Paris and a provincial France seemingly removed from the war. For the first bicycling sequence in *Lacombe Lucien*, jazz buff Malle chose a 1942–43 recording in which Reinhardt replaced violinist Stéphane Grappelli with a clarinetist.
8. A youthful supporter of the neo-Royalist Action Française movement, Mohrt (1914–2011) was a prolific author of novels, essays and historical studies as early as 1941. In his longtime role as an editor at Editions Gallimard, he specialised in twentieth-century American fiction. Mohrt was elected to the Académie Française in 1985.
9. Cited in Hewitt 2000: 86 and French 1993: 93.
10. 'There are some Jewish girls who are incredibly beautiful… Compared to them, other women look like mares… That's right, old boy: mares… I had a Jewish

fiancée once, some time back… Incredibly stacked, and incredibly wealthy' (Malle and Modiano 1975: 79). The figure of the hypersexualised Jewish woman goes back at least as far as Baudelaire (see his 'Une nuit que j'étais près d'une affreuse Juive' [1857] poem in the 'Spleen et idéal' section of *Les Fleurs du mal*).

11 I thank Maurice Samuels, Marie Ferran and Patrick Ferran for their input on this topic.

12 Destrée blurs semantic differences between the nominal *Juive* (with a capital 'J') and the adjectival *juive* (whose non-capitalised form ought to translate as 'Jewish') when she translates *être juive* as 'being a Jew'. The nominal form strikes me as reductive and racialised, with parallels to film titles such as Jean Rouch's *Moi, un Noir* (1958) and Ousmane Sembène's *La Noire de…* (1966).

13 In this, Horn recalls Louis Jouvet's Monsieur Edmond in Marcel Carné's *Hôtel du Nord* (1938) who laments that '[his] life is not an existence'.

14 Early titles considered for the film included *Le Milicien: Fils du soleil* ('The Militiaman: Son of the Sun') and *Lucien*.

15 Hugo Frey writes that when Pierre Cousteau (1906–1958) fell seriously ill, Malle offered a blood transfusion after learning that he and Cousteau shared the same blood type. Even though the effort failed, a biographer of Malle, Bernard Violet, considered Malle's offer an elegant gesture and sign of support for a dying man; see Frey 2004: 76 and Violet 1993: 150.

Bibliography

Andrew, D. and S. Ungar (2005) 'A Page in History: Alain Resnais' *Stavisky* (1974) and … the 1930s', in *Popular Front Paris and the Poetics of Culture*. Cambridge, MA: Harvard University Press, 15–51.

Austin, G. (1996) *Contemporary French Film: An Introduction*. Manchester: Manchester University Press.

Billard, P. (2003) *Louis Malle: Le rebelle solitaire*. Paris: Plon.

Bonitzer, P. and S. Toubiana (1974) 'Entretien avec Michel Foucault', *Cahiers du cinéma*, 251/2, 5–15.

Bory, J.-L. (1974) 'Servitudes et misères d'un salaud', *Nouvel Observateur*, 481 (28 January), 56–7.

Carrard, P. (2010) *The French Who Fought for Hitler: Memories from the Outcasts*. New York: Cambridge Univ. Press.

Feste-Guidon, A. (2012) '*Lacombe Lucien*: un film de Louis Malle sous influence modianesque', in M. Heck and R. Guidée (eds) *Patrick Modiano*. Paris: L'Herne, 246–52.

Forbes, J. (1993) *The Cinema in France: After the New Wave*. Bloomington, IN: Indiana University Press.

French, P. (1993) *Malle on Malle*. London: Faber and Faber.

Frey, H. (2004) *Louis Malle*. Manchester: Manchester University Press.

Golsan, R. (1996) 'Collaboration and Context: *Lacombe Lucien*, the Mode Retro, and the Vichy Syndrome', in S. Ungar and T. Conley (eds) *Identity Papers:*

Contested Nationhood in 20th-Century France. Minneapolis, MN: University of Minnesota Press, 139–55.

Golsan, R. and P. Watts (eds) (2012) 'Literature and History: Around *Suite Française* and *Les Bienveillantes*', *Yale French Studies*, 121.

Greene, N. (1995) 'La Vie en rose: Images of the Occupation in French Cinema', in L. Kritzman (ed.) *Auschwitz and After: Race, Culture, and 'the Jewish Question' in France*. New York: Routledge, 283–98.

Hewitt, L. (2000) 'Salubrious Scandals/Effective Provocations: Identity Politics Surrounding *Lacombe Lucien*', *South Central Review*, 17, 3, 71–87.

Higgins, L. (1992) 'If Looks Could Kill: Louis Malle's Portraits of Collaboration', in R. Golsan (ed.) *Fascism, Aesthetics, and Culture*. Hanover, NE: University Press of New England, 198–211.

Jacob, G. (1974) 'Entretien avec Louis Malle (à propos de *Lacombe Lucien*)', *Positif*, 157, 29–34.

Jankowski, P. (1991) 'In Defense of Fiction: Resistance, Collaboration, and *Lacombe Lucien*', *Journal of Modern History*, 63, 3, 457–82.

Kael, P. (1974) 'The Current Cinema: *Lacombe Lucien*', *New Yorker*, 30 September, 94–100.

Kedward, H. R. (2001) 'The Anti-Carnival of Collaboration: Louis Malle's *Lacombe Lucien* (1974)', in S. Hayward and G. Vincendeau (eds) *French Film: Texts and Contexts*, 2nd edn. New York: Routledge, 227–39.

Kleinberger, A. (2010) 'Patrick Modiano: co-scénariste de la mémoire historique. A propos de *Lacombe Lucien* (Louis Malle, 1974)', in A.-Y. Julien (ed.) *Modiano ou les intermittences de la mémoire*. Paris: Hermann, 446–64.

Malle, L. (1987) *Au revoir les enfants*. Paris: Gallimard.

Malle, L. and P. Modiano (1975 [1974]) *Lacombe Lucien*; trans. S. Destrée. New York: Viking.

Marie, M. (2003) *The French New Wave: An Artistic School*; trans. R. Neupert. Malden, MA: Blackwell.

Mohrt, M. (1974) 'Louis Malle, *Lacombe Lucien*', *Nouvelle Revue Française*, 257, 115–17.

Nettelbeck, C. (2006) 'Modiano's *stylo*: A Novelist in the Age of Cinema', *French Cultural Studies*, 17, 1, 35–54.

Nettelbeck, C. and P. Hueston (1986) 'D'un clown collabo à une France juive: *Lacombe Lucien*', in *Patrick Modiano, pièces d'identité: écrire l'entretemps*. Paris: Lettres Modernes, 53–64.

Ory, P. (1981) 'Comme en l'an quarante. Dix années de "Rétro Satanas",' *Le Débat*, 16, 109–17.

Ott, S. (2011) 'Looking for *Lacombe Lucien* in Southwestern France', *Proceedings of the Western Society for French History*, 39, 290–9.

Paxton, R. (1972) *Vichy France: Old Guard and New Order: 1940–1944*. New York: Norton.

Samuels, M. (2006) 'Metaphors of Modernity: Prostitutes, Bankers, and Other Jews in Balzac's *Splendeurs et misères des courtisanes*', *Romanic Review*, 97, 2, 169–81.

Sartre, J.-P. (1988 [1948]) *'What is Literature?' and Other Essays*. Cambridge, MA: Harvard University Press.
____ (2008 [1949]) 'What is a Collaborator?', in *The Aftermath of War (Situations III)*; trans. C. Turner. London: Seagull, 41–64.
Singerman, A. (2005) 'Histoire et ambiguïté: un nouveau regard sur *Lacombe Lucien*', *French Review*, 80, 5, 1058–68.
Southern, N. C., with J. Weissgerber (2006) *The Films of Louis Malle: A Critical Analysis*. Jefferson, NC: McFarland.
Suleiman, S. (1995) 'The Jew in Sartre's *Réflexions sur la question juive*', in L. Nochlin and T. Garb (eds) *The Jew in the Text*. London: Thames and Hudson, 201–18.
____ (1999) 'Rereading Rereading: Further Reflections on Sartre's *Réflexions*', *October*, 87, 129–38.
Vincendeau, G. (1996) *The Companion to French Cinema*. London: Cassell.
Violet, B. (1993) *Cousteau, une biographie*. Paris: Fayard.
Zimmer, C. (1974) 'La Paille dans le discours de l'ordre', *Temps modernes*, 336, 2492–505.

CHAPTER FIFTEEN

Memory, Friendship, and History in Au revoir les enfants

Sandy Flitterman-Lewis

> 'A haunting and timeless truth.'
> – Louis Malle (1988: v)

Louis Malle's 1987 film about a childhood wartime memory that had haunted him for forty years proves as disturbing and powerful for audiences thirty years after its release as it was in its initial run, evoking the essential reciprocity of personal and historical memory across the cinematic field. Hugo Frey characterises this work by calling Malle 'a memorial activist ... a filmmaker who repeatedly engage[s] with the meaning of the past' (2004: 90). French audiences of the 1980s were, for the most part, still embroiled in the arguments and contradictions of the Occupation, while contemporary audiences often see both times, the 1940s and the 1980s, as distant historical moments whose evocative resonances barely whisper to them. And yet the power of intense experience combined with distanced yet compassionate observation, enlightened by the revelation of newly significant historical information, is capable of transcending time and crossing generations. Most of the film is a recognisable New Wave-like representation of childhood friendship, maternal attachment, curiosity and youthful bonding, while the last few sequences wake us from our nostalgic reverie to face the cold historical truth of the Final Solution and Vichy France's eager participation in it.

Audience familiarity with the exact events is not necessary, yet the historical and symbolic specificity of this film makes it extremely timely and relevant. It challenges us with our own questions of conscience and moral obligation at a time when these are continually and excruciatingly called into question. The film is set in January of 1944 at a Catholic boarding school near Fontainebleau; Malle's statement in voice-over at the film's close comes from somewhere between New York (as per the preface to the screenplay), Paris and Le Coual, in 1987. Referring to the sight of his denounced Jewish friend being marched away by the Gestapo he states: 'Over forty years have passed, but I will remember every second of that January morning until the day I die.' With this poignant personal intervention, the fictive spell is broken and fictional narrative becomes evidentiary document of a very specific past, and a warning for the future. Story becomes History and personal reflection becomes a social and moral call to action. Likewise, film spectatorship is transformed from passive absorption in a compelling narrative to active engagement with issues in contemporary history.

The film opens at the Paris Lyon train station where young Julien Quentin (Gaspard Manesse) delivers an emotional farewell to his mother, as students returning from winter vacation board the waiting train. A subtle irony is set up as Madame Quentin waves to them and says 'Bonjour les enfants', something that will trace the distance between the relatively minor separation anxiety of this bourgeois kid and the very tragic separation (preceded by other invisible separations) of the ending, where the phrase that titles the film 'Au revoir les enfants' – uttered by Père Jean as he accompanies his three charges to their, and his own, deaths – punctuates the overwhelming and memorable sadness of the scene. It is clear from the very beginning of the film, and by the preponderance of close-ups, that this is Julien's story; the fact that he is a proxy for Malle himself, although surmised, is only established with certainty by the ending quote. With this opening we are thus plunged into the world of adolescent boys, and every attendant activity, though occurring against the backdrop of the Nazi occupation of France and its Vichy counterpart near the end of the War, seems ordinary enough. Yet we notice, with a subtle sense of dread, that the varied signs of this Occupation will coalesce as the historical details (redolent of the vicious ideology and hatred characteristic of the era) move from simple background to motivating foreground and transform the story of innocence and joyful exuberance into one of unwitting betrayal and brutal cruelty, and thus into an iconic representation of the age. By the end of the film it is not only Julien's story, but also that of the hidden Jewish children, and beyond that, the story of a generation's tragedy that is ours as well.

A short summary of the action will help to trace this evolution. Once maternal goodbyes are said, the film's credits appear over the movement of the train, as a forlorn Julien watches the landscape speed by. This will create a parallel with the ending close-up of a devastated Julien, suddenly and painfully aware of the unspeakable cruelty of the world as he now sees it, while Malle as the director attests to the power of that vivid memory, thus integrating the represented self with the actual self, and historical catastrophe with personal trauma. The opening credits end with a dedication, as the young students march past a sign designating 'Carmelite Convent. School of Saint John of the Cross', and Malle's own children are evoked: 'For Cuotemoc, Justine et Chloë.' These credits, signs of authorship and production, will disappear until the film's end, when Malle makes his final statement, one that brings us back to the reality outside of the world of the film, and emphasises the central place of children in the Malle oeuvre, this time in the context of historical awareness. In an interview Malle has said that he feels that today's young generation can relate very well to the context of 1944: 'It gave me hope, because I could suddenly see that children of today watching this film would be seized by what was going on…' (French 1993: 178). Malle thus forges a revised cinematic relation to history, one in which moral, ethical and political imperatives combine to create a new kind of film spectatorship through the powerful evocation of a distant past with crucial implications for the present and the future.

Almost as soon as Julien arrives at the school he is introduced to one of three new boys that the headmaster, Père Jean (Philippe Morier-Genoud), has brought in – a young, fairly awkward, quiet boy named Jean Bonnet (Raphaël Fejtö), who is immediately taunted by the others. He's a stranger in their midst, but Julien's participatory hostility gradually turns to curiosity and then to friendship, as the two grow closer by degrees until the catastrophic final scenes. Within the relatively enclosed spaces of the school (the classroom, the dormitory, the refectory, the schoolyard, the air-raid cellar, the chapel) – except for a number of forays into the village, including the public bathhouse, lunch at a fancy restaurant, and one frightening event amid the boulders of the Fontainebleau park – the film gives a fairly accurate representation of the daily life and adolescent energy of the boarding school. It is a world apart, where the safety of ritual and the commonality of experience offer a kind of protective shield for the more disturbing considerations of the age. But this atmosphere functions really as authenticating background for what becomes the heart of the story: Julien's recognition of Jean's Jewish identity (and its significance, retrospectively determined, in history). From that point on, in the middle of the film, the narrative gradually transforms its focus from Julien's experience to historical reflection.

In 1987 the issue of 'hidden children', those Jewish boys and girls who sought protection from extermination by assuming false identities either with compassionate families or with those who sought to profit from the crisis, was barely acknowledged. The first International Conference of Hidden Children took place in New York City in 1991, four years after the film came out. Most who participated thought their experience was unique; the conference changed that and gave way to organisations that encouraged accounts of the now-grown children about their experiences in hiding. In 1987 the few references to this phenomenon were absorbed in Holocaust literature, but Malle's choice to make this film acknowledges his political commitment, as a non-Jew, to this widespread, yet fairly unknown situation. Of course, the fate of some hidden children was much worse – most of those discovered or denounced perished in Auschwitz, with no one left to tell their stories. Malle gives voice to at least one of these, in the context of his own personal revelation. And what he conveys in making the film is his own horror as a child which gave him the desire to become a filmmaker: 'In 1942, we would see children my age wearing the yellow star. I would ask, 'Why? Why him and not me?' No one had a good answer. From that moment on, I felt that the world of adults was one of injustice, deception, false explanations, hypocrisy and lies […]. And following that morning in January, when Bonnet left, the feeling became a certitude' (Insdorf 2003: 91)

The growing importance of the Holocaust imprint on this childhood memory finds concrete expression as the film progresses. And the film which, as noted, seems to be at first glance about childhood innocence and its loss becomes a narrative of historically tragic proportions. As the friendship between Julien and this mysterious boy

Fig. 1: *Au revoir les enfants* (1987): Jean and Julien wrapped in blankets.

warms, the reality of the hostile threat becomes more visible. The thread of increasing reference to the anti-Semitic attitudes that undergird the Holocaust gains prominence. This can be traced in the film through a set of subtle and symbolic clusters in categories beginning with the letter M: Mothers, Memento, Milice, Movies, Music, Murder and Memory. Either they are foregrounded in specific events or situations, or they are alluded to across the text, creating a symbolic network of references that become central to the film's meaning.

Mothers

The most obvious examples of the Mother are the farewell scenes of Julien and his elegant haute bourgeoisie mother (played by Francine Racette). More than once he buries his head in her ample fur, expresses the need to be near her (and she for him), and articulates his adulation through the somewhat desperate appeals. Yet to the fullness of Mme Quentin's presence to her son and her avowals of a similar desire to be together, we can contrast the absence of Jean Bonnet's mother, alluded to in short conversations that subtly suggest the tragedy of most Jewish mothers of the Holocaust, something even Holocaust literature itself tends to elide, with its focus on surviving children, and the scarcity of available maternal writing. Here, however, a letter falls from Jean's desk, and an unresponsive Julien reads it. The poignant tones of Julien's dispassionate voice-over ironise the tenderness of the text: 'My little darling, as you'll understand, it is very hard for me to write to you. Monsieur D. is going to Lyon and has offered to mail this letter. Your aunt and I are going out as little as possible.' Julien responds with an unfeeling 'your mother's up to something', as the reality of hunted Jews in hiding has not yet taken hold of him. Later in a completely innocuous and friendly exchange, the privileged Julien tells Jean about the skill of his family cook, Adrienne. But he doesn't understand the absence of a family cook for Jean who sets him straight by stating that his mother, who does all the family cooking, is a very good cook, while the enormity of the tragedy of Jewish families is evoked under the surface. Family cooking is one of the ways in which Jewish culture is transmitted, the way it surrounds its young. Jewish cooking can suggest a familial embrace and in this context it is a sign of an impossible longing.

Memento

A reminder of the past, a keepsake. Late one night Julien awakens to see Jean place two candles on his bed and say a prayer in a foreign language: *Baruch Atah Adonai…* This evokes the candle-lighting ceremony performed every Friday night in Jewish families for the Sabbath. The meal is central, there are flowers and special dishes, the family is around the dining table, and the table becomes a sort of secular altar. Deriving from the fourth Biblical commandment, 'Remember the Sabbath and keep it Holy', it is meant to be a celebration of the family through a weekly observance. 'The Joy of Sabbath' is the title that Leon Ringelblum used for his documentation of Jewish life in the Warsaw ghetto contrasting optimistic humanism with murderous brutality. The Sabbath designates a day separate from usual daily activities and is especially seen as a time of familial togetherness. These resonances are unknown, even strange, to Julien but those familiar with Sabbath customs will understand the longing attached to the ritual and the drive toward preservation that Jean performs. Nevertheless, this is after the discovery of Jean's real name and provides further confirmation of an affinity in spite of strangeness; Julien's curiosity is piqued and his sense of connection to this 'outsider' grows. In speaking of this sequence, Malle confirms that he didn't see it himself, but was told about it by someone who did. Skeptics will point out that true hidden children did not dare make their religion visible; however, Malle's interest in including this scene attests to the affirmative portrait of Jewish identity in the context of the widespread cultural anti-Semitism of the War years, and Julien and Jean's growing affinity in spite of different religious backgrounds and their contrasting cultural acceptance.

Milice

The oversised black berets of the Milice, the French fascist police force formed in 1943, make their emphatic appearance in the fashionable restaurant, 'Le Grand Cerf'. A French paramilitary organisation created by the Vichy regime ostensibly in order to combat the French Resistance, their xenophobic stance allows them to harass Jews in the name of patriotism. The appearance of these men here, a demonstration of the servile collaboration associated with this group, is solely to exercise the ill-gotten authority by terrorising an elegant Jewish diner. 'Madame, we serve France, our country. This man has insulted us.' Patriotism is evoked in defense of an extreme reaction to the very presence of a Jew, demonstrating the ideology of racial elimination contained in French policy, and it foreshadows the fate of Jean and his two compatriots. The display of cold hatred nevertheless allows the Quentin family to express a kind of solidarity with Jews, something that Jean silently observes, while the dynamics of the power-wielding French Right provide an occasion for some drunken Wehrmacht soldiers to feign gallantry. By this time, we know about Jean's dark secret, and Malle gently alludes to the atmosphere of terror evoked for this hidden child. The theatrical quality of the episode also affords an opportunity to relate several points of view regarding the Jews in France: Mme Quentin espouses a quasi-liberal view, although she still abhors Jewish Socialist leader (and former President of the Council) Léon Blum; others in the restaurant challenge the Milice and side with the Jewish gentleman. Malle also foregrounds the incipient anti-Semitism of the fascist social culture, something that will be played out tragically at the film's end.

Movies

As an antidote to this dynamic scene of tension, and after the maternal visit with its promises of a future reunion at Mardi Gras (and more subtle contrasts between the childhood realities of the two boys), a diversion planned as an amusement by the monks takes place. After some fiddling with the unfamiliar equipment, the whole school settles down to watch a projection of Charlie Chaplin's *The Immigrant* to the musical accompaniment by Mlle. Davenne and M. Florent who play a Rondo Cappriccio by Saint-Saëns. The primitive viewing conditions, the benches, the equipment, the makeshift score, do not mitigate the pure joy that this movie brings its audience. Although they have presumably seen it many times, Chaplin's gentle comedy mixed with pathos enthralls children and adults alike. All join in shared laughter, in a momentary utopian vision of community. Even the besieged kitchen helper, Joseph, seated next to Père Jean in a stunning portrait of contrasts, laugh together; '[It] is a tender moment, a moment of forgetfulness' (Malle 1988: 65). But it is a forgetfulness tinged with longing for the two hidden children (shown in close-up) whose vision of freedom evoked by the Statue of Liberty will never be realised. The Chaplin film continues as the ship full of immigrants sails into New York Harbor, and Malle emphasises, in dreamy, poignant close-ups, the doomed faces of two of the hidden children, Jean and Negus, contrasting with the eager, aspirational wonder of Julien, whose world is still one of possibilities. It is hard to ignore the unexpected symbolism of the Statue of Liberty in *The Immigrant*, as it reverberates beyond the film-within-the-film to show its audience the possibility of freedom that exists at the margins of the contemporary crisis. It also suggests Malle's renewed perspective on his homeland as he crafts his fiction from his own position as 'immigrant' in New York City.

Music

The friendship between Julien and Jean finally solidifies, joyfully, around music. At first, earlier in the film, Jean's proficiency with a piano sonata by Schubert earns the admiration of the music teacher Mlle Davenne (Irène Jacob) and the resentment of the untalented student (in this case), Julien. It establishes something of a cliché, although this has proven to be true historically: pre-War Jewish families encouraged musical appreciation and talent. Here it becomes one more hurdle for Julien to overcome in his hesitant trajectory toward friendship; he will replace rivalry with fellowship. Resentment later turns to admiration, after a series of bonding incidents, including being found on the road by German soldiers after some terrifying moments alone in the woods, the revelatory lunch at 'Le Grand Cerf' that Jean seems bemused to watch, and Julien's protective fibbing that allows Jean to miss choir practice in the sanctuary. The realisation of this friendship is depicted in sublime moments of sharing, lyricism, and laughter at the piano. The two boys play a boogie-woogie duet, after Jean shows Julien how to embellish the low notes with his left hand. Jean has been playing the tune solo when Julien enters the music room, and in a selfless gesture of sharing, Jean shows Julien literally how to 'make music together'. An air raid isolates them further in the room, they hide from everyone, and to the surrounding eerie silence of the raid, laughter and rolling chords fill the place. As Malle describes it in the screenplay, 'Later. Standing up at the keyboard, they are playing a four-handed boogie. JULIEN is doing the bass, BONNET is improvising on the high notes. Peals of laughter' (Malle 1988: 65). This wordless musical solidarity, coming as it does amid the silence of the deserted music room and courtyard, reinforces the idea that the two boys have created a kind of magically separate universe, impervious to the prejudices and hatred of the surrounding world. Each boy has his part, and they are in coordinated concert with each other. Lyrical reciprocity, musical creation, shared friendship, joyful hilarity – all are depicted, even if only momentarily, in this exhilarating scene.

Murder

And yet, as noted, beneath this story of youthful friendship and solidarity lies a subtext of murder: mass extermination as a political ideology and the social reverberations surrounding it. 'Why do we hate the Jews?' asks Julien of his older brother. 'They're smarter than us. And also for crucifying Jesus Christ.' Still dissatisfied, Julien notes that the Romans killed Christ. With one last effort at comprehension, Julien asks, 'Is

Fig. 2: *Au revoir les enfants*: Father Jean and the three Jewish boys being marched off.

that why they have to wear the yellow star?' evoking one of Malle's most vivid wartime memories. Of the roughly 76,000 Jews deported from France, 11,403 of them were children. Most of these died at Auschwitz or in the detention camps along the way. Yet 75% of France's Jews survived the war, and many of them (if not all) were children. While there are no figures that cover the number of hidden children, it is certain that most who were saved were protected in some way. Malle's intervention at the film's close has two parts. Before he cites the memory that has troubled him for forty years, he summarises the conclusion to the final scene: 'Bonnet, Négus and Dupré died in Auschwitz, Father Jean in the camp at Mauthausen. The school reopened its doors in October 1944.' This is the fate that befalls the semi-fictional characters in Julien Quentin's world and the return to normality that historically elides it. But as Malle himself attests by this closing quote and its forty-year impact on his memory, this is an actuality-based fiction. Each of the three boys had counterparts in history. In a boarding school called 'Sainte-Thérèse de l'Enfant Jésus' in Avon, three Jewish children were hidden: Jacques Halpern (Jacques Dupré), Maurice Schlosser (Négus) and the most important one, Hans-Helmut Michel (Jean Bonnet). After their arrest they were transported to that antechamber to Auschwitz just northeast of Paris, Drancy. From there they were sent on Convoy 67 to their deaths, just a few weeks after their arrest. Upon their arrival at the extermination camp, death was immediate (see Braunschweig and Gidel 1989: 39–48). As for Père Jean, whose real name was Lucien Bunel, later Père Jacques, he was literally the exemplary man of faith, notably imbued with four enduring characteristics: 'a deep religious faith, a tireless work ethic, an active love of learning, and a staunch sense of social justice' (Murphy 2006: 11). He died in Mauthausen one week after the liberation of the camp, having insisted on staying there until the last Frenchman was repatriated, and succumbing to his weakened state caused by the debilitating conditions of the prison. While none of this aftermath is represented in the film, aside from Malle's terse, elliptical commentary, there is plenty of evidence in the film of the murderous xenophobic ideology that makes this ending inevitable.

When Doktor Muller of the Gestapo enters the classroom on that fateful morning, he is looking for Jean Kippelstein, one of the Jews denounced by Joseph the scullery boy. Having been punished for his black-market trading while the rich boys go free, but not knowing exactly who they are, Joseph denounces the school for hiding 'some Jews'. The tactic Muller chooses is in keeping with the prevailing anti-Semitic ideology that necessitates hiding in the first place. He searches for that suspicious boy who averts his gaze. Triumphant because he's been led to his prey by the errant glance of Julien, he appeals to a perverse form of patriotism. When Kippelstein is discovered, Muller instructs: 'This boy is not a Frenchman. This boy is a Jew. Your teachers have committed a serious crime by hiding him. The school is closed.' And out in the courtyard as the rest of the boys are lined up while the captives make their way out, he says, 'We're not your enemies. You have to help us rid France of strangers, of Jews.' In each of these statements lies the normalised xenophobia that became government policy and presided over a vicious cleansing of France of all who were designated as other. It is a revulsion at this particular form of murderous hatred that provokes Malle's voice-over at the end of the film and instills a humanist commitment to social values that marks his filmmaking career.

Memory

Until fairly recently, and certainly a decade or two after *Au revoir les enfants*, the situation of hidden children in France seemed like a secondary, if compelling, tributary to World War II histories. It is only with the increased revelation of the tragedy known as the Vel' d'Hiv – named for the Winter Cycling Stadium in Paris where, on 16/17 July 1942, Jewish families were rounded up by French police and held for a week with neither food nor water until transported to Pithiviers or Drancy on their way to certain death in Auschwitz – that the tragedy of Jewish children was highlighted. This was the first time that whole families were arrested, and it made the danger for every Jewish child palpable. Malle himself refers to the widespread knowledge of this event, and he was only twelve at the time. Most did not know exactly what would happen to the Jews in the East, but they certainly knew that it was tragic. The revelation has been gradual but forceful, and the emphasis on the tragedy of the children as well as on the collective responsibility of the French nation has intensified, including at the highest level of the State.

Memory is the catalyst for Malle's return to France, its form is the film *Au revoir les enfants*. When he revisited this very vivid school time memory he reworked the raw material of recollection with the contributions of other witnesses, others who had been in or around the school at the time. He was not interested in a detailed docu-

Fig. 3: *Au revoir les enfants*: Farewell as Remembrance.

mentation of events, but rather in the reconstruction of the emotional impact of the situation of shock, plumbing its historical significance from the distance of decades in order to give the viewer a visceral experience of history, to renew compassion. In saying 'Memory is not frozen, it's very much alive, it moves, it changes' (French 1993: 167), he refers to his own process, the working through of what was personally traumatic into a historically and emotionally significant film. He started work on the film from the last sequences, the most vivid to him, and tried to avoid sentimentality and cliché. Of the authorial intervention at the end he says: 'These lines were the first thing I wrote before I even started the screenplay. […] [The] fact that I would inject my own voice – suddenly jumping forty years – that was my intention. […] I knew it *had* to be my voice. I thought it was important for people watching the film to understand at the end that this story was a true story and actually came directly from my memory' (French 1993: 181, 182). Memory as authenticating instance, without the visual cues or dreamy reflections that indicate a cinematic past. This is the method that Louis Malle has chosen in order to create the impact and visceral experience of history and the contemporary renewal of commitment and compassion. Free of any restrictive category of film (childhood, New Wave, personal reflection, Holocaust film) and yet partaking of all of them, *Au revoir les enfants* engages our own sense of responsibility in the face of evil and encourages us to confront that evil, to welcome it so that we might enact change.

Bibliography

Braunschweig, M. and B. Gidel (1989) *Les Déportés d'Avon. Enquête autour du film de Louis Malle, Au revoir les enfants.* Paris: La Découverte.
French, P. (1993) *Malle on Malle.* London: Faber and Faber.
Frey, H. (2004) *Louis Malle.* Manchester: Manchester University Press.
Insdorf, A. (2003) *Indelible Shadows: Film and the Holocaust.* Oxford: Oxford University Press.
Malle, L. (1988) *Au revoir les enfants: A screenplay*; trans. A. Hollo. New York: Grove Press.
Murphy, F. J. (2006) '*Au revoir les enfants*: Père Jacques and the Petit-Collège d'Avon' (Criterion Collection DVD release).

CHAPTER SIXTEEN

Atlantic City: When Sound Meets Utopia

Francesca Cinelli

'Unlike the conventional city, Atlantic City had a single purpose, the boardwalk was a stage, upon which there was a temporary suspension of disbelief, behavior that was exaggerated, even ridiculous, in everyday life was expected at the resort [...]. The town was a gargantuan masquerade, as visitor deceived visitor [...]. And people wanted to be deceived, to see life other than it was, to pretend to be more than they were.'
– Charles E. Funnel (1975: 23)

The notion of the American dream suggested in *Atlantic City* (1981) is based on the identity and history of the eponymous city. Baptised 'the American Utopia' in 1920, 'a fantasy of [the] ideal world [for] the sturdy middle-class millions' (Bryant 2004: 19),[1] the city is still cloaked in its utopian dimension, even if tatters are all that remain of its former self. During the 1980s, which set the stage for the film, the city bore only a hint of its past glory but had yet to surrender. It was replete with projects, investors, activity and crowd of dreamers who, carried away by visions of their American dream, maintained the myth of Atlantic City and its emblematic beachfront – or at least tried to revive it.

To assess the state of this American utopia, Louis Malle's film focuses on three couples representing two different generations who take part in its pursuit: one generation yearns nostalgically for the glory days it enjoyed during the 1940s while the other one lives in the present and witnesses the attempted rebirth that occurs between the demolition of buildings and their construction. The main characters live in a modest building that is about to be razed. They share the same will to abstraction and sometimes the same disavowal of reality and fascination with money. Their fantasies differ only in the forms they take. For some, like Sally and Lou, the dream of grandeur is based on a rather timeless notion of luxury and sophistication, while for others – Grace, Dave and Chrissie – this same dream is more contemporary and in rather bad taste.[2]

Lou, an old failed gangster,[3] is smitten with Sally, his next-door neighbour, and passes himself off as a former hitman who now survives by taking bets and taking care of Grace, a vulgar, disabled former beauty queen and the shrewish widow of a small-time gangster – 'the embodiment of tackiness and tastelessness against which Lou must rebel' (Southern 2006: 197). By night, Sally is a waitress at a casino's oyster bar; by day, she is an apprentice croupier. She aspires to work on the Côte d'Azur, lured by the prestige she attributes to it. Her husband Dave and sister Chrissie, a flower child who is pregnant with Dave's baby, arrive at her home unannounced. Dave, an unscrupulous opportunist, has stolen a bag of cocaine from some mobster in Philadelphia; he hopes to sell it for a good price on Atlantic City's drug scene. Chrissie sees the world from the hippie's peace-and-love perspective, adopting the principles of various beliefs and philosophies with an exaggerated naïveté.[4]

Music and sound effects are essentially diegetic, but often falsely so. To reflect the pretenses displayed by the characters and by the city they inhabit, these two elements are fashioned after the film's protagonists – bigger than life. They affirm and sometimes reveal the discrepancy, created through the cinematography, between the reality and the utopia that Atlantic City sustains. In other words, there is a difference between the situation in which the protagonists find themselves and that to which they truly aspire. Building on their frustrations, the soundtrack adds a theatrical dimension to their illusions, flirting with the burlesque in the contrast that defines its relationship to the image and the relationship that each of the characters, individually or as a couple, has with the utopia that inspires them.

An opera aria epitomises Sally and Lou as well, through its association with the fantasies in which he sees the image of this elegant young woman as it is evoked by the music. A horror film's soundtrack, a mise-en-abyme created by a television that is left on, becomes the soundtrack of Grace's lost illusions. Ordinary noises, whether they are part of the city or the protagonists' personal lives, are amplified to emphasise the comparison that brings fantasy and reality into opposition. In these instances, the film's sound is positioned on the cusp between pit music and screen music, to use Michel Chion's terminology (1994: 80–1). Due to its increased volume, the aural narration has an energy similar to the one that defines the city under construction, which is caught between past and future, and the main characters, who live between reality and their fictitious selves. Sound thus serves the characters' grandiose dreams, which are tied to a combination of gambling and drug deals.

Through the relationships of the three couples presented in key sequences, I now propose to analyse the functioning of audiovisual devices used to create this dynamic, in which music and sound effects emphasise the theatrical aesthetic of the film. Not only are the selected sequences representative of the role given to the soundtrack, but they offer an in-depth reading of the utopia that the characters construct themselves around in tandem. They cover more specifically the first part of the film and the very end of it, one conveying an understanding of the stakes between sound effects and music, the other, essentially a musical overview.

Sally and Lou

The film opens with a close-up of two yellow lemons and a woman's hands holding an inexpensive knife and slicing the fruit into quarters on a little wooden cutting board. The sound associated with the action is also a 'close-up' in the sense that its amplification dominates the image, or at least competes with it, shaping the viewer's impressions and the meaning conveyed by the scene. The tone of the soundtrack is made clear by the emphasis placed on the sound of the juice being squeezed from the lemons and the punctuating thump of the serrated blade hitting the wood while the viewer receives almost no visual information about the character other than her hands. The aural amplification underscores both the characters' modest reality and the idealised way in which they perceive themselves.

In this first shot, prominence is given to the alternating sounds of the lemons' pulpy flesh and the blade striking the board; there is no background noise or any other aural pollution. The opposition of the two sounds represents Sally's desires as they come up against an entirely different reality. She dreams of the sensuality of an elegant, sophisticated life in her ideal location, Monaco, with its casinos and the easy life that the Riviera symbolises for her. The sound of the knife on wood represents a cold and hard reality. Set in opposition is the highly sensual sound generated by the lemon's flesh, which represents Sally's dreams. The sound of reality does not seem to deter Sally from her ambitions, the closest of these being a 'purification' ritual, which rather than eliminating the corruption at its root only masks it. The sound imbues the scene with a depth of meaning that the images alone could not provide. This dynamic is established in the next scene in which we see Sally holding a lemon slice in her hand and pressing the 'play' button on a cassette radio sitting on the windowsill in her kitchen, where the scene takes place. A static close-up of the object highlights the contrast between the object (the cassette player) and the surprisingly good acoustic quality of the *Casta Diva* aria being played. The tape recorder mechanism indicates the very modest social context that Sally is trying to eradicate by devoting herself to this ritual. The same principle applies to the cutting of the lemons. The sound effects are amplified: the mechanism with its sounds of plastic and metal symbolises the relation-

Fig.1: *Atlantic City* (1981):
Lemon ritual.

ship between dream and reality, between the cheap device and the opera diva, between the inexpensive knife and the sensual delight of the lemon flesh.

Although far from *Norma* this is still a solemn and sensual ceremony, with its altar, singing, and sacrifices: a 'purification' ritual, motivated by the desire to suppress the smell of the fish that Sally sells to earn her keep [1:06:43]. This odour reminds her of her current employment and social status, which are obstacles to the fulfillment of her dreams. Décor and accessories highlight the gulf between the young woman's 'operatic' desire and the banality of her reality: reminiscent of neon lighting, a harsh light bulb hangs above Sally's head, clearly representing the moon that illuminates the priestess as she begins her ritual. Tired old curtains partially drawn back inside the window frame, fading flowers standing upright in a bistro carafe, two apples sticking out of a pot, and a few other knick-knacks complete the picture. Once the camera and the soundtrack have indicated this disparity, the ritual begins, supported by a much wider and longer shot that ends with a reverse tracking shot as the *Casta Diva* aria resounds from beginning to end. The volume does not reflect the modulation that should result from the camera's backward movement. Instead, the aural emphasis is placed on the ideal and the projections it generates. The amplified sound contradicts the images and the angles that frame them, further emphasising the contrast with reality that the two characters seek to evade.

The scene's oneiric dimension becomes all the more significant as we view the scene through the eyes of Lou, a secret admirer whose nightly ritual is to watch Sally's own, as he will later reveal to her: 'I watch you […]. The place where we live – I watch you' [1:06:17]. The camera is placed in Lou's apartment window directly across from Sally's, and it then turns toward Lou to reveal his physical presence. He is always linked to the young woman through musical effects, but visually separated from her by his own curtains behind which he moves. Lou is followed by the camera, which is far enough away from him that it draws the attention to himself and away from Sally, who disappears from the scene long enough for him to be introduced. The music is as loud at his home as it is at hers: the two characters are linked by one common ideal. Lou sees the young woman as she wishes to be perceived. Their expectations intersect and are communicated to the viewer through this aspect of the soundtrack, even before Lou appears on the screen. As she applies the lemon juice to her torso and arms, which she slowly bares, the camera lens follows Lou's gaze at first, and then invites us, through a reverse tracking shot that brings him into the screen, to be voyeurs – rather than admirers – alongside him. Lou then withdraws behind his curtains and turns to present a three-quarter profile to the camera, revealing that he is a lower-class old man. This gives the scene a somewhat less romantic feeling, but does not rule out the possibility of a relationship developing between the two since Lou is handsome and elegant,[5] and elegance is just the thing to fuel Sally's dreams. Looking pensive, sad and tired, Lou lights his cigarette. At that very moment, *Casta Diva* is interrupted by a mechanical noise from Lou's lighter, which is similar to that made by the cassette radio. For an instant, the viewer focuses on Lou and the modesty of his circumstances as it is signaled by the functional sound of his lighter and the shabbiness of his curtains. In this case, his fantasy of success is embodied by Sally – by her beauty as well as by her ritual. However, both in the viewer's mind and in Sally's awareness of her current situation, Lou would have to attain a higher social rank and greater financial situation for this illusion of harmony to be turned into reality (as the rest of the storyline enables him to do).

Sally is nothing like the high priestess in *Norma* nor does she have anything in common with a courtesan, although she certainly dreams of a similarly sophisticated life. In *Atlantic City*, the dream constructed around gambling money can be seen as a cult whose goddess she hopes to become, the sort of goddess that the city would be willing to accept – an operetta goddess. This interpretation is confirmed by Lou's perception of her as he stands watching at his window; there is a fire in his eyes that she rekindles. Her presence, symbolised by the operatic aria when she is off-screen, helps Lou negate the sometimes brutal vulgarity of the world of Grace, with whom he shares his life. In Nathan C. Southern's words:

> Lou's exalted vision of Sally is partially an illusion – just as her vision of him ('Teach me stuff…') is based on fantasy. Lou essentially perceives Sally as something of an Olympian goddess, his ticket to spiritual redemption. In a moment that is nothing short of inspired, just after Grace seats on her bed and rhapsodizes about pumps with goldfish swimming in her heels, Malle overlays the beginning of the aria on the soundtrack, and what begins, for the first few seconds, as non-diegetic – a parody of Grace's sense of class and sophistication – soon reveals itself to be diegetic. It is, in fact, Sally's recording of Norma, descending from the upstairs; Lou begins to drink from his bottle of wine but slowly raises his head and closes his eyes and absorbs the music as if the goddess herself is casting down her blessings. (2006: 198)

During this scene, Grace cruelly reminds him that he is worthless and that he works for her. The difference between the two universes becomes even more marked as she persists in her attack, describing the pair of clear plastic shoes with live gold fishes swimming in the heels that would make her walk with an elegant daintiness [12:00]. A dispirited Lou hears the *Casta Diva* aria coming from upstairs: he raises his head toward the sound, a beatific expression on his face. He forgets, if only for a moment, his situation [11:28 to12:25].

Dave and Chrissie

The next scene relies on the same type of sound effects. Shot during the day, it stands in stark contrast to the intimacy of the night scene that precedes it. It is not exactly clear where the scene takes place; what matters is *what* is taking place and how it continues to be articulated. The soundtrack contributes to the understanding of the diegetic sound and the sound that is now clearly extradiegetic. Such a contrast is accentuated by the abrupt shift from the operatic aria to the loudly animated street, which corresponds to the rather rough editing of the visual elements. This audio-versus-visual opposition highlights the difference between the kind of dream that Sally and

Lou represent, which is sophisticated, classic and compatible with the timelessness of the image of luxury and sophistication on the one hand, and the dream sought by new characters, which is tumultuous, noisy and so devoid of sensuality and elegance that it could be described as vulgar, on the other. They also dream of an alternative social condition, but in a different way. They personify another aspect of the American utopia, which is that of a new generation deprived of the social codes in which Lou (as well as Grace and to a certain extent, Sally) still believes and which Dave and Chrissie dismiss.[6]

In this new scene, a car starts loudly. When the driver hits the gas, the *Casta Diva* aria is silenced in a barely perceptible aural cross-fade and the music immediately gives way to the urban cacophony of footsteps, traffic and scarcely audible snatches of conversation. A tracking shot creates the image of Dave, a troubled young man with a 'granola' or hippie look to him. It is later revealed that he is Sally's husband and currently her sister's boyfriend. Dave watches a man going into a phone booth, pretending to make a call and leaving a suspicious-looking package on the upper edge of the booth's interior. The man hangs up, the sound amplified once again, and leaves as a church bell begins to chime repeatedly in the distance. It looks as if a countdown has begun at this specific moment since it can only be heard once the man has replaced the receiver, left the phone booth and moved on. Just as Dave enters the phone booth to steal the package, psychedelic music begins to play softly and then quickly prevails over the bell's chiming, which then ceases. The progression of bell to music, both of which are out of the character's range of hearing, signals danger in the subtle difference between reality and idealised world that it implies. Because this is actually a cocaine delivery, the aural shift emphasises not only the entry into a disturbing universe but also illustrates the nonchalant and thoughtless nature of Dave's actions. He thinks only of the 'master plan' that he is putting into effect and the profit he hopes to make by selling the drugs. The chiming bell and the music hint at a possibility; the muffled sound is all the more striking given the music's genre and low volume, which both intimate that this is a minefield that could blow up at any moment. This suggestion is confirmed in the next scene when drums erupt in the music and the camera follows Dave and Chrissie as they carry their bundles of clothes along the road. It only lasts for a few seconds and resembles a drumroll introducing a clown show. The characters, however, do not appear to live up to the ambitions announced by the drums, which are now silenced and soon replaced by the diegetic sound of traffic and their footsteps.

The countdown symbolised by the church bell thus implies that Dave does not 'hear' the reality of the situation in which he is involved. Largely drowned out by street noise, the tolling lingers above the thief's head, and as such constitutes a tacit warning that speaks of immanent justice – at least the code of justice adopted by the underworld, the milieu in which he is now committing a crime.[7] The church bell is almost inaudible, its tone monotonous: it does not bode well for the future. With respect to the music, the introduction of the psychedelic piece is paired with shots that indicate the character's insouciance and heedlessness. These two characteristics echo the imaginary nature of the hippie movement (spirituality, free love and recreational drug use) with which Dave will more clearly be identified once he is on the road with his girlfriend. The psychedelic music during the scene is an indication of the thief's state of mind: he is not only at odds with the crime he has just committed but also with his self-image and the image that his couple projects (although full of contradictions, his girlfriend is a caricature of a hippie and displays a naïveté that Dave does not share). The disparity created by the music continues when the dealers come to the phone booth to collect the drugs and are stunned to find them gone: despite a prevailing air of unconcern, Dave's attitude clearly stems from the denial of the situation's reality and the danger it represents. On the screen, sinister-looking gangsters – the intended recipients of the package – screech up in their car after Dave has left the scene of the crime.

The next scene shows Dave and a very pregnant Chrissie, loaded down with their bundles and walking along the side of the road. Exhausted but behaving with a certain indifference, they hitchhike. The visual editing is accompanied by the previous scene's psychedelic music. When the couple appears in this new setting, a loud drum sound is added, which works on two levels: first, it marks the official and spectacular entrance of a couple that is even more unlikely than the previous one; second, and more importantly, this entrance is cut short because the couple they imagine themselves to be lacks consistency. The music and drumming stop after a few seconds, once again overcome by traffic noises, more gently this time, and then by the sound of their feet as they walk on the gravel beside the road. This is certainly an ironic wink at the so-called Hippie Trail, the path that brought the hippie subculture of the 1960s and 1970s from Europe to South Asia. It was a utopia founded on the rejection of society and a quest for spirituality: to put it mildly, the route that our couple takes has no basis in such a philosophy.[8] The reference to the Hippie Trail also points out that this movement was out of fashion by the early 1980s, thereby emphasising the limited viability of the couple's plan which jumbles up spirituality, love, or family[9] with money, drugs and the Mafia. In search of an identity, they end up chasing chimeras, each lost in their own realm of confusion. The trip they are taking has none of the exoticism or spirituality of the Hippie Trail, even though the roads from Atlantic City and Katmandu both offer escape from a conventional life, the former being more illusory than the latter to which it refers.

The psychedelic music fails to bring Dave and Chrissie together in a common fantasy[10] and gives way to 'real' diegetic sounds of traffic and specifically to the amplified sound of their footsteps on the gravel. This, too, is a mechanical noise, cold and devoid of all sensuality, an irregular noise of dragging feet, boredom and a poorly oiled mechanism. The swish from the last two cars driving by before the soundtrack focuses on the sound of their footsteps conjures up the rolling Atlantic Ocean waves that await them. Equally lacking in poetry, the distant sound of an approaching engine is a segue into the next scene, in which the hitch-hiking couple sits unsecured on a flat-bed truck carrying cinderblocks. Dave slumps while Sally looks at the landscape. As they enter the city, she is thrilled to see a funfair attraction – a huge plastic elephant; to get Dave's attention, she exclaims, 'Oh wow! Look! It's Ganesh! It's a sign from Heaven!' [4:13]. The level of her disconnect is reinforced by a further detail: at the elephant's feet is a sign that reads 'Welcome to Atlantic City', thus presenting the city as an invitation to perpetuate this split between reality and ideal, and inviting the public to participate in theatrical conventions. Meanwhile, the saturated sound of the truck's engine can be heard. As soon as a joyful Chrissie becomes convinced that the funfair attraction is a Hindu god, this sound gradually merges with the roar of the ocean, which can be seen in the background. First, seagulls can be heard calling in the sky; the cries are then joined by the sound of the waves and the traffic, creating a realistic soundtrack of the city that exists outside of the casinos and boardwalk. Then the credits end with the filmmaker's name: after this long introduction from *Casta Diva* to Ganesh, the film invites the viewer to enter Atlantic City after having revealed the audio-visual dynamic that defines the two couples' relationship to the American Dream.

Grace and Lou

The aging couple formed by Grace and Lou is haunted by the past and, more specifically, by the widow's rancor: she thinks that the mediocrity of her old lover keeps her from entertaining her dreams of youth and beauty. She reproaches him for this, constantly reminding him of his failure and his inability to make her happy: 'You're the big time thief! Mister Master Mind! Mister ten most wanted!' [11:33]. Bedridden for years by ailments that are partially imagined, she harasses him and makes him feel guilty, ultimately ensuring his continued presence.

In the first half of the film, the only music paired with Grace fails to express the grand dream of being a princess that she seems to have experienced up until her husband's death, but the reverse is true of the décor: she is eaten up by the loss of her illusions, which she cloaks in the authority she wields with such animosity. The horror film's soundtrack (harrowing music, a cat's shrieks and a woman's screams) playing on the television when Lou comes in with Dave, which emphasises the so-called magic that Dave is proposing,[11] betrays her fear of losing the man who actually validates her utopia by having somehow shared her life since she arrived in Atlantic City. The same holds true for the sound of the service bell that links their two apartments and which she frantically rings when she needs him: the sound effects operate as a subtext, revealing both the darkness of Grace's thwarted ideal and the panicky fear that the prospect of her companion's indifference provokes. The service bell symbolises the way their couple functions: theirs is a game of dependency in which the dominant partner

Fig.2: *Atlantic City*: Grace's (Kate Reid) kitschy bedroom.

is not necessarily the one we believe it to be. Witness the dialogue when Lou is late coming to prepare Grace's food in her apartment:

> *Grace*: Here I am ringing this bell like Charles Laughton in *The Hunchback of Notre Dame*! Is that what you want for me? To become a hunchback whining for you?
> *Lou*: What else with your eggs?
> *Grace*: You work for me, Lou! The cigarettes you put in your mouth, I pay for! I ring this bell and you get down here.
> *Lou*: You got no ketchup.
> *Grace*: Why the hell don't you get some?! [8:45]

It is only when Lou moves up in the world with the sale of his loot (the cocaine stolen by Dave, who has just been killed by the dealers he robbed) and asserts himself sexually and caringly that Grace imperceptibly begins to relinquish her bitterness-fueled hatred (the service bell is henceforth silent throughout the film). In fact, after this 'miraculous' resale, Lou returns home in the evening, amazed by what is happening to him: its sound amplified, *Casta Diva* resounds throughout the building. With eyes full of desire, he briefly stands at the window to watch Sally's ritual, goes out onto the landing, hesitates before his neighbour's door, and then descends the stairs like a young man. The aria continues to play, only stopping when he enters the widow's room.

After sending Chrissie (who has spent the afternoon with Grace) away, Lou puts on a record from another era; it is light, joyful swing music from the days of their youth. Grace, who is pretending to be asleep, suddenly smiles for the first time in the film. He takes off his pants, slips under the sheets beside Grace, and the viewer can infer the movement of his hand between the legs of his companion who, surprised but delighted, allows this to happen. In the meantime, a swing tune that does, after all, reflect her true character is playing. In the next few scenes, she will soften and recount her youth to Chrissie with pride, her eyes and voice full of dreams, the diegetic music coming from a record player:

> I came here during the war, Betty Grable Look-Alike Contest. The boardwalk! Filled with hundreds of Betty Grable look-alikes! From all over America, selling war bonds… [almost singing] 'On the boardwalk in Atlantic City, life would be peaches and cream' […] I met some boys, Lou, and Cookie Pinzer, who I later married… Atlantic City became my home. [1:29:35–1:30:15]

During the final scene, which takes place after Lou has gone with her to sell the rest of the cocaine, they walk on the boardwalk together as the same swing music plays, except this time it is extradiegetic: *Song of India* informs the entire sequence, not just the couple. The selection's volume is low, as if it were muted so as not to disturb the magic that has just occurred in their life. The American dream is back in play and Atlantic City is back at centre stage. No other sound disrupts this state of grace, nor is the music's volume amplified. Only the peaceful sound of their steps can be heard.

The camera leaves them and lingers on a big hotel that is being demolished by a crane equipped with a wrecking ball. The swing music, an evocation of the city's zenith, continues for a few seconds as the camera remains on this image of a disappearing past: it appears as an ageless vessel that suggests the durability of the American dream. The building was little more than a ghost of the city's past glory, made in the image of Lou and Grace, who live in the nostalgia of their dreams. Its physical presence will vanish and give way to another spectacle, to further excesses: the world of casinos.[12] However, the city does not lose its soul, which is symbolised by Tommy Dorsey's music and which the hotel will not take with it when it goes. The wrecking ball strikes the building, each blow activating cymbals that, as in a circus or a music-hall, announce some sort of daring exploit: musically represented here are all the transitions that the city has undergone. The percussions punctuate the medley that plays as the final credits begin to roll: all of the musical styles that were heard in the United States and Atlantic City (city and film) between 1940 (the year the couple first met) and 1980 (the year that they reconnected with their utopia) are played in succession over the still frame. The image of the grand hotel laid bare thus wraps past, present and future in a single embrace, introducing the notion of eternal renewal: the city may change its profile but it will still embody the grandeur and decadence of the American utopia.

Matching the pace at which the wrecking ball strikes, the grand hotel's demolition proceeds slowly, each blow leaving the impression that the different eras evoked will appear from a magician's hat. The stone itself, as it falls to the repeated blows, speaks and attests to what it has witnessed. It does so definitively, through the soundtrack. Each selection of music carries with it the clichés that the American dream may have taken on depending on the era, and the lines from the excerpts selected support this: 'Glad to see you're born again / Atlantic City, my old friend. / Be there when I bet on 10 / I bet on you' (*Atlantic City (My Old Friend)*); 'We will walk in a dream / On the boardwalk in Atlantic City / Life will be peaches and cream / There, where the salt-water air brings out a lady's charms' (*On the Boardwalk in Atlantic City*). Thus, played in chronological order are: *Song of India*, *Casta Diva*, free jazz, *Atlantic City (My Old Friend)*, *On the Boardwalk in Atlantic City*, a psychedelic rock instrumental (probably AC-DC),[13] country music, smooth jazz, psychedelic music inspired by East Indian music and *Casta Diva* once again. Despite the final blow of the wrecking ball heard during the credits, the Bellini aria continues to play: the illusion lives on, surpassing its physical representation and characterised by musical theatre that, when linked to the title, lends the city a certain virtue.

Notes

1. Simon Bryant here quotes the words of Bruce Bliven, a writer for the *New Republic* at the time.
2. 'Malle and Guare employ structural parallelism in the sense that Lou and Sally are each torn between the same two worlds – the world of the classy and polished … and the world of the everyday, the grotesque and the gaudy' (Southern 2006: 197).

3   In the words of his current boss, 'he used to run numbers for the dinosaurs' [24:13].
4   She refers to Hinduism and its principles several times, as well as to Buddhism ('Nam-myoho-renge-kyo'), which she adapts, depending upon the situation.
5   This makes the voyeuristic setup even more layered, according to Susan Sarandon (in a telephone interview with Nathan C. Southern, 18 November 2004): '[what] really made it interesting for Louis was the voyeurism and then the possibility that if you cast it correctly, that [Lou Pascal] wasn't some horrible old man but an elegant guy, so there's actually the possibility that something might happen' (2006: 189). I would add that it is also fed by the principle of a gap, which partly underscores the soundtrack.
6   Dave, suddenly a ready-for-anything dealer, cares nothing for social, mafia or family codes. Chrissie is unencumbered by codes, mostly out of naïveté. Pregnant with Dave's baby, she leaves with him to end up with her older sister Sally, who also happens to be Dave's wife (Dave having abandoned her to flee with Chrissie). This rejection of social conventions does not cause either one of them any real moral uncertainty.
7   It is worth noting that this aerial, quasi-divine bell will be contrasted with the household bell that Grace activates with a system of belts to call Lou from her apartment downstairs. This is for him an unwelcome reminder of the true nature of their strange, aging couple. Twice in the film, the camera follows him as he uses a pair of socks to muffle the sound meant to bring him to heel but which he wants to ignore: first, as he irons his clothes and prepares to go out [4:42–5:20], and later on, as he passively participates in cutting the cocaine with talcum powder, an operation that Dave pretends is a magic trick [29:18].
8   In the French edit of the film an additional scene is inserted between the phone booth sequence and the moment where Chrissie makes her entrance. Driving towards Atlantic City, the couple happily lists all the consumer goods that the proceeds of the drug sale will enable them to purchase. They are clearly disoriented and their utopia is more consumer-oriented than spiritual: 'We can buy anything? Stereo? – Oh Yeah, the finest! Quadriphonic! – Headphones? Biggest? – Oh yes! Biggest! – Aw! I want all of this because we can get! – All right! – And when the baby comes, I want flowers, music boxes and balloons and butterflies – Right! – Yeah! Right! – I want acid … I want acid so we can learn from the baby's wisdom – All right! – Yeah? – Oh yeah! [she continues as the car dies and Dave cracks up] […] Dave, do you know what else I want? I want a hang diver and I want the baby to start skydiving real early and I also want his face to be tattooed!' [2:53–3:58].
9   Chrissie is impregnated by her sister's husband and she will later suggest that the three of them should share the baby.
10 To indicate their separation and absolute enmity, two musical styles personifying Dave and Sally are set in opposition to each other. During a fight where Dave tries to dominate Sally, he stops *Casta Diva* without asking her permission and switches to a folk-music station, and then Sally puts the opera aria back on. This is repeated until Sally turns the radio off. The absence of music lends a presence to

what is happening. For Sally, the dream is one of elegance (opera, *Norma*) while for Dave, it is of the common (the radio). Beyond the content of the dialogue and décor, the music proves that these two have radically different dreams and worlds [12:48–13:15].
11 Dave is at Lou's place weighing the stolen cocaine as he cuts it with talc and invites his host to participate in the activity: 'Do you like magic? Pass your hand over the scale […] That's two thousand dollars! … Say *abracadabra*! … That's four thousand dollars!' [28:40–29:17].
12 'Here is the building! A shame, it was a resort in the old days. It was a real work of art. They are going to tear it down now to build a casino', Lou tells Dave as they walk in front of it [27:20].
13 Only *Song of India*, *Norma*, *Atlantic City (My Old Friend)* and *On the Boardwalk in Atlantic City* appear in the credits.

Bibliography

Bryant, S. (2004) *Boardwalk of Dreams: Atlantic City and the Fate of Urban America*. New York: Oxford University Press.
Chion, M. (1994) *Audio-Vision: Sound on Screen*. New York: Columbia University Press.
Funnell, C. E. (1975) *By the Beautiful Sea: The Rise and High Times of That Great American Resort, Atlantic City*. New York: Knopf.
Malle, L. (1981) *Atlantic City*. DVD. Burbank: Warner.
____ (2005) *Atlantic City*. DVD. Paris: Arte Vidéo.
Southern, N. C., with J. Weissgerber (2006) *The Films of Louis Malle: A Critical Analysis*. Jefferson, NC: McFarland.

CHAPTER SEVENTEEN

Between Conversation and Conversion: My Dinner with André

Tom Conley

Thirty-plus years after the fact, we can wonder if Louis Malle's bio-filmography *My Dinner with André* (1981) is an object of history or a tagline. Shot in a style that was either an anachronism or a nasty wager, for viewers then and now the feature would seem slow, static, without compass or purpose, self-indulgent, consumed with palaver. Compressive in its unity of time and place, bereft of montage and movement, it invites cinephiles to wonder why it was done as it was. It would be proof of a conversation that in his path-finding study of New Wave cinema T. Jefferson Kline imagines the words an American couple share when viewing a film, like *My Dinner with André*, so lacking in 'action, plot, or normal character development', that they can only conclude they have been watching a 'French movie' (1992: 1).[1] Would Malle have taken a cue from Gustave Flaubert who had indicated to Louise Colet that he wanted to write a novel in which nothing happens? If critic Jean-Pierre Richard has famously noted about boredom or the entropy of history in *Madame Bovary* and *L'Éducation sentimentale*, 'people eat a lot in Flaubert's novels' (1954: 119), in the same vein, the characters *talk a lot* in *My Dinner with André*. In 1981 the feature no doubt confirmed what so many viewers sensed to be the signature of French cinema: words and no action.

But in this feature somehow – somehow and somewhere – something happens between the interlocution and the frame in which the exchange takes place. In what follows the contention is that *My Dinner with André* has the trappings of a mystical narrative, and that its form bears the attributes of a *mystic fable*. Understood from these two angles, in the first instance the latter is an ever-repeated story of an unlikely and even extraordinary 'event' that takes place within the most common and often innocuous circumstances. In the midst of everyday life, a sudden or even protracted experience of alterity changes a person's way of thinking and living. For historians and anthropologists of religion such events include any number of chance encounters or moments 'that give a new sense of ease, allow a breath of fresh air to enter one's life. The song of a bird that reveals to the shaman his vocation, the spoken word that pierces the heart, the vision that turns one's life upside down – these are decisive experiences, indissociable from a place, a meeting, a reading, but not reducible to the means that convey them' (De Certeau 1992: 17), alienating the self from the one in which an individual had been accustomed to live. A mystic event is one that comes forward 'from some unfathomable dimension of existence', from elsewhere, 'under the sign of a melody, a spoken word, or a vision' (1992: 18).[2] In the second instance, from the standpoint of moviegoers and moviemakers, the experience would be the very matter of cinema *tout court,* the seventh art comprising any number of 'thwarted fables' in which a narrative, done and undone by the play of images and language, somewhere becomes a mystical experience in what it makes of the most everyday phenomena, and no less, when a hand turns a doorknob, a closed window is opened, or a cup of coffee is raised to a person's lips (see Rancière 2001: 16 and 2011: 11–13).

My Dinner with André is composed of three sequences. Of a duration of slightly under four minutes, the first records one of the two protagonists (Wally, played by Wally Shawn) coming into view in an industrial area in lower Manhattan, an urban zone or *terrain vague* strewn with detritus and garbage.[3] Speaking (voice-over) of his life in times past and present to the spectator who would be his silent interlocutor or analyst, he tells how he has learned upsetting news of the condition of a former friend (André Gregory, played by André Gregory) who, despite being down and out, has invited him to dinner in at an elegant restaurant (the 'Café des Artistes' at 1 W. 67th Street) far above their station, be it in both lives or in lower Manhattan. Wally walks along Canal Street, rides in the subway to Columbus Circle, enters the restaurant, and finds himself out of place. Lasting about an hour and half, the second and longest sequence begins with Wally's entry into the checkroom and dining area. André arrives, a waiter seats the couple at their table, and the conversation, the meal and the departure from the restaurant take up about 140 minutes that follow. The last sequence, not even a minute long, records Wally watching the city pass by as he rides homeward in a taxi late in the night. For much of the time André spills the story of his recent life onto his friend who listens alertly, nodding now and again, after taking an entrée identical to André's before ordering two roasted quails for the main course. Wally hears about

Fig. 1: *My Dinner with André* (1981): New York subway ride.

how his friend has traveled to Poland, Scotland and elsewhere, to places of altitude high and low; how he has had hippy-like encounters with collectives whose members believe in a boundless world; how certain rituals have aroused lugubrious fantasies of death. As the major sequence progresses, critics keenly note, caught in the undertow of André's stories of his travels, Wally intervenes to defend and illustrate a life that has never led him far from home. Echoes of Gide's parable of the meeting of the good and prodigal brothers notwithstanding (1958: 475–91 ['Le Retour de l'enfant prodigue']), in view of André's dubious panache, Wally, a concentrated New Yorker, holds his ground. He implies that the daily drudgery he experiences as a struggling artist (having none of the distinction of the clientele for which the restaurant is famous), confined to the New York Island, beginning with a cup coffee and ending in the same place at the same hour, keeps him going.

Not a great deal when measured against the duration of a good French meal, the two hours and a quarter the couple spends at a table in the corner of the restaurant, at the edge of the bar and the dining room, seem to confirm that the film, executed with Racinian concision, becomes an essay on conversation set within the frame of Aristotelian poetics. The opening shots that record Wally walking along the clutter of lower Manhattan in bright sunlight find their counterparts at the end at night when, in transport, peering from behind the side window of the taxicab that drives him home, Wally sees in their passage, bathed in an eerie fluorescent glow, many of the familiar places he has known since childhood. Coupled with the 'real' time of the meal, the minutes and seconds in which Wally travels to and from the restaurant suggest that the event of the film itself is couched in duration acutely felt at the table, while the awareness of it comes afterward, in strong and stirring contrast to what was shown at the beginning.

When André and Wally exit the restaurant at its closing hour something has happened. In the return home, when, as if through a glass darkly – or the window of a New York taxi at midnight – Wally sees familiar things quite differently, the effects of André's words redounding in his thoughts, the film ends at the threshold of a *conversion*. It would be a fable, what in the time of Shakespeare was defined as 'a lie, fib, leasing, false tale', an 'unlikelie thing reported; also, a Comedie or Enterlude' (Cotgrave 1611: np).[4] Its heritage reaches back to Aesop and forward, for the sake of this essay, to a *lai,* cousin of the *Fables* that in her Anglo-Norman French of the twelfth century Marie de France delivered before her public of listeners. Her 'Bisclavret' (literally 'cleaved in two') tells the tale of a knight who periodically becomes a werewolf. A commuter to and from a chateau and a forest, a man who 'leads two lives', Bisclavret tells his wife of his sojourns in the woods. His words prompt such alarm and fear that she forsakes their bond (she filches the clothes he leaves at his appointed spot of transformation) and commits to another lover who eventually becomes her spouse. Locked in his animal guise, having become canine, or literally *entre chien et loup*, he demonstrates such unstinting faith in his suzerain that ultimately justice is done when he indicates the perpetrators of the wrong done to him. A story that medievalists deploy to attract unwary students into their fold, 'Bisclavret' begins with a line that seems fitting for what we see in Malle's film. Pondering his absence, prior to hearing her husband tell of his sylvan ways, the spouse says, 'My lord, in the days and hours you are gone I am so upset that I suffer to the bottom of my heart, and I fear that I'll lose you. If you don't reassure me, I really risk dying. Tell me where you go, where you are, where you lead your life' (De France 1994: 128).

In the dialogue (and much of Marie's *Lais*) *translation* is at the core of the tale. Translating himself into a different state of being, going on a mystical voyage into a sylvan world, Bisclavret undergoes a conversion. The wife's query about *u conversez* (where you 'converse') is understood as 'what life you live'. For *My Dinner with André* it could be said that Bisclavret's conversion takes place in the visual and aural registers of his conversation, that is, between the written and spoken language he uses to describe how he lives in a perpetually 'translating' condition of being. In his empathy for André Wally stands at the edge of a conversion. Seeing and hearing his interlocutor's words, he is tempted to imagine himself in the forest and hinterlands of Scotland, or amidst the strange people in the most remote areas of eastern Europe. Wally's transport into those places depends on a mode of transport in which one is at ease – a chair, what for the *précieux* in a salon or café des artistes would be *une commodité de la conversation*, adjacent to a table overseen by a vigilant waiter. The commodity that allows the conversion to take place is at once the chair at the restaurant and the film itself, the 'metaphor' that enables Wally's displacement in a world where otherwise he goes nowhere.

The film becomes a mystic fable. Built as much upon its performance as its style and manner, Malle's fable oscillates between familiarity and alterity. In the section of *La Fable mystique* titled 'Figures du sauvage', Michel de Certeau tells the tale of Jean-Joseph Surin's first account (circa 1630) of an event that took place, in transit, in a mode of conveyance. In its *editio princeps* Surin writes of it in a letter he sends to his reverend fathers of an experience of astonishment and ecstasy about a conversation he had with a young man, illiterate perhaps, during a voyage in a coach rolling over the countryside of southern France:

> In the coach, I found myself next to a young boy, about eighteen or nineteen, simple and extremely rude in his speech, utterly illiterate, having spent his life in the service of a priest; but for all that, suffused with good graces and inner gifts so endearing that I've never seen any of the same kind. Only God had instructed him in his spiritual life, and yet he spoke of it to me with such sublimity and solidity that everything I've read or heard pales in comparison what with what he told me.
>
> Just as I had first discovered this treasure, I departed from the company to be with him as much as I could, sharing with him all my meals and my conversations. Outside of the words we exchanged, he was continually in prayer, in which he was so sublime that his beginnings were ecstasies, in his words, which are imperfections from which our Lord had delivered him. [...] What I found particularly remarkable in the speech of this boy is an admirable prudence and extraordinary effectiveness. ... Finally, I took leave of him with a thousand pardons that he asked me to have spoken with so much pride. (Quoted in De Certeau 1982: 283, 285)

De Certeau meticulously reconstructs the itineraries of the transmission of the letter. One of them that went along a 'northern' path, in four manuscripts (in archives in Chantilly, Paris, Brussels and Semoine) and fourteen printed editions, generally titled 'le berger illumine' (the enlightened shepherd) or 'les secrets de la vie spirituelle' (the secrets of spiritual life) dating from 1631 to circa 1700–1730; the other, its counterpart, in two manuscripts (Carpentras and Paris) and two printed editions (Nantes and Paris from 1635 to 1698), took a 'southern' route. After thirty pages devoted to the history of the circulation of the tale whose effect is crystallised in Act III, scene 2 of Molière's *Dom Juan* (1665) when the protagonist meets the poor man from the forest, a sense of conversion comes not merely in the narration itself but in the author's process of reconstructing it, of telling the story over and again of an otherwise anodyne encounter and its aftereffects. An iteration, Certeau's account of its shape and circulation belongs to the event of the story itself. Hence the end of the chapter, as if it were the end of Malle's movie, becomes part of an illumination shared with the memory of the event and, as in the circulation of a film, its retelling in new and different circumstances:

> Each of the interpretations that mark and plot the circulation of the story is a manner of understanding it and at the same time a speaker of the group who, at a moment, along the way 'encounters' the young man or shepherd. It only marks off another stop in a story set under the sign of the coach – a voyage in the text, a myriad voyage in fundamental formation of a double weave. The story can only be 'reviewed and corrected'. As in past times, it mixes the reciprocal aspects of a 'conversation' among a few people; it is at once our reading of Surin [or for Malle, André's story of his travels], his reading of the event and our knowledge of the present through a 'relation' with this past. (De Certeau 1982: 321)

The mystical aspect of *My Dinner* – or, say – 'My Conversation' – *with André* could not be clearer. Unrelenting as it may be, in myriad close-ups André marks the beginning of many of his remarks with an index finger raised. In counter-shots, set behind Wally's balding pate, the camera records André speaking, his pursed lips and his eyes glazed, recalling his emergence from unearthly realms, from dark rituals and nocturnal Sabbaths. The words have a fabulous and mystical flair. That his ventures are memories, or that the 'relation' they establish with Wally cannot be discerned becomes the stake and substance of the film. Seen today, over a gap of thirty-six years, its iteration becomes its mystical fable, and perhaps too, what makes the conversation resist stylistic or formal analysis. The confined décor in which the dialogue takes place draws attention to the scriptural and even graphic character of the voices. Infrequent cutaway shots seem to serve to be 'shifters' or minimal units of visual variety conferring depth of time and space upon the setting. In the pervading orality of the exchange over dinner the film draws attention to a loose montage of close-ups and reflections (André's face often doubled in a mirror behind the table) that may – or may not – bear on what is happening. Hence the 'event' owing to the chance and necessity, or even the vagaries, of the conversation: the exchange acquires visual force in the constant variation of point of view that slightly offsets our expectations. We are told that in classical cinema the '180° rule' holds firm, and so also the composition of shot/reverse-shot of characters in dialogue. Generally, voice-in and in medium close-up, the speaker is seen over a shoulder and a neck, temple, ear or partially visible head of the interlocutor in the foreground, often in soft focus to put the origin of the uttered speech in sharp focus. Some directors (such as Fritz Lang or Alfred Hitchcock) draw attention to visuality of these exchanges by showing us that the interlocutor is seeing through glasses, which cues the lenticular character of the scene. On occasion directors use two-shots to establish the setting of the dialogue and determine how the characters are set before a background, especially when the waiter enters the frame and stands between them. Malle follows these conventions *to a degree,* but with shifts and changes that call attention to the drift of the speech (mostly André's) and interlocution (Wally's interventions) while holding, neither visible nor invisible, a productively bothersome cinematic presence. The rhythm of shot/reverse-shot underscores how the one speaks and the other listens. The speaker is not always voice-in. Sometimes the camera cuts in the middle of a remark to register how the one may or may not react to the other. Now and again the camera, drawing near to André, suggests that what he says is of special import, but only to invite the viewer to consider his hairline and even wonder if the rascal might be wearing a wig; to follow the creases and wrinkles of André's face, the aquiline physiognomy, or the thin lips reminding us that in the evolutionary scheme of things he is closer to a monkey than a human; to fancy how, like an aroused canine, he bares his teeth when speaking with exceptional intensity. Without specific recall of Bruegel's prints of the domiciles of *the fat and the lean,* or Roman Polanski's early film of the same title (*Le Gros et le maigre,* 1961), the camera draws attention to André's thin and hungry aspect, his face seemingly tanned, through contrast with Wally's pudgy and even wimpy pallor. Sometimes, as if in a portraiture, the characters are isolated in the frame, but often they are anchored in the setting where, as the narrative insists, they do not belong.

Yet, on several occasions, generally in the middle of the film, the camera studies André in profile, as if speaking to himself as much as to Wally, while he looks down upon what the viewer imagines to be the remainders of the quail, fruit, parsley and rice on his plate. Seen in the mirror behind him, his face is doubled, even split [51:50, 54:04, especially 1:03:02, 1:30:15 and elsewhere], such that not one but two André's address Wally who remains on the other side of the frame. At first guess, because the camera and its operator are never reflected in the image, the doubling simply happens. Or does it? Would the six or seven occasions when he is seen be sign, as the currency of psychoanalysis in the early 1980s would have it, of an *Ichspaltung,* of a divided self, a 'bisclavret' of sorts, on display before both interlocutor and viewer? Would recourse to reflection be a prod for reflection on reflection? Or an indication, as Wally later 'reflects' in the taxi en route to Soho (voice-off and face-in), watching illuminated store windows passing by while his face is reflected on the rear window of the cab? The moments where the camera – either slyly or as if unbeknownst to itself – doubles the figure in the frame, on the viewer's part a host of associations come forward only to be

Fig. 2: *My Dinner with André*: Reflection(s) (Wally Shawn and André Gregory)

dismissed or set aside. On occasion André's reflection [1:09:43] is eclipsed by Wally's face (his bald head bearing resemblance to a lunar form), seen over and above the stemware and sparkling water glasses that stress the lenticular aspect of the film. Yet the relation of the camera to the conversation remains unresolved. As if in a psychoanalytic séance, listening passively to the conversation, the camera becomes, like the spectators and the waiter, a third party of the conversation, an implicit figure moving about and around the dinner table.

The camera could also have – but we can't know for sure – a role analogous to the waiter. In philosophical terms the waiter might be the 'intercessor', the *other* or an agent of alterity who both serves the couple and is unsettling. It is hard to tell if, as in many French restaurants, the waiter is savvy, of intelligence, know-how, elegance and poise that humiliate those at the table (in the classical scenario of a master-slave relation), or if he is merely a wizened professional, at their service, who does his job. His full head of white hair betrays an impression of quiet wisdom. His gravelly voice and foreign accent suggesting that he is a person displaced by the events of World War II, he comes from elsewhere, he is other, but a fixture in the setting. An outsider whose crisp demeanor disturbs, the waiter is 'an old man', but also a *garçon,* a mute speaker standing over the table and in front of the bar, an interloper who both intimidates and reassures. He often enters the scene his body reflected on the mirror adjacent to the table before he arrives at the table. When he does, he reminds the interlocutors of reality. For an instant, in what would be a mere cutaway, a detail that has everything and nothing to do with the action, the film cuts to a close-up of the dinner plate on which sit a pair of shrunken squabs next to a monticule of rice and fruit *en confit.* Are they merely two overcooked squabs or analogues of Wally and André? Like the waiter, they are both what they seem to be and, unnamable, something else.

Wally looks intently at André. Seated in front of a mirror that displays the back of his head whose bald spot makes it appear tonsured [1:49:31], his face gets obfuscated, as if in a wipe, when the shadow of the waiter passes by. Amidst sparse piano notes recalling Satie, the screen fades into black. For the first time in the film the image – for the duration of a full second – shifts from reference to the waiter to pure abstraction, before cutting into the last (and third) sequence, beginning with a shot taken from the inside of a moving taxi, that draws attention to illuminated store windows and

Fig. 3: *My Dinner with André*: Early 1980s lower Manhattan.

vehicles zipping by. It is within the moving 'mode of transport' or *metaphor*, a car, that Wally wonders what has happened. What had begun in innocuous conversation in the Café des Arts has led to reflection of mystical temper. The film ends with Wally in the monadic enclosure of the cab, his face in close-up, almost pressed against its side window, in a pose which forces recall of the first shot, when the film comes into visibility after the front-credits in white on a black background – beginning when he first emerges into view, minuscule, from behind the cab of the rig of a parked semi in the industrial district of lower Manhattan. Of complementary – one begins with the day and the other ends in the night, one is a long shot outdoors and the other a close-up in the confines of the cab – the two sequences before and after the dinner are more than exposition and conclusion.

In the first shot the parked and moving modes of transport point to a social and physical topography, the haunts of painters and screenwriters in the industrial quarters of lower Manhattan (before its real estate became a playground of the rich and famous), but also to the hieroglyphic aspect of the film in which things seen become signs of things unseen. In the microseconds of the first shot Wally becomes a visible point in the depth of the frame at the very moment the film locates itself in a discernible space and place. In the following shots, swimming in his own reflections, as if walking aimlessly across lower Manhattan in his thoughts, he appears lost in traffic, depressed, almost disconsolate, pressed in the space seen through a lens of long focal length. In the bright and broad daylight of an urban landscape he sees through a glass darkly. Everywhere, in the streets, but especially adjacent to the graffiti on the walls and windows of the subway car in which he rides en route to 59th Street, he ambulates amidst all kinds of writing. Conversely, in the final shots, in expression of an obscure illumination he contemplates the city through the bright window in the dark of night. He is moved by what has happened over the course of the dinner, a séance or session that has forced him to consider where he is and, given that he is a laboring playwright, if and how he moves in a boundless world extending beyond Manhattan.

Hence the tenor of the last sequence of 44 seconds: to his surprise, following André's remark about how memory is capricious and fleeting, at a moment when voice-over turns the interlocutors into mute speakers, just as André sets some bills on the table under the eyes of the waiter, Wally recalls that André has paid the bill. The waiter cuts across the frame, blackening the image [1:48:33] that cuts immediately to a tracking shot taken from the inside of a cab speeding down what seems to be Fifth Avenue. Looking at the camera, perplexed, Wally retreats into what becomes a stream of thought [1:49:31] he voices in his passage from upper to lower Manhattan. The ride in the taxi, an otherwise guilty pleasure that he is hard put to afford, becomes the very metaphor – the mode of transport – from the meeting and the meal to an obscure illumination extending beyond what he beholds of the city flashing by. In voice-over, while immobile mannequins in elegant store windows cross the frame: 'There wasn't a street, there wasn't a building that wasn't connected to a memory in my mind' [1:49:54]. As he attaches memories to the unnamed places the camera stops in very brief intervals to designate the sites that prompted the recall. No longer in the lower depths of the subway, in the Cartesian seclusion of the cab, in consort and concord with the moving images, as he had not in the opening sequence, he sees and thinks differently. Folding the title of the film into its spoken matter, in the best of mystical scenarios, Wally's last words belong to a conversation that through our participation becomes a conversion. 'When I finally came in, Debbie was home from work. And I told her everything about my dinner with André' [1:50:10]. When the title of the film, its last spoken words, slips into the passage that fades into night, there takes place a conversion.

Notes

1 'French movie, Bill', he adds, 'has become a refrain encapsulating a perception of the (often unpleasurable) sense of cultural difference that separates French from American cinematic expression' (1992: 1–2).
2 Having used the cinema of Marguerite Duras as a contemporary expression of mystical experience (see De Certeau 1982: 48–50), the same author later studies its historicity (De Certeau 2013: 19–50, esp. 49).
3 As if it were displacing the heritage of Italian neo-realism, into New York, before settling on Canal Street proper, the camera locates the first of the protagonists in what Gilles Deleuze has called an 'anyplace-whatsoever' (1983: 286).
4 In the same vein Malle, the director, would thus be a 'fabloyeur', someone 'given to tell tales, talke idly, prate foolishly, to fable, to fib it' (Cotgrave 1611: np).

Bibliography

Cotgrave, R. (1611) *A Dictionarie of the French & English Tongues*. London: Adam Inslip.
De Certeau, M. (1982/2013) *La Fable mystique: XVIe-XVIIe siècle*. Paris: Gallimard.
____ (1992 [1968]) 'Mysticism', *Diacritics*, 22, 2, 11–25; trans. M. Brammer, from the entry 'Mystique', in *Encyclopaedia Universalis* [Vol. 15]. Paris: Encyclopaedia Universalis, 1030–6.
De France, M. (1994) *Lais de Marie de France*. Paris: Garnier-Flammarion.

Deleuze, G. (1983) *Cinéma 1: L'Image-mouvement*. Paris: Éditions de Minuit.
Gide, A. (1958) *Romans. Récits et soties. Œuvres lyriques*, eds Y. Davet and J.-J. Thierry. Paris: Gallimard.
Kline, T. J. (1992) *Screening the Text: Intertextuality in New Wave French Cinema*. Baltimore, MD: Johns Hopkins University Press.
Rancière, J. (2001) *La Fable cinématographique*. Paris: Éditions du Seuil.
____ (2011) *Les Écarts du cinéma*. Paris: La Fabrique.
Richard, J.-P. (1954) *Littérature et sensation*. Paris: Seuil.

CHAPTER EIGHTEEN

Vanya on 42nd Street: Inventing a Space of Creation

Sébastien Rongier

There is No Such Thing as Louis Malle's 'Last Film'

Following the success of *Au revoir les enfants* (1987), and despite the disappointment of the Academy Awards,[1] Louis Malle embarked on a series of new projects at the end of the 1980s. With the Hollywood production of *Eye Contact* having proved a dead end,[2] he returned to the vague project of a liberal modern adaptation of Chekhov's *Cherry Orchard*, which was to become *May Fools* (*Milou en mai*, 1990). The film took audiences by surprise, and was predictably not very well received in France. Yet a dialogue with Chekhov's work had begun, a familiarity that led to Malle's involvement with the production of *Vanya* by André Gregory and his troupe. While making another film (*Damage*, 1992), Malle and his friend John Guare, playwright and the scriptwriter of *Atlantic City* (1980), developed a common passion for Marlene Dietrich, spurred by the publication of Maria Riva's book on her mother. This convergence became Malle's new grand project. Meanwhile, the director's cardiac problems continued to worsen. After a tense and difficult shoot, followed by the theatrical release of *Damage*, Malle underwent heart surgery. He then resumed the Dietrich project with Guare. The script took shape, as did the casting, with Uma Thurman set to play the role of Dietrich. Filming was planned for the summer of 1995. With preproduction underway, the project was already far along. Such large-scale Hollywood productions are often punctuated by periods of relative inactivity; while waiting on his coming film, Malle took the opportunity to check in with his friend André Gregory. He had declined to make a short documentary of rehearsals for *Uncle Vanya*, as he had been busy making *Damage*. In the spring of 1994, Malle took advantage of a well-timed break and immersed himself in Gregory's proposed project to direct what would become *Vanya on 42nd Street*. Filming was quick, convivial and animated – from 5 May to 19 May 1994, with the last shot filmed at 2am (see Billard 2003: 524). The film was released in American theatres on 19 October 1994. However, after this enchanted interlude, Malle became gravely ill, and the *Marlene* project was definitively abandoned. Louis Malle died on 24 November 1995. *Vanya on 42nd Street* was thus his last film.

If Chekhov's play is a story of old age, dilapidation and failure, Malle's film is an adventure of friendship and admiration, an impulse of creation and companionship. Perhaps this is Malle's testament, hidden away in the film: creation and friendship, beyond the play's crepuscular theme and time-ravaged décor. The film was shot at the New Amsterdam Theater, which had been abandoned for nearly forty years, but had been home to the Ziegfeld Follies during their glorious heyday between 1913 and 1927. The location thus lent itself particularly well to the melancholic spirit of Chekhov's play, since the theatre on 42nd Street still had traces of its magnificent Art Nouveau décor, while having considerably deteriorated over several decades of neglect. The stage, gnawed away by rats, had become totally unusable; *Vanya on 42nd Street* was filmed among the seats in the auditorium.[3]

Vanya on 42nd Street was first and foremost the fruit of a long-term venture undertaken by André Gregory and a small troupe of actors that he had assembled for a project in the form of an aporia: to rehearse and work on Chekhov's *Uncle Vanya* for its own sake, beyond all finality of a performance; to create a space of free and disinterested creation around David Mamet's adaptation of the play. Wallace Shawn, Brooke Smith, Julianne Moore, Larry Pine, Georges Gaynes, Ruth Nelson, Phoebe Brand, Jerry Mayer and Lynn Cohen thus came together between 1989 and 1994 to work on the play and its characters, to form an improbable troupe for a unique and unending project, bringing to it their personalities, their enthusiasms and their sorrows. The plan proposed by Gregory throughout their years of work was simple: no décors, no costumes, no intentional props and no continuous acting, but, rather, improvisations as encounters took place. Sometimes, Gregory and his associates organised mini-events around the work, sharing rehearsals with an audience of a few friends, including Malle. The latter was among the happy few (eight audience members per session) who, in 1991, at the Victory Theater on 42nd Street, witnessed the small troupe at work. That same year, however, Gregory's wife died, along with Ruth Nelson, who was playing the part of the nurse. The sudden deaths brought the *Vanya* venture to a halt. By late 1993, André Gregory and Wallace Shawn had begun working together on other projects. Shawn confessed to his friend that he missed the character of Vanya; they subsequently decided to contact Malle in order to resume the venture, in particular the documentary project that had been impossible during the making of *Damage*.

Malle was no stranger to the two men, having collaborated with them on the film *My Dinner with André* (1981). In the early 1980s, Shawn began circulating a script stemming from conversations with Gregory about his travels and experiences. It was a highly unlikely project, based solely on a discussion between two friends over a meal. It was this difficulty that seemed to attract Malle. He accepted the proposition, and showed his two thespians how to go about making a film instead of a play. The making of the film included an experimental working phase that sealed a relationship of mutual trust among the three artists. It was not a forgone conclusion, given that the project combined Gregory's life, Shawn's writing and Malle's cinematic direction. What could easily have been a battle of egos became an intense and amicable artistic experience. It was also a complex task preparing the set so as to arrange the camera angles and give substance to the life of the restaurant. Filming took place in a vacant luxury hotel, as though there were a particular tropism between Shawn and Gregory's filming locations and their projects. Upon its release in the US in 1982, *My Dinner with André* enjoyed a very favorable reception from critics and moviegoers alike.[4]

When Malle decided to direct *Vanya on 42nd Street*, he was by no means setting out to make a testamentary work, despite his past health concerns; the film is entirely the opposite. True, Chekhov's work is sombre, and portrays a society in decline and the pitiable aging of men; true, Malle himself felt time slipping by and old age creeping up on him. Yet this would be to impose a hasty retrospective reading on a work that, on the contrary, is based on energy, experimentation, enthusiasm and the decades-long desire to make a collaborative work with Gregory and Shawn. *Vanya on 42nd Street* is indeed Malle's last film, illness having interrupted the other projects being developed by the director, but it is in no way a *testament film*. The speed with which it was produced, the richness of its friendships and Malle's aesthetic choices make the film a harnessing of human and artistic experience that is far removed from any testamentary statement.

The notion of a 'testament film' is rather loose, and somewhat dubious. Any director's final film is fairly quickly labeled 'testamentary'. Yet are all final films testaments, if we consider a testament as a legacy, a gesture for posterity in which one's main ideas and heritage are displayed? Some final films undeniably possess such a dimension, through a conscious reflection on, and representation of, death – for instance, John Huston's *The Dead* (1987). But can the same be said about the final film of Billy Wilder (*Buddy Buddy*, 1981) or of François Truffaut (*Vivement Dimanche!* [*Confidentially Yours*], 1983)? How does Stanley Kubrick's *Eyes Wide Shut* (1999) constitute the cinematic testament of its director? If one considers the work of Alain Resnais, one might wonder how a film such as *Vous n'avez encore rien vu* (*You Ain't Seen Nothin' Yet!*, 2012) is any less testamentary than his final film *Aimer, boire et chanter* (*Life of Riley*, 2014). And Alfred Hitchcock's last film, *Family Plot* (1976), is only testamentary if one considers nothing but the director's cameo (the appearance of his silhouette through the door of the Registrar of Births and Deaths). The paradox becomes impossible to fathom in the case of a *hapax film*: is Charles Laughton's *Night of the Hunter* (1955) a testament film? Daniel Serceau poses the question: how sure can one be that a director has made 'his final film with the full awareness that it is the "last time"?' He notably cites the example of Jean Renoir 'delivering the cutting of *Juliette et son amour* as if ready to begin filming, and, on 12 February 1979, the day of his death, mentioning an idea for a new novel' (1998: 14). It must be admitted that a number of so-called testamentary films only become so through pure chance.

The general problem of the testament film is that of the teleological classification of the final film. Finality raises profound questions about the nature and place of a body of work, but also about the particular moment of its completion, what brings it to an end, what makes it a finished whole. The problem is that of the value added *a priori* to an artist's last creation. If one considers a testament as a voluntary and deliberate act, as a gesture anticipating imminent or approaching death, then the notion of 'testament film' deserves to be refined. Some filmmakers, such as Nicholas Ray or Manoel de Oliveira, have taken up the question. Ray and Wim Wenders co-directed *Nick's Movie* (1980), a documentary film that follows the director of *Johnny Guitar* in his last days. Similarly, de Oliveira, who died at the age of 106, indicated that *Gebo and the Shadow* (*O Gebo e a Sombra*/*Gebo et l'Ombre*, 2012) was not his 'testament film', even if it was his last film. He wished the autobiographical documentary *Visit or Memories and Confessions* (*Visita ou Memórias e Confissões*), directed in 1982 but only released after his death in 2016, to be known as his testamentary work. One could reel off any number of references and examples, or focus on the specific case of actors who died during the making of a film (with both the general and specialised press tending to be slightly too quick to turn a given film into an immediate obituary). One must therefore question the meaning of the notion of 'testament film' and envisage criteria that would clarify it, between factual circumstance, the director's wishes and the film's aesthetic stakes. Such a questioning is evidently far from trivial, and could not possibly be resolved in a few lines, for it involves an interrogation of the director's intentions and the situation and context of the film's production, but also the critical analysis that the film's final nature may or may not entail. If one considers the situation of *Vanya on 42nd Street* in the life and work of Malle, it is difficult to reduce it to a testament. When Marie-Thérèse Journot declares that '*Vanya on 42nd Street* will hardly spawn a host of imitations' (1999: 54) one can take it that, on the contrary, she is substantiating the film's non-testamentary nature. Its atypicality and desire for experimentation make it a gesture of experience and renewal, far from the idea of closure and completion that a testament would imply. That said, it no doubt still remains to analyse the film's heritage in light of the contemporary use of video on the theatrical stage. It is perhaps amid this blurring of aesthetic boundaries and genres that Malle's film strikes a chord.

A Jazz Chorus Without End

How is it that a work as precise and polished as *Vanya on 42nd Street* could have been edited and filmed so quickly? The film was rapidly prepared, produced outside the usual constraints, and above all was shot in barely two weeks in a forgotten and abandoned location. While *Damage* had been a difficult and exhausting shoot, *Vanya on 42nd Street* was a happy and fulfilling one, both for Malle and for Gregory's troupe of actors.

The film's production unquestionably benefited from the different experiences of its protagonists. The work carried out by the trio of *My Dinner with André*, first of all, created a climate of trust that buoyed *Vanya on 42nd Street*. The development of the venture led by Gregory was a further considerable force in this cinematic experience. The actors, well-seasoned in a variety of approaches and improvisations based on Chekhov's play, were able to enter freely into the new variation on their work with and around *Vanya*. The film has a paradoxically improvisatory feel,[5] relying on the layers of experience that had enabled the troupe's companionship leading up to the new shared experience of Malle's filmmaking. The place of jazz in the director's life, and in this film in particular, is doubtless no coincidence. The recompositions performed by Malle rely both on the precedence of the *Vanya* venture and on a taste for shifting dramatic form. They make it possible to open up new potentials in the space of creation and the improvisations of the actors.

Music, and jazz in particular, is doubtless at the heart of Malle's aesthetic affair with cinema.[6] His collaborations with jazzmen were numerous – sometimes dazzling and trenchant, as with Miles Davis for *Ascenseur pour l'échafaud* (*Elevator to the Gallows*, 1958), or casual and lighthearted, as with Stéphane Grappelli for *May Fools*. For *Vanya on 42nd Street*, Malle called on the young saxophonist Joshua Redman, who wrote and performed the music in the film. Playing on tension and release in the horns (a solo saxophone and trumpets in counterpoint), jazz accompanies the shots of the city in the opening of the film. In *Vanya on 42nd Street*, there is nothing nocturnal about it, nothing of the darkness of *Elevator to the Gallows*. The swing has spirit, much like the joyous appearance of the band of actors. The extradiegetic music stops once the actors enter the New Amsterdam Theater. The music's return cannot be reduced to a simple improvised punctuation; on the contrary, it is an underground presence, never disappearing, moving constantly throughout the film. Jazz in *Vanya on 42nd Street* is like the imprint of reality: it accompanies the bustling crowds, and subtly irrigates the film when Gregory marks the breaks between the different acts of the play [at 27:30, and again after 1:00:40]. Vanya's monologue [39:00] nevertheless merits particular attention. Following a disastrous lovers' quarrel with Yelena (during which one can already hear the sounds of the city blending with the actors' words), Vanya reflects on his condition and his calamitous existence. During the monologue (the only one in the film), the muffled faraway sound of a saxophone can be heard, making the source of the music undecidable. Is it extradiegetic, or is it part of the porosity of the real already indicated by the urban noise? It's impossible to determine, but perhaps the music points to Malle's decision to keep the character as close as possible to the real – in other words, to jazz. The music of the Joshua Redman Quartet returns during the final credit sequence, highlighting the complexity of an artistic experience that is at once theatrical, cinematic and musical. Overall, Redman's musical subtlety allows for a consubstantiality between the film and its music. The musical structure is both the urban imprint of New York (a now-classic dimension) and a subtler evocation of the work done by the actors. Their experience over the years, between rehearsals and improvisations on Chekhov's *Vanya*, is comparable to a jazz aesthetic. There is thus an intricate mix, a profound aesthetic affinity between jazz (both in its general structure and its particular use by Malle in this film) and the performance of the actors under Gregory's direction. This relationship is hinted at discreetly at the start of *Vanya on 42nd Street*; it deepens throughout the film, and is fulfilled in the final credits, as we will see.

In a 1960 interview with the magazine *Jazz Hot*, Malle explained the role of Miles Davis's music for *Elevator to the Gallows*: 'The music contributed significantly to the film's success. It gave it its tone, its atmosphere – and when I say atmosphere, I mean it in the noblest sense. Miles Davis's music maintains a kind of general tone, a kind of ambience from start to finish, and gives the film its unity' (Malle 2000: 84). This observation about the music for *Elevator to the Gallows* could just as easily apply to Malle's work with the music of Joshua Redman for *Vanya on 42nd Street*. Redman's music is certainly not to be confused with that of Miles Davis: the saxophonist is closer to Sonny Rollins or John Coltrane than to Davis's modal jazz.[7] Nonetheless, in addition to their collaboration with Malle, the two musicians share a taste for shifting the boundaries between musical genres. Here, the comparison between them is mainly based on Malle's use of music in his films.[8] Redman's jazz irrigates the whole of *Vanya on 42nd Street* in a subterranean manner, and maintains the sense of the actors' performance as it comes and goes, between improvisation, reinterpretation and delicate freedom. For this film, Malle seizes on jazz's ability to work on improvisation, to *organize chance* (see Mouëllic 2000: 59). In a way, Redman's music simultaneously reveals and consolidates the unique moment of creation encapsulated by the performance and filming of *Vanya on 42nd Street*. Furthermore, Malle's musical approach is of a piece with his work as a director and with the rhythm of the film.

Cinema/Theatre Dialogue: From Heritage to Undecidability

The specific case of the relationship between film and theatre is complex, for it is based as much on historical and technical matters as on aesthetic questions. The connection seems evident, so fluid are the positions of actors (who, throughout their training and career, continue to go back and forth between film and theatre) and directors, but the relationship between these two artistic forms is deeper and more fraught, even if this constant circulation already highlights the intensity of the exchanges.

With early film, from the Lumière brothers' 'views' to the first cinematic works, frontal perspective, a fixed point of view and a principle of unity (unity of time, place, and action) prevailed. The technical constraint thus immediately corresponded to an established aesthetic convention of theatre. The space, even the real space of the views, became a stage. The influence of theatre was confirmed and strengthened with the 'tableau' approach to filmic fiction. The cinematic 'tableau' involves a stationary camera placed before a décor with a painted backdrop; the staging of the scene is a function of the décor, and not of the cinematic frame. The tableau shot is that of a closed world that implies technical and aesthetic constraints: no movement, a single point of view (that of the audience member seated in the orchestra), establishing shot type filming (with actors seen from head to toe), no depth of field, cursory editing and the establishment of a fourth wall. The development of editing, and then of talking films (despite the prevalence of theater actors), caused forms to shift and enriched the specificities of cinema.

There remains the thorny question of the cinematic adaptation of a theatrical work, whose differential relation must be studied independently of any value judgement. The question can indeed be a trap if it leads to a hierarchy among the arts. To escape a restrictive reading of adaptation, one could envisage the relationship between artistic forms (and hence between film and theatre) in terms of erosion. In an article entitled 'Art and the Arts' (1967), the philosopher Theodor W. Adorno examines genre and notes its vacillation in modern times; the boundaries between genres have become uncertain, 'their demarcation lines have become eroded' (2003: 368). He adopts a dynamic negative critique in order to analyse this process of erosion or fraying (*Verfransung*). The 'blurring of the clean divisions between different genres of art' (2003: 371) reveals the anxieties of a civilisation, and signals an uneasiness with regard to the principle of unity. Erosion is a sign of resistance through fragmentation and editing, which highlights a contradiction and exposes art to its difference. Rather than filling in the gap that makes an art an art, erosion explores this dynamic tension. According to Adorno,

> Every work possesses materials that are distinct from the subject, procedures that are derived from the materials of art, as well as from human subjectivity. Its truth content is not exhausted by subjectivity but owes its existence to the process of objectification. That process does indeed require the subject as an executor, but points beyond it to that objective Other. This introduces an element of irreducible, qualitative plurality. (2003: 375)

Art no longer lies within a concept that subsumes the arts, but is on the contrary the expression of an overflowing and a dissatisfaction, which Adorno assumes through a dialecticisation of art and the arts. The notion of erosion allows for an escape from the constraints of a univocal definition, a way of evoking the uneasiness and the fragility of what is thinkable in aesthetics. Here, non-knowing becomes the experience of art, which allows the foreign to enter into it. Faced with *territorial discipline*, Adorno envisages a critical paradigm in which artistic form is *tension*. Erosion is a movement that subtracts from the notion of genre and the unity of art, a strictly historical movement of the evolution of the dialogue between the arts. It thus makes it possible to prolong the dialogue between film and theatre without falling into the delicate ruts of adaptation. This dialogue henceforth becomes a play of hybrid forms that complicate the relationships among forms in general.

Vanya on 42nd Street is not an adaptation of Chekhov, insofar as Malle's ambition was not to adapt Chekhov's text, but rather to present a project happening in the theatre. How does one cinematically write a shared experience in which the set is an isolated space, but one that has to do directly with a collective relationship that is renewed with each performance? The relationship between film and theatre implies two distinct materials, the one being narrative and audiovisual (iconographic and acoustic), the other being the oral and corporeal performance, direct and immediate, of an often complex narration. Doubling the theatrical work with its cinematic formulation necessarily implies discrepancies and variations. Adapting a dramatic work for the cinema is 'the persistence of a thematic and the variation of a material' (Ropars-Wuillemier 1970: 131) – in other words, a flexible conception of adaptation that is not stuck in a dialectics of faithfulness and betrayal. We thus move from a work of adaptation to a logic of *reading*, which is to say a transcription and a displacement, a logic of discrepancy that establishes a complex relationship between the thematic and the aesthetic material. As has been suggested, what Malle sought to film was the act of creation: that of Gregory and the actors (see Lemarié 2013). The film subverts the tradition of adaptation by proposing a cinematic experience that blurs category lines, a discrepancy that makes the cinematic object undecidable: it is a gesture of erosion. For Marie-Thérèse Journot, *Vanya on 42nd Street* is the work of a 'documentary maker' (1999: 52). While it is undeniable that Malle relied for this film on his long involvement with the genre, can one really call *Vanya on 42nd Street* a simple documentary? If the film benefits from experience in the documentary domain, its ambition cannot be reduced to that of a report, a recording or filmed theatre. What's more, the film is not external to the venture that it presents; it has become an integral part of André Gregory's process. As has been pointed out, 'Louis Malle is not actually recording a scenography; he is establishing connections and bringing tensions to light' (Lemarié 2013: 161). The cinematic approach involves a reflection on the vacillation of boundaries (theatre, fictional film, documentary film): an erosion of forms. A veritable cinematic reading of theatre, *Vanya on 42nd Street* shifts the boundaries between genres and examines the place of the director as audience member in a flexible experience that primarily stages the fragile moment of the space of creation.

The film opens with images of the reality of 42nd Street in New York. The shots show the moving crowd of anonymous faces from which those of the actors soon emerge, starting with Wallace Shawn leaning against a wall in the street and watching the movement of the city, particularly a young woman on roller blades. The very first image of the film is perhaps not as trivial as it may seem. It shows the green sign indicating the number of the New York street, and below it another sign that reads 'No Standing', as if the film's opening were already indicating a project, a movement, a dynamic. This mobility is found in the cuts between the city shots, which place us in the midst of daily life among ordinary people, their outfits, their behaviours (a man is drinking a bottle of water, one woman is on her skates, another scratches her nose, two men are talking on a street corner, another looks off into the distance, and the crowd is walking). One by one, from the chaos of the crowd, familiar faces emerge: that of a motionless Wallace Shawn, that of André Gregory. This *emergence* is important, for it cinematically underscores the actors' place. They come from the real, from ordinary daily life, carried along by Joshua Redman's music. They remove themselves from it for a cinematic and theatrical experience, but never cut themselves off completely. From one shot to the next, all the actors gradually converge on the same meeting place: a dilapidated and abandoned theatre, a space that has been forgotten and gnawed away by time. This is where the *run-through* of the play, rather than a performance, takes place, even if a few audience members are invited (beginning with the viewer of the film). This is consequently neither a recording nor an adaptation, but a theatre experience to which the film constantly calls attention through a series of distancing effects, as though to keep reminding the audience of the film's strange status, its process of erosion. This claim to reality is never erased in the film. It begins with the actors' outfits, which are those of their daily life in New York, the imprint of reality always prevailing from this point of view. It also comes through in the props, which perfectly exploit the ambivalence between a theatrical situation and the banality of the real. In effect, if the jingling of a cluster of bells, a prop taken from a bag, subtly announces that the run-through has begun [5:22], the plastic cup with 'I ♥ NY' written on it [1:22:25] is, for its part, a clear distancing effect, in order to balance the text and the actors' work against the strict unfolding of the plot. The police barriers cutting through the ruined theater [1:07:33] produce the same effect. Subtler is the use of sound during the very intimate dialogue between Vanya and Yelena. Throughout the conversation [36:12], one can hear the background noise of the city, the movement and honking of cars, weaving a strange melody of the real in between the words of the two unhappy Russian characters.

An Aesthetic of Interweaving

The aim of *Vanya on 42nd Street* is first of all to render the space of creation undecidable, to show a vacillation that is also a rapture (that which enraptures, and that which takes away). Getting a first-hand look at the actors' experience and reconstituting the layers of that experience is above all to give the audience, via the production, a taste for indetermination. Yannick Hoffert is likewise in favour of referring to the 'hybrid status' of Malle's film, a status that would not reduce it to a documentary, but that would be achieved through 'interweaving effects' (2010: 204).

Where are we? In New York at the end of the twentieth century, or in the heart of Russia a century earlier? Is it Larry Pine talking, or Dr. Astrov? The director has to work with the texture of the text, interlacing the tissue of words by Chekhov and the actors in a distinctively cinematic way. If the text is etymologically a *tissue*, the interweaving performed by Malle is cinematic, constituting an organic slippage. It is as though the New York reality of the beginning of the film never fully gave way to Chekhovian Russia – as though, in the end, the New York of the dramatic runthrough never disappeared beneath the late-nineteenth-century Russia of Chekhov's play. Everything seems to vibrate together like an unending dissolve, except that here, Malle's production does not resort to such a device, and adopts an infinitely more precise approach. The actors enter the run-down theatre on 42nd Street, a site oozing former glory and slow decline, not unlike Professor Serebryakov. As they come in, the actors are chatting about the passing doubts and hassle of their daily lives, creating a falsely banal bonhomie. In the fifth minute of the film, we see Lynn Cohen, sitting on a bench and rummaging in her bag, talking with Julianne Moore about her need to go swimming at the pool: a perfectly trivial situation, if one ignores Larry Pine and Phoebe Brand behind them, sitting at a table and similarly chatting. The shot ends with the departure of the two women and the immediate arrival of Wallace Shawn, who sits on the same bench, the shot closing in on him alone. The following shots take us to other exchanges, other conversations. Four shots later [5:27, just after the jingling of the bells), we see a medium shoulder shot of Shawn [5:30', his eyes closed in concentration or weariness. He slides down and lies on the bench. The voice of a woman off camera asks, 'Drink?', and a male voice replies, 'Oh, no, no thank you…,' while the camera slowly rises in a lateral tracking shot to show Larry Pine and Phoebe Brand still seated at the table. A few shots earlier, we had seen them chatting warmly as they sat down, with Larry confessing that he was swamped with the work of rehearsing two plays simultaneously. Larry refuses Phoebe's offer of a drink; she presses him, asking, 'A little vodka?' With the word 'vodka', we realise that we are sliding … like

Fig. 1: *Vanya on 42nd Street* (1994): Performance or run-through?

Shawn on his bench. This sliding is the transition from actor to character, from Shawn to the character of Vanya, from Pine to the doctor. Shawn's movement that leads to the movement of the camera thus brings us into the theatrical fiction. Thanks to a doubly cinematic link (an off-camera voice and a lateral tracking shot), we pass from the situation of the actors to that of the run-through. Malle interweaves the two universes in a cinematic slippage.

We find this same passing effect at the end of Larry Pine/Astrov's monologue. He kisses Phoebe Brand/Nanny. While the previous shots have shown a frontal view, the kiss allows for a match cut of face and back [6:43], which emphasises the link between the two characters; it serves above all to show the audience of the run-through, which has well and truly begun. Between the doctor and Nanny framing the shot on either side, we can see the seven audience members, and in the middle of them André Gregory attentive and smiling. The audience is thus in the filmic counter-shot, shifting the idea of a fourth wall, and uniting, perhaps even conflating, the audience of the film with

Fig. 2: *Vanya on 42nd Street*: Actors and 'audience'.

the audience present at the run-through. Here again, the filmic slippage creates an instability of places and gazes. The play of blurring and interweaving is the same when the film adopts the play's multi-act structure. The second break in the run-through is brought about through cinematic means, as though the rhythmical regulation of the film were extending beyond the acts of the play while accompanying them at the same time. After the intense exchange between Sonya (Brooke Smith) and Yelena (Julianne Moore), whose final laugh truly seems to reveal the layers of years of rehearsals and exchanges, an off-camera male voice breaks the tension. The following shot shows Gregory standing up and saying with a smile, 'Let's take a little break' [1:00:40]. The play of transition from film director to theatre director, from off-camera to on-camera voice, is a new and subtle slippage, allowing one to understand the dialogue of forms and artists.

The Art of the Prosopon

Who are the faces we watch for two hours?

Both a theatre mask and a face in the culture of ancient Greece, *prosopon* literally means 'gaze toward', i.e. the idea of a relation. What's more, the connection between mask and face in Greek tradition involves less a question of dissimulation than one of substitution or weaving. Françoise Frontisi-Ducroux unpacks the etymology as follows: the 'word *prosopon* also comes from the root word *ops* ['eye, face'], yielding *proti- (or pros-) opon' (1995: 20). It thus signifies 'that which faces the eyes of another'. The face, in Greece, is above all that which presents itself to the view of another. This is the paradigmatic situation of a relationship between individuals. The face-prosopon implies the identity and authenticity that one finds in the Latin term *persona*, which refers to a theatre mask, to a character in a play, and to a person.

Malle's film works on the effects of porosity in the actors' situation, that play between reality and representation that is opened by the slippages and interweavings of the production. It is interesting to re-watch the beginning of the film in light of the characters' attributes: is Wallace Shawn's waiting not like that of Vanya, who has likewise watched the world go by? Does not the complicity between Brooke Smith and Julianne Moore, who arrive together, announce the reconciliation between Sonya and Yelena? Do Larry Pine's casual manner and the way in which he separates the two actresses to talk to Julianne Moore indicate what is going to happen? Similarly, it is unsettling to hear Larry confessing to Phoebe his fatigue, his exhaustion from the multiple activities he is taking on ... rather like Dr. Astrov, perhaps? If we have shown that the cinematic production, the music, and the editing accompanied the run-through, *Vanya on 42nd Street* is above all a film showing the actors' performance. Malle works in ten-minute-long takes, thus giving the actors the time to settle into their performance. The latter is accompanied and amplified by the framing choices, zeroing in on the faces. The actors, like Chekhov's text, open up in this filmic intimacy, which does not stop Malle from taking his own approach here and there, as with Yelena's monologue. Following a conversation with Sonya, Yelena finds herself alone. She reflects, meditating on the young woman's situation as well as on her own, equally

Fig. 3: *Vanya on 42nd Street* Yelena's (Julianne Moore) 'face-prosopon'.

attracted as she is to Dr. Astrov. This interior monologue is above all a cinematic moment, since the minute-and-a-half of intimate reflection is a close-up sequence shot of Yelena/Julianne Moore's face. Her words are spoken in voice-over: no sound comes from her mouth, and her face alone reflects those words of cinema. This inner prayer of Yelena places us before an experience of *prosopon*: the cinematic speech of the (theatrical) character shows the face of the person (Julianne Moore) interpreting her character, all of which highlights, via the close-up, a relation between the audience and the vacillation of the *persona*.

The end credits depend on this same infinite slippage between actor and character, run-through and reality. The play comes to a stop, but the lights remain dim, like the crepuscular air of the play's end. André Gregory and all the actors return, as though for a final bow. They are around the table. But something of the tissue of theatre remains with this light, and with Wallace Shawn's concentration, which seems to last after the last words spoken by Sonya. Accompanied by Redman's music, the film ends on a series of close-ups on each actor, indicating their names and roles, as though the experience were being prolonged with these faces in shadow. In this final moment of the film, the cinematographic and the theatrical continue to invent an intimate choreography, slipping into an uncertain space, that of the gaze and the face.

* * *

Vanya on 42nd Street is not Louis Malle's last film. It is neither a testament nor a funeral oration. On the contrary, it is a place of life and of exchange that goes beyond just the director, since above all it welcomes the work of André Gregory and his actors. What is woven through the images of *Vanya on 42nd Street* is a space of creation and friendship, with Chekhov and against death. The paradox of this project is that the film does not fix a particular moment in the work undertaken by André Gregory Wallace Shawn, and all the actors who came together to interpret Chekhov's *Uncle Vanya* over the years, in an unusual and informal way. Malle's film shows the unending run-through of all the possibilities of a troupe. Perhaps this is what *Vanya on 42nd Street* captures most intensely: the spirit of a troupe. What the faces framed by Malle allow us to see is indeed the inner space of an experience: in this respect, *Vanya on 42nd Street* is Chekhovian. But what it shows first and foremost is the life of creation at work. As such, if the notion of 'testament film' has any meaning for this film by Louis Malle, it is that of inviting the audience to re-watch all the director's films, and to forge the critical meaning of an artistic journey and the evolution of a life's work.

Notes

1   In 1988, at the 60th Academy Awards, *Au revoir les enfants* competed in the category for Best Foreign Language Film. Louis Malle was convinced that the Hollywood statuette would not get away from him this time, after the failures of *Lacombe Lucien* and *Atlantic City*. His disappointment was immense when Gabriel Axel's Danish film *Babette's Feast* was eventually crowned by the Academy of Motion Picture Arts and Sciences.
2   In 1985, Malle and John Guare visited Sicily and began work on the screenplay for *Eye Contact*, a comedy about the remarriage of two specialists of ancient Greece against a backdrop of political and police intrigue. William Hurt and Diane Keaton were in line for the lead roles, but the project failed to advance. Malle abandoned it during the filming of *Au revoir les enfants*. Once he returned to the *Eye Contact* project, he intended to give the lead role to his last wife, Candice Bergen. This lighthearted comedy never materialised.
3   In 1994, after Malle's film shoot, the theatre was bought by the Walt Disney company. It was renovated, and has since been home to musicals by the animation studio.
4   For a more extensive analysis of that film, see chapter seventeen in this volume.
5   See Mouëllic 2011. It is clearly not a question of mistaking Malle for John Cassavetes, but simply of emphasising that Malle was able to capture the improvisatory layers of the work of Gregory's troupe in *Vanya on 42nd Street*. The choice of Joshua Redman enhances the singularity of improvisation through music, the underground accompaniment of an artistic gesture, and the aesthetic dialogue between two forms of a single work of improvisation.
6   For a more exhaustive treatment, see chapter ten in this volume.
7   See 'This is My Point', conversation with Joshua Redman (Ratliff 2008: 127 ff).
8   We might also think of the place of Ry Cooder's music in *Alamo Bay* (1985).

Bibliography

Adorno, T. W. (2003 [1967]) 'Art and the Arts', in *Can One Live After Auschwitz? A Philosophical Reader*, trans. R. Livingstone. Stanford, CA: Stanford University Press, 368–88.
Billard, P. (2003) *Louis Malle. Le rebelle solitaire*. Paris: Plon.

Frontis-Ducroux, F. (1995) *Du masque au visage*, Paris: Flammarion.
Hoffert, Y. (2010) 'Effets de tissage dans *Vanya, 42ème rue* de Louis Malle', in Y. Hoffert and L. Kempf (eds) *Le Théâtre au cinéma. Adaptation, transposition, hybridation*. Nancy: Presses Universitaires de Nancy.
Journot, M.-T. (1999) '*Vanya, 42ème rue* de Louis Malle: une expérience sur les rapports entre théâtre et cinéma', *CinémAction*, 93 ('Le théâtre à l'écran'), 51–5.
Lemarié, Y. (2013) '*Vania 42e rue*, de Louis Malle: voyage dans le monde des morts', *CinémAction*, 146 ('Tchékhov à l'écran'), 154–63.
Malle, L. (2000 [1960]) 'Le problème de la musique de film', *Jazz Hot*, 155, 14–15.
____ (2007) DVD *Vanya, 42ème rue*. Coll. 'Les Films de ma vie,' Mayfair Entertainment International.
Mouëllic, G. (2000) *Le Jazz. Une esthétique du XXème siècle*. Rennes: Presses Universitaires de Rennes.
____ (2011) *Improviser le cinéma*. Crisnée: Yellow Now.
Ratliff, B. (2008) *The Jazz Ear: Conversations Over Music*. New York: Times Books.
Riva, M. (1992) *Marlene Dietrich by Her Daughter*. London: Bloomsbury.
Ropars-Wuillemier, M.-C. (1970) *De la littérature au cinéma. Genèse d'une écriture*. Paris: Armand Colin.
Serceau, D. (1998) 'Le Film testamentaire', *Contre Bande*, 4 ('Les Films testamentaires').

INTERVIEW

Truth and Poetry: An Interview with John Guare (New York, 7 October 2015)

Philippe Met

Later described by former artistic director of Lincoln Center Theater Gregory Mosher as one of a handful of dramatists who reshaped the face of contemporary American theatre, John Guare was already an accomplished and acclaimed playwright (with such plays as *The House of Blue Leaves* [1971] and *Landscape of the Body* [1977], or the Tony Award-winning rock musical, *Two Gentlemen of Verona* [1971]), when he first met Louis Malle in his native city of New York in 1979. Although they went on to make only one film together, the iconic *Atlantic City* (1980) for which Guare was nominated for an Academy Award (in the Best Screenplay category), the two men enjoyed a close friendship until the director's untimely demise and collaborated on a number of unique and promising projects that unfortunately never made it to the screen, including the one inspired by Henry James's 1897 novel *What Maisie Knew*, a version of which script is published for the first time in this volume.

Meeting Louis Malle and Making Atlantic City

Philippe Met: I'd like to start by asking about the circumstances of your encounter with Louis Malle.
John Guare: It was wonderful. He called in this very parlor; I've lived here a long time. The phone rang, it was July, and he said, 'Are you the man who wrote the play that was at the Public Theater last year, *Landscape of the Body*, with Shirley Knight?' I said 'yes', and he said, 'All right, could I come see you, I want to talk about a movie.' I said, 'Come now', so he came right over. I loved Louis' films, *Lacombe Lucien* and *Murmur of the Heart* in particular. It turned out he had the money to make a film – it had to be a thriller, starring Susan Sarandon and an unnamed bankable male star, and it was to be made with Canadian money (from, I believe,

a rabbi or a dentist from Winnipeg). In that year, 1979, every dollar spent making a Canadian movie was tax-free, but Louis said he had nothing to film, and asked if I had any ideas for a film.

PM: How did you hit on the idea of building a story around the town of Atlantic City?

JG: Strangely, I had been in touch with a childhood neighbour from when I was a kid in New York, a man named Tony Rey, who had left the Waldorf and moved out to Atlantic City to take over the Chalfonte-Haddon Hall. He was a man who was bringing gambling to Atlantic City. My mother was old friends with his wife, and even bought stock in Atlantic City, Resorts International – it was going to be big. What was happening to Atlantic City was in the papers a lot. I knew Louis' strength as a documentary filmmaker, and I said, 'I think our answer might be in this new world of gambling coming to Atlantic City'. And he said, 'When can we go?' We said 'let's go down tomorrow'. I called up Tony Rey in Atlantic City and he said he would see us. We went down early in the morning. He took us through Resorts International, which was just opening. And there were all these beautiful women shucking clams and oysters. I said, 'What is that?' Tony said, 'If they want to be dealers, they have to work here three months at this slave job, at the clam bar, to prove that they are dependable, before they're allowed to be trained as blackjack dealers.' Louis and I thought, 'Well, there's Susan's part. Whatever the story is, she's going to be behind that clam bar.' And going through all of Atlantic City that day, thanks to Tony Rey, we even met Skinny D'Amato (a longtime close friend of Frank Sinatra's). We went to Skinny's house, and I found a picture book there called *Atlantic City* and in it there was a picture of a gangster convention in 1929 with Al Capone and in the top back of the picture, there was a young guy smiling. And we thought, 'whoever that is, that's our gangster today, forty or fifty years later'. We wanted to show that the old Atlantic City – those gangsters' glamorous world – was being torn down, and this one brand new casino was hopefully the start of a renaissance in Atlantic City. We had a great day: we were there for about twelve hours, made notes, came back – and we talked all night. Louis, who had to return to France the next day, said that the problem was that in order to qualify for the tax dollars, this picture had to be finished wrapping by 31 December 1979. It was now 29 July. We had five months. Louis asked, 'Do you think you can come up with something?' I replied 'Sure' and he said, 'Come in two weeks with the first draft to Le Coual' (his home in the south of France). Adele (my wife) and I flew over. I worked and worked with Louis. Then the producers came down, we read it to them and they said, 'Great.' That's when we started sending it off to people.

PM: Apart from Susan Sarandon, what actors did you and Malle have in mind for the film at that point?

JG: We knew Lou, the aging gangster, was a good part. We thought, 'Who's the best?' Well, Laurence Olivier is the best, he was an entertainer, a great actor. But his work schedule didn't make it possible to film; due to his health he could only function something like 45 minutes a day. The next day we said 'let's get a great American'. We went to Henry Fonda, and he too was medically challenged. We went through a number of people. Robert Mitchum. He opened up his hotel door and he'd just had a face-lift. He said, 'It's interesting, but I only play 43 now.' And then, about the seventh choice, we suddenly said, 'Burt Lancaster'. We hadn't come to him originally, because of *The Killers,* his first movie, what he brought to it… We sent it to Burt, and within a couple of days he said, 'Yes.' It was that simple. We just went to work and we were writing all the way through filming. We started at the end of October in Atlantic City and all the interiors were shot in Montreal, that's why there's lots of Canadian actors, Robert Joy, Hollis McLaren and Kate Reid, who was my great friend. We sent the part of Grace, the woman in bed, first to Ginger Rogers, and she said, 'I did not end my career to appear in pornography, this script is pornographic.' So we went to Kate Reid, who was only 49 at the time, and she looked about 80, so it was great.

PM: *Atlantic City* was Burt Lancaster's last great film and his role as Lou arguably one of his best performances. What was he like on the set?

JG: Burt behaved terribly. Louis and him did not get along. Burt was overacting, acting big, and Louis would say, 'No, Burt, bring it down, bring it down.' And Burt turned to the cast one day and said, 'Okay, we're going to do two takes from now on. The first take will be the way it should be done, and the second take will be what the little frog wants.' Burt was a … ham bun. He never came to dailies … and after a week or so, Louis said, 'I should just ruin this man', because he was horrible to Susan Sarandon. He liked me; I was the first writer he had met in fifteen years; he'd never met a writer who was working on a movie, who was there all the time. And Louis said, 'If I was destructive and really suicidal, I would print only his performance and ruin his career, but I'd ruin mine right along with it – but it might be worth it.' But then he did piece together a reel of the way he wanted Burt. Burt went, 'Oh' and never apologised, but listened to Louis after that, and gave a beautiful performance. But Louis really had to fight to get it out of him.

PM: I believe your wife also appears in the film…

JG: Yes, Adele plays the flower girl when Lou and Sally go buy flowers to send back to Moose Jaw for Dave's funeral. Louis said, 'I want Adele to play the flower girl, not because of her relation to you, but because she's the only human being I know who can stand Monsieur Lancaster and the complete nothingness that he is!' Anyway, it was one of the happiest times in my life. When I think about happiness, it was writing that film, and then filming it. We finished it on New Year's Eve, 1979 – we couldn't believe it. We came back to our hotel and had a big party to celebrate finishing it. We got a lot of pizzas and put them in the oven, and somebody turned the oven on and we came into the kitchen in the flat we were staying in in Montreal and flames came out of the boxes. Smoke was pouring out, and Adele said to Burt, 'Look, look, it's on fire, help me put out the flames.' And Burt replied, 'I'd say this is a fire', and he shut the oven and walked out – we never saw him again. So that was that.

PM: The film is all ambient sound, but was there ever a score?

JG: Michel Legrand had written a full score for it and we had a rough cut of the picture with the score, but the film just rejected it. Oddly, there was a soundtrack with the music that never appeared in the movie.

PM: Regardless, the film was a major success…

JG: It went to Venice and won. We still didn't have any distributors, but Paramount picked it up, and they were very miffed because they had the pictures *Reds* and *Ragtime*, which were supposed to be getting all the attention and cost a fortune to make, and our film was getting the awards. Paramount was not happy with the picture because it screwed up their books. Anyway, it was nominated for five Oscars, didn't win one, and Louis and I became really close friends.

PM: What was your next big project with Louis Malle?

JG: After he finished cutting *Atlantic City* Louis went right to Richmond, Virginia, to shoot *My Dinner with André* (with Wally Shawn and André Gregory), but while we were still working on *Atlantic City*, the Abscam scandal had come to light in Miami, with FBI agents dressing up as Sheikhs to entrap congressmen. The story was so lunatic it was hilarious. We wrote a script on that and were going to film with John Belushi and Dan Aykroyd. It was called *Moon Over Miami*.

PM: This was a couple of years after *Atlantic City*…

JG: Yes, two or three years… Louis directed a play of mine in the meantime and then we did this film. John Belushi had been a nightmare… He kept coming up to our office; we'd have to go to dinner with him, and he was so drunk and so stoned that you'd say goodnight to him and he'd appear five days later at the office not having been home, or to sleep. Manic, crazy, he wanted to slam dance around the office and throw himself against the wall. And we thought, 'how are we going to get through with that?' And then he was dead within a week of that, so the picture just collapsed.

PM: What was Louis Malle's next move?

JG: Louis wanted to make a comedy, so he went into *Crackers*, with Wally Shawn. How he'd met Wally is pretty incredible. In those days, you would take your script to the copy shop to be duplicated, and so after finishing writing *Atlantic City* (right here at my place) we went to the copy shop on 10th St. and 6th Ave., so we could then send the script to the producers and the agents. We were waiting in line when a playwright friend of mine, Wally Shawn, came in to give something to me, and I introduced him [to Louis]. So it was all serendipitous and congenial.

Life in the US

PM: Speaking of Wally Shawn and André Gregory, what type of 'group', if any, did you form with them?

JG: We were never a group. Louis went to London where Wally and André were performing and testing *My Dinner with André* on stage at the Royal Court. I believe it was performed on a slowly revolving table, so the audience watched the conversation; it kept spinning around. Louis watched and studied it; then they went to Richmond, as I mentioned, and filmed it there in about four weeks. Wally and André had their own life with Louis. Wally stays home and is making films; Louis and I liked the same kind of social life – we liked going out and drinking as well as seeing movies and shows all the time.

PM: And André Gregory was just traveling the world…

JG: Yes. I can't remember an evening where it was ever a 'gang' with Wally, André and John. We all liked each other, but Louis and I had a much more social relationship. Which is where the projects came from, because we talked all the time, we were trying to find the next project. It was fun to do. That whole period was very, very happy. At the end of *Atlantic City*, he broke up with Susan Sarandon and met Candice Bergen – and they were married months later that summer. So it was a very happy time for Louis.

PM: Except for the break-up with Susan Sarandon which, I think, was very difficult.

JG: It was very difficult and painful for Susan, but Louis was comfortable with Candice in a way he had never been with anybody else, including Alexandra [Stewart], or Gila von Weitershausen, the mother of Cuotemoc, or his first wife, Anne-Marie [Deschodt] … His American time was a very happy time. He was happiest in New York and Le Coual; those were his two comfort zones. And he'd go out to California with Candice who still had a house there. He was the one who read the pilot of *Murphy Brown* and told Candice that she should do it, that it was the perfect part for her.

PM: The fact that he moved to the United States certainly didn't help in terms of his 'visibility' in France, and is perhaps one of the reasons for the critical neglect of his work at that time, and even today. To what extent do you think he was aware of this, and would you say he ever had any intention to make it in Hollywood?

JG: No, he already had his life. Louis loved New York, he loved being here. He didn't have any of the baggage of what his life was in the class restrictions and class divides in Paris. And then Louis was only happy working. He was a born filmmaker. If it didn't work out, on to the next. What I loved about him was that he was always in the now. Had he lived longer, I don't think Louis would have ever been interested in writing his memoirs. So I don't think he ever thought about his critical standing. He didn't think about his position in France. The question was, 'Can I get another project?'

PM: I'm curious, again, about how American or Americanised Louis might have felt – or was it really not a consideration for him. Did he feel a little bit torn between France and the United States? How did he adjust to his New York life?

JG: He was an incredibly cosmopolitan guy. He was a Frenchman, he was very funny, but there was never a sense of him being an outsider.

Books and Abortive Projects

PM: Would it be fair to say that a shared passion for literature was an important component of your friendship with Louis Malle?

JG: Very much so, and right from the start. Back in 1979 when Adele and I went to France to meet Louis, with a first draft of the *Atlantic City* script, and we were on the train coming down from Paris, the closer we got to Cahors where Louis was picking us up, the more I realised I had only seen him twice before, here in New York and that day in Atlantic City. I said to myself, 'I hope we get along.' We pulled into the station, got off the train, and as we were walking to the car, I said 'I saw you reading a book on the platform, what book was it?' – just to say something – he was as nervous as I was. 'Oh yes,' he replied, 'it's a wonderful book, that nobody knows, called *Les Mystères de Paris* by Eugène Sue,' and out of my pocket I took the exact same book, in English, *The Mysteries of Paris*. We hugged each other and knew everything was going to be all right. So that was that moment with that synchronicity of our tastes – we really both were interested in the same things. That's how we became friends.

PM: Didn't you work with Louis on a project around Henry James' *What Maisie Knew?*

JG: Yes, in the late eighties. Again, we were talking about our projects every time we'd meet. That one would have been perfect for Louis because the novel is from the viewpoint of a seven-year-old child, aware of nothing, and through her eyes we understand the degradation of her mother and father, the moral chaos of the life that she was living with complete unawareness. That was just up Louis' alley.

PM: This is arguably even truer of another crucial yet equally doomed project of Louis Malle's, based on *Victory*, a novel by Joseph Conrad. He revisited it at several points in his life until he finally had to throw in the towel…

JG: We had talked a lot about that project. In a sense *Victory* is not unlike *The Great Gatsby*, in that it's a great anecdote, beautifully told, but very hard to dramatise. And the mystery of Lena, who is the sexual focus in the book, is all done by innuendo and Conrad's tone, so that when you take his voice out of that story, the bare bones are not thrilling. It's about someone coming to get us and kill us. Similarly, you can't make a great movie out of *The Great Gatsby* because it's about Fitzgerald's voice, and when you remove that voice from it, you're left with an anecdote.

PM: How did your final project with Louis Malle, 'Dietrich and Marlene', come about?

JG: Fred Schepisi had shot the movie *Six Degrees of Separation* (1993) based on a play and a screenplay I had written. I came out to postproduction at MGM and was going to stay with Louis and Candice. The question you always had when you met Louis was, 'What are you reading?' This time I said, 'Louis, I'm so embarrassed, I just finished reading something hypnotic, *Marlene Dietrich (by her daughter Maria Riva)*.' He took me by the arm and we went into the house and into his bedroom: there, by the side of his bed, was the same book. We talked all day about why that book meant so much to us. We loved as filmmakers the fact that she and von Sternberg had devised this character of Dietrich and they knew it worked when there would be a butterfly shadow under her nose, and every light had to get that, so she only acted with mirrors, she didn't play against the actors. So I wrote that screenplay and John Calley was going to produce it at I forget what studio. Uma Thurman was going to do it, and Milena Canonero was designing it. We were going to shoot it in Rome, of all places, because we could replicate there what Beverly Hills and California looked like in the thirties. We wanted to see if we could tell a biography of somebody in one day. One day in the life of Marlene Dietrich, the highest-paid woman in America during the lower depths of the depression. It was a comedy about that. Milena was getting the plans ready and she brought them to Louis because they were going to start the next week. Louis asked, 'What are these?' and she said, 'They're for the movie.' And his response was, 'What movie?' She knew he got nervous before a film, but this was really different – he didn't know what she was talking about. She called John Calley and said, 'I think you should put a hold on this film because something's wrong with Louis.' Indeed that was the start, the first sign of the sickness that would kill him, and it was a terrible time. His death was just really the end of something.

PM: What would you say was the main draw for you and Louis with such a project? The Pygmalion syndrome?

LM: Capturing the image – the director and the star collaborating and creating a third entity, and how that's created with light. Louis always said that poetry is in black and white. And it was about that relationship of the director to a star. And how von Sternberg grew to hate it… The screenplay took place on the day that von Sternberg vanished from Dietrich's life, and she was trying to get him back. And it was about that, saying, 'Who am I if the director doesn't create me?'

PM: And had you talked about the cast?

JG: Uma Thurman was going to play Dietrich. Uma was 23, while Marlene was 33… Marlene would approve of that, having a 33-year-old being played by a 23-year-old. Uma would have been wonderful because she is incredibly stylish.

PM: And for von Sternberg?

JG: Stephen Rea.

PM: What became of that project after Malle's premature death?

JG: Almodóvar was very interested in it and flirted with it as his first English-language film. Uma brought it to him and they did a reading of it and he loved it. Then Almodóvar and I met, and he realised, wisely, as did Ingmar Bergman, that he could not work in English. It's a pity because it was so specifically geared to Louis – or to someone like Almodóvar – that nobody else knew how or why to do it. Louis' obsession with the camera, and the poetry of the camera, and being that realistic with the poetry of the camera, and the creation, the director's role in creating a star, that relation of the actors… Bardot, Moreau, Alexandra Stewart and Gila von Weitershausen – he had worked in creating their image. Louis adored women and knew how to frame them. So the idea was to make a film about the ritualising of that worship and why von Sternberg, the director, had finally become repelled by his creation, and had to leave it, and how Dietrich tried to get him back.

PM: More generally, how would you characterise your collaboration with Malle? If we take the example of *Atlantic City*, would you define it as a team effort, or were you writing the script based on ideas that you had discussed and debated with Louis Malle?

JG: With *Atlantic City* a lot of it was on the fly as we were trying to solve an immediate problem. At one point I wrote and wrote and wrote, and Louis took the script, tore out like fifty pages and said, 'We're going to end it here. Find the end here.' And I did. But it was a collaboration in that I was writing it for Louis. Specifically, for the Louis that I was learning to know.

On the Set

PM: Since you were on the set of *Atlantic City* for the entire duration of the shoot, and mentioned the difficult relationship between Burt Lancaster and Louis Malle, how would you describe Louis Malle as a director on set? Was he calm, or nervous? Was he an actor's director?

JG: Oddly, I had forgotten this… Once he got the camera set and knew where it was going to be placed, Louis shut his eyes and listened intensely – to determine if the rhythm of the scene was right… He was so brilliant that he 'cut off' his eyes while filming in order to listen to it. Because he could hear the truth of it. He wasn't distracted. His eye did not distract him. Louis once said, 'The eye is a whore, it believes anything. But once you put sound in it, that's when you get truth. Sound brings truth and black in film brings poetry.' I'd forgotten that's what had first struck me. That Louis would clench his fists and screw up his face and then say, 'All right, cut!' He knew which was the right take. He would say, 'Okay, print that.'

PM: And what about the general 'climate' on the set?

JG: People adored Louis because he respected everybody. He wasn't a dictatorial director. He realised that everybody on that set was there for the specific purpose of getting the scene right. So everybody was of equal value once the shooting was started.

PM: John Guare, thank you so much for sharing all your memories.

JG: It's a pleasure to talk about Louis. I love Louis and I miss him, but when I get to talk about him, I'm very happy because he's a key part of my life… I had no brothers or sisters growing up. And Louis is the first intimation I've ever had of what it would be like to have a brother. He was great. Difficult and great and always, always interesting.

Thanks to Melissa Dunlany for the initial transcription.

VARIA
(PREVIOUSLY UNPUBLISHED MATERIAL)

LECTURE

Notes for a Lecture to be Given by Louis Malle on the Queen Elizabeth 2

Below is the transcription of rough, often elliptical, notes (twenty pages, handwritten; family archives)[1] jotted down in preparation for a lecture that Louis Malle delivered aboard the Queen Elizabeth 2 in the early/mid-1980s.[2] Not only does it constitute a uniquely retrospective look at his own career by the filmmaker, but it more largely sketches the lineaments of a cinematic *ars poetica* – perhaps in lieu of the autobiographical, or Proustian, project on his youth he seems to have toyed with a couple of years prior, as is attested in the Louis Malle Archives by a loose sheet related to his 'little madel[e]ine'.[3] The endnotes are mine in an effort to clarify some of the opaque or elliptical references inherent to the notational, self-directed nature of the document.

– Philippe Met

Anecdote – My Dinner with André:

Private screening. Lady somewhat connected with show business. She loves the picture. Then added: 'I saw your name – what did you exactly do?' Compliments – a lot of work. But wants to give the impression it is completely improvised.

I have been at times a cameraman, an editor, a producer, a writer, but I think of myself as a director. Director in UK – metteur [en scène]. What is it? Technically, your function is to say 'action' and 'cut'. Not difficult, but … De Sica.

In a lot of American movies, the producer is the captain of the ship. He buys a book, hires a writer, 4 weeks before shooting hires the director, controls the cutting. Works sometimes. Ex: *Witness* Peter Weir

My way of working, coming from French New Wave, the director is the boss. Architect. In a typical film of mine I'll pick the original concept. Then develop it into a treatment, with or without a writer.

Then the various drafts of the screenplay, plus raising the money (so many different ways), hiring the actors…

Then production: the technicians and crew, the casting, the locations, the sets, the costumes, the lighting. Directing the actors. Being the first spectator. Obsession with continuity. You are the only one who knows. Ex: *Atlantic City*, the staircase – 8 scenes in a day and a half.

Post production. Editing. You know scenes are not shot all at once, but you cannot even imagine the monkey business that goes on in a cutting room. That's when the structure, the rhythm, the style of the film are given their shape, also correcting and improving actors' performances. Ex: *Feu follet* – Venice

After, the campaign – 'pluggin'' – check everything, and then wait. The hardest part by far to sell it. It's happened to me to see a picture opening and closing almost right away, a year and a half or 2 years going down the drain in 2 weeks. There is no business like show business.

I take the full responsibility, since I pretend to control everything. But I know too much to ignore it is a collaborative medium, everybody's contribution is essential, because it is such a demultiplied [sic] process. Sometimes I envy writers and painters – alone. But I thoroughly enjoy working with a lot of people.

Of course, of all the collaborators, actors are the key. They're on the screen and we're not. Homage.

How does one become a director?

Lots of ways, even film schools, although I don't much believe in them.

I come from a family light years away from show business. I was 13, and for reasons I can hardly understand today I had decided I was going to be a film director. Call it an extreme case of what they call vocation. I had 2 older brothers and both refused to join the respectable family business, making sugar. I was making very pretentious artistic little films with my father's 8mm camera, and one day I went to see my parents and told them: 'Maybe it's better if I let you know right away, I have decided to become a director, and nothing else.'

My mother was so stunned, and so angry, I suppose, she had a reflex – slapped me in the face (the only time…). Now, I have always wondered if they had said 'of course Louis, what a wonderful occupation, we are delighted'. I might have wanted to become a fireman in the next 15 minutes.

All these years I have been grateful to my mother. Her reaction 'gelled' my decision. That very moment I'd reached the no-return. I would be a director, and I would make it.

I am often asked, 'what should I do to become a director?' They must be discouraged by all means. If their motivations are superficial they'll move to something else. If they really want it they'll ignore your advice.

Now, it takes luck. Very early I had a lucky break.

When I was 18 my parents gave up and let me join the film school of Paris University if I would also study law and economics. The following spring Cousteau asked for a trainee. I jumped on the opportunity, spent the summer on Calypso, learnt how to scuba dive and became an underwater cameraman. At the end of the summer, C. asked me if I'd stay, in charge of photography and cinematography. Thrilled – 19.

[in the margin: Homage to J[acques]Y[ves]C[ousteau]]

Followed 4 extraordinary years. Greece and antique wrecks, Red Sea. Persian Gulf – Abu Dhabi – Seychelles Islands before *Silent World* – Golden Palm in Cannes, raves from Picasso, Oscar.

Next year – *Elevator to the Gallows*

I learned my craft. I had a great time. I was thrown into the real world à Andrea Doria[4] Sharks – currents – cold. Highest part at 220 feet. We lost a 19-year-old diver. Then I broke my 2 eardrums. I decided it was time to go back to normal life. And somewhere in the back of my head…

Silent World was a big hit. So at 24 a producer gave me a shot at directing from a detective novel. I was terrified.

[in the margin: The youngest person on the set.]

The first week of shooting I don't think I slept one hour. I was wandering in Paris nightclubs, expected to be fired every morning. Terrified of actors/fishes.

Lalla Azar anecdote.[5]

Miles Davis improvised score.

Prix Louis Delluc (the French critics' prize) before release. I was rolling. 3 months after that, I started shooting another pix, *The Lovers* – we were fast in those years. It turned out a big critical success and a scandal hit all over the world. Venice Festival. Controversy: the bishop. That one bed scene. My naïveté. In the US an exhibitor (saw him 2 years ago) was put in jail because of me, went all the way to the Supreme Court in Washington. Today it could be shown at Sunday school, so innocuous compared to what has been done since. So here I was, at 25, I had made it. Because I spoke English, Columbia Pictures offered me a 3 picture deal, that I wisely turned down – sweet smell of success…

My years with Cousteau saved me. I still loved documentaries, and decided I would alternate my fiction work with going back into the real world. Hold the camera myself – away from the artificial world of the sound stage. I am probably the only director to do that systematically. Truffaut anecdote *Day for Night*. 5 features in a row. Talks about what he knows – making a film about making a film. Delightful result. But he took a sabbatical…

So I went on with my career. In fiction, I realised little by little my interest with actors. Showing off my technique at the beginning, then realising actors are the only ones on the screen.

Several sabbaticals. The main one: India.

[in the margin: Italy/Mexico/Amazon]

Divorce, desire to start from scratch.

An extraordinary experience. Self-search.

Also, over the years I was approached by American studios and producers on various projects.

America intrigued me. I came almost every year, one pretext or another. As aspiring directors, we admired American films, and Hollywood, of course, was the Mecca of filmmaking, the temptation, the dream, for many of us.

Polanski at the Cannes Festival: 'Louis, you speak English. Go to Hollywood. They have those huge, wonderful cranes.' But I never use cranes…

Then, because of my interest in jazz, the book on Bellocq + a historical book on Storyville, interview of an old woman who remembered being born in a whorehouse, a prostitute's daughter, Violet the child prostitute, those years, the corruption, different standards.

I came to NY, made a deal with Paramount.

Now, I'd come for 6 months, and it took 2 years. Pictures take more time in the US (more money involved and more of an industry).

Everything about *Pretty Baby* was harder than I expected, and in the meantime, I fell in love with America, and decided to stay.

It was a real challenge, taking a chance. In France, I was one of 4 or 5 directors who could do almost anything they wanted. In America, you're as good as your last picture's gross at the box-office. But it was a new start, my curiosity which had somehow fallen asleep in France, was all out again.

I was also extremely welcome. American hospitality. Supported by critics – with ups and downs – a somewhat unique position, knowing enough about a culture to go beyond clichés and ready-made concepts, but being an outsider, I did not take anything for granted, kept asking questions – to myself and to my entourage like looking at the American scene with a slightly different angle. I have tried to maintain that.

What are the differences?

In Europe, directors are stars. Fellini mobbed in Rome, a la Sophia Loren. In America, except for a few director celebrities – usually for the wrong reasons – they are hardly mentioned.

Tonite Show anecdote. Pretty baby: scandal because of subject. Controversy has followed me, and I have cultivated it. I like to provoke and disturb and force the spectator to reconsider preconceived ideas. Swifty Lazar,[6] then my agent, tries to put me on the show. Answer: 'As a policy we don't take directors on the show. Directors are not verbal.' Eventually they took Brooke Shields. She is not extremely verbal, but she is gorgeous-looking…

Another difference, it was an industry. It is basically about money. My saying…

Slowness of the process. I like to pursue a momentum. When it's ready let's go.

In Hollywood, development deals. They pay to see. Hire a writer, sometimes a director.

1 out of 70

The power – who has control. In Europe, it's accepted it's the director. Not in the US, with a few exceptions. The producer. That's why I am usually my own producer.

But I can't substitute for the actors. The stars have the power. Which is all right (? Travolta getting final cut after *Saturday Night Fever*. Dangerous). The problem with American actors is their entourage, and their fear entourage. Now I hardly had an agent in Europe, developing my own projects, but US actors have agent, manager – sometimes 2 – a business manager, a couple of lawyers (American habit).

All these people have to have their say, they interfere, some are good, most are obnoxious, but the result is you take a lot of meetings.

Fear and paranoia. For good reasons. We're in an age where movies are mostly aimed at the teenage market, with teenagers on the screen. The result is instant stardom, which doesn't last. In old Hollywood a serious star would last 10 years or more, they often had a lifetime career. Today you can be on the cover of People magazine, and forgotten a year later. Rebecca de Mornay end of 83. Very hot. Could not meet her. 2 years later, I see her on a plane, she is desperately looking for work – very destructive.

Also, among the solid stars, the fear of failing, the obsession with their image. Impossible to depart from it.

[in the margin: ex. comedians]

John Belushi Continental Divide / Bill Murray The Razor's Edge / Clint Eastwood venturing into comedy[7] – at Xmas.

Ambient paranoia in Hollywood – because it is a company town. And a code of status symbols. Ex. when I got to L.A. for *Pretty Baby*, red carpet treatment. Gorgeous office at Paramount Studios. Parking place with my name. Trouble started when I parked the tiny 2-door Honda I had rented between a Rolls Royce and a Mercedes. I hate big cars. And because I learned how to drive in a Bentley, RR don't fascinate me as the ultimate achievement.

In fact, I realised quickly L.A. was not for me. Too suburban. I like the city; I like the country. The weather is wonderful, but in the morning you don't go to the window.

And seeing only movie people.

In France, outside work, my circle of friends was pretty much outside show business. Matter of sanity. All they talk about is deals, and I surprised myself becoming involved in this paranoia. Decision not to read the trade papers.

Quickly I moved to NY, a great city, closer to my roots, everybody speaks English with an accent, the great Cosmopolis.

Because it is such a competitive business, loyalty is not excessive.

My friend the young executive. Sent him the script. 6 weeks of limbo – not one phone call. The day the picture is a 'go', he calls me to tell me how much he loves the script.

Shooting is no different. There is not so many ways of making movies. – In India

My excessive involvement. My sempiternal presence on the set. My constant readiness to change. I find disorder very creative, and it was hard on the *Pretty Baby* crew, used to a more orderly approach. I am fed up working with an artist […]

American crews are great. I have worked mostly with New York crews, younger and faster and more enthusiastic than L.A. crews.

So I was in America, after the release of *Pretty Baby*, a little controversy, a success d'esteem, I had contributed to American mass culture by bringing Brooke Shields to the world.

The next one was *Atlantic City*. I'll talk about it later.

A movie I have not made à [in the margin:] John Guare / Moon over Miami / Belushi Aykroyd / Abscam – / swindler hired by FBI to frame politicians / Development deal / Belushi crazy / First draft / He dies / no way to replace me [*sic*] / script a little

Since, I have shot a documentary in Minnesota, about a small farming community, to be aired by PBS this fall.[8]

And *Alamo Bay*, a project close to my heart, based on true incidents. I put my best into it. About the painful process of integrating

The reactions 10th anniversary – a certain hostility – people don't want to see it.
[in the margin: Crazy Dustin[9]]

Now, *My Dinner with André*, an odd proposition, a challenge, outside the film industry.

André and Wally, friends.

Their script. Sure, send it. I say yes. Let's work.

First, why not Dustin and Redford.

It's us. It's about us.

Yes, but it's not you. From now on you're actors playing those parts.

Rehearse switching roles.

And to prove them art is reality reinvented and reorganised, I take them to Ginger man.[10] Impossible.

Interesting example of what film acting is about.

The naturalist school. You become the character. You are the character using different techniques.

Now the opposite. Diderot. Paradox of the comedian. Sincerity and natural are an actor's worst enemy. If he pretends to be the character he is only a fool faking against an artificial environment – a paradox, but some truth in it.

Brecht. The point is not to be the character, but to show the character. The famous distantiation. Your role is to inform the spectator. No identification.

When casting, I try to imagine something exciting happening between the character in the script and the personality of the actor. An interplay, going from complete identification to what we call counter-casting which can be very creative. [typecasting boring Poitier]

But what fascinates me with actors is the unconscious part of their personality, what they don't know about themselves.

Ex.: Maurice Ronet. *Feu Follet*. Childhood – refusal to be an adult à suicide. His walk – insecure, clumsy first steps. I didn't tell him.

Excesses of trying to be the character specially with mediocre actors. The mother in *Lacombe Lucien*.[11]

Ed Harris, *Alamo Bay* – the best of American acting. *Fool for love*. Glenn.[12] Immersion in physical and mental environment. A fisherman and a redneck. Instinct. And then letting himself into the character, almost passively.

My advice always to beginners. Relax. Learn to be passive. Let it happen to you.

Film actors are worried. They miss an audience to be confronted with to tell them something.

In films is has to be the director. First and only spectator. I am under the camera and you do it for me.

That's why so many actors are cute on the screen, I mean not just Shirley Temple, but the macho guys especially, Clint E, Arnold Schw[arzenegger], Sly Stallone, because they don't have an audience to play with, to keep them under control, they are alone, and they want desperately to please and nobody to check them, and they go overboard.

Truffaut anecdote; Hitchcock *Torn Curtain*; Brooke Shields

Back to My Dinner, these 2 guys playing their own parts

after weeks of rehearsing, learning lines, taping (I'd show them what I didn't like; what I liked was for me) until they said 'He'

on stage at the Royal Court in London demonstrate that it was only for movies. Losing the intimacy. But an audience – some laughs. Good Lord, it is a comedy. And also it's not only what they say, but the way they say it, what they don't say, what else they betray, sometimes the opposite of what they are saying. Maybe we have an interesting movie here.

shooting. After the money was finally put together (it is not a movie) a very comfortable shoot. 10 days. Could've been done in 2 days. Richmond ballroom Jefferson perfect sound stage.

The mirrors, my suggestion, very difficult to light. B.G.[13] as mobile elements, always a life in the B.G., without intrusion.

First week, we see everything. Decide to reshoot almost everything.

The day he was inspired.

Editing – key to filmmaking. See your mistakes, try to correct them.

Had to be seamless, a flux – when it's actually incredibly cut. Must no show. No awards for the editor.

Result my anecdote – like it has been shot in 1 afternoon, with these friends improvising their discussion. I was proud of myself.

Atlantic City.

Project falling apart. Canadian producers. Laurel and Hardy type, with a book. I say no. Come back. Carte blanche. John Guare. We talk about A[tlantic]C[ity]. Rent a car. One day in A[tlantic]C[ity]. Always the starting point – a strong visual impact.

We see it as a metaphor of America, maybe.

Tax shelter. Has to be finished by Dec 31. We're early August. Incredible rush. I like that.

Casting. Burt and Mitchum. Facelift. Burt enthusiastic about part. But still dealing with old macho image.

Very difficult scene. Lots of magic hour. Needs overcast. Five weeks of sun. We had to come back.

Picture completed. The easy part. Goes to Venice Festival. Wins.

No US distribution. Turned down by everybody until Barry Diller.

Then we don't know how to market it.

Then release – rave reviews, success d'esteem.

At the end of the year, divine surprise, a rainfall of awards: L.A., then NY, then national (a sweep – excessive).

5 key nominations. Miss Oscar for Burt.

Ray Stark's story. In my films you know everything about the characters in the first 10 minutes.

That's why we'll never be mainstream Hollywood, J[ohn]G[uare] and myself. We're working again together – my future may be in America. It's hard. This one is about Americans living in Europe.[14] A transition?

Notes

1. My thanks to Justine Malle for generously providing a copy and giving me permission to transcribe it for this volume.
2. Surprisingly, I have been unsuccessful in pinpointing a more precise timeframe, either in archival documents or through personal testimonies.
3. 1230-B228.
4. Name of an Italian ocean liner that was involved in one of history's most infamous maritime disasters (July 1956). Malle was part of the perilous dive to inspect the sunken wreck which cost an American diver his life and resulted for the aspiring director in ruptured eardrums.
5. Leonide Azar edited Malle's first two films (*Elevator to the Gallows* and *The Lovers*).
6. Irving Paul 'Swifty' Lazar (1907–1993) was a talent agent representing many celebrities in Hollywood (as well as in the book publishing industry).
7. Malle is presumably thinking of films like *Bronco Billy* (1980), *Any Which Way You Can* (1980) or *City Heat* (1984).
8. Although he started filming *God's Country* in 1979, Malle was unable to complete it (due in part to PBS's financial difficulties) until he returned to this much-changed community for a follow-up in 1985.
9. Probably a reference to Dustin Hoffman whom Malle tried in vain to rope in for the main lead part in *Moon Over Miami* after Belushi's death.
10. 'The Ginger Man' was the name of a restaurant where Malle subjected his two actors to a rehearsal during an actual meal.
11. In what must have been accompanying notes on directing actors, Malle specifies: 'The woman in Lacombe Lucien. Peasant woman. About the extras, she says, "they don't walk like that" but they should.' (Malle family archives).
12. In 1983 Ed Harris made his debut on Broadway in one of Sam Shepard's best-known plays, *Fool for Love*. That same year he played the astronaut John Glenn in *The Right Stuff* (dir. Philip Kaufman)… alongside Sam Shepard.
13. Background.
14. Malle is likely referring here to a film project scripted by John Guare under the title 'Eye Contact' centered around two American archaeologists conducting excavations in Sicily. Eclipsed by the successfully concurrent *Au revoir les enfants*, it will never see the light of day despite revival attempts a couple of years later.

TREATMENT

Script of 'The Loner' by Louis Malle

Introduction
– Philippe Met

Film scholarship all too frequently tends to neglect a dark or submerged continent of the history of world cinema – what I have elsewhere attempted to theorise under the appellation of 'phantom cinema' (Met 2008: 61–5), i.e. the nebula of films that somehow never made it to the shooting or production stage, yet subsequently and continuingly haunted their creators. Doomed, failed, shelved, abortive, stillborn, unmade – whatever modifier one might use to qualify such 'nonfilms,' they oftentimes exist and persist, even if in not-immediately-recognisable avatars. As a matter of fact, Louis Malle once went so far as to make this phenomenon a habitual punctuation of his oeuvre: 'Every time I finish a film, I return to one of these projects, I toy with it for a while, and then I let it go, for one reason or another. It is a peculiar step in the progress of my work, almost a ritual!' (Mallecot 1978: 22). Admittedly, some of the limited critical or monographic literature on Malle does list, if not comment upon, the numerous film projects that throughout his transatlantic career the director had worked hard, albeit in vain, to bring the screen,[1] many of which have now been deposited at the Bibliothèque du Film/Cinémathèque Française by the legal successors. Inevitably, said documents run the preproduction gamut, from a few hastily jotted ideas by way of outline to bare-bones synopses to treatments to continuities or fully-fledged screenplays to shooting scripts. The most insistent and/or nearest-to-completion ones include various versions where 'genetically' inclined critics will be assured to find a lasting gold mine. As for the non-advent of such filmic endeavors, it originated from an equally wide range of causes: the usual financial entanglements; the perceived unripeness, imperfection(s), or even impasse of the writing; the disruption and diversion brought on by concurrent or competing projects; or, more radically, the interruption of death, be it that of an A-list actor already approached and cast for the leading role (John Belushi, in the case of *Moon Over Miami*), or of the director himself (the already greenlighted *Dietrich and Marlene* was cut short by Malle's untimely demise).[2]

In several instances, however, those misfired attempts eventually morphed into other more successful projects, occasionally along intermedial lines. A stage version of the script for *Moon Over Miami* (both by John Guare) was thus performed at the 1987 edition of the Williamstown Theater Festival. Similarly, some elements of 'Eye Contact' *aka* 'I Hate My Life', another scenario penned by Guare, patently migrated to his 1992 Broadway play, *Four Baboons Adoring the Sun*, while others were more tacitly re-invested in, precisely, the successive scripts based on – or, to use Malle's own words, 'suggested by' – Henry James's 1897 novel, *What Maisie Knew*. The latter efforts never saw the light of day, but in their turn fed into the remarkable adaptation of Maria Riva's biography of her late mother, screen icon Marlene Dietrich, which due to copyright issues cannot unfortunately be reproduced in the present volume.[3] Indeed, the Henry James and Marlene Dietrich projects alike are essentially and strikingly narrated through a child's point-of-view (onto parental behavioural aberration), with the attendant blend of naïveté, or innocence, and forced maturity. Such a structural device arguably harks back to a constant, early concern in Malle's cinema, as exemplified by *Zazie dans le métro* (1960) and *Pretty Baby* (1978)[4] in particular – that of 'always trying to have the children look at the adults' (Cott 1978).[5] But the Malle connoisseur will have no difficulty identifying in the pages that follow other thematic threads that run through the director's filmography: solitude, (ir)responsibility, parental substitute, sexual betrayal, social or societal corruption, etc.

Entitled 'The Loner' and dated 'end nov. 1990', the modernised adaptation of the Henry James story presented here was shortly preceded by a first *frappe*, or typewritten draft, with not only a distinct date ('end 09/90'), but a different heading ('Poor Monkey') – both authored by Malle only[6] and with mere minor variations between them. A degree of confusion arises, however, regarding putative variant iterations, notably one composed by John Guare, relocating the action from Hollywood to a Caribbean island and bearing the intriguing title 'The Manchineel Tree'. Although missing from the Bibliothèque du Film/Cinémathèque Française archives, Pierre Billard (2003: 502) as well as Nathan C. Southern (2006: 346) mention its existence (with a confusing spelling in the latter case: 'The Manchiméel Tree'). Since Guare himself does not appear to have kept any physical trace of it – or a clear recollection of the actual specifics of what he wrote beyond title and concept ('a tree that kills')[7] – this even more spectral script will likely remain a tantalising mystery, an ever-receding mirage…

As it stands, the more domestic, yet poignant 'The Loner' is mostly faithful to the source material, in terms of both letter (despite the altered chronotope and the renamed protagonist) and spirit (the careful avoidance of melodrama, for example – significantly, Malle's young Sophie is recurrently described as on the verge of tears rather than crying outright), even if it throws a scathing critique of Hollywood lifestyle into the mix. Last but not least, this document should be approached by readers for what it is: a preliminary step in the adaptational process – already fairly developed, but necessarily destined to be revisited and further refined, or even redirected and rechanneled.[8] In other words, a *traitement* providing but the initial lineaments or raw contours of what was never brought to fruition, but might have been the first screen transposition of note – possibly in the vein of a certain classical American cinema[9] – of Henry James's masterwork.[10] Whether an unfilmed screenplay such as this one is, to put it in oxymoronic terms, a successful failure – or a victorious defeat (to refer back to one of Malle's most obsessive, ill-fated project sparked by Conrad) – is, in the end, a matter of appreciation…[11]

...

MALLE 1215 B 291

PROJET DE FILM

SCÉNARISTIQUE
Traitement
'The Loner'
1 doc. dactyl. [64f.]

Auteur:
Louis MALLE

[f. 1] THE LONER
Suggested by H. James 'What Maisie Knew'

End of class in a very proper, old style elementary school in Los Angeles. Boys and girls in uniforms say good-bye to their teacher. Outside the building, school buses and car-pooling mothers are waiting.
Sophie, a 6-year old blonde with pig-tails, is picked up by a young English woman, Michelle. In the car, they babble like mother and daughter.
They stop in front of a large fake-Tudor house in the Beverly Hills flats. Sophie enters, runs to the pool. She is late for her swimming lesson, runs through the patio, kisses her father, Bill, a handsome man in his forties, who is playing poker with his friends, a raucous, hard drinking bunch.
At the pool, she undresses rapidly, next to the tennis-court where a tall, great looking woman in her late thirties plays a tough game with a man ten years younger. She is Diane, Sophie's mother. Her partner, Claude, speaks with a British accent. Diane plays hard. Her ball hits the net, she angrily throws her racquet, a woman with an athletic body and a flaring temper. (Henry James describes her 'violent splendor' and 'hard stare.')
Sophie takes her lesson in the pool with the swimming teacher. She sees Michelle coming from the house bringing a tray with a snack, soon followed by Bill, a glass in his hand, tipsy. He sits on the bench next to Michelle and, as they watch Sophie, they exchange small talks.

Michelle is the little girl's new nanny. At some point, Bill mentions that he just lost five grand.

Meanwhile, Diane and Claude finish their game. She wins and enjoys it. She rewards Claude with a kiss and a hug, as they walk to the pool. So far, all seems wonderful, the life of the rich and famous. But when Diane sees her husband, the mood changes abruptly.

[f. 2] BILL says something nasty like:

'You look like a jock.'

DIANE:

'You're drunk!'

Michelle stands up and leaves, crossing Claude. Exchanges of looks, quick presentation.

Claude comes to Bill and introduces himself. A young British actor, with excellent looks and manners, he plays a supporting part in Diane's current movie. Bill looks him up, turns to his wife with a crude remark. Keeping their voices low, Diane and Bill exchange insults.

NOTE: As in the rest of the story, we see and hear everything through Sophie's P.O.V. She is a keen observer of her entourage of grown-ups. She is wise and witty, but not smart-ass, or a cute monster à la Shirley Temple. Diane is a famous actress on her way down from the top. Bill a screenwriter who has not written in a long time.

Later, Sophie finishes her supper in the kitchen, attended by Michelle and China, the Filipino house-keeper. Michelle reads aloud 'Little Red Riding Hood.' As she turns a page, Sophie finishes the sentence. Michelle is stunned. SOPHIE: 'I know the book.'

As Sophie climbs the stairs to her room, she hears Diane screaming at Bill in the master bedroom. She stops by the door and sees her parents in the middle of an ugly fight. [f. 3] They exchange vicious, sordid, absurd arguments mostly about money and their extra-marital relations. Bill, drunk, tries to stand still in the middle of the room, turning slowly to face Diane who paces back and forth like a fury. She does most of the talking (his whoring, his drinking, his gambling, he does not work, spends all the money she makes, he is a terrible example for Sophie).

BILL:

'Shut up you goddam slut!'

Diane throws things at Bill, one of them breaks at Sophie's feet. She picks it up, it is a framed photograph, her father and mother as smiling newly-weds.

Michelle comes up the stairs and tries to take her away, but Sophie resists and keeps watching and listening, eyes wide open. Bill tells Diane she is the worst mother. Diane hits him, he hits back, it becomes a street fight. She is very strong and he is very drunk, she jumps on him, he trips and falls, she kicks him. It is grotesque and disgusting. When Bill stand up, he sees Sophie in the door, Michelle behind her. He goes to Sophie but Diane runs and grabs her.

DIANE:

'Don't touch her, you drunk! She is mine, mine, mine,…'

BILL:

'You didn't even want her, remember? If it was not for me, you would've gotten rid of her. You don't give a damn about her!'

[f. 4] They pull Sophie back and forth like a tug of war. The scene is unbearable and Michelle can't help moving forward to Sophie's rescue.

Bill gets back to his senses. He picks up his jacket, goes quickly down the stairs, muttering 'Shame on us, Goddam shame on us!'

and leaves.

Diane, holding Sophie very tight keeps screaming at him. When he is gone, she cracks up. We're not sure if it is true or acted, but she sobs loudly, tightening her grip around Sophie. The little girl, after a while:

'Mommy, you hurt me. Your belt hurts me.'

Diane lets her go. They look at each other, a moment. Sophie has a brave smile. The phone rings. Diane goes to answer. Michelle takes Sophie to her room.

Later. Sophie in bed, eyes open. Michelle kisses her goodnight. Diane enters the room. She has changed into a negligee.

DIANE

'You can go now. I am staying home to-night. Be here to-morrow at 8.'

Michelle leaves.

Sophie plays with a doll in a long dress

SOPHIE

'Mommy, isn't she pretty? But I lost one of her shoes. We looked everywhere.'

She tries to keep the conversation about the doll, but Diane leans over her.

[f. 5] DIANE

'Do you love me?'

A beat, then SOPHIE:

'Yes, I love you very much.'

DIANE

'What's the matter?'

SOPHIE

'You never asked me before.'

DIANE

'It's because of you, only because of you that I stayed with your father who has been so horrible to me. You understand?'

SOPHIE

'Yes… You're not going to stay with him anymore?'

DIANE

'Soon, it'll be us, just us…'

They snuggle. Sophie is all love and sweetness. Diane is tender, but tense.

The doorbell rings.

SOPHIE (jumps up)

'It's daddy! He came back! He is sorry and misses us…'

She runs to the window, pulls the curtain and sees Claude at the door, looking up.

Diane grabs her, in a fit of anger.

DIANE

'No, it is not your Daddy and I'll make sure you never see him again.'

[f. 6] SOPHIE (shaken):

'But I thought…'

DIANE

'It doesn't matter what you think! And you'll have to learn to keep your thoughts for yourself.'

She leaves. Sophie stays in the middle of her room, then goes for her doll, starts undressing her. She scolds her for being spoiled and selfish.

Next day. Michelle picks up Sophie at school when they see Bill coming out of his car. Sophie runs to him, he grabs her, whirls her around.

BILL

'You want to go to the beach? Both of you?'

MICHELLE

'Well, I don't think…'

SOPHIE:

'Yes, yes, come! Please come with us'

MICHELLE

'I don't think Mrs. Farange…'

Bill puts his hand gently on her mouth.

BILL (whispering)

'I've only to look at you. You're the only person who can save my daughter.'

On the sun deck of a Malibu beach-house, right on the ocean, Sophie undresses and puts on a bathing-suit. The house is comfortable, a big kitchen, a living-room, three rooms upstairs. Sophie is at home, Bill and Diane have rented this house for a long time. Michelle comes down the stairs, wearing a bikini.

[f. 7] SOPHIE

'It's Mommy's!'

She laughs.

MICHELLE

'It's a little big.'

She starts laughing too. Her hair taken down, she is not the shy Nanny anymore, but a young woman, sensual and poised. Sophie takes her hand and they run to the water, followed by Bill carrying drinks.

Sophie builds a huge sandcastle, at sunset. Behind her, Michelle and Bill sit in the sand, drinking and talking. He makes her laugh, he seduces her.

In the kitchen, Bill makes French toast, Sophie's favorite dish. She flips the TV remote control, stops to watch a commercial for Diane's movie-to-come, which includes a few seconds with Claude.

BILL (yelling)

'Turn that off!'

MICHELLE looks at her watch, says:

'Shouldn't we go back?'

just as Bill brings the French toast.

They watch a video cassette of 'Mary Poppins,' all three singing along with Julie Andrews. Michelle has a lovely voice and soon they let her sing alone. She says she wants to be a singer, she takes lessons, she works as a nanny in the meantime.

[f. 8]

BILL
'You have a green card?'
MICHELLE
'Not yet.'
He has put his arm around her shoulder, filled her glass. All evening, except for a couple of mean words for Diane, he is charming, witty, sarcastic, and very handsome, although one can't help notice he is twenty years older than Michelle. Sophie's eyes go from the television set to the two grown-ups. She sees Michelle attracted to her father and enjoys the happy time. The phone rings, Bill picks up, listens for a second, hangs up.
Sophie is asleep on the living-room floor. She opens her eyes: Bill and Michelle are kissing on the sofa.
She is in bed now, in her little room. Michelle sings her a lullaby. Sophie turns towards the wall, smiling. Michelle kisses her and leaves the room.
The little girl, alone, eyes open, listens to the powerful roll of the ocean, soon mixed with the chuckling and snickering that often precedes love-making.
In the middle of the night, noise and light wake Sophie up. Diane shows up with a detective and a photographer. The whole scene is like a cinematic nightmare in slow motion, Diane kidnapping Sophie in a blanket, Bill trying to get dressed in the master-bedroom next door, threatening the photographer who keeps flaring flashlights, Michelle naked in the bed, screaming, fighting for the sheet with the detective.
Diane overplays the scene.
[f. 9] DIANE
'Slut! Slut! Fucking my husband in front of my daughter…'
She turns to Bill who now fights with the detective.
DIANE
'See you in court!'

A few months later, divorce in court. Diane, dressed to kill, works hard on seducing the judge and playing the victim. Bill seems absent-minded. Their lawyers argue fiercely. The judge asks questions to Sophie.
JUDGE
'Which one of her parents would she prefer to live with?'
SOPHIE
'Both of them, if I could.'
She says she would like to stay in the same school. She has no other relatives in Los Angeles, only a grand-mother in a retirement home on the East Coast.
She is brave, very poised. She says she understands the situation, her parents don't love each other anymore, so they should not live together. Diane takes her in her arms and kisses her, provoking a nasty remark by Bill's lawyer, and another clash between the two parties.
It is clear that Diane and Bill's fight for Sophie's custody has more to do with pride and hatred than with love for the child.
[f. 10] The judge makes his decision: the house in Beverly Hills goes to Diane, Sophie will live with her. She will spend the weekends with her father, who keeps the rented beach-house. Bill has to pay alimony.

Defeated, Bill gets nasty. He starts shouting and insulting the judge who tries to shut him up.
Outside the court house, Diane appears triumphant before a crowd of journalists and photographers, holding Sophie by the arm like a trophy. Claude waits quietly in the background, next to Michelle. Bill comes out fuming, pushes the newsmen, gets in his car with Michelle and leaves, chased by paparazzi.

A few weeks later, China, the Filipino house-keeper, is rushing Sophie who is late for school. In the patio, Diane pumps iron with her personal trainer. Very concentrated, sweating in a tight leotard, she projects a dark, brutal sensuality. Sophie walks by, watches her for a second, waiting for Claude who comes out, half-dressed. He is driving her to school.
In the car, Sophie looks at him, then abruptly:
SOPHIE
'Are you scared of Mommy?'
CLAUDE
'Very!'
He laughs and lights a cigarette.
[f. 11] SOPHIE
'You shouldn't smoke before breakfast'
CLAUDE
'I know.'
With his hair disheveled, his boyish charm, he does not look like a grown-up to Sophie.
SOPHIE
'I think you're my best friend.'

Sophie at school, a short scene to show her with her peers. She is tough, bossy with them. The teacher likes her quick wit, her sense of humor. We see her play with a little boy called Simon.

In the house, Sophie plays alone in her room. China calls her. She slides down the banister, runs into the kitchen, sits down for supper.
China watches 'Entertainment tonight.' They announce a scoop, a tape shot in Las Vegas by a tourist. Sophie sees Bill and Michelle coming out of a building, just married. They are surrounded by a brawly bunch of Bill's poker friends. He is very drunk, she is radiant, sweet-looking in a flowery dress. He slants, but she holds him tight. The voice-over comments ironically: 'Two months after his sensational divorce, Bill Farange, Oscar-winning screen-writer, marries Michelle Harrison, who was his daughter's governess. She is 22, he is 45.' The journalists quiz each other: 'which year did he win his Oscar?'
[f. 12] MALE JOURNALIST
'The ceremony took place at 3 in the morning'. 'Must have been quite a shock when he woke up the next day.'
FEMALE JOURNALIST (laughing)
'John, you're not a romantic. We wish them to live happily ever after.'
Diane and Claude have entered the kitchen, dressed to go out, they watch too.
DIANE

'She got what she wanted. Look at them, he is twice her age.'
''Claude wishes them happiness; she snaps at him.
SOPHIE
'Are you going to get married too?'

Sophie and Claude visit Diane on a movie-set. As they walk in, red light, buzz. 'It's a take!' Diane, in a cabaret costume, is mowed down by a sub-machine gun. She falls, covered with blood. Extras spread away screaming. Sophie cries 'Mommy!' and runs to Diane. Claude grabs her just before the 'Cut!'

Diane stands up, her dress torn apart by the fake impacts. She turns to the director.
DIANE
'It was great. You printing it?'
DIRECTOR
'No.'
[F. 13] DIANE
'Why?'
DIRECTOR
'You started falling before the blow.'
She starts arguing with him. Sophie comes to her.
SOPHIE
'Are you all right, Mommy?'
Diane kneels down and holds her tight. ''The set photographer shoots at random. He knows a photo opportunity when he sees one.

Diane throws a dinner-party. A few guests have already arrived. A-list. Sophie wears an embroidered long dress with smocking; she is very excited and silly, dances around the grown-ups, hits a waiter carrying a tray. Nobody pays attention to her. Claude welcomes the guests, until Diane makes a regal appearance down the stairs, just in time to greet Sid Daimler, a very short balding studio chief, obviously the guest of honor. Salaams. Sid compliments Diane on her dress.
SOPHIE
'Do you like MY dress?'
Sid laughs and lifts her up. He is a jovial and friendly shark. Introduced to Claude, he exclaims:
'Here is the lucky fellow! You look good, you look too good. We're all jealous of you.'
Sophie takes Claude's hand:
SOPHIE
'I am going to marry him when I grow up.'
[f. 14] The guests laugh.
SIDNEY
'What about your Mommy?'
SOPHIE
'She does not mind. She works all the time. We share him.'
More laughs.

This is the one scene when Sophie is what one expects her to be all the time, a spoiled brat. China tries to take her upstairs to bed. She runs away, hides behind the grown-ups, until Claude grabs her, brings her to the stairs.

CLAUDE

'Old girl, stop behaving like a fool. I don't like you one bit to-night.'

Sophie looks at him, tears in her eyes.

SOPHIE

'I was just trying to be nice... I hate you.'

She runs up the stairs, pushing away China.

She undresses and gets into bed alone. She cries. Loud party noises, Diane's high-pitched laugh. Sophie holds a post-card of the Vegas strip. One reads: 'I am so happy! Miss you. Michelle.' The door opens, Claude comes to bed. She turns away.

CLAUDE

'Good night, old girl.'

SOPHIE

'Where is Mommy?'

CLAUDE

'She is busy with the guests.'

[f. 15] A moment, then Sophie throws herself into his arms, sobbing. Later, next to the ramp upstairs, Sophie builds a castle with blocks and watches the grown-ups having dinner. Diane has Sid on her right, Claude sits at the other end of the table.

Friday afternoon.

Michelle picks up Sophie at school and drives her to the beach in Bill's old Bentley. She tells her about the wedding, how happy she is.

MICHELLE

'Your father is my husband, so now I am your little mother.'

She has changed, speaks faster, wears make up, expensive clothes. She shows Sophie her ring.

MICHELLE

'Your dad is a darling. I bring him luck, you know. He won a bundle at the crap-table. And it's all thanks to you. You brought us together.'

Sophie loves the idea.

SOPHIE

'Yes, I brought you together.'

They enter the beach house. On the sundeck, Bill plays a loud game of poker with his buddies. He sits Sophie on his knees.

BILL

'Poor little monkey! I missed you. I missed you so much I married your Nanny.'

Everybody laughs drunkenly. Sophie looks at Michelle, who smiles tensely. The gambler next to Bill takes Sophie on his knees: 'Bring me luck!'

[f. 16] She is carried around the table, the men tease her, pinch her, tickle her. She laughs at first, then it gets rough. Michelle rescues her. While they build a sand castle, Michelle confides her views of the future to the little girl, a serious grown-up conversation. She plans to quiet Bill down, get rid of his gambling friends and put him back to work. He might have to go to a clinic for a while, get off the habit. Meanwhile, she will pursue full time her singing career, she has a new teacher, she is auditioning next week for background vocals at a recording studio.

MICHELLE
'I can work now. Soon I'll be an American citizen.'

If everything goes her way, she wants Bill to appeal to the court for Sophie's custody. In the conversation, the little girl mentions how much she loves Claude.

SOPHIE
'You should come and see us.'

MICHELLE
'I don't think your mother would like it.'

Dinner. Bill is cooking. His buddies are still around. Several women have joined the party. Michelle talks to a young man. Bill has lost heavily and is very drunk, very loud. He asks Sophie about 'your horrible mother and her gigolo' and follows with a series of the coarsest insults. He turns against Michelle who tries to calm him down. He wonders why he married her: she can't cook, she is broke.

[f. 17] 'She must have something we don't know,' says a buddy. Roaring laughter.

The doorbell rings; Michelle opens to Fred, Bill's agent. They have a few whispered words, interrupted by Bill.

BILL
'Did you bring the dough?'

Fred takes Bill apart. He produces a bundle of money, but before giving it to Bill, he wants him to sign a contract, a rewrite job for a Canadian movie that Bill had previously turned down.

Bill signs on the table next to Sophie.

BILL
'You see, I've become a whore, just like your mother.'

Sophie is in bed, sleeping. Bill comes in, pushing away Michelle who tries to keep him from waking her up. He gets on his knees by the bed and they snuggle. Such sadness in his eyes. Sophie holds him as if he was drowning.

SOPHIE
'Pop, you smell terrible. Go to bed.'

When Sophie comes down the next day, she finds her father reading the Sunday papers on the deck, while Michelle sings arpeggios in the kitchen, in a great mood, until Bill can't stand it any longer and sends her to the market.

Bill fixes himself a Bloody Mary in the kitchen, watched by Sophie who is eating cereals. The doorbell rings. Bill goes to open, a woman walks in, not young, heavily made up.

[f. 18] She comes to visit the house which is soon up for rent. Bill takes her around, the woman knows who he is and is obviously seduced by his charm and good looks. Sophie watches them go upstairs, enter the guest-room. The door closes.

Michelle comes back loaded with shopping bags. Sophie helps her. Michelle asks for Bill.

SOPHIE

'He went for a walk. Let's go find him. Catch me.'
She starts running towards the water.

Sunday afternoon.
Claude comes to pick up Sophie. She kisses Michelle good-bye.
SOPHIE
'Come visit us. You promise?'
Michelle looks at Claude.
MICHELLE
'May be. But I'll call first.'"
In Claude's little British convertible, Sophie asks about age differences.
SOPHIE
'Is it true Michelle could be Dad's daughter?'
CLAUDE
'Technically, yes. If your father had married very young.'
SOPHIE
'Then she should be my sister.'
She likes the idea. She goes on.
[f. 19] SOPHIE
'You too, you're much younger than Mommy.'
CLAUDE (laughing)
'I don't think she has in mind to marry me.'
SOPHIE
'Wouldn't you like it? I mean being my second father?'
CLAUDE
'Of course, old girl. But there are other considerations.'
SOPHIE (after a beat)
'I don't think I would like it.'
Claude tells Sophie she has a new governess.
SOPHIE
'How is she?'
CLAUDE
'I don't know.'
SOPHIE
'Is she as pretty as Michelle?'
CLAUDE (laughing)
'I doubt it.'

Sophie enters Diane's bedroom, runs into her arms. Diane is busy packing.
SOPHIE
'Mommy, you're leaving?'
DIANE
"I'm going on location to-morrow. Somebody has to work. Your father has not paid a cent since the divorce. I'll have to sue him. Did he say anything?'

[f. 20] Sophie (a beat)
SOPHIE
'Yes.'
DIANE
'What?' (Silence). 'Will you please tell me what he said?'
SOPHIE (she whispers)
'He said to tell you you're a nasty horrid pig.'
Diane turns to her, eyes flaring. Sophie moves back quickly.
DIANE
'He was drunk, of course.'
She resumes packing. She hands a garment to Claude.
DIANE
'Darling, could you return this to Ralph Lauren to-morrow?'
SOPHIE whispers to Claude
'You're not going with her?'
CLAUDE
'No.'
SOPHIE
'Good.'
The bell rings.
DIANE (to Sophie)
'It must be your new Nanny.'
Sophie runs down the stairs and almost bumps into a small woman in her fifties, holding a shabby canvas suitcase.
She introduces herself, an unpronounceable Polish name and adds: 'You call me Mrs. D.' She wears thick glasses, a hat, a strict old-fashioned suit. She has a bit of a moustache. Diane comes down the stairs.
[f. 21] DIANE
'From now on, you're under this lady's care. Mrs. D., you can teach her a little discipline.'

In pajamas, Sophie washes her teeth, swallows the rinsing water. She hears Mrs. D.'s voice: 'Hurry up, Sophie!' She goes to Diane's room to say good night, stops at the door when she sees her mother with Claude in a tight embrace on the bed among the suitcases. She gets into her bed.
MRS. D.
'What about your prayer?'
Sophie looks at her, surprised.
MRS. D.
'Don't you say a prayer every night?'
Mrs. D. makes her kneel down with her and recite the Pater Noster. She adds at the end.
MRS. D.
'God bless Mommy, God bless Daddy.'
Sophie repeats and goes on.
SOPHIE

'God bless Claude, God bless Michelle.'
Mrs. D.
'God bless little Clara.'
Sophie
'Who is little Clara?'
[f. 22] Mrs. D.
'My daughter. She died a long time ago. She was a little younger than you. She was an angel.'
Mrs. D. has tears in her eyes.
Mrs. D.
'She is your little dead sister.'
Sophie
'Did she look like me?'
Mrs. D.
'No. She had long black hair.'
Sophie
'Why did she die?'
Mrs. D.
'She was very sick.'
Sophie
'I thought only old people died. She is not going to come back?'
Mrs. D.
'Not in this world.'
Sophie asks questions about death.
Sophie
'Where do you go when you die?'
Mrs. D.
'All children go to heaven near the Lord.'
Sophie
'Can you take your toys with you? etc. …'
As they converse, Mrs. D. picks from a box of sweets on the bed table. Sophie wants to take one, Mrs. D. stops her.
[f. 23] Mrs. D.
'You brushed your teeth.'

Sophie in class, day-dreaming. The teacher asks her a question. She does not hear. Everybody laughs. Furious, Sophie pushes Simon, a cute boy next to her.
Later. Art class. Sophie, very concentrated, finishes a drawing. Simon wants to know what it represents. She explains.
Sophie
'On the left, Bill and Michelle, by the ocean, on the right, Claude and Diane…'
Simon
'Are they kissing?'
Sophie
'Yes! In the middle, me and Mrs. D.'

Simon kisses her.

Mrs. D., Claude and Sophie are putting decorations on a big Christmas tree in the living-room of the house. Claude holds a ladder for Sophie who ties a golden star to the top of the tree. He tickles her, she falls in his arms. Laughing hysterically. Then Claude turns to Mrs. D.

CLAUDE
'I am sure you've never been tickled in a long time.'

He runs after her around the tree, she giggles like a teenager. The doorbell rings. China opens to Michelle, very pretty in a jogging suit.

[f. 24] MICHELLE
'Hey, everybody. I promised I'd visit…'

She came to town for a singing lesson and decided to drop by. She is a little uncomfortable, but Sophie runs into her arms and introduces her to Mrs. D.

SOPHIE
'She is my Pappy's wife. I mean, his new wife.'

They have tea in the patio. They talk about Christmas coming. Michelle sits against the sun, her hair shining, and is the center of attention. Claude sits next to her.

MICHELLE
'I miss England so much at Christmas. Don't you?'

Mrs. D., sulking, eats a lot of cookies.

Michelle says Bill has started writing again, he went to Toronto for a few days. She hopes Sophie will spend Christmas with them at the beach. She asks Claude about his plans. He does not know yet, has not heard from Diane.

SOPHIE
'Why don't we all go to the beach for Christmas? Me, Claude, Mrs. D.'

CLAUDE
'What about your Mommy?'

SOPHIE
'Mommy too!'

They all laugh, except Mrs. D. who announces she will spend Christmas Eve with her sister in Orange County.

[f. 25] Claude takes Michelle to her car. Sophie sees them through the open door, engaged in a conversation. She explains to Mrs. D. that Michelle was her Nanny before she married Bill.

MRS. D.
'Is that so? Well, I don't think it's proper for her to come here when your mother is away.'

SOPHIE
'Oh she would never come when Mommy is here. Mommy detests her.'

MRS. D.
'How did she know your mother was not here?'

SOPHIE
'Claude must have called her.'

MRS. D.

'Are they friends?'
SOPHIE (proudly)
'Oh yes, because of me. I put them together.'
Claude comes back, looks at his watch.
CLAUDE
'I have one hour for you, girls. Let's play a game of cards.'
As he goes to get the cards, Sophie whispers to Mrs. D.
SOPHIE
'I love him. Don't you?'
MRS. D.
'It seems like everybody loves him. He makes me think of a butterfly.'
SOPHIE
'A butterfly?'
She laughs. Claude comes back with the cards.'
[f. 26] SOPHIE
'You know what? Mrs. D. thinks you're a butterfly.'
CLAUDE
'I hope she means it as a compliment.'
MRS. D. (blushing)
'Don't be so sure!'
SOPHIE
'Let's play!'

Sophie is in bed, Mrs. D. tells her the story of Abraham and Isaac. Sophie keeps interrupting. She wants to know why Abraham wants to kill his son.
MRS. D.
'Because the Lord ordered him.'
SOPHIE
'Then the Lord is mean.'
Mrs. D. tries to explain the Lord is only testing Abraham. Sophie won't have it and little by little, they get angry at each other.
SOPHIE
'If the Lord asked you to kill me, would you do it?'
Mrs. D. gets very upset and ends up in tears.
MRS. D.
'The Lord took my little Clara away and if I am a good Christian I must say "thank you Lord." But I am not a good Christian.'
[f. 27] At school, children kiss their teacher good-bye with many 'Merry Christmas' and 'Happy holidays.' Sophie is invited by Simon to a Christmas party.
Outside the school, she is met by Mrs. D. in a black dress. She asks Sophie if she would come to a church and light a candle for little Clara who would be 25 this day.
Inside a vast Catholic church. The space, the light, and the silence make a strong impression on Sophie. A few faithful attend Vespers and sing with the priest, accompanied by the harmonium. Mrs. D. praying, head down. Lips muttering, almost barbaric.

They both light a candle and leave. As they drive back, Sophie asks questions about God.
SOPHIE
'Don't we ever see him?'
MRS. D.
'Very rarely. He sometimes appears to people.'
SOPHIE
'Like a witch. A good witch.'
MRS. D.
'Certainly not! Witches don't exist, only in fairy tales. God is one and only, he watches us everywhere, every time. He sees you but you can't see him.'
SOPHIE
'Even if I look very hard?'

As they enter the house, China tells them Diane has returned. Sophie rushes upstairs to her mother's room and finds her [f. 28] in a chair, attended by a hair-dresser, a make-up man and a manicurist, all trying to work on her at the same time. Claude, in a robe, takes Sophie apart.
CLAUDE
'You don't have to mention Michelle's visit to your Mom. She wouldn't like it'

Later, Diane and Claude leave for the theater. She wears a flashy evening dress, he has a double-breasted tuxedo, a great sight for Sophie as they come down the stairs, answering questions to a couple of journalists. Cameras follow them to a stretched limousine.

Sophie is in bed, sleeping. She wakes up hearing her mother's voice. Diane comes and kisses her. Sophie pretends to sleep. Diane and Claude are drunk, they hold each other. Diane is gay and silly. She starts undressing.
CLAUDE (sententiously)
'The movie is terrible, and we're bad in it.'
DIANE
'Who cares? They loved it.'
They leave the room.

Next morning, Sophie is having breakfast. Diane enters the kitchen, wearing dark glasses. She grabs the paper, finds the Calendar section and starts reading. Quickly, she turns mad.
[f. 29] DIANE
'The bitch! The bitch!'
She turns to Claude who just entered.
DIANE
'I thought she liked me. She once told me I had guts.'
CLAUDE
'You sure it was a compliment?'
DIANE

'Oh shut up! You want to know what she says about you? (she reads) 'Claude Burley, the young British actor who was so attractive in the B.B.C. series "Bristles" seems miscast and bored..."

CLAUDE

'Here goes my Hollywood career!'

He does not seem too struck down. Sid Daimler has joined them, as jovial as ever. He tries to soothe Diane.

SID

'Aah! They're barking. We're the caravan."

He has come to take her back to location. He is very friendly with Sophie and Claude.

Diane leaves in a frightful mood. She has to work on Christmas Eve, she says. She asks Mrs. D. to call the beach and arrange for Sophie to spend Christmas with her father.

CLAUDE

'When are you coming back?'

DIANE

'My work comes first, understand? Why don't you make plans for yourself?'

[30] CLAUDE

'How could I make plans if I don't know...'

DIANE (cuts him)

'You're so dreadfully vague. Let me tell you something, you're simply not serious...'

Diane as usual uses attack as the best defense and she ends up blaming Claude for everything, including the bad reviews.

She leaves with Sid.

Sophie is on holiday. The week before Christmas goes by in a series of short scenes. This is a happy time for her with Claude and Mrs. D.

Sophie and Claude, on the tennis-court. He shows her how to play a backhand, he stands against her, holding her arm back and forth. Mrs. D. watches. Claude puts a racket in her hand and drags her to the court. Side by side, Sophie and Mrs. D. try to hit the balls Claude sends them. A lot of misses, a lot of laughs. Mrs. D. out of breath whispers to Sophie.

MRS. D.

'Isn't he wonderful? A real gentleman!'

The three of them stop at Robinson's. They buy presents for Diane, Bill, Michelle, Simon and each other. As they bring their loot to the wrapping desk, Claude whispers to Sophie.

CLAUDE

'How are we going to pay for all this?'

[f. 31] SOPHIE

'I don't know.'

CLAUDE

'Charge it. Your mother has an account.'

They go to the cashier.

CASHIER

'Will this be cash or charge?"

SOPHIE (suave)
'Charge it to my mother, Mrs. Diane Farange.'
The cashier looks surprised.
CLAUDE
'It's perfectly all right. Mrs. Farange called the manager.'
CASHIER
'Can we reach her on the phone?'
SOPHIE
'She is on location in Arizona.'
The cashier consults with her boss, comes back and starts punching the cash machine.
SOPHIE (whispers to Claude)
'She'll be mad at us.'

Simon's Christmas party. Children and parents exchange presents; Sophie gives hers to Simon. She is photographed with him, his mother and his father. They ask about Diane and Bill.
SOPHIE
'They're working.'
Later, the kids are playing when a Santa Claus makes a [f. 32] theatrical entrance. He staggers and speaks loudly, like a drunk. Sophie is thrilled when she recognizes Claude. He is very funny, lets the kids harass him. They love him.

They go back to the house. China tells them Diane has called. No message, she can't be reached and will call back. They play cards. Sophie cheats again and again. She can't stand to lose. Claude protests, threatens to leave the game. Then he teases Mrs. D., whose hand keeps plunging into a box of chocolate. He grabs that hand and holds it.
CLAUDE
'Pretty hand you have, Agneska.'
Mrs. D. blushes.
SOPHIE
'Let's play hide and seek!'
They start running around the house, chasing each other, ignoring China's protests. At some point, Claude shows Sophie Mrs. D.'s plump shape hiding inside a curtain. He puts his arms around the curtain and grabs her by surprise. She shrieks and ends up in a tight embrace with Claude who takes her around the room mocking a voluptuous tango. Mrs. D. has lost her glasses and does not see anything. Next time, Mrs. D. looks for Claude and Sophie, finds them in a tiny closet. Sophie, seated on his lap, is in heaven. Claude stands up.
CLAUDE
'I got to get dressed.'
[f. 33] SOPHIE
'Oh no!, you're not going out?'
CLAUDE
'I am afraid so, old girl. A boring dinner with a director. Got to find a job. I'm broke.'

Sophie, sulking, runs up to her room. She locks the door and stands against it, refusing to open to Claude. She hears Mrs. D.'s voice.

Mrs. D.
'You love children, don't you?'
Claude (laughing)
'No, I don't. I grew up with four younger brothers, enough for the rest of my life.'
They move away. Sophie silently unlocks the door and opens it a couple of inches.
Mrs. D.
'You love Sophie.'
Claude
'Yes, I love this little girl. She moves me… Ah well… (he laughs) maybe I am a family man, Agneska.'
Mrs. D.
'Then you should marry a family woman, have children of your own. This is not a proper life for a man like you.'
Claude
'There are no family women that I know of.'
Mrs. D. protests.
Claude
'Take Diane. She won't hear of children. But she can't help the one she's got.'
[f. 34] He takes Mrs. D. by the arm into Diane's bed-room.
Claude
'Agneska, I have something to ask you.'
He closes the door, whispering. Sophie, from the landing, can't understand anything of their conversation.

Sophie and Mrs. D. are having dinner in the kitchen. Claude comes in, impeccably dressed, offers China to drop her at the bus-stop on Sunset. They leave.
Alone, the little girl and her governess discuss about Claude, how much they love him.
Sophie
'Don't we have the best time with him! The three of us… You know what I was doing in my room before dinner? I was praying God to keep Mommy away until I go back to school.'
Mrs. D.
'Sophie! You love your Mommy and you should not say that.'
Sophie
'I love her, but I don't miss her, now that I have you. I love Daddy too, but sometimes I dream we're running away, Claude and you and me, running away for good.'
Mrs. D.
'Poor darling! I know exactly what you feel. But you know, he might not be with us much longer. He is thinking of going back to England.'
Sophie
'How do you know?'
[f. 35] Mrs. D. (smiling)

'Well, he leans on me. I try to give him good advice. He has a wonderful nature, but he is weak. He needs help from somebody who can understand him… (she sighs) I wish I could save him.'

SOPHIE
'From what?'
MRS. D.
'Oh just from awful misery. Your mother who treats him so badly. And now Michelle…'
SOPHIE
'Michelle?'
MRS. D.
'He sees her.'
SOPHIE
'You mean just the two of them?'
Mrs. D. nods.
SOPHIE
'It's not true! He would've told me! How do you know?'
MRS. D.
'He didn't tell me, but I know'
Sophie suddenly has a fit of anger.
SOPHIE
'You don't know anything!'

[f. 36] Night. Sophie has a brutal nightmare. She wakes up screaming. Mrs. D. runs into the room. Sophie throws herself into her arms, sobbing. She tries to explain her dream, Diane killing Claude with a big knife, then chasing Sophie around the house.

Day before Christmas Eve. Sophie packs her little suitcase. She has a terrible argument with Mrs. D. about which dress she should wear to her father's to-morrow night. She has put on the dress she wants to wear. It is too big for her but she loves it.

SOPHIE
'Claude gave it to me.'
Claude comes in from outside.
SOPHIE
'Where were you?'
CLAUDE
'I went to my agent to pick-up residues. Santa Claus's money!' From behind his back he brings out two presents, for Sophie a Barbie doll whose nylon hair grows down to her feet, for Mrs. D. a book of photographs of Poland.
The three get into Claude's small convertible. Mrs. D. can hardly fit in.
MRS. D.
'I have to start a diet after Christmas.'
She has a bag with her, she is going for two days to her sister's house in Orange County. They drop her at the bus station. Sophie must then go to the dentist with Claude. Mrs. D. says so many good-byes. She almost misses her bus. She is funny and warm and touching.

[f. 37] Sophie in the dentist-chair. The doctor finds a cavity and begins to drill. She makes a fuss. Claude holds her hard and tells her a joke. Sophie starts laughing so hard the dentist has to stop.

Back in Claude's car, he offers to take her to a movie but first they'll stop by the Beverly Hills Hotel for a milk-shake.

While Sophie sips on her drink in the little coffee-shop of the hotel, Claude has a hard time convincing her that the earth is round.

SOPHIE

'How do you know?'

CLAUDE

'Well, that's what everybody says. But I know it's true. I got it from an astronaut.'

SOPHIE

'You know an astronaut?'

CLAUDE

'I know hundreds of astronauts. I was one myself in a terrible movie.'

A pretty girl, the starlet type, seated next to them, laughs. Claude turns to her and starts a conversation. Sophie does not like it. She stands up.

SOPHIE

'I am finished. Let's go see "Dumbo."'

[f. 38] Claude gets her very crossed when he writes down the girl's phone number. He makes fun of Sophie as they leave.

CLAUDE

'Who do you think you are? You're going to spend Christmas with your Dad and Michelle, what about me? I should stay alone waiting for your mother?'

At this very moment, they pass by the Polo lounge and hear a laugh, a high-pitched theatrical laugh, unmistakably Diane's. Sophie runs inside the lounge and sees her mother seated in a booth with Sid. He is whispering something in her ear and she laughs again, when Sophie throws herself into her.

SOPHIE

'Mommy, you're here!'

Diane is stunned for a second, but she immediately counter-attacks.

DIANE

'What are YOU doing here?'

She lifts her eyes and sees Claude. Conversations have stopped around them. Diane stands up and walks imperiously to Claude.

DIANE

'What is the meaning of this? You take my daughter to a bar?'

CLAUDE (smiling)

'Surprise! We thought you were in Arizona.'

DIANE

'As you can see, I am not in Arizona. Will you answer my question?'

SOPHIE

'I was having a milk-shake at the Coffee-shop.'

[f. 39] She has taken Claude's hands and comforts her mother. Diane takes her by the shoulders.

DIANE

'Go and sit with Sidney. I have to talk to him.'

CLAUDE (in a burst of anger)

'That won't do. She stays with me. And stop posturing. You gave her up a long time ago.'

DIANE

'How dare you? My own child…'

She presses Sophie hard against her belt, then pulls her towards Sid's table. But Sophie holds to Claude's hand and she finds herself in a tug of war another time.

Somebody laughs at a table nearby. Claude sees the anguished expression on Sophie's face. He lets her go, turns to Diane.

CLAUDE

'You bitch!'

They go into the garden, exchanging insults in low voices. Sophie sits in the booth, as far away as she can from Sid.

SID

'You want a juice? A glass of milk?'

Sophie says no, her eyes fixed on Claude and her mother.

SID

'Sophie, you must not believe any harm of your mother. You don't know how fond of you she is.'

SOPHIE

'She is fond of me?'

SID

'Tremendously. But she thinks you don't like her.'

[f. 40] SOPHIE

'I think I love her more than she loves me.'

SID

'You're wrong! Listen to me! Your mother is an angel, a true angel, but she's had so much to put up with, so much to suffer…'

Sid is very sincere, very convincing. He gets Sophie's full attention as he explains how much Diane is misunderstood, how great a person she is.

SID

'She is trying to recover now, with my help. But she loves you. She keeps telling me about you.'

SOPHIE

'She does?'

SID

'Yes she does. She cares so much about you.'

Sophie looks at him. She is moved now. She believes him.

SOPHIE

'And you? Do you love her?'

SID

'Oh yes I love her! And you too! We both want you to live with us.'
SOPHIE
'Now?'
SID
'Soon. When she gets better.'
SOPHIE (a trace of suspicion)
'Didn't you tell me once you are married and have two daughters?'
[f. 41] Sid is taken aback. He does not know how to handle this one, but Diane comes back. She collapses into the booth, silent, like out of breath. Sid takes her hand.
SID
'You're exhausted, darling. It must've been dreadful…' Diane gazes ahead. Sid continues.
SID
'I told Sophie how much you love her. She understands you need a rest.'
DIANE
'I am sick of everybody. I want to be alone.'
SID
'I know. We'll go to that spa where you'll rest for some time. Sophie knows we love her and when we come back…'
Diane cuts him furiously.
DIANE
'She hates me! He has taken her from me and now she hates me! (she turns to Sophie) He has set you against me and you've been won away and your dreadful little mind has been poisoned! You've no more feelings for me than a fish!'
Sophie stands up with such anguish on her face that Sid tries to stop Diane. But she goes on.
DIANE
'Go to him! He is waiting for you. He'll take you to your horrible father or wherever he wants! Go! Go! I'm not your mother anymore!'
[f. 42] Sophie looks at her, a long stare, then she runs away and finds Claude in the lobby. He takes her hand and they walk out without a word. Sophie cries, quietly.

They drive to the beach. Sophie has her little suitcase on her knees. Claude puts his hand on her knee.
CLAUDE
'You know what I keep thinking all the time? You Sophie, so sweet, so loving, how can you be the child of such a monster?'
SOPHIE
'She didn't really mean what she said. She was angry. I know her.'
CLAUDE
'And now I am taking you to your father, who is just as bad as she is.'
SOPHIE
'But Michelle is not. Will you stay with us at the beach?'
CLAUDE (laughs)
'Me and your father?'
SOPHIE

'When shall I see you again?'
CLAUDE
'I don't know. It's time for me to go back to England.'
SOPHIE
'You can [missing verb] with me and Mrs. D. Mommy and Sid won't be back for a long time.'
CLAUDE
'That you don't know! She changes lovers in a whiff.'
[f. 43] SOPHIE
'Then take me with you in England.'
CLAUDE
'There's an idea! With Mrs. D.?'
SOPHIE
'If you want. Or just the two of us.'

They stand by Bill's door in Malibu. It is locked and nobody answers. They walk around and check the sundeck and the back.
CLAUDE
'I should've called. They were not expecting you until to-morrow. I wonder where Michelle went.'
SOPHIE
'I thought you'd know. Haven't you seen her?'
Claude looks at her.
CLAUDE
'Why do you say that?'
SOPHIE
'Mrs. D. told me.'
CLAUDE
'Well, I met her once at a party…'
He stops, uncomfortable under Sophie's inquisitive stare.
CLAUDE
'You know what? Let's drive up the coast and visit my friends in Ojai. Maybe we'll sleep there and I'll drive you back to-morrow. What do you say, old girl?'
Needless to say, Sophie is thrilled.
[f. 44] What follows is a musical montage, a series of dreamy, almost unreal moments for Sophie.
- Claude drives his convertible through luscious orange groves. Sophie, her head bent backward, looks at the trees that seem to close down on her. They are lost.
CLAUDE
'I've been here only once.'
The night falls. They get deeper and deeper into the grove, the path narrows until the little car is stuck in the mud and stalls. The silence is filled with noises, birds, branches cracking, the wind. Sophie is scared and loves it. They hear a strident neighing, a horse appears suddenly, mounted by an old man in a cape. Without a word, he helps Claude to pull the car.

As they get out of the grove, they see on a hill in front of them a large building, like a baroque castle with several towers, lit like a Christmas tree. It is a hotel. They go to the desk. There is no room available, Claude insists, Sophie mutters a prayer, the phone rings, somebody cancels. They follow a long corridor behind a very young bell-boy, almost a child, who insists on carrying their luggage.

They make their entrance into a large formal dining-room full of guests. Sophie wears her Christmas dress, Claude a dark suit. He holds her arm. Everybody looks at them as the maître d' takes them to their table. Sophie is in heaven and behaves with great poise. They order. Claude suggests a [f. 45] cheese burger but Sophie chooses a very complicated entrée. They make fun of the other guests who keep staring at them. Claude, gay and relaxed, starts talking about his younger brothers. He describes a tightly knit and loving family, a house full of noise and mischiefs, a very eccentric father.

SOPHIE
'I would like so much to meet them.'

She remarks he never talked about his family before. She asks about his mother.

CLAUDE
'She died three years ago.'

He says it was a terrible shock for him. His father encouraged him to come to this country. Sophie looks at him, the flame of the candle flickers on his face, he looks so young and fragile. He forgets he is talking to a little girl and tells her of his life in Los Angeles, his restlessness in the company of women, his fascination for Diane. As he talks, Sophie looks around at the waiters who seem to slide silently on the carpet, the glittering silverware, the huge chandelier. Claude takes her hand.

CLAUDE
'Time to go to bed, old girl. Thank you for a lovely evening. I have such a happy time with you.'

Sophie looks at him, she wants to say something but she is overwhelmed by her emotions.

[f. 46] She is in the bathroom, singing and playing with her little plastic toys. She hears Claude who calls her from the room, tells her to hurry up and go to bed. She turns and sees him in the room talking on the phone. She rushes out of the tub, dries herself quickly and comes into the room just as he hangs up.

CLAUDE
'Did you wash your teeth?'

SOPHIE
'Yes.'

CLAUDE
'Get to bed.'

She runs around the room until he catches her. She throws herself at his neck and kisses him. She says she wants to sleep in his bed.

SOPHIE
'I'm scared, I can't sleep alone. And I want to snuggle with you.'

He puts her in her bed and improvises a Christmas tale. She falls asleep.

She wakes up in the middle of the night, crying. She looks around, scared in this unfamiliar room, until she sees him sleeping in the other bed. She kneels by him and gently touches his face.

The next day, they park by the Malibu house, hear Michelle singing. She runs to them, kisses Claude, takes Sophie in her arms.

[f. 47] SOPHIE

'Where is Daddy?'

Michelle explains she has not seen him in a week. She has learnt from Fred, his agent, that Bill never went to Toronto. Michelle is worried, very tense, angry at Bill. She does not know where to find him, she has no money, the house lease is expired, the new occupants come in right after Christmas, she does not know where to go. She cracks up, starts sobbing and throws herself into Claude's arms.

MICHELLE

'Darling, I'm so sick of all this! And I've missed you…'

Sophie stares at Claude who comforts Michelle awkwardly. He turns, they exchange a look. Sophie runs to the beach. She runs and runs, as if she wanted to kill herself.

The three of them have lunch in a pizzeria by the ocean. Sophie eats silently, Michelle does all the talking. She tries to be cheerful and positive.

MICHELLE

'Don't worry, Sophie. I am in charge now. After all, I am your step-mother and I'll take care of you, with Claude. The three of us! We're a family, the best you ever had!'

Sophie smiles. Michelle takes Claude's hand.

SOPHIE

'Like I brought you to Daddy.'

Claude laughs, followed by Sophie. After a time, Michelle starts laughing too.

[f. 48] As they leave the table and walk back, Michelle makes plans. She says she might be hired for this recording, Claude will get a job, they'll rent an apartment. She holds Claude by the waist. He says he very much wants to go back to England.

MICHELLE

'Let's all go back to England!'

Claude takes Sophie's hand.

A Rolls Royce is parked in front of the house, chauffeur waiting. They find Bill in his room; packing clothes. He is dressed formally, wears a tie. He goes to Sophie.

BILL

'Where were you, monkey. I'm looking for you.'

Michelle starts yelling at him. He resumes packing without answering her questions. She gets mad and grabs him. Claude holds her back. Bill turns to him.

BILL

'I understand you're screwing all my wives. You have poor taste, my boy.'

He then tells Michelle she is free to do what she wants; she can go to hell as far as he is concerned.

BILL

'Just remember to get out of here before to-morrow, the cleaners are coming.'

Michelle gets hysterical

MICHELLE

'If you think you're going to get away with this! I'll sue you! If you want a divorce…'

[f. 49] BILL

'A divorce? Why should I want a divorce? I was drunk when you married me. I don't remember anything.'

He stops suddenly. As nasty as he is, he does not have his usual spunk. He sits on the bed. His voice is tired. His tone changes.

BILL

'Do we have to go through this? It's Christmas Eve. Why don't you have a nice time with your boy-friend and let me go quietly with Sophie?'

MICHELLE

'Where are you taking her?'

Bill gets up without answering, calls the driver and closes his suitcases. Sophie goes to him.

SOPHIE

'Where are you taking me?'

BILL

'To the house of a friend, if you don't mind spending Christmas with your father.'

Sophie looks at Claude and Michelle who hold each other. The driver comes and takes the suitcases. Bill stops by the door.

BILL

'Adios, Michelle. Sorry for all this. If you really want a divorce, you know my lawyer. I won't be here.'

Sophie follows him. She kisses Claude and Michelle good-bye.

CLAUDE

'So long, old girl.'

[f. 50] Bill pushes Sophie with her little suitcase into the back of the Rolls-Royce, helped by the chauffeur.

BILL

'Gaston, we're going back home.'

GASTON

'Very well, Sir.'

They ride silently. Bill seems in pain. He drinks water and sweats profusely. He looks at her, puts his hand around her shoulder. She rests her head against his arm.

BILL

'We made such a mess of your life, poor monkey.'

She suddenly has tears in her eyes.

SOPHIE

'Oh, Poppy! Poppy!'

The car enters the Bel Air gate and stops in front of a grand house, all lights out. A butler opens the door, they move to a huge salon, overfurnished in fake 18th century French, with wood panels, chandeliers, and 'more curtains and cushions, more pictures and mirrors, more palm-trees drooping over brocaded and gilded nooks, more little silver boxes scattered over little crooked tables and little oval miniatures hooked upon velvet screens'[12] than Sophie had ever seen in her life.

BILL

'This is the house of a dear friend of mine.'

Sophie
'She must be very rich!'
[f. 51] 'Not only she is rich, she is a remarkable woman. A countess. You will like her. She keeps asking about you.'
Sophie moves about the room, looking at the objects and paintings. Bill points out certain things, how precious they are, a Sevres vase, a portrait of Madame Roland, 'a famous lady of the French Revolution.'
The butler comes back with a glass of milk for Sophie, a Perrier for Bill. There are a lot of servants in the house, very busy dressing a huge table in the dining-room, a bar in a corner of the salon, trays of appetizers on every table.
Bill sits down, takes Sophie on his knees.
Bill
'You know, monkey, I shall soon be off to Europe.'
Sophie jumps up.
Sophie
'With Michelle?'
Bill
'Don't be a little ass.'
Sophie
'With the Countess?'
Bill
'I plan to live and work in France for a while.'
Sophie
'I won't see you anymore?'
Bill
'It depends. What I want to hear, you know, is whether you'd like to come along?'
[f. 52] Sophie (gasps)
'Me? You want me to come with you?'
Bill gets up, goes to the chimney, his back to her.
Bill
'Must I understand your answer is no?'
Sophie
'Dear Papa, I'll go with you anywhere.'
Bill turns around, looks at her intensely.
Bill
'Do you know anything about your horrible mother? I can't find trace of her.'
Sophie
'She went to a spa with her friend Sid. She won't be back for a while.'
Bill
'That's what I'd heard. She's off with that dwarf. She cares about you as much as if you were a kitchen maid.'
He steps back and leans over her, threatening.
Bill
'Do you mean to say you'd really come with me?'

SOPHIE
'I'll do anything in the world you ask me, papa.'
BILL
'That's a way of saying "No, thank you"! You don't want to go at all!'
And as if to expose all that goes against it: he does not have custody and would be forced to go back to court, he will travel a lot in Europe, what about school?'
[f. 53] It is obvious he has no room for Sophie in his future plans, and wants the little girl to turn down his offer.
Sophie listens to him carefully, sees how uncomfortable he is.
SOPHIE
'It might be easier if I stayed here with Claude.'
BILL
'Your mother's fellow! But he is out, don't you understand?'
SOPHIE
'Well, he likes Michelle, and they both like me.'
BILL (laughs)
'You little rascal! You've settled it with the other pair!'
SOPHIE (boldly)
'Well, what if I have?'
BILL
'Don't you know they're awful?'
SOPHIE
'No, they're not. And they love me tremendously.'
BILL
'Do you know why? You're a jolly good pretext.'
SOPHIE
'For what?'
BILL
'Why, for their game.'
SOPHIE
'Well then, that's all the more reason.'
[f. 54] BILL
'Reason for what?'
SOPHIE
'For being kind to me.'
BILL
'Do you realize that in saying that you're a monster?'
SOPHIE
'Me? A monster?'
She suddenly loses her aplomb.
SOPHIE
'Take me with you, then. Somebody must take care of me, you or Mommy, Mrs. D., Claude, Michelle. Somebody!'
The scene is interrupted by the entrance of the Countess.

Bill calls her Francine. She is petite, in her forties, dark in every way, hair, skin, eyes. She wears a satined long black dress and is followed by two Pekinese dogs who bark at Sophie. The little girl looks at her as if she was the wicked witch.

She addresses Sophie with a strong French accent.

COUNTESS

'Here she is! She is very pretty. She looks like you, Bill. What is your name, little girl?'

She takes Sophie in her arms, but not too close. It is clear she has no interest in children. Sophie pulls back from her. The Countess goes away to give orders to the servants, comes back, offers chocolates to Sophie.

[f. 55] COUNTESS

'It is very nice of you to come to my party. You'll be the only child and I am afraid you'll be very bored. But if you're going to live with us, you'll have to get used to it. Do you have a better dress?'

While she speaks, she moves around, fixes flowers, pulls a chair. Bill goes to the bar.

BILL

'Believe it or not, she does not want to live with us. She turned down my offer to go to Paris.'

SOPHIE

'I didn't!'

THE COUNTESS

'We're not going to Paris until next spring anyway. Don't you remember I have promised to visit my friends in Tahiti?'

She sees Bill opening a bottle of gin.

COUNTESS

'Bill, what are you doing?'

She takes the bottle from him.

COUNTESS

'You promised.'

BILL

'One drink…'

COUNTESS

'Not a drop. Have a little courage in front of your lovely daughter.'

And she forbids the barman to serve Bill any liquor.

[f. 56] Sophie watches her father. For the first time, he looks old, and pitiful. Francine takes her by the arm.

COUNTESS

'I am sure we'll get along fine. You can help your father get rid of his terrible habit of drinking. Go upstairs quickly and change. I don't have a children's room but you can stay in the little guest-room on the third floor.'

She calls the chamber-maid.

COUNTESS

'Emmenez la petite à la chambre verte, qu'elle se change. Coiffez-la surtout, elle a l'air d'une sauvage.'

SOPHIE

'What did she say?'

The first guests arrive, a French couple.
COUNTESS
'Chers amis, quel plaisir…etc.'
Sophie runs to her father.
SOPHIE
'Poppy, I want to go home.'
BILL
'Are you crazy? Go and change for dinner.'
SOPHIE
'It's a grown-up dinner. They don't even speak English.'
BILL
'You can eat in the kitchen if you want.'
SOPHIE
'I prefer to go home.'
[f. 57] BILL
'I can't let you go. Your mother is away.'
SOPHIE
'Mrs. D. will be home. She'll take care of me.'
Francine comes back in the salon with more guests.
COUNTESS
'What is it now? Aren't you going to get dressed?'
BILL
'She is a heartless little beast!'
He whispers something in Francine's ears. She turns angrily to Sophie.
COUNTESS
'You're nothing but trouble! Gaston can't drive you. I need him here to serve (to the butler) Henry, call a taxi.'
Sophie waits in a corner of the entrance hall, holding her little suitcase. Guests keep pouring in. A yellow cab stops outside the door. She goes to kiss her father good-bye, both of them very uneasy.
SOPHIE
'Pappy, I don't have any money for the taxi.'
Bill searches his pockets. He goes to Francine. She picks up her purse, takes out a wad of money and pushes it into Sophie's hand.
COUNTESS
'Take this. Christmas present from your Dad.'
[f. 58] Sophie rides back home with an immigrant cab-driver who hardly speaks any English. She gives him directions. They stop in front of Diane's house. She handles him the wad of money, all hundred-dollar notes.
DRIVER
'No change.'
He picks a hundred dollar, gives her back the rest with a smile.
Sophie walks to the door and rings. China opens. She is on her way out, loaded with Christmas bags.

CHINA
'Sophie! What happened? Where is your papa?'
Sophie does not answer. China has to leave, her children are waiting for her, she is late. Yet she can't leave Sophie alone.
SOPHIE
'I am fine. Claude will come back soon.'
CHINA
'Are you sure?'
She gives Sophie a big hug 'Happy Christmas.'

Sophie is alone in the house. Only the big Christmas tree is lit. She stays in front of it, on the verge of tears, but she does not cry.
The bell rings. She runs to the door. It is a messenger who brings a big gift-wrapped parcel.
[f. 59] MESSENGER
'For Mrs. Farange. Is she here?'
SOPHIE
'No.'
MESSENGER
'Can you sign?'

Sophie has put on her nice dress and opens the many presents under the Christmas tree. Many of them are for Diane, some are toys for her. She plays with them. She talks to herself, stops, hearing a noise. She starts singing 'Rudolf, the red nose deer,' louder and louder.
One of the presents is a Christmas pudding. She devours it. On her back, she looks up at the tree lights.
SOPHIE
'Mommy! Mommy! Mommy! Mommy!...'

Christmas morning. She sleeps on the floor, by the tree, wrapped in a shawl. She wakes up hearing the door lock. Claude enters. She runs to him.
SOPHIE
'You came back!'
CLAUDE
'What are you doing here?'
Sophie looks at Claude, unshaved, tired.
SOPHIE
'And you?'
[f. 60] CLAUDE
'I came to pack my stuff. I'm flying back to London this afternoon.'
SOPHIE
'Will you take me?'
CLAUDE
'Where's your dad?'
SOPHIE

'I'll tell you. Let's eat. I'm starving.'

They have a mock formal Christmas lunch at the dining-table, with candles, silverware and all kinds of leftovers from the fridge. Sophie gaily tells Claude of her encounter with Francine, the wicked witch. She describes her, the house, the French servants. She imitates her accent. Claude laughs. She concludes.

SOPHIE
'I told Poppy I preferred to stay with you.'
CLAUDE
'What did he say?'
SOPHIE
'He called me a monster. But they won't have me anyway. They're going to travel. You have to take care of me now.'
The doorbell rings. Claude opens to Michelle who does not see Sophie at first. She kisses Claude.
[f. 61] MICHELLE
'I'm sorry I'm late. I went to see my friend Andrea, she talks a lot. But she lent me money for the plane.'
She sees Sophie in the dining-room.
MICHELLE
'Sophie!'
Claude talks to her in whispers. Sophie stares at them. Michelle comes to her, takes her in her arms.
MICHELLE
'Poor darling! What's going to happen to you?'
CLAUDE
'She wants to come to London with me.'
MICHELLE
'Do you think we can do that?'
CLAUDE
'Why not?'
MICHELLE
'Are you serious? We don't have enough money.'
SOPHIE
'I can pay for my ticket. Poppy gave me money.'
Michelle seems hesitant, then she laughs and kisses Sophie.
MICHELLE
'All right, we'll kidnap you and we'll wait to hear from them. You'll be my little hostage.'

Michelle packs Sophie's clothes. She talks about London. Sophie stands by in silence.
[f. 62] MICHELLE
'By the way, where is your passport? You have a passport, don't you?'
SOPHIE
'I think it's in Mommy's room.'

MICHELLE
'Get it. I'll call British Airways for your seat.'
Sophie goes to her mother's room where Claude is packing. She looks at him a moment.
SOPHIE
'Do you love her?'
Claude does not answer.
SOPHIE
'I don't think you do.'
CLAUDE
'What if she loves me?'
SOPHIE
'Mrs. D. is right. You're weak. You let women take advantage of you. You were scared of Mommy and now you're scared of Michelle.'
CLAUDE (laughs)
'You seem to know everything! I am not scared of you, though!'
SOPHIE
'Because you don't love me.'
CLAUDE
'I love you more than anyone, old girl.'
He kneels down and takes her in his arms. He whispers.
CLAUDE
'You're the only one I've loved outside of my family.'
[f. 63] SOPHIE
'I'll come with you to London, but not with her.'
CLAUDE
'Sophie, you know you can't ask me that.'
SOPHIE
'I know.'
She holds him very tight.

Sophie and Claude play cards in the kitchen. Michelle sits with them. She looks at her watch.
MICHELLE
'The taxi should be here any minute.'
The front door opens, Mrs. D. comes in. She is stunned to see the three of them. She starts asking questions. A cab-driver appears, takes the suitcase by the door.
SOPHIE
'Don't take this one…'
She turns to Michelle.
SOPHIE
'I'm staying with Mrs. D.'
Michelle goes to say something. Claude stops her. They exchange good-byes.
SOPHIE (to Michelle)
'You do love him, don't you?'
MICHELLE

'Of course I do.'
[f. 64] SOPHIE
'Then don't do it only for just a little while.'
MICHELLE
'A little?'
SOPHIE
'Like all the others. Do it always!'

They leave. Sophie sits down in a chair. She does not cry. Mrs. D. looks into the fridge. There's nothing left.
MRS. D.
'I'll go quickly to the market. You come with me?'
Sophie says no. She plays in her room alone.
Or she watches a Christmas fairy tale on TV. …

Notes

1. Outside of Pierre Billard's biography (*passim*), see Mallecot 1978: 73–6 ('Pour une filmographie imaginaire…'); Southern 2006: 341–47 ('Appendix A. Lost Horizons – Selected Unfinished Malle Projects, 1949–94'); Malle 2005: 103–6.
2. On both occurrences, see interview with John Guare.
3. The brilliant, madcap script, *Dietrich and Marlene*, would definitely warrant standalone publication, as would another gem hidden from view, despite its varied, lustrous facets, that Malle strived to chisel periodically, not to say compulsively, since early on – now single-handedly, now with the aid of writers like Daniel Anselme and Patrick Modiano, or his then-partner, Susan Sarandon – inspired by Joseph Conrad's *Victory* (1915).
4. It barely needs pointing out that the pedophiliac undertones in 'The Loner''s poker game sequence (f. [15]-[16]) are strongly reminiscent of young Violet's lot in the Storyville brothel of *Pretty Baby*.
5. In that same interview with Jonathan Cott, the filmmaker also mentions the examples of *Phantom India*, *Murmur of the Heart* or *Lacombe, Lucien*, and goes on to claim that 'If there's anything moral in [his] pictures, you have to find it in the close-ups of those children in [his] films looking at you.'
6. Hence a fair number of Gallic turns of phrase throughout, which have been kept unaltered in the present transcription (minor typos or spelling errors have, however, been edited for clarity.) In point of fact the archival dossier marked 'MALLE 1007 B185' contains a manuscript, in Malle's own handwriting, of the first nineteen pages of 'Poor Monkey'. In private email correspondence (29 August 2017), John Guare confirmed that he was not involved in either version.
7. Private email correspondence with P. Met (29 August 2017). Originally known as *árbol de la muerte*, the fruit and milky sap from the manchineel are highly toxic and potentially fatal.

8   In the late 1970s, Malle even went so far as to define a screenplay as 'a mere rough draft, a bare skeleton devoid of flesh, a pious hope': 'everything is there except the essential' (Mallecot 1978: 64).
9   One might also think of an RKO 'B' unit film like *Curse of the Cat People* (Gunther von Fritsch and Robert Wise, 1944), which Malle's script increasingly, if covertly, seems to evoke with its distressing depiction of Christmas time and a somewhat otherworldly fairy tale-like mood (all coming to a head through the French countess in the role of the wicked witch).
10 In 2012, directors Scott McGehee and David Siegel released a same-titled adaptation of James' novel, setting the plot in present-day New York City and markedly toning down the sombre mood and dark humour of the original.
11 My thanks to the Louis Malle Estate for granting me permission to reproduce the script and to Régis Robert at the Bibliothèque du Film/Cinémathèque Française for his assistance in gaining access to it in the Louis Malle Archives (1008-B185).
12 Malle is quoting from the Henry James text.

Bibliography

Billard, P. (2003) *Louis Malle. Le rebelle solitaire*. Paris: Plon.
Cott, J. (1978) 'Fires Within: The Chaste Sensuality of Director Louis Malle' (interview), *Rolling Stone*, 262 (April 6); http://www.rollingstone.com/movies/features/the-chaste-sensuality-of-director-louis-malle-19780406 (accessed 15 September 2017).
Malle, J. (2005) 'Amère victoire. Les projets non réalisés de Louis Malle', *Positif* (December), 538, 103–6.
Mallecot, J. (1978) *Louis Malle par Louis Malle*. Paris: Editions de l'Athanor.
Met, P. (2008) 'Pour un cinéma fantôme: autour du *Harry Dickson* d'Alain Resnais et de Frédéric de Towarnicki', *Positif*, 565 (March), 61–5.
Southern, N.. C., with J. Weissgerber (2006) *The Films of Louis Malle*. Jefferson, NC: McFarland.

AFTERWORD

Wes Anderson

Three-quarters of the way through *Place de la République*, a fly-on-the-street documentary observing the various *habitués* of that Parisian square, a woman we have gotten to know well over the course of the film (she sells wigs from a sidewalk-stand) interrupts her own narrative to say to someone off-screen, 'I know who you are, by the way. And I know it's your birthday today. How old are you?'

The camera pans to the film's director for the one and only time, and he is Louis Malle, and he says, surprised, reluctant, sheepish: 'I'm forty.'

I was forty, myself, when I saw this scene by one of my very favourite artists in any medium, and this breaking-of-the-spell, this peek-behind-the-curtain which he chose not to leave on the cutting-room floor moved me suddenly and sharply.

My own experience was this: one evening in 1988, as a third-string projectionist in the student cinema at the University of Texas, I inexpertly threaded *Au revoir les enfants* through the gate and watched it from the booth's six-inch glass portal. I was transported enough that I missed every reel-change. The next afternoon, I read Pauline Kael's old *New Yorker* review of *Murmur of the Heart* in the magazine-archives at our school library. I walked across the campus, checked-out a laser-disc from the A/V collection, and watched the movie twice a year for the subsequent two-and-a-half decades. On VHS, I saw the masterpiece he made with John Guare about faded – or more like demolished, or more like only-*imagined*-in-the-first-place – grandeur (*Atlantic City*). On Betamax, I saw the masterpiece he made with Wallace Shawn set entirely at a table in a restaurant (*My Dinner with André*). At noon on the Friday it opened, I saw the masterpiece he made with Michel Piccoli about The Events of May '68 set entirely at a house in the country (*May Fools*). *The Fire Within*, possibly my favourite of all, inspired me to make a whole movie of my own.

He died in 1995, and I remember reacting to his death with the kind of grief I probably ought to have reserved for a person I actually knew. When I bumped into him in his documentary, fifteen years later, revived on the street, my own age, I recognised the movie-maker I had most aspired to be.

Who else has made films of such spectacularly wide-ranging subject-matter, fiction, non-fiction, adapted from books, dreamed-up in his imagination, mined from his own most personal experiences? Who else has been so deeply beloved by such a strikingly diverse cast of collaborators? The young co-director to Jacques Cousteau, the maverick outside the *nouvelle vague*, a highly curious and adventurous man who found peoples' stories to tell all over the world: who else has created a body of work so *complete* as Louis Malle's?

FILMOGRAPHY

1953
Crazéologie
5 minutes
Director: Louis Malle
Production: IDHEC
Screenplay: Louis Malle
Cast (main actors): Nicolas Bataille, Pierre Frag, Bernard Malle

1954
Station 407
18 minutes
Director: Louis Malle
Production: Jacques-Yves Cousteau

1955
La Fontaine de Vaucluse
14 minutes
Director: Louis Malle
Production: Office de recherches sous-marines

1956
Le Monde du silence (US/UK: *The Silent World*)
86 minutes
Co-Directors: Jacques-Yves Cousteau, Louis Malle
Production: Société Filmad & Requins associés
Cinematography: Edmond Séchan
Editor: Georges Alépée
Sound: Yves Baudrier

1957
Ascenseur pour l'échafaud (US: *Elevator to the Gallows*; UK: *Lift to the Scaffold*)
90 minutes
Director: Louis Malle
Production: Nouvelles Éditions de Films
Screenplay: Louis Malle, Roger Nimier (from the novel by Noel Calef)
Cinematography: Henri Decae
Editor: Léonide Azar
Sound: Raymond Gauguier
Music: Miles Davis
Cast (main actors): Yori Bertin, Jeanne Moreau, Georges Poujouly, Maurice Ronet, Lino Ventura

1958
Les Amants (US/UK: *The Lovers*)
88 minutes
Director: Louis Malle
Production: Nouvelles Éditions de Films
Screenplay: Louis Malle, Louise de Vilmorin (from *Point de lendemain* by Dominique Vivant Denon)
Cinematography: Henri Decae
Editor: Léonide Azar

Sound: Pierre Bertrand
Music: Brahms String Sextet No. 1 in B Flat Major
Cast (main actors): Jean-Marc Bory, Alain Cuny, Jeanne Moreau

1960
Zazie dans le métro (US/UK: *Zazie*)
92 minutes
Director: Louis Malle
Production: Nouvelles Éditions de Films
Screenplay: Louis Malle, Jean-Paul Rappeneau (from the novel by Raymond Queneau)
Cinematography: Henri Raichi
Editor: Kenout Peltier
Sound: André Hervé
Music: Florenzo Carpi
Cast (main actors): Vittorio Capriolli, Catherine Demongeot, Jacques Dufilho, Carla Marlier, Philippe Noiret

1961
Vie Privée (US/UK: *A Very Private Affair*)
103 minutes
Director: Louis Malle
Production: Progefi, Cipra (France)/CCM (Rome)
Screenplay: Jean Ferry, Louis Malle, Jean-Paul Rappeneau
Cinematography: Henri Decae
Editor: Kenout Peltier
Sound: William Robert Sivel
Music: Fiorenzo Carpi, J. Max Rivière, Jean Spanos
Cast (main actors): Brigitte Bardot, Marcello Mastroianni, Nicolas Bataille, Jacqueline Doyen

1962
Vive le Tour
18 minutes
Director: Louis Malle
Production: Nouvelles Éditions de Films
Cinematography: Ghislain Cloquet, Jacques Ertaud, Louis Malle
Editor: Suzanne Baron, Kenout Peltier
Music: Georges Delerue

1963
Le Feu follet (US: *The Fire Within*; UK: *A Time to Live and a Time to Die*)
110 minutes
Director: Louis Malle
Production: Nouvelles Éditions de Films
Screenplay: Louis Malle (from the novel by Pierre Drieu La Rochelle)
Cinematography: Ghislain Cloquet
Editor: Suzanne Baron
Music: Erik Satie (by pianist Claude Helffer)
Cast (main actors): Jeanne Moreau, Bernard Noël, Maurice Ronet, Henri Serre, Léna Skerla, Alexandra Stewart

1964
Bons Baisers de Bangkok
15 minutes
Director: Louis Malle
Production: ORTF
Cinematography: Yves Bonsergent

1965
Viva Maria
115 minutes
Director: Louis Malle
Production: Oscar Danciger, Louis Malle
Screenplay: Jean-Claude Carrière, Louis Malle
Cinematography: Henri Decae
Editor: Suzanne Baron, Kenout Peltier
Sound: José B. Carles
Music: Georges Delerue
Cast (main actors): Brigitte Bardot, Paulette Dubost, Georges Hamilton, Jeanne Moreau

1967
Le Voleur (US: *The Thief of Paris*)
120 minutes
Director: Louis Malle
Production: Nouvelles Éditions de Films
Screenplay: Jean-Claude Carrière, Louis Malle, with dialogue by Daniel Boulanger (from the novel by Georges Darien)
Cinematography: Henri Decae
Editor: Henri Lanoe
Sound: André Hervé
Cast (main actors): Jean-Paul Belmondo, Geneviève Bujold, Charles Denner, Marie Dubois, Françoise Fabian, Julien Guiomar, Marlène Jobert, Paul Le Person, Martine Sarcey

1967
William Wilson, from *Histoires extraordinaires* (US: *Spirits of the Dead*; UK: *Tales of Terror*), a film in three parts
40 minutes (entire film: 121 minutes)
Director: Louis Malle
Production: Les Films Marceau-Cocinor (Paris), PEA Cinematografica (Rome)
Screenplay: Daniel Boulanger, Louis Malle, Clément Biddle Wood (from the short story by Edgar Allan Poe)
Cinematography: Tonino Delli Colli
Editor: Franco Arcalli, Suzanne Baron
Music: Diego Masson
Cast (main actors): Brigitte Bardot, Alain Delon, Danièle Vargas

1968
Calcutta
105 minutes
Director: Louis Malle
Production: Nouvelles Éditions de Films, Elliott Kastner
Cinematography: Étienne Becker, Louis Malle
Editor: Suzanne Baron
Sound: Jean-Claude Laureux

1969
L'Inde fantome (US/UK: *Phantom India*)
378 minutes (7 episodes, 54 minutes each)
Director: Louis Malle
Production: Nouvelles Éditions de Films, Elliott Kastner
Cinematography: Étienne Becker, Louis Malle
Editor: Suzanne Baron
Sound: Jean-Claude Laureux

1971
Le Souffle au cœur (US: *Murmur of the Heart*; UK: *Dearest Love*)
110 minutes
Director: Louis Malle
Production: Nouvelles Éditions de Films/Marianne (Paris), Vides Cinematografica (Rome), Franz Seitz Filmproduktion (Munich)
Screenplay: Louis Malle
Cinematography: Ricardo Aronovitch
Editor: Suzanne Baron
Sound: Jean-Claude Laureux, Michel Vionnet
Music: Charlie Parker
Cast (main actors): Benoît Ferreux, Daniel Gélin, Michel Lonsdale, Lea Massari, Gila von Weitershausen

1974
Lacombe Lucien
137 minutes
Director: Louis Malle
Production: Nouvelles Éditions de Films/UPF (Paris), Vides Film (Rome), Hallelujah Films (Munich)
Screenplay: Louis Malle, Patrick Modiano
Cinematography: Tonino Delli Colli
Editor: Suzanne Baron
Sound: Jean-Claude Laureux

Music: Django Reinhardt and the
  Quintet of the Hot Club de France
Cast (main actors): Pierre Blaise,
  Stéphane Bouy, Aurore Clément,
  Holger Löwenadler

1974
Humain, trop humain
75 minutes
Director: Louis Malle
Production: Nouvelles Éditions de Films
Cinematography: Étienne Becker
Editor: Suzanne Baron
Sound: Jean-Claude Laureux

1974
Place de la République
94 minutes
Director: Louis Malle
Production: Nouvelles Éditions de Films
Cinematography: Étienne Becker
Editor: Suzanne Baron
Sound: Jean-Claude Laureux

1975
Black Moon
100 minutes
Director: Louis Malle
Production: Nouvelles Éditions de
  Films/UFP (Paris), Vides Film (Rome)
Screenplay: Louis Malle
Cinematography: Sven Nykvist
Editor: Suzanne Baron
Sound: Luc Perini
Music: Richard Wagner (arranged by
  Diego Masson)
Cast (main actors): Joe Dallesandro,
  Thérèse Giehse, Cathryn Harrison,
  Alexandra Stewart

1976
Close Up
26 minutes
Director: Louis Malle

Production: Sigma-Antenne 2
Cinematography: Michel Parbot
Editor: Suzanne Baron
Music: Erik Satie
Cast (main actors): Dominique Sanda

1978
Pretty Baby
110 minutes
Director: Louis Malle
Production: Nouvelles Éditions de Films
Screenplay: Polly Platt
Cinematography: Sven Nykvist
Editor: Suzanne Baron, Suzanne Fenn
Sound: Don Johnson
Music: Jelly Roll Morton et al. (adapted
  and arranged by Jerry Wexler)
Cast (main actors): Keith Carradine,
  Antonio Fargas, Frances Faye, Susan
  Sarandon, Brooke Shields

1980
Atlantic City
105 minutes
Director: Louis Malle
Production: Cine-Neighbour
  (Montréal), Selta Films-Elie Kfouri
  (Paris)
Screenplay: John Guare
Cinematography: Richard Ciupka
Editor: Suzanne Baron
Sound: Jean-Claude Laureux
Music: Paul Anka, Vincenzo Bellini,
  Michel Legrand
Cast (main actors): Burt Lancaster,
  Michel Piccoli, Kate Reid, Susan
  Sarandon

1981
My Dinner with Andre
111 minutes
Director: Andre Gregory, Wallace
  Shawn
Production: The Andre Company

Screenplay: Louis Malle
Cinematography: Jeri Sopanen
Editor: Suzanne Baron
Sound: Jean-Claude Laureux
Music: Allen Shawn, Erik Satie
Cast (main actors): Andre Gregory, Wallace Shawn

1983
Crackers
92 minutes
Director: Louis Malle
Production: Universal
Screenplay: Jeffrey Fiskin (from the 1958 film *I soliti ignoti* by Mario Monicelli)
Cinematography: Lázló Kovács
Editor: Suzanne Baron
Music: Pal Chihara
Cast (main actors): Sean Penn, Wallace Shawn, Donald Sutherland, Jack Warden

1985
Alamo Bay
99 minutes
Director: Louis Malle
Production: Tri-Star-Delphi III
Screenplay: Alice Arlen (from *New York Times* articles by Ross E. Milloy)
Cinematography: Curtis Clark
Editor: James Bruce
Sound: Danny Michael
Music: Ry Cooder
Cast (main actors): Ed Harris, Amy Madigan, Ho Nguyen

1986
God's Country
95 minutes
Director: Louis Malle
Production: PBS
Cinematography: Louis Malle
Editor: James Bruce
Sound: Jean-Claude Laureux, Keith Rouse

1986
And the Pursuit of Happiness
80 minutes
Director: Louis Malle
Production: Pretty Mouse Films (New York)
Cinematography: Louis Malle
Editor: Nancy Baker
Sound: Danny Michael

1987
Au revoir les enfants
103 minutes
Director: Louis Malle
Production: Nouvelles Éditions de Films, MK2 Productions, Marin Karmitz (Paris), Stella Film and NEF (Munich)
Screenplay: Louis Malle
Cinematography: Renato Berta
Editor: Emmanuelle Castro
Sound: Jean-Claude Laureux
Music: Camille Saint-Saëns, Franz Schubert
Cast (main actors): Raphaël Fejtö, Gaspard Manesse, Francine Racette, Philippe Morier-Genoud, François Négret

1989
Milou en Mai (US: *May Fools*; UK: *Milou in May*)
108 minutes
Director: Louis Malle
Production: Nouvelles Éditions de Films, TF1 Films (Paris), Ellepi Film (Rome)
Screenplay: Jean-Claude Carrière, Louis Malle
Cinematography: Renato Berta

Editor: Emmanuelle Castro
Sound: Jean-Claude Laureux
Music: Claude Debussy, Stéphane Grappelli, Wolfgang Amadeus Mozart
Cast (main actors): Paulette Dubost, Michel Duchaussoy, Miou-Miou, Michel Piccoli

1992
Damage
110 minutes
Director: Louis Malle
Production: Nouvelles Éditions de Films, Skreba (UK)
Screenplay: David Hare (from the novel by Josephine Hart)
Cinematography: Peter Biziou
Editor: John Bloom
Sound: Jean-Claude Laureux
Music: Zbigniew Preisner
Cast (main actors): Juliette Binoche, Rupert Graves, Jeremy Irons, Miranda Richardson

1994
Vanya on 42nd Street
119 minutes
Director: Louis Malle
Production: The Andre Gregory Company
Screenplay: David Mamet (from *Uncle Vanya* by Anton Chekhov)
Cinematography: Declan Quinn
Editor: Nancy Baker
Sound: Tod A. Maitland
Music: Joshua Redman Quartet
Cast (main actors): Phoebe Brand, George Gaynes, Andre Gregory, Julianne Moore, Larry Pine, Wallace Shawn

INDEX

Academy Award, 5, 232
Adorno, Theodor W., 132–3, 237–8
Agamben, Giorgio, 40. *See also* animals
Alexandre, Serge, 195
Alexandrov, G.V., 132
Algeria, 3, 37, 74, 77, 100, 101, 102, 104–5, 192, 193
    FLN (Front de libération nationale), 192
Alice in Wonderland (Carroll), 11, 96n1
Althusser, Louis, 51
anarchism, 13, 159, 160, 161–2, 168, 169
Anderson, Wes, 9, 15
animals, 10, 20, 24, 38, 39, 40–41, 42, 45, 69, 93, 146
    marine animals, 7, 26, 27, 43–4
anti-Semitism, 14, 99, 102, 105, 185, 188, 190, 192, 203, 204, 205, 207
Antonioni, Michelangelo, 101–2, 104
Armstrong, Louis, 128, 135
Arts (newspaper), 100
Atlantic City, 210–21
Audé, Françoise, 38
Aurel, Jean, 6
Auschwitz, 202, 207, 208
automatic writing, 11, 86, 88, 89, 95, 125.
    See also Surrealism
Azar, Leonide, 34

Bardot, Brigitte, 6, 10, 38, 73, 74–8, 79, 80, 81, 82–4
Barnow, Eric, 44

Baron, Suzanne, 3, 56, 58, 61, 154
Barthes, Roland, 51, 54, 127
Bataille, Georges, 2, 118, 125
Bataille, Nicholas, 129
Baudelaire, Charles, 13, 108, 167, 190
Bazin, André, 12, 25, 36, 64, 66, 69, 99, 110, 114, 175
Bechet, Sidney, 12, 128, 129, 135, 136, 140
Becker, Étienne, 50, 55, 57, 176
Beghin sugar empire, 123
Belmondo, Jean-Paul, 73, 156, *163 fig. 1*
Bergen, Candice, 8
Bergson, Henri, 38, 44
Berri, Claude, 194
Bertolucci, Bernardo, 108, 194
Bertucelli, Julie, 10, 63, 64
Besson, Luc, 8
BIFI, 13, 161
Billard, Pierre, 5, 103, 110, 111, 113, 130, 159
Binoche, Juliette, 157
Blaise, Pierre, 72, 84
Blier, Bertrand, 9, 84
Bobet, Jean, 25
Bolden, Buddy, 137
Bolkan, Florinda, 82
Bory, Jean-Louis, 189, 194
Botticelli, Alessandro, 191
Bourdieu, Pierre, 39
Brand, Phoebe, 233, 240, 241
Brasillach, Robert, 186, 195

Brecht, Bertolt, 53, 189
Bresson, Robert, 6, 34, 35, 38, 103, 129, 134, 166, 180
Breton, André, 54, 58, 88, 93, 94, 95, 97, 103, 160, 174
British Petroleum, 20
Bruegel, 227
Brussels, 159, 226
Bujold, Geneviève, 156
Buñuel, Luis, 125, 129

Cahiers du cinéma (journal), 6, 51, 52, 65, 66, 99, 100, 189
Calef, Noël, 42, 100
Calypso (ship), 7, 19, 20, 23–4, 27, 28, 34–7, 39, 45
Campan, Véronique, 127
Camus, Albert, 100, 128, 134, 135
Canby, Vincent, 55, 82
Cannes Film Festival, 5, 6, 24, 35, 59, 159–60
Cardonne-Arlyck, Elisabeth, 12
Carrière, Jean-Claude, 104, 118, 125, 160
Carroll, Lewis, 11, 96n1
Cavalier, Alain, 100, 129
Cavani, Liliana, 51, 194
Chabrol, Claude, 6, 99
Chancel, Jacques, 126, 141
Chapier, Henri, 5
Chaplin, Charlie, 153, 205
Charbonnier, Georges, 88
Chautemps, Camille, 195
Chauvin, Louis, 137
Chekhov, Anton, 14, 100, 118, 232–6, 238, 240–44
Chevrier, Alain, 95
Chion, Michel, 56, 127, 133, 211
Christie, Julie, 80
Ciment, Michel, 11
Cinelli, Francesca, 14
Cinémathèque Française, 2, 13, 28, 161
cinematography, 35, 36, 39, 93, 156, 169, 180, 211, 243
  cinematographers, 3, 6, 35, 102, 186
cinéma vérité, 36–7, 40, 64, 66, 67. *See also* direct cinema
  difference from direct cinema, 46n15
Citroën, 49, 50, 54, 58
Clair, Philippe, 51

Clarke, Kenny, 131, 140n3, 141n10
Clausewitz, Carl von, 185
Clément, Aurore, 190
Clément, René, 101
close-ups, 38, 44, 56, 57, 147, 148, 150, 154, 155, 157, 176, 183n5, 187, 201, 212, 228, 229
  of animals, 2, 22, 93
  of faces, 43, 54, 57, 93, 146, 153, 205, 243
  medium close-up, 55, 90, 149, 153, 191, 227
Club St. Germain, 130, 131
Cocteau, Jean, 11, 109–10, 111, 114, 149, 154, 169
Cohen, Lynn, 233, 240
Colet, Louise, 222
Coltrane, John, 237
Colvile, G., 86
communism, 52, 100, 103, 181, 188, 189
Communist Manifesto (Marx/Engels), 53
Communist Party, 51
Conley, Tom, 14, 37
Conrad, Joseph, 7, 13, 99, 175
Consenstein, Peter, 92
Cooder, Ry, 12, 127
Cortade, Ludovic, 13,
counterpoint, 55, 127–42, 236
Cousteau, Daniel, 192
Cousteau, Jacques, 19–33, 110
  Calypso, 7
  as cameraman, 5
  Cousteau period, 9
  Le Monde du silence (film), 19, 34–48, 55, 134
  narration, 19
Cousteau, Pierre, 192, 197n15
Crawley, T., 75

Damascus, 181
Daney, Serge, 51–2, 53
Darien, Georges, 13, 100, 160–61, 163, 164, 169
Dassin, Jules, 156, 162
Davis, Miles, 6, 12, 102, 128, 129, 130, 135, 236, 237
Debord, Guy, 53
Decaë, Henri, 6, 34, 102, 156
De Certeau, Michel, 225, 226

De Chappotin, Johan, 194
De France, Marie, 14, 224
De Gaulle, Charles, 120
De Jean, Joan, 107, 110
Deleuze, Gilles, 38, 39, 41, 42, 92, 135
Delli Colli, Tonino, 186, 187, 191
Delon, Alain, 10, 72, 73, 82, 83, 84
Deneuve, Catherine, 72
Denis, Claire, 146
Denon, Dominique Vivant, 37, 42, 51, 100
De Oliveira, Manoel, 235
Depardieu, Gérard, 84, 194
Depardon, Raymond, 10, 59, 65
Deschamp, Claude, 152
Deschodt, Anne-Marie, 80
De Scudéry, Madeleine, 37
Desnos, Robert, 150
De Vilmorin, Louise, 34, 111
De Voisins, Jean-Bertrand, 186, 190
Dien Bien Phu, 12, 117, 136
Dietrich, Marlene, 124, 161, 232,
direct cinema, 10, 20, 22, 36–7, 49–62, 64, *176 fig. 1*, 177. See also *cinéma vérité*
  difference from *cinéma vérité*, 46n15
Disney, 9, 21, 27
Disney, Walt, 66
divers, 19–33
documentaries, 7–12, 34–48, 50, 51, 59, 61, 63–71, 73–4, 86, 93, 117, 235, 239
  Algeria, 193
  Cousteau, 19–33, 37
  documentary technique, 64, 65, 77, 89, 126, 128, 134, 137
  India, 13, 73, 174–84
  Ophul, 106, 188
  short documentary, 20, 100, 232
dolphins, 24, 26, 45
Doniol-Valcroze, Jacques, 99
Drach, Michel, 58
Drieu La Rochelle, Pierre, 11, 100, 101, 102, 104, 105, 145, 186
Dubost, Paulette, 118, 122
Dumas, Frédéric, 20, 23, 24, 28, 31n30, *43 fig. 3*
Dumont, Louis, 180
Duvivier, Julien, 8

Eades, Caroline, 9
Eastmancolor, 20
editing, 3, 20, 22, 49, 64, 75, 100, 153, 169, 175, 214, 226, 237, 238, 242
  continuity editing, 91, 93, 152
  Cousteau, 26, 27
  editors, 3, 22, 56, 58, 61, 180
  Humain, trop humain (film), 54, 61
  Silent World (film), 34, 36
  Zazie dans le métro (film), 91, 93, 94
Eisenstein, Sergei, 53, 132
Epstein, Jean, 153, 174
Ertaud, Jacques, 22
Esquire (magazine), 104, 193
Etcherelli, Claire, 58
Eurocentrism, 130
Evein, Bernard, 147–8
existentialism, 100, 130–33

factories, 10
  automobile factory, 34, 40, 49, 50, 53–8, 61, 66, 69
  sugar factory, 117, 123
Falco, 22, 23, 24, 27, 28
Faure, Elie, 188
Fejtö, Raphaël, 201
Fellini, Federico, 73, 82, 104, 175
feminism, 6, 107
Ferry, Jean, 74–5
Feste-Guidon, Aurélie, 195
Filteau, Claude, 107
Firestone, Cinda, 52
Fitzgerald, F. Scott, 103, 148, 155
Flaherty, Robert, 99
Flaubert, Gustave, 160, 222
Fleishman, Ian, 11
Flitterman-Lewis, Sandy, 14
Fordism, 50, 58. *See also* Taylorism
Foucault, Michel, 189
Frag, Pierre, 129
France. *See also* Paris
  box office, 21
  Côte d'Azur, 211
  German occupation of, 7, 13–14, 49, 99, 101, 105–6, 127, 185–99
  Lyon, 65, 203
  Resistance, 105, 189–90, 192, 193, 194, 204
  Vichy, 13, 185, 188, 193, 194, 195, 200, 201, 204
Franju, Georges, 66, 100

Frèche, Gaston, 136
French, Philip, 5, 67, 75, 80, 89, 112–13, 125, 128
French Foreign Legion, 101
French Resistance, 105, 189–90, 192, 193, 194, 204
French star system, 72, 84
Frey, Hugo, 6, 200
Frontisi-Ducroux, Françoise, 242

Gaullism, 13, 49, 53, 100, 188, 189
Gaynes, Georges, 233
Gégauff, Paul, 99
Geneva, 75–7
Germany, 79, 117, 186, 194
  occupation of France, 7, 13–14, 49, 99, 101, 105–6, 127, 185–99
Gestapo, 13, 105, 106, 117, 119, 186, 187–8, 189–90, 191–4, 201, 207
Gide, André, 224
Giraud, Thérèse, 52
Godard, Jean-Luc, 6, 38, 39, 53, 56, 65, 74, 90, 99, 101, 159, 169, 182
Golsan, Richard, 193, 196
Gondry, Michel, 8
Grapelli, Stéphane, 12, 127, 236
Graves, Rupert, 157
Greece, 175, 242
Greene, Bob, 137
Grégoire, Stéphanie, 6
Gregory, André, 14, 222–31, *228 fig. 2*, 232–9, 241–2
Gréville, E. T., 9, 20
Guare, John, 15, 232
GXXX, 86, 88

Hamlet, 11, 108, 110
Harris, Sue, 10
Hart, Josephine, 11, 108
Henriot, Philippe, 188
Higgins, Lynn, 193
Himalayas, 22
Hitchcock, Alfred, 6, 99, 103, 227, 234
Hitler, Adolf, 190, 194
Hodeir, André, 128
Hoffert, Yannick, 240
Hollywood, 5, 8, 78, 100
Holocaust, 14, 202, 203, 209
Hot Club de France, 127, 128, 187

Huston, John, 100, 162, 234

Ichac, Marcel, 22, 23, 30n22
IDHEC (The Institute for Advanced Cinematographic Studies), 7, 24, 35, 124, 129, 132, 180
immigration, 10, 63, 64, 66, 70,
India, 28, 34, 69, 73, 104, 124, 159, 174–84. See also *Phantom India*; *Song of India*
Indochina, 44, 101, 116–26, 136
Ionesco, Eugène, 124, 129
Irons, Jeremy, 157
Italy, 74, 76, 79, 82
  Spoleto, 74–8

Jackson, Tony, 138
Jacob, Gilles, 58, 159–60, 194
James, Alison, 89
James, Henry, 15
Jankowski, Paul, 194
Jarry, Alfred, 129, 160
jazz, 12, 15, 23, 102, 117–18, 127–42, 187, 219, 235–7
Jazz Hot (magazine), 128, 129, 130, 132, 236
Jeunet, Jean-Pierre, 8
Jewish children, 14, 117, 200–209
Jews, 168, 185–6, 190, 203–8
Joplin, Scott, 137
Journot, Marie-Thérèse, 235
Joyce, James, 166

Kael, Pauline, 186
Karmitz, Marin, 53
Kassovitz, Mathieu, 8
Keaton, Buster, 3, 153
Kedward, H.R., 193
Kleinberger, Alain, 195
Kline, T. Jefferson, 11, 222
Kodachrome, 20
Kracauer, Siegfried, 38, 44, 45n4, 66
Kubrick, Stanley, 234

Lacan, Jacques, 51, 134
La Huchette (theatre), 124, 129
Lang, Fritz, 227
La Parisienne (newspaper), 100
Laplantine, François, 39
Lasserre, Henri, 194

Last Tango in Paris (film), 108, 114n1
Laughton, Charles, 218, 234
Laurent, Jacques, 100
Laureux, Jean-Claude, 50
Leacock, Richard, 10, 64, 65
Le Coual, 7, 200
Leenhardt, Roger, 120
Lefebvre, Henri, 54
Le Figaro Littéraire (journal), 77
Left Bank, 10, 39, 100, 104
Leiris, Michel, 13, 175
Le Pen, Jean-Marie, 99
Leroi-Gourhan, André, 42
Leroy, Alain, 12, 36, 104, 119, 152, 160
Les Temps modernes (journal), 101, 189
Leterrier, François, 130
L'Humanité (journal), 51
Libération (newspaper), 50
Linklater, Richard, 9
Littell, Jonathan, 195
lobsters, 26–7
Lomax, Alan, 129, 130, 137, 138, 139
London, 101, 159, 161, 166, 167
Los Angeles, 8
Losey, Joseph, 100, 194
Löwenadler, Holger, 190
Lukács, Georg, 52
Lumière brothers, 60, 90, 237

Machu, Frank, 27
Malle, Françoise, 12, 116, 118, 122–4
Malle, Justine, 12
Mallecot, Jacques, 7, 106,
Malraux, André, 106, 153, 155, 177, 180
Mamet, David, 233
Manesse, Gaspard, 201
Marcorelles, Louis, 65
Marie, Michel, 189
Marker, Chris, 39, 64, 65, 66, 100
Marxism, 52, 58
Mastroianni, Marcello, 10, 73, 75, 104
Mauron, Charles, 112
Mauss, Marcel, 57
May '68, 118, 120
Mayer, Jerry, 233
Melville, Jean-Pierre, 102, 156, 194
Met, Philippe, 13, 15
Mexico, 4, 75, 78, 79, 80, 104, 192
Miami, 15, 70,

Michelot, Pierre, 131, 141n10
Miles, Sarah, 80
mise-en-scène, 13, 14, 25, 37, 39, 49, 146–7, 148–9, 151, 152, 153, 155, 159, 177
Mitry, Jean, 23, 38
Modiano, Patrick, 11, 13, 49, 100, 105, 185–6, 188, 189, 190, 191, 192, 194, 195–6
Mohrt, Michel, 189
Molière, 226
Monroe, Marilyn, 76
Moore, Julianne, 233, 240, 242, 243
Moore, Michael, 65
Moreau, Jeanne, 6, 10, 43, 72, 73, 78, 79, 80, 101, 102, 110, 111, 113, 151
Morin, Edgar, 39, 40, 64, 66, 67
Morin, François, 51
Morris, Eroll, 65
Morton, Jelly Roll, 12, 129, 130, 135, 137, 138, 139
Moscovitz, Ferdinand, 59
Murnau, F. W., 99
Murphy Brown (sitcom), 8
Museum of Modern Art (MoMA), 137

Nagra recording system, 10, 65, 66
Nazis, 49, 101, 102, 201. *See also* France, German occupation of; Germany, occupation of France
Nelson, Ruth, 233
Némirovsky, Irène, 195
Nettelbeck, Colin, 133
New Amsterdam Theater, 14–15, 233, 236
New Orleans, 128, 129, 136–7, 168
New Wave, 5, 6, 10, 11, 14, 39, 65, 67, 86, 91, 99, 104, 182, 209, 222
New York, 8, 15, 137, 147, 200, 202, 205, 223–4, 236, 239, 240
New York Film Festival, 100
New York Times, 55, 82
Nicaragua, 70
Nichols, Bill, 63–4
Niger, 39
Nimier, Roger, 11, 34, 100–102, 104, 105
Noiret, Philippe, 90, 91
nonfiction, 63–71
Normand, Jean, 109
North Africa, 101
 Egypt, 147
nouvelle vague. *See* New Wave

OAS, 101, 103, 104
objectification, 78, 238
octopus, 26, 27, 31
Orpheus, myth of, 49, 108–10, 111, 112–14
Orpheus (film), 109, 110, 111, 149
Ory, Pascal, 189
Ott, Sandra, 194
Oulipo, 11, 87–9, 92, 95, 96n2. *See also* Surrealism
    Oulipian automatism, 11, 86, 87–92, 95

Painlevé, Jean, 23, 25, 26, 44, 45
Paris, 49, 51, 82, 117, 120, 186, 188, 193, 208, 226
    film location, 6, 8, 37, 39–41, 76, 90, 91, 101–2, 104, 133, 150, 154, 200–201, 207
    jazz, 128, 130, 131, 136
    Left Bank, 10, 39, 100, 104
    Right Bank, 49, 51, 52, 100
Paris-Match (magazine), 193
Parker, Charlie, 12, 117, 128–9, 135 *fig 2*, 136
Pautrot, Jean-Louis, 12
Paxton, Robert O., 188
Perec, Georges, 60
Perrault, Pierre, 51
Pétain, Philippe, 188, 193
Philibert, Nicolas, 10, 63, 65, 70
photography, 20, 21, 29n4, 44, 87, 110
    underwater photography, 9, 19–33, 182
Piaf, Edith, 59
Pine, Larry, 233, 240–41, 242
Platt, Polly, 129, 138
Poe, Edgar Allan, 10, 82, 163
Polanski, Roman, 227
Pompidou, Georges, 55
Porter, Melinda Camber, 71, 86
Poste Parisien radio studio, 2, 130
Prédal, René, 5
Preminger, Otto, 102
Prokofiev, Sergei, 132
Proust, Marcel, 13, 169
Psycho (Hitchcock), 55
Pudovkin, V. I., 132

Queneau, Raymond, 11, 41, 42, 86, 88, 89, 90, 95, 100, 129

Racette, Francine, 203
Randal, Georges, 156, 160, 161–9,
Rappeneau, Jean-Paul, 74–5, 100
Ray, Nicholas, 100, 235
Rebatet, Lucien, 99, 192
Redman, Joshua, 12, 15, 127, 236, 237, 239, 243
Reinhardt, Django, 12, 127, 140, 187
Renaud, Henri, 136
Renoir, Jean, 8, 122, 152, 234
Resnais, Alain, 38–9, 53, 66, 99, 100, 194, 195, 234
Rezorri, Gregor von, 75
Richard, Jean-Pierre, 222
Rigaut, Jacques, 103
Robichaux, John, 136
Robinson, Edward G., 187
Roger, Jean-Henri, 53
Rohmer, Eric, 99
Rollins, Sonny, 237
Romano, Marcel, 130
Ronet, Maurice, 1, 3, 73, 101, 104, 112, 113, *145 fig. 1*, 146, 150, 151, 153, 155, 160, 180
Rongier, Sébastien, 14
Rose, Al, 137, 138
Rossellini, Roberto, 134, 179
Rouch, Jean, 10, 35, 39–40, 44, 45, 64, 65, 66, 67
Roud, Richard, 100
Rousseau, Jean-Jacques, 178
Rozier, Jacques, 76
Russia, 240
Ruttmann, Walter, 41

Saint-Laurent, Yves, 195
Salle, Jérôme, 23
Samuels, Maurice, 190
Sarandon, Susan, 4, 84
Sartre, Jean-Paul, 13, 100, 132, 140, 185, 186, 190, 194, 196
Satie, Erik, 13, 104, 147–9, 228
Saulnier, Jacques, 156
Sautet, Claude, 100
Schilling, Derek, 10
Schlemilovitch, Raphaël, 195
Schlöndorff, Volking, 15
Séchan, Edmond, 24, 27
Sellier, Geneviève, 76

Serceau, Daniel, 234
Serres, Michel, 109
sex, 50, 52, 76, 91, 118, 119, 125, 136, 138, 155, 156, 157, 191, 218
Seyres, Jacques, 152
Shakespeare, William, 224
sharks, 21–2, 27
Shawn, Wallace (Wally), 14, 223, *228 fig. 2*, 233–4, 239, 240, 241, 242, 243
silence, 34–48, 133, 134, 135, 178, 206
Simon, Michel, 194
Skerla, Lena, 146
Smith, Brooke, 233, 242
Sondheim, Stephen, 195
Sontag, Susan, 87, 89, 93, 96
Soulez, Guillaume, 9
soundtrack, 12, 56, 65, 66, 67, 68, 102, 127, 130–42, 148, 182, 211–21
South Asia, 216
Southern, Nathan C., 6, 74, 214
Spain, 186
Stavisky, Alexandre, 195
Stendhal, 2, 99
Stewart, Alexandra, 1, 152
submarines, 45–6
Surrealism, 86–9, 93, 94–5, 96n2, 96–7n3, 103, 104, 122, 124, 129, 175
 automatic writing, 11, 86, 88, 89, 95, 125
Switzerland, 188
synchronous sound, 10, 49, 56, 65, 66, 132

Taffin, Tony, 152, 153
Taillez, Philippe, 23
Taylorism, 10, 50, 58. *See also* Fordism
television, 20, 21, 104, 125, 179, 211, 217
 ORTF, 60, 65
Thomas, Dylan, 166
Thurman, Uma, 232
Time (magazine), 78
Tiphaine, Bernard, 154–5
Toubiana, Serge, 50
Tour de France, 25, 34, 40

Tourneur, Maurice, 8
Truffaut, François, 6, 99, 234
turtles, 2, 24, 26, 40, 45

Ungar, Steven, 13
United Artists, 78, 79, 80
United States, 5, 7, 8, 15, 63, 65, 66, 76, 129, 133, 219, 234
US Library of Congress, 130, 137

Vadim, Roger, 6, 73, 75, 82
Varda, Agnès, 39, 65, 66, 100, 104
Verne, Jules, 21, 114
Vertov, Dziga, 41, 45n4, 52, 53
Vian, Boris, 129, 130, 135, 136, 137
Vichy France, 13, 185, 188, 193, 194, 195, 200, 201, 204
Vietnam, 3, 101, 104
 My Lai massacre, 193
Vincendeau, Ginette, 76, 189
Visconti, Luchino, 82
Voisin, Roger, 161, 165

Wagner, Richard, 45
Welles, Orson, 82
Wenders, Wim, 235
Wexler, Jerry, 136
whales, 21, 22
Whitman, Walt, 9
Wilder, Billy, 234
Williams, Alan, 10
Wise, Robert, 102
Wiseman, Fredrick, 10, 64, 65, 70
Wolman, Gil, 53
World War I, 137, 164–5, 188
World War II, 44, 102, 117, 129, 186, 208, 228
writers, 99–106

Yanne, Jean, 51

Zimmer, Christian, 189

GPSR Authorized Representative: Easy Access System Europe, Mustamäe tee
50, 10621 Tallinn, Estonia, gpsr.requests@easproject.com

www.ingramcontent.com/pod-product-compliance
Lightning Source LLC
Chambersburg PA
CBHW030300010526
44108CB00038B/840